MODERN AUSTRIAN WRITING

MODERN AUSTRIAN WRITING

LITERATURE AND SOCIETY AFTER 1945

Edited by Alan Best and
Hans Wolfschütz

Oswald Wolff · London

Barnes & Noble Books · Totowa, New Jersey

© 1980 Oswald Wolff (Publishers) Ltd.
London W1M 6DR

Published by
Oswald Wolff (Publishers) Ltd., London
and
Barnes & Noble Books, Totowa, New Jersey

British Library Cataloguing in Publication Data
Modern Austrian Writing
    1. German literature – Austrian authors – History and Criticism
    2. German literature – 20th century – History and criticism
    I. Best, Alan
    II. Wolfschütz, Hans
    830'.9'9436   PT3818

ISBN   UK 0–85496–067–8
        US 0–389–20038–7

PHOTOSET, PRINTED AND BOUND IN GREAT BRITAIN BY
REDWOOD BURN LIMITED
TROWBRIDGE AND ESHER

Contents

Acknowledgements

The editors are grateful to the government of the Federal Republic of Austria for the generous financial support given to this project. They also wish to acknowledge their debt to Dr. Wolfgang Kraus, President of the 'Österreichische Gesellschaft für Literatur', whose advice and encouragement was unstintingly given and to Dr Bernhard Stillfried, Director of the Austrian Institute in London for his assistance. Mention must be made of the facilities extended by Professor Viktor Suchy and his colleagues at the 'Dokumentationsstelle für neuere österreichische Literatur' in Vienna for the provision of much invaluable material. The editors wish also to thank the University of Hull for granting them study leave to undertake this project and the Sir Philip Reckitt Trust for financial support to enable study to be undertaken in Vienna. A final acknowledgement is due to colleagues in the Department of German at the University of Hull for their many helpful comments and suggestions.

A.D.B./H.W.

Editorial Note

Titles of primary texts are given in German throughout the book, followed by an English translation. The translated title is intended as a guide to the non-specialist reader and may not be identical with the title under which a translation has been published. All quotations in German have been translated into English and will be found either immediately adjacent to the German (if short) or in the notes at the end of each chapter. Translations throughout are by the individual contributors.

I The Emergence and Development of the Second Republic

Hans Wolfschütz

The history of modern Austria is, above all, the record of a people who have learnt to live with the past. The traumatic loss of geographical area and political stature which accompanied the collapse of the Austro-Hungarian monarchy in 1918 has, over the years, been assimilated and digested to allow present-day Austria to take full political and economic advantage of its current role as a non-aligned state.

Few Austrians today give a second thought to the fact of their country's existence as a wholly independent and neutral state. Rebuilt from the devastation bequeathed from the Third Reich in 1945, the Second Republic of Austria has more than proved itself as a stable, highly affluent and socially progressive state enjoying, in addition, the democratic maturity so crucially lacking in the ill-fated First Republic of the years between the two World Wars. The younger generation of Austrians, growing up in an atmosphere of political consensus well-nigh unique in a European context, have come to regard the mutual suspicions, self-doubts and self-destructive ideologies which still manifest themselves from time to time amongst their parents' generation as anachronistic foibles of little contemporary import. Even so, it is the memory of the strife-torn, turbulent days between 1918 and 1945 and the high price they exacted in human terms, that explains the emergence and development of the political unity and the policy of economic co-operation which characterize the Second Republic.

Dr Adolf Schärf, who as Socialist Vice-Chancellor was to play a decisive part in the negotiations which led to the Austrian State Treaty and who was later elected as the third President of the newly-formed Second Republic, writes in his memoirs of the moment when he realized that his vision of Austria as part of a greater Germany was no longer valid. It was in 1943, as he was listening

1

to an emissary of the German resistance movement explaining the nature of the Greater Germany (including Austria) which would be formed after Hitler and his regime had been overthrown. Schärf records that he interrupted the man curtly and declared: 'The Anschluß is dead. Any affection the Austrians felt for the German Reich has been driven out of us'.[1]

Here is a man, who had never felt drawn to the National Socialists, acknowledging that he had been awakened to the reality of a political ideology which many leading politicians of all leanings had shared during the First Republic. Schärf's rejection of the 'Anschluß', and all it represented, is symptomatic of a shift in attitudes amongst the greater part of the Austrian people and its timing is no less significant. The year 1943 was crucial for the subsequent development of the Second Republic. It was then that the Allies declared their intention, in the so-called 'Moscow Memorandum', to re-establish Austria after the war as an independent state; it was also then that, for the first time, leading representatives of the various political groupings inside Austria, hitherto at daggers-drawn with one another, came together in a spirit of close co-operation to evolve a common programme to establish a new form of independence for their country. At the same time, a decisive shift in the progress of the war in the Allies' favour provided the impetus for the hopelessly and disastrously fragmented resistance groups to see if they too could work under one umbrella, as indeed with some exceptions they agreed a year later.

The creation of a new national awareness thus went hand in hand with the breaking-down of the historical barriers of ideological differences. This was, however, not the result of a sudden inspiration but the logical outcome of a process of sober consideration, the direct result of the political reality created by Nazi rule in Austria after 1938. As a consequence, the political climate into which the new Austria of 1945 emerged was incomparably more favourable than that 'enjoyed' by its counterpart the First Republic in 1918–19.

The First Republic (1918–1938) was the product of somewhat rather embarrassed and politically naive manoeuvrings across the negotiating table. The problem confronting the politicians in St Germain was what should be done with over six million German-Austrians who were left after the national aspirations of the other former constituents of the Hapsburg monarchy had been satisfied. There could be no question of integrating them into Germany, since this addition to the Reich in its hour of defeat was tantamount

2

to a direct contradiction of the war effort. The only acceptable conclusion, as far as the victors were concerned, was to create a new state for the German-Austrians, but with no great confidence that the infant would survive.

Doubts as to the life expectancy of this new 'Deutsch-Österreich' as it was initially called, were well-founded, not least because the citizens who had had state and nation-hood forced upon them considered its reduced status an affront. The *Wiener Freie Presse* dismissed the Treaty of St Germain and 'Deutsch-Österreich' in September 1919 in a characteristic outburst:

What has our new state to do with this peace, which makes minor concessions but drags our wounds through the dust? We have lost our freedom, our nation has been eradicated and millions of our fellow-countrymen have been delivered to the arbitrary rule of foreigners. How can such a peace possibly serve the progress of mankind? We have not lost a war, we have lost our identity. The six million souls herded together under a convenient label have nothing in common and have lost all say in world affairs.[2]

The *Wiener Freie Presse* spoke here for many people, and in a manner not unlike the German reaction to the 'Shameful Peace' of Versailles. Yet despite the hollow pathos and empty words of a 'nation destroyed' which subordinate the reality of the multinational Hapsburg monarchy to the myth of a unified nation the besetting Austrian dilemma of the post-1918 period is evident. The common bond of the German language was not considered sufficient justification for political independence and, in any case, too many German-speaking regions had been ceded to the new states emerging from the debris of the old monarchy. It was thus almost inevitable that the German Austrians should turn to the ethnic considerations which the Allied powers had half-heartedly applied, and take them to their only logical conclusion: unification with Germany. This was the only way in which they felt able once more to 'have their say' in affairs of state. This 'Anschluß' mentality was virtually incorporated into the political framework of the First Republic; Article 2 of the Constitutional Law which the provisional National Assembly passed unanimously in 1918 declared that 'Deutsch-Österreich' was 'an integral part of the German Reich'.

The general consensus which rejected the concept of Austrian independence was, however, wholly absent when it came to deciding what form the new 'größeres Ganzes', the new greater unity so beloved by the Austrian mind, should take. The conservative element in the population, if it was not considering a reincarnation of the old multi-national Hapsburg state, was drawn towards Germany both for economic reasons and by its fear of internal revolution. The working-class, organized in the Social Democratic Party, sought an 'Anschluß' on nationalistic grounds and from the conviction that by enlarging the state it would be more readily able to create a society on Marxist-Socialist lines.

There was thus no positive basis on which to found an independent parliamentary democracy. The only common-ground was negative – a mutual antagonism towards the newly created state – and it was inevitable that the parties would retreat into a total commitment to the success of their own particular ideology, whether this was the political catholicism of the Christian Social Party or the Marxist determinism of the Social Democratic Party. The most ominous feature of this ideological encampment was the creation of para-military units whose presence merely served to engender an atmosphere of subterranean civil war long before the actual outbreak of open hostility.

The storm finally broke in the 1930's. Between 1933 and 1934 the Austrians saw the end of their parliamentary democracy, the establishment by the ruling Catholic-conservative alliance of a 'Ständestaat', a Christian Corporate state, unsuccessful insurrections against this development by the Socialists and an attempted Putsch by the Austrian Nazis. Growing international isolation and the failure of the two traditional political camps to settle their differences even when faced with the common threat of National Socialism almost inevitably led to the end of the First Republic in March 1938.

Whether the massive celebrations which greeted Hitler's arrival in Vienna or the almost unanimous 'Yes' vote sanctioning the 'Anschluß' in April 1938 were an expression of genuine pro-National-Socialist feeling among the majority of Austrian people at the time is open to question. This enthusiasm could in part be explained by the fulfilment of the pan-German aspirations evident throughout the First Republic though doubtless many, as in Germany in 1933, were carried away by an irrational hope that a new age was about to dawn. After all, they had already lost their democratic rights, the economic situation could hardly become worse and the vast majority of Austrians had grown up owing their allegiance to the concepts and values of the Hapsburg monarchy and felt little enough responsibility for this small republic forced into being by external political factors.

The grim reality of 'Anschluß' soon dispelled such optimistic dreams and illusions as might have been cherished. 70,000 Austrians were arrested in its immediate aftermath, the name 'Austria' disappeared from the map to be replaced by the term 'Ostmark', the Eastern March, as part of a rigorous process of 'Gleichschaltung', the co-ordination of all areas and aspects of life to the National-Socialist pattern. The dreams of a measure of independence within the framework of Greater Germany was ruthlessly shattered by Austria's relegation to a province governed from Berlin. While none of the other parties went so far as the Communists, who called for open resistance, the 'Germanization' carried out by the Nazis rekindled the long-standing animosity felt for the Germans by many Austrians, including not a few 'Austro-Nazis'. The break with the 'Anschluß' ideology, to which Adolf Schärf referred, began now and was intensified by the horrors of the Second World War and the increasing brutality of the Nazi authorities. Norbert Leser considers the seven years of 'lost independence' to have been an effective shock therapy, without which the preconditions for the new start after 1945 would have been unthinkable:

> Yesterday's victors and vanquished were thrown together in the prisons and concentration camps of the Third Reich, at the front or in the air-raid shelters at home. Thanks to this unsought opportunity they were able to enlarge their intellectual horizons and acquire the broader political awareness which had not been able to exist in the First Republic. It took first-hand experience of the lessons of National Socialism to bring these old rivals to their senses and to bring home to them that Austria's independence and self-sufficiency was something to be treasured. Like democracy, it was until they no longer enjoyed it that they appreciated how much they had lost. The terrible detour of National Socialist oppression was perhaps necessary, in order to create the psychological basis on which Austria's future after 1945 could be built.[3]

There could be no 'tabula rasa' in the Austria of 1945, no 'Jahr Null'. The presence of the First Republic could be sensed in every development which now began to take shape – if only as a warning example of what should not be done this time. The politicians responsible for their country in the first two decades of its new existence felt themselves to some extent at fault for past events. They had all grown up in the First Republic and some of them had played prominent roles in the opposing political camps and, while there were none among their number tainted by National Socialist involvement or sympathies, they had nonetheless involuntarily paved the way for the Nazi interregnum through their own political stubborness. They had learnt by bitter experience that the only hope in the future was a policy of co-operation across the political barriers.

This newly-found unity was reflected in the composition and policies of the first provisional government formed in April 1945 immediately after the surrender of Vienna to the Soviet forces. It was made up of Socialists, Catholics and Communists and was led by Dr Karl Renner, who ironically enough had been the first Chancellor of the First Republic in 1918–19. The coalition government then had been purely provisional and had broken up in 1920 as a result of irreconcilable ideological differences; now, in 1945 it considered itself to be more than an executive instrument for political decision imposed from outside; it saw itself above all else as the standard-bearer of the universal Austrian desire to gain national independence and to reconstruct the country from the considerable debris of the war.

There were, however, serious obstacles in the path of such ambitions and in many respects the external political climate was far less favourable for an independent Austria than had been in the case of 1918. Like Germany, Austria was divided into four occupation zones and its capital placed under four-power control. There was no general agreement amongst the Allies as to how Austria should develop in the years to come. The Western powers did not recognize the Renner cabinet as an 'all-Austrian' government until October 1945, despite the terms of the 'Moscow Memorandum' of 1 November 1943 in which Britain, the United States and Russia had accorded Austria the status of first victim of National Socialist aggression, affirming their intention to re-establish her as an independent state. Then, however, the Allies were more concerned with weakening Germany's position than with the good of Austria. Immediately after the collapse of the Third Reich only the Soviets showed an apparent interest in Austrian independence while the British, for example, were still considering the establishment of a central European Danubian Federation which would combine Austria and Southern Germany.[4]

A further problem was posed by the unequivocal reference in the Moscow Memorandum to Austria's responsibility for 'participating in the war on the side of Hitlerite Germany' which left the young republic in a most uncomfortable situation, neither victim nor yet collaborator. Technically a victim of Nazi Germany, Austria had no-one with whom she could sign a peace treaty; as a collaborator she could scarcely be granted the benefits accorded to such genuinely liberated countries as Belgium or the Netherlands. Consequently, Austria was obliged to pay reparations and her government, even after free elections, was subject to the strict control of the Allied Council.[5]

Many observers have suggested that these first elections of November 1945 were only allowed because the Soviet Union believed that the Communist Party would do well. But, despite the heavy price the Communists had paid in human terms in their struggle against the National Socialists, and despite (or perhaps because of) the support they received from the Soviet Occupying Power, they suffered a substantial defeat. The large majority of the Austrian electorate opted for the parties which were the direct heirs of the two traditional camps of the First Republic and which had campaigned on a platform of parliamentary democracy on Western lines. The Christian Democratic People's Party, the 'Österreichische Volkspartei' (ÖVP) gained a small absolute majority, with the Austrian Socialist Party, the 'Sozialistische Partei Österreichs' (SPÖ), as the second largest faction. Leopold Figl (ÖVP) was appointed Federal Chancellor with Adolf Schärf (SPÖ) the new Vice-Chancellor.

The elections of 1945 set the course for the internal development and political topography of Austria for the next two decades. Despite the parliamentary dominance of the ÖVP, the coalition of the two major parties, which included the Communists until 1947, was not ended until 1966. In subsequent elections the ÖVP retained its position as the strongest political party but the pattern of voting reflected a strong Austrian desire for some measure of power-sharing. On a number of occasions the Socialists were only narrowly defeated, while the various minority parties met with little success. Under the Austrian Constitution the Federal President is elected by direct suffrage, and in each election since 1951 the Austrian voters have consistently returned a candidate from the

SPÖ almost, it seems, as a deliberate counterweight to the succession of Conservative (ÖVP) Federal Chancellors. Although the role of the Federal President in Austria is purely formal, and such a vote might not be seen to be of major significance in terms of everyday politics, the fact remains that the President's role in times of crisis is decisive.

Much of the ideological dead-weight had been jettisoned by the two major parties in Austria after 1945 as they moved towards the political centre. The old Christian Socialist Party had re-christened itself the Austrian People's Party in a concerted effort to break with the past and the implications of the authoritarian 'Ständestaat'. Like the West German Christian Democrats, whose Ahlen manifesto of 1947 proclaimed the CDU as a party for social reform, the ÖVP in the immediate post-war period evinced a similar reforming attitude, acknowledging a strong sympathy which it felt towards the British Labour Party and Clement Attlee.[6] The effects of the American-financed European Recovery Programme (Marshall Aid) are among the main reasons which later led to a gradual shift to the right – a further parallel to the West German CDU under Konrad Adenauer.

For their part the Austrian Socialists could see themselves as victims both of National Socialism and the Catholic 'Ständestaat'. Nonetheless, as Norbert Leser comments:

> Their attitude to the traditions of the old party was from the start ambivalent. They paid due lip-service to the traditional ideals but their day-to-day policies deliberately avoided all trace of the pre-war attitudes and consigned the treasury of Austro-Marxism to the darkest oblivion.[7]

The Socialists discarded their long-held antagonism to the conservative camp which had gone hand-in-hand with the conviction that a Socialist revolution was a matter of time, and embraced a policy of necessary and pragmatic co-operation within the framework of a capitalist society. The long-standing schism between evolutionary and revolutionary Socialists was clearly resolved in the former's favour.

The integration back into society of the erstwhile 'Austro-Nazis' represented a further successful political rapprochement, although in this case the consequences were not always as auspicious. The NSDAP had been banned in 1945 and half a million former members of the party, ranging from insignificant sympathisers to prominent members of the party machine, had been listed and excluded from participation as voters or candidates in the first elections. This, however, was virtually the sum of Austria's 'Vergangenheitsbewältigung', its attempt to come to terms with the immediate past. It would be unrealistic to suppose that such a large block of voters would long be ignored and they were assiduously wooed by the various political parties in the second elections, held in 1949. The major beneficiary was the newly-permitted Association of Independents, the 'Verband der Unabhängigen' (VdU), which was returned to parliament as the third largest political faction although both major parties also gained support from this new source. The VdU subsequently changed its name to the more appealing 'Freiheitliche Partei Österreichs' (FPÖ), the Austrian Freedom Party, thus staking its claim to be a liberal party; up to 1970, however, it had to be content with the role of an isolated and impotent political opposition.

In opening their doors to former Nazi sympathizers – 'instant political baptism' as it was mockingly labelled – the political parties made a major contribution to the stability of the Second Republic, and as a consequence the spectacular growth in support of the neo-Nazi NPD in West Germany during the 1960's was not evident in Austria. This is not to say that the trappings and attitudes of the Nazi past did not linger on in the Second Republic; they were to be found in old comrades' associations, student organizations and the like. Whilst such organizations were rarely more than insignificant anachronisms on the fringe of society, the lenient verdicts or inexplicable acquittals which some Nazi criminals secured at their trials in Austria caused far greater concern, particularly abroad. This leniency, too, must be seen against the background of the very conscious attempts of the Austrians to minimalize internal conflict as much as possible and to avoid any kind of polarization within society.

A more positive reflection of this tendency to minimize internal conflict can be seen in the policy of constructive co-operation between the two sides of industry. In the early days of the First Republic the Austrian Social Democrats had demanded a radical socialization of the economy but had failed to make any practical impression on the extensive range of private ownership. The Socialists of the Second Republic accepted the re-establishment of a free market economy from the start, and contented themselves with

9

nationalizing key industries (especially heavy industry) and the banks. It had been the social concessions made to the workers in 1918–19 which the Austrian middle-class had blamed for their own precarious economic situation in the inter-war years. The fear of the 'red menace' eventually led them to a strategy of political despair and the establishment of the corporate state with its prohibition on independent trade unions. In 1945 the middle-class showed that it had learnt that more was to be gained by the integration of employees' organizations into the political and economic process and by the expansion of social welfare than by a policy of continuous suspicion and open conflict.

This new post-war consensus was considerably aided by the establishment of a highly centralized employees' organization embracing the various trade unions but owing allegiance to no one party, although inevitably the Socialist voice was clearly heard in its deliberations. The Austrian Federation of Trade Unions, the 'Österreichische Gewerkschaftsbund' (ÖGB), comprising sixteen different unions and recruiting individual workers to membership on a wholly voluntary basis, played an active part in the economic reconstruction from the early days of the Second Republic. In an attempt to curtail inflationary tendencies and to stimulate investment in the economy five wages and prices agreements were concluded between 1947 and 1951. These were general, across-the-board agreements whose prime aim, recognized and accepted by both sides of industry, was the promotion of economic growth – an early hint of the so-called 'social partnership' which would evolve in Austria in the late 1950's.

Although wages and prices agreements made a significant contribution to the prevention of wage disputes, they could not completely prevent social unrest. This was primarily linked with the immediate social effects of Marshall Aid. The Austrian government had decided to accept Marshall Aid in 1948, despite protests from the Soviet occupying power, but had also been obliged to accept the conditions under which such aid could be used to further industrial recovery. This meant the abolition of agricultural subsidies and the raising of food prices inside Austria to the higher level then current on the international market. Inevitably, when the wages and prices round of 1950 left the increase in wages considerably in arrears of the new level of prices, there was an outcry; Austria found herself faced with the first, and up till now the only, serious internal crisis in its post-war history.

The Communists called for a general strike and large sections of the Socialist working population defied the advice of their leading representatives and were prepared to join in. The trade union leaders and the Socialist party machine were ultimately successful in their attempts to draw their members back from an out-and-out confrontation, aided no doubt by the spectre of the Communist take-over in neighbouring Czechoslovakia two years earlier. The co-operation of the employees' organization with the government in this crisis was instrumental in enabling Austria to secure integration into the Western economic orbit, a process completed in 1953 when the country was accepted into the OECD (the Organization for European Co-operation and Development), despite the presence of a Soviet occupying force in the eastern 'Länder', and the fact that the State Treaty granting Austria full independence was still some two years in the future.

The ten-year delay between the cessation of hostilities and the conclusion of the State Treaty can be directly attributed to the Cold War which enveloped the former Allies. While the Western powers had readily renounced all claim to reparations and had assisted Austria's economic reconstruction their political and strategic priorities in effect obstructed the realization of Austria's emergence as an independent state.[8] As far as the United States was concerned, Austria was a constituent part of Western Europe and, as such, a strategically important link between the future NATO allies Italy and the Federal Republic of Germany. Austrian initiatives towards a state treaty which were guided by a concept of neutrality akin to that of Switzerland struck the Americans as both unrealistic and fraught with danger in the face of what was seen as the military threat of the Soviet forces in Europe. Against this background the coalition government stood firm in its efforts to preserve the unity of the country, knowing full well that only the complete withdrawal of all the occupying forces, Western and Russian, and a commitment by the Austrians themselves to neutrality would enable this ambition to be realized.

After Stalin's death in 1953 relations between East and West improved. According to the then State Secretary Bruno Kreisky one of the by-products of the Berlin Conference on Germany of 1954 was a significant shift in attitudes to the Austrian question. He argues that the prospect of an Austrian State Treaty was used by the Soviet Union to demonstrate to the world the end of Soviet expansionism and the dawn of a new era of political co-existence.[9] The

11

negotiations leading up to the State Treaty found the Soviet Union prepared to moderate their demands for reparations and willing to return former 'German assets' which they had confiscated; at the same time the Western powers managed to overcome their strategic scruples. The State Treaty was finally signed in May 1955 and by October of the same year all occupying forces had left Austrian soil. Under the terms of the Constitutional Law passed by the National Assembly, Austria was to become and remain a neutral state in perpetuity; it was a neutrality akin to that of Switzerland in that it was founded on political and military non-alignment and was explicitly Western and democratic in its ideology.

It was undoubtedly the prevailing international climate which enabled the State Treaty to be successfully concluded. In the context of the mild thaw in East-West relations which characterized the years from 1953–1956, a neutral Austria, sharing frontiers with two member countries of both NATO and the Warsaw Pact, gained in importance as a buffer zone. This was particularly evident during the Hungarian rising in October 1956, when the existence of a non-aligned country may well have been an important factor in dissuading the United States from the course of a more direct intervention in Hungary. Yet, as the Hungarian example also shows, the emergence of Austria as a sovereign and neutral state was a matter of seizing a favourable moment.

The Hungarian government under Imre Nagy had clearly envisaged a neutral status for their own country outside the Warsaw Pact, but the ruthless suppression of such aspirations by the Russians was an obvious indication that they were not prepared to allow Austria to serve as a precedent within their own sphere of influence. Indeed it is doubtful whether the Russians would have agreed to the Austrian State Treaty had it been negotiated after the events of October 1956, although it could equally be argued that it was the voluntary withdrawal of Soviet troops from territory they had been occupying which provided the kindling for the Hungarian rising. The 'Austrian solution' is and has remained unique. Successive West German governments have set their face against any suggestion that Germany should be reunified as a neutral state, the latest of which was made in early 1979, though the topic can generate considerable popular discussion – if not always founded in political reality.

Having chosen Switzerland as the model for her own neutrality Austria has consistently interpreted her neutral status in her own individual way. This is as much deliberate policy as a consequence of her geographical location which makes her more susceptible to tensions between East and West. Unlike Switzerland, Austria never regarded neutrality as an obstacle to full membership of the United Nations, which she joined in December 1955, immediately after the State Treaty had come into force. Successive governments of the Second Republic have adopted an active role in world affairs ranging from participation in UN operations in the Congo, Cyprus and the Middle East to acts of a humanitarian nature as, for example, granting sanctuary in both 1956 and 1968 to thousands of Hungarian and Czechoslovakian refugees or providing a transit camp for Jewish emigrants from Russia during the 1970's. The location of influential international organizations in Vienna, the choice of Austria for important political negotiations and, not least, the election and subsequent re-election of Dr Kurt Waldheim in 1971 and 1976 as Secretary-General of the United Nations, all testify to Austria's new-found self-confidence in the political role which even a small state can play in a world dominated by two power-blocs. This role in the interest of peace and international co-operation may indeed be interpreted as a more positive, outward-looking reflection of the First Republic's self-centred wish to have its 'say in world affairs'.

Nevertheless, in spite of international recognition as a successful peacemaker, Austria's relations with her immediate neighbours have not always been free from tension. Successive governments have been faced with two major issues which have impaired Austria's relations with Italy and Yugoslavia. Both disputes centred on the vexed question of the rights of national minorities: the Austrians in the South Tyrol, which had been ceded to Italy under the Treaty of St Germain, and the Slovenian minority in Carinthia, the most southerly of Austria's federal 'Länder'. Both disputes were originally linked with territorial claims; the Austrian demand for the re-incorporation of the South Tyrol being matched by Yugoslav claims to that part of Carinthia with a Slovenian population. The territorial claims were soon dropped, but the interests of the varying minorities were defended with passion.

The Paris agreement of 1946 between Italy and Austria – the so-called Gruber/de Gasperi agreement – had made provision for equal rights for the German-speaking population of the South Tyrol and had promised autonomy to the province of Bolzano, but this had not been fully implemented by the Italians. Relations between Italy and Austria suffered accordingly and were at a low ebb in the 1960s as a result of acts of terrorism by German-speaking extremists in the South Tyrol. The dispute was not settled until 1969, and by then there had been debates on the subject at the United Nations and long and arduous negotiations between the two countries; under the terms of the new agreement, greater power was to be given to the provincial authorities of the German-speaking area without, however, granting full autonomy to the region.[10]

Where Austria had been the champion of minority rights in Italy, in Carinthia the boot was firmly on the other foot. Under the terms of the State Treaty, Austria was obliged to safeguard the interests of the Slovenian minority, but had failed to fully face up to her responsibilities in this regard. During the late 1950's Austrian procrastination over the implementation of both Slovenian and German as languages of instruction in schools gave rise to tensions with the Yugoslavs, who regarded themselves as the guardians of the Slovenian minority. In the 1970's the conflict spilled over once again, this time provoked by apparently trivial causes. The Austrian government had decreed that the 'Ortstafeln', the boundary signs of towns and villages in South Carinthia, should no longer be in German alone, but in Slovenian as well. When these new signs were erected, they were defaced or removed under cover of darkness by self-styled German-Carinthian patriots, and the overtones of German nationalism in the public pronouncement of some local politicians resurrected an ideological spectre which most Austrians had trusted was dead and buried.

Austria's difficulties with Italy over the South Tyrol also caused problems on the economic front after the establishment of the European Community by the Treaty of Rome in 1957. The six original signatories to the treaty sought to create an economic unit which would absorb and replace individual national economies, but the long-term goal of political as well as economic unity never raised the question of Austria or, indeed, other neutral countries ever becoming full members of the Community. Despite her economic dependence on the six member countries, and particularly on West Germany, Austria had no intention of ignoring the State Treaty and her obligations of neutrality. Her alignment with EFTA (the European Free Trade Area) in the 1960's was a different matter since EFTA's aims were wholly economic and were restricted to the abolition of customs barriers between the various mem-

14

bers. After the failure of the United Kingdom (the guiding hand behind EFTA) to gain entry to the European Community in 1962–63 the Austrian government responded to the threat of increasing trade discrimination against her goods by the Community members by trying to secure individual terms for herself. This move failed; it was blocked by Italy (a direct repercussion of the dispute over South Tyrol) and vetoed by France, while the Soviet Union reminded Austria very firmly of her obligations as a neutral state.[11] Austria and other non-aligned states of EFTA were eventually accommodated in 1972 by an agreement with the enlarged European Community of ten members which took account of the political obligations and neutral status of the various signatories. This agreement was fully implemented by 1977, abolishing tariff and trade barriers for commercial and industrial goods.

Austria's growing international stature in the years following the State Treaty must in some measure be due to the secure foundation provided at home by the eleven years of continuing political co-operation between the two major parties in the so-called 'Grand Coalition'. As a 'national government' the coalition alliance had made a major contribution to the conclusion of the State Treaty itself. As the representative of over 80% of the population it could fairly claim overwhelming popular support for the goal of Austrian independence. By 1955, however, it had served its main purpose. Austria was free, it had a stable economy, the 'Anschluß' mentality had been replaced by a new national consciousness and the ideological differences of the past had been bridged by a broad measure of democratic understanding; why, then, did Austria continue with a form of government for which there was no longer any political necessity?

In the first instance, neither of the two major parties was in a position to govern on its own. Neither party had an absolute majority in parliament and neither was willing to enrol the Freedom Party as a junior coalition partner in view of its dubious right-wing reputation. In addition, neither coalition partner was inclined to renounce the executive power it had by then secured for itself. When it came to elections neither party went to the people to argue for an absolute majority for itself, but rather to argue why its opponents should not receive an absolute majority for its policies. Both parties tended to revert to emotive slogans all too often designed to evoke the shadow of the First Republic in the minds of the electorate.

Indeed, for all their personal friendships and successful co-operation in government the leading Austrian politicians of the 1950s and early 1960s seemed to have been haunted by the last vestiges of the political suspicions which had bedevilled the First Republic, and simply could not bring themselves to contemplate or seriously consider the possibility that their political opponents might assume office in their own right. It took a new generation of voters and politicians, a generation brought up in the traditions of the Second Republic and owing allegiance to no other body, to dispel such shadows, break up traditional party loyalties and create sufficient political fluidity in voting patterns to allow one or other of the major parties a chance of securing an absolute parliamentary majority. Thus it was not until 1966 that Austria elected its first one-party government, the ÖVP under its leader Chancellor Josef Klaus. The then opposition party, the SPÖ, had to wait until 1970 for its turn in office. The 1970 elections returned the SPÖ, under the leadership of Bruno Kreisky, as the largest parliamentary party but without an absolute majority. After eighteen months of minority government with the FPÖ as a junior partner, the Socialists called a snap election in 1971 and were returned with an absolute majority, a position they retained in the elections of 1975 and 1979.

Coalition is by definition a matter of compromise, of avoiding extremes and seeking a 'middle way', and it must be said that as a result the political atmosphere in Austria in the early 1960's became increasingly stagnant. Long over-due reforms, particularly in education and social matters were further delayed, and the absence of any meaningful political debate meant that the trivia of political life (for example, whether to allow an entry visa to Otto von Hapsburg, the current head of the dynasty), received disproportionate attention. The high level of consensus necessary to support a coalition government led to decisions being made outside parliament and behind closed doors. The only opposition party, the Freedom Party (FPÖ), was too weak to exercise any effective criticism of the government's activities. Government was by 'Koalitions-ausschuß', the coalition committee, and in parliament itself the governing parties eschewed conflict in favour of a united political front.

In such a stultifying atmosphere, where the expensive cultural splendour of Herbert von Karajan's regime at the Vienna State Opera was generally acclaimed as the jewel in Vienna's crown, intellectual life tended towards the purely provincial if not downright complacent. It was as if there were an unspoken agreement not to indulge in any form of activity which might suggest discontent with the achievements of the pre-war reconstruction. The coalition committee made its decisions 'in the public interest' carefully screened from public scrutiny in parliament and in this it was soon joined by the so-called 'Parity Commission', established in 1957.

By far the most powerful institution in Austrian political life, the Parity Commission has no basis in law and yet makes recommendations – which are acted upon – in the most crucial of all political areas, the development of social and economic policy. It meets regularly once a month under the Chairmanship of the Federal Chancellor and is composed of representatives of the government, the Trade Union Federation, the Council of Austrian Chambers of Labour, the Federal Economic Chamber and the Presidential Conference of the Chambers of Agriculture. Membership is thus representative of the full cross-section of the political scene, ensuring that the Commission's recommendations will almost always be followed by the government of the day whatever its political hue.

The Parity Commission enshrines the principle of social partnership, the guiding light in the early wages and prices agreements of the Second Republic. It owes its existence in no small measure to the efforts of the Austrian Trade Union Federation, whose aims, as formulated by one of its leading officials are: 'to come to terms with the current situation as realistically as possible, so that we can choose the most practical course of action.'[12] For Klenner this means self-discipline in the interest of continuing economic growth, a far cry indeed from the demands for free collective bargaining so close to the hearts of his British trade union colleagues.

The consequences of such a pragmatic approach include removing the political element from confrontations between labour and capital, and securing the practical benefits of economic expansion, a better standard of living for broad sections of the population. In Austria contentious issues tend to be settled at the negotiating table; the Austrians proudly inform foreign journalists and industrialists that the average length of a strike in their country can be measured in seconds! Industrial harmony has led to the virtual eradication of poverty in modern Austria. The welfare state was vigorously expanded, particularly in the 1970s, and even in an age of world-wide recession the level of employment remains high and the rate of inflation within acceptable bounds, well below the 10% so keenly sought after in some other European countries.

The Austrian trade union movement has thus secured a considerable voice in economic affairs by its positive contribution to the country's economic prosperity, but this influence has had to be bought at a price. Compromise has been inevitable and critics of the social partnership point to the lack of communication between trade union leadership and grass-root membership, to the tendency towards increased bureaucracy and paternalistic decision-making; they also claim that the emphasis on economic growth has, in fact, led to a deterioration in the relative financial position of the white and blue-collar workers with a marked deterioration in the conditions of the lower paid.[13] Whatever the merits of such claims it is self-evident that the trade union movement in Austria no longer considers its role to be that of a pressure group or negotiating body soley responsible to its own membership. It has undoubtedly been very successful in its attempts to reconcile conflicting sectional interests, and the country as a whole has benefited from this new concept of trade union activity. It should not, however, be forgotten that these gains have been made in a climate of continuous economic growth and increasing affluence; it remains to be seen whether such social partnership as a form of sublimated class-conflict (Bruno Kreisky) can survive the strains of a period of serious economic recession. The inevitable conflict of loyalties between national and sectional interests will prove the acid test, and it may well be that harsh economic realities will resurrect traditional antagonisms. It is a dilemma the Second Republic has not yet had to face.

Unlike the British 'social contract' of the 1970's, social partnership in Austrian terms implies a fundamental change in the understanding of pluralistic democracy. Whilst on the one hand undermining the power of parliament, it also incorporates a wide cross-section of interests in affairs of state. It is in short a continuation of the principle of power-sharing in Austrian political life beyond the political demarcation of the end of the coalition era. Even after 1966 and the first one-party government, neither of the two major parties has been wholly excluded from the effective process of decision-making.[14]

The 'Proporz', another specifically Austrian phenomenon, serves much the same function. One of the most widely-practised of Austrian conventions the 'Proporz', as its name suggests, secures a proportional appointment of official positions according to party affiliation in all aspects of public life. Only undertakings that are private in the strictest sense of the word escape its ramifications. The

18

'Proporz' evolved as a further manifestation of the Grand Coalition during which both governing parties filled appointments to 'their' ministries with their own men. Political balance within individual ministries was assured by allocating an appropriate number of positions to the coalition partners. In several ministries this was to be seen at the very top where an ÖVP minister would have to work with an SPÖ state secretary and vice versa. In practice, of course, certain areas were traditionally held by the different parties: the Ministry of Education, for example, was controlled by the ÖVP while the SPÖ exercised control over nationalized industry.

As a consequence, membership of both major parties, which was in any case high, grew to a size almost unique in European terms, for it was not merely the top positions which were allocated on a proportional basis, but such patronage extended over virtually the whole social hierarchy. As Bluhm so rightly comments, Austria 'enjoyed' an extensive system of patronage in which the party rank and file were well taken care of.[15] The demise of coalition government had little effect on the 'Proporz' and the Second Republic has justifiably been described as a 'Parteibuch-Republik'.[16] Despite increasing political mobility and a marked improvement in the position of independents, job prospects are still closely linked to party affiliations. Whilst this may prevent the creation of an all-powerful one-party state and may guarantee a fair representation in public life of the opposition parties, it tends to reduce political interest and commitment to a purely pragmatic if not cynical concern for material well-being and career advancement.

The peculiarly Austrian version of pluralistic democracy with its emphasis on consensus politics, social partnership and 'Proporz' has enabled a state of political relaxation to develop. The 'end of ideology' – in itself the dominant ideology in the technological age – has perhaps gained more ground in Austria than in the other European parliamentary democracies, and it may well be that such a result was the inevitable reaction against the beleaguered mentality which so bedevilled the First Republic. The two major parties, once deeply entrenched in their respective ideological bases, have now become virtually interchangeable, as was explicitly shown in the results of the most recent general elections in May 1979. The SPÖ, traditionally a party of change and reform, managed to increase its absolute majority in parliament, thanks not merely to the outstanding personal merits of Chancellor Kreisky, but also to a concerted electoral commitment to continuity and stability, stealing the clothes off the ÖVP's back. Hence they were able to stifle the inevitable charges of lethargy levelled against any party that has enjoyed nine years in office.

It is most improbable that Austria will ever revert to the attitudes of the First Republic, even if the Austrian economy were to come under severe strain. The greatest dangers now facing the Second Republic are a tendency towards complacency and a general reluctance to practise constructive self-criticism. Criticism there is, ranging from petty bickering to prophecies of gloom and despondency, and the failure of national sporting heroes to live up to expectations is greeted with the same, almost apocalyptic response as is the liberalization of the laws controlling abortion.[17] The Austrians themselves are by no means sure that they inhabit the idyllic, fairy-tale land suggested by their tourist brochures or indeed by such divergent figures as Pope Paul VI and the Soviet politician Mikoyan.[18] But in all their self-criticism and scepticism the political structures underpinning the state all too often receive short measure. Stability, for all its positive effects, has also resulted in political apathy, particularly amongst the younger generation. Thus the wave of political and ideological involvement which swept Western Europe and America in the late sixties found but a faint echo amongst Austrian youth. The generation conflict in Austria took a literary and cultural rather than political aspect.

There are, however, signs of a gradual shift in the political climate which extends beyond the mere transfer of political power from one party to another. As the Atomic Energy referendum of November 1978 indicates, the Austrian people do not regard themselves as lobby fodder. Despite the concerted efforts on the part of government, industry and the trade unions to persuade the nation to approve the peaceful use of nuclear power within Austria, the referendum showed a finely balanced decision in favour of the 'Noes'. Such a result, however narrow the rejection, marks an independence and political awareness not noticably evident in Austrian history. The rejection of the use of nuclear power also threw some doubt on the absolute priority given to economic growth, a priority which had virtually ensured Austria's 'mini-economic miracle'. These far-reaching economic implications, together with the growing popularity of referenda in general, suggest a desire to be more directly involved in the democratic process free from organized interest, a desire which could well set the wheels of political evolution in motion once again.

20

NOTES

1. Adolf Schärf, *'Österreichs Erneuerung 1944–1955'*, Vienna 1955, p. 20. Quoted in: Erika Weinzierl/Kurt Skalnik (eds), *Österreich. Die Zweite Republik*, Graz/Vienna/Cologne, 1972, vol.I, p. 15.
2. Quoted in: Bruno Kreisky, 'Der Staatsvertrag und die österreichische Neutralität. Ein historischer Überblick', in: *Neutralität und Koexistenz. Aufsätze und Reden*, Munich, 1975, (= neue edition List), p. 38.
3. Norbert Leser, 'Das Österreich der Ersten und Zweiten Republik', in: Norbert Leser/Richard Berczeller, *Als Zaungäste der Politik*, Vienna/Munich, 1977, p. 128.
4. cf. Fritz Fellner, 'Die außenpolitische und völkerrechtliche Situation Österreichs 1938. Österreichs Wiederherstellung als Kriegsziel der Alliierten', in: Weinzierl/Skalnik, op.cit., vol.I, pp. 63f.
5. cf. Gerald Stourzh, 'Der Weg zum Staatsvertrag und zur immerwährenden Neutralität', in: Weinzierl/Skalnik, op.cit., vol.I, p. 206.
6. Kurt Skalnik, 'Parteien', in: Weinzierl/Skalnik, op.cit., vol.II, p. 202.
7. Norbert Leser, 'Das Erbe der Revolutionären Sozialisten', in: Leser/Berczeller, op.cit., p. 71.
8. cf. Rudolf G. Ardelt/Hanns Haas, 'Die Westintegration Österreichs nach 1945', in: *Österreichische Zeitschrift für Politik und Wissenschaft*, 4(1975), 379–99. cf. also: Karl Gruber, *Ein politisches Leben. Österreichs Weg zwischen den Diktaturen*, Vienna, 1976.
9. Bruno Kreisky, 'Der Staatsvertrag und die österreichische Neutralität', op.cit., p. 27.
10. cf. Stephan Verosta, 'Außenpolitik', in: Weinzierl/Skalnik, op.cit., vol.I, pp. 318f.
11. ibid. pp. 329f. cf. also: Alois Brusatti, 'Entwicklung der Wirtschaft und Wirtschaftspolitik', in: Weinzierl/Skalnik, op.cit., vol.I, pp. 479f.
12. Fritz Klenner, 'Interessengruppen', in: Weinzierl/Skalnik, op.cit., vol.II, p. 189.
13. cf. for example: Egon Matzner, 'Funktionen der Sozialpartnerschaft', in: Heinz Fischer (ed), *Das politische System Österreichs*, 2nd rev.ed., Vienna, 1977, pp. 437f.
14. cf. Anton Pelinka, 'Von der Koalition zur Einparteienregierung', in: *Revue d'Allemagne*, 6 (1974), No.1, 37.
15. William T. Bluhm, *Building an Austrian Nation*, New Haven/London, 1973, p. 73f.
16. 'a card-carrying republic' 'Parteibuch – Republik', in: *Die Furche*, 18.4.1979.
17. cf. an article by the former Austrian Minister of Education Theodor Piffl-Perčević in which he equates the legalization of abortion in Austria with the end of the Second Republic: 'Heimlicher Staatsstreich gegen Österreich. Die Zweite Republik endet mit der Freigabe ungeborenen Lebens', in: *Die Presse*, 12/13. 1. 1974.
18. Pope Paul VI referred to Austria as an 'island of the blessed', on the

occasion of a state visit to the Vatican by the then Federal President Franz Jonas in 1971, and Mikoyan is said to have called Austria 'fast ein Paradies', 'almost a paradise'. The latter comment is quoted by Ernst Fischer in the last chapter of his memoirs (*Das Ende einer Illusion: Erinnerungen 1945–1955*, Vienna/Munich/Zurich, 1973).

22

II The Austrian Tradition:
Continuity and Change

Alan Best

Vienna in the years immediately following the Second World War, the Vienna of Orson Welles and *The Third Man*, may be seen as the nadir in a succession of humiliating contractions from the erstwhile glory of that city's role as capital and focal point of the Hapsburg dynasty. A divided city in an occupied country it could not even claim to match Fritz Hochwälder's ironic disparagement of its reduced post-imperial status – namely that it had declined in status from metropolis to capital of a minor Alpine republic. Those who returned to Vienna in 1945 and the years immediately after were reminded at every turn of what had been lost beyond recall. The architectural rubble of an erstwhile Hapsburg splendour represented the last remnants of an idea which had been potent enough to sustain generations of Austrians in the past, the question was: who was to show the way forward?

Hans Weigel's comment on the paucity of post-war literary talent: 'Die österreichische Literatur besteht derzeit aus zwei Autoren, aus dem Lernet und dem Holenia'[1] became a by-word, for Alexander Lernet-Holenia's criminal and adventure novels enjoyed considerable popularity and seemingly lacked any real literary challenge, since many of his generation had either failed to survive the war or were never to recapture after 1945 the vigour and quality of their pre-war work. Indeed, in many respects the seven years from the *Anschluß* to 1945 proved an insurmountable obstacle for those Austrian writers who had been born prior to 1918, and many of the works which reached the general public in Austria after 1945 had in fact been completed, or at least begun, prior to 1938.

Of the major literary figures, Kraus, Roth and Horváth had died before the war began, Zweig and Musil died in 1942, Werfel in 1945 and Broch remained in exile in the United States until his death in 1951. His novel *Der Tod des Vergil* (The Death of Vergil, published in German in 1947), consisting to a considerable extent of an inner

23

monologue covering the last eighteen hours of Vergil's life (during which time the poet questions the relevance of the *Aeniad*, which he is inclined to destroy on the grounds that what he once thought was valid now strikes him as mere aestheticism), and the posthumous publication of Musil's gigantic novel *Der Mann ohne Eigenschaften* (The Man without Qualities, 1952), one of the less well-read works of narrative fiction, although both landmarks of considerable literary significance, echoed rather forlornly in a void.

Those who had fled and those who had stayed in Austria and survived were now joined by a younger generation born after 1918 for whom the Third Reich was the dominant experience and the backcloth against which they had begun to write. All three groups shared a common sense of disorientation, neatly expressed by Hans Weigel in 1952:

> Aus der Fremde ist ebensowenig eine Literatur zurückgekehrt, wie sie aus den Trümmern aufgetaucht ist. Auch wer bei den Siegern Zuflucht fand, hat den Krieg verloren. . . . Uns, die wir in deutscher Sprache schreiben, sind große Tote als Vorbilder gegeben, Kafka und Musil und Broch, von den Lebenden aber keine Meister unserer Sprache. Die Richtzeichen sind: Joyce und Malraux, Camus und Sartre, Wilder und Gide und Proust. Der Rest ist Zuckmayer.[2]

'Der Rest ist Zuckmayer' is a deliberate historical echo. Having assisted at the dismemberment of the Hapsburg Empire Clemenceau is reputed to have pointed to what was left after the various national aspirations had been gratified and commented: 'What's left is Austria'. Weigel's words are even more pessimistic given the fact that the remaining 'Austrian' Carl Zuckmayer was born in the Rhineland and only lived in Austria between his migration from Berlin in 1933 to his departure for Switzerland in 1938. Though married to an Austrian, he chose not to return to Austria after the war but, like Hochwälder, settled in Switzerland.

Weigel, who himself did so much to promote and encourage a new generation of Austrian writers after the war, also offers an intriguing argument as to why Austrian literature managed to ride the effects of National Socialism and emerge relatively unchanged, while in Germany everything was reckoned *ab initio*. Many critics have argued that there was no 'Nullpunkt' in Austrian literature, others that there were several. Weigel comes close to establishing yet another 'Austrian myth', and yet his argument has considerable merit:

> Die eigentliche Geburtsstunde Österreichs war fünf Minuten vor dem Untergang Österreichs: der 12. Februar 1938. . . . Das österreichische positive Bewußtsein ist eigentlich damals erst entstanden und ich glaube nicht, daß ohne diese vier Wochen von Februar – März 1938 die große Wiederkehr des Österreichischen im Jahre 1945 möglich wäre. . . . Durch das Leben in der Emigration und durch das quasi-abstrakte Denken an Österreich war Österreich ein unverlierbarer Begriff geworden . . .[3]

This 'positive Austrianism' explains why Austro-Hungary does not loom so large in the calculations and works of what can well be termed the transitional generation of Austrian writers after 1945 as it had before 1938. The Third Reich had effectively broken what vestiges of political continuity there had been between the Hapsburg Empire and the First Republic, the situation required a critical appraisal which took note of the political realities, dispensed with myth and yet drew on the positive aspects of the defunct Hapsburg era. After 1945 the 'Hapsburg myth' went underground, reappearing either in costume-piece revivals or borrowed clothes; before 1938 the critique of the Hapsburg era which permeates the first part of Musil's novel *Der Mann ohne Eigenschaften* with its brilliant analysis of the weaknesses and self-delusions of Hapsburg Austria, or which is found in Joseph Roth's *Radetzkymarsch* (Radetzky March, 1932) and Werfel's *Der Abituriententag* (Reunion Day, 1928) and *Das Trauerhaus* (The House of Mourning, 1927) generally subsumed under the aegis of the imaginary state 'Kakanien'[4] although by no means without bite, was very much from within, accepting if not tolerating the Hapsburg rubric. The enthusiasm with which Fritz von Herzmanovsky-Orlando's 'Tarockanien'[5] was greeted in the 1950s, an ironical and highly-personalized gloss on Austria's glorious past, coinciding as it did with the State Treaty and the creation of the 'new' Austria is a significant indication of the popular search for continuity without the discipline of historical realism. Herzmanovsky-Orlando's play *Kaiser Joseph und die Bahnwärterstochter* (Emperor Joseph and the Railwayman's Daughter) was successfully staged by the Burgtheater in 1957 and together with his novel *Gaulschreck im Rosennetz* (How Jaromir von Eynhuf Frightened the Horses, written in 1928, available in a new edition after the war in 1957) it reflects the panoply of Austro-Hungary as many wished to remember it. Herzmanovsky-Orlando wrote to please himself but he nonetheless struck a chord in popular sentiment that was eagerly received.

Almost inevitably, any Austrian is drawn towards the Hapsburg era – (where else indeed is he to look for his cultural roots?) – but the illusory nature of imperial unity and a nostalgic longing which chose to believe in myth as if it were reality had been aspects of an inward-looking and a-political attitude to life which had failed to recognize National Socialism for what it was in the 1930s. The tenacity with which the Austrian public clung to the past is well revealed by an incident from the 1960s. A film version of Roth's *Radetzkymarsch* provoked considerable popular outrage by including a scene in which the emperor was shown in his nightshirt. This was not how the Austrians wished to remember Franz Josef or what he stood for!

'Kakanien' had been posited as a supra-national entity, but in reality the Austro-Hungarian Empire had never managed to fuse its multiplicity of peoples into a genuine nation; nonetheless, it was the surface image of a unified Empire to which those who felt overwhelmed by events beyond their control tended to withdraw, and the more the House of Hapsburg showed signs of inner decay the greater the task-force of volunteers who stepped forward ready to shore up the edifice. The disintegration of Hapsburg Europe after World War I was not, however, so much the work of politicians in a distant capital as the consequence of former Hapsburg subjects stepping out of a looking-glass world into a reality which, although harsher and of brief duration, was at least theirs to command.

Apart from Joseph Roth's novels, a significant indication of the mood of the Austrian literary scene in the years immediately after 1945 is provided by *3. November 1918*, a drama by Franz Theodor Csokor (1885–1969). This, the first part of what was to be a European Trilogy, was completed by 1936, but the first complete, uncut production in Vienna did not take place until 1949. The play transcends the immediate political trauma of 1918 to provide audiences in post-war Austria with a sense of national identity and direction. The Viennese public had found Ödön von Horváth's abrasive criticisms of their heritage in *Geschichten aus dem Wiener Wald* (Tales from the Vienna Woods) too bruising when that work was revived in 1948 and sought reassurance that there had been more to the First Republic than Horváth's picture of a world dominated by the ethos of the *Kleinbürger*. This public accepted Csokor's play because it discredited the illusion of Hapsburg unity and yet at the same time suggested that a new and true Austria had risen phoenix-like from the ashes of the Hapsburg Empire, a phoenix that could rise for a second time now 'in einem Reich, das aus Menschen gebaut wird and nicht aus Nationen und Grenzen.'[6] *3. November 1918* offered reassurance that there was a way forward and allowed the prospects for an eventual Second Republic to continue the ideals of the First. A further bonus was the fact that this much-sought sense of continuity was undisturbed by any direct evocation of National Socialism, although the discerning ear can sense the problems as yet beneath the surface, and it is not easy to disregard the sound of machine-gun fire at the close of the play when 'Hapsburg' turns on 'Hapsburg'.

Csokor was born in Vienna, and if he at times seems to succumb uncritically to the 'Hapsburg philosophy' the complexities of his own ancestry help explain this susceptibility. He had Serbian and Croatian blood from his father's side and Hungarian, Czech and German blood from his mother's; he was, in short, a walking em-bodiment of 'Hapsburg unity'. In addition, Vienna, though it can never be taken as representative of Austria as a whole, can, in the late nineteenth and early twentieth centuries, be likened to the Empire under anaesthetic. The outward image is of a harmonious blend of races and cultures, but in the capital at least, the political stresses and strains were dulled by the 'Wiener Luft' and its capacity for absorbing moral and political considerations in a social round devoted both to pleasure and to the world of the creative imagina-tion. *3. November 1918* may well mark the transition from Haps-burg myth to Austrian myth, for its institutionalization was assured in Csokor's later years when it was performed each October 26 (The Austrian National Day) at the Burgtheater in Vienna. A film ver-sion made in 1965 is further evidence of the emotive appeal con-tained in a play conceived some thirty years earlier.

3. November 1918 is set in a military convalescent home, a former tourist-hotel high up a mountain pass in Carinthia in early Novem-ber 1918. The hotel is empty except for a handful of officers and enlisted men and a nurse. Between them the soldiery provide a geo-graphical polyglot of Hapsburg Europe bound together by a common cause and common tongue. They all speak

das alte, leicht dialektische sogenannte k.u.k. Armeedeutsch,

27

gefärbt durch die besondere nationale Zugehörigkeit eines jeden.[7]

However, it is not clear whether this reflects Csokor's acceptance of the unifying spirit of the Hapsburg era or represents an implicit criticism of its essentially superficial and illusory nature. Their shattered bodies, relics of a former human splendour, epitomize the straits to which Austro-Hungary herself has been reduced by the war; they are brothers on the surface, their uniform testifies to this – but they have yet to learn how fragile this bond is.

Oberst Radosin, the senior officer and career soldier, lives for the imperial idea. He is a relic from the past as his preoccupation with Xenophon's Anabasis, the march of ten thousand ancient Greeks, indicates. Radosin draws hope for the present from his study of the past, unaware that, as he does so, the present is passing him by. It is a peculiarly Austrian characteristic. What Radosin admires in the Ancients:

> Denn je weiter die weg waren von ihrer Heimat, desto mehr sind sie richtige Griechen geworden, nicht Athener, Spartaner oder Thebaner[8]

is a vain illusion in contemporary terms. He is a refugee from reality who draws his strength from a misplaced belief in an inner bond drawing his fellow officers together in the interests of a 'Vaterland über den Völkern'[9] and yet, as the snows which have held this outpost of Hapsburg power in animated suspension melt, Csokor indicates the self-delusion of such a supra-national myth, the very cornerstone of Hapsburg propaganda. Kaczuik, the sailor who brings news of defeat and revolution, provides the catalyst that turns Hapsburgers into nationalists. He gives his suspicious audience a lesson in instant political geography, using his bayonet on a 'k.u.k.' railway map from the hotel lobby to cut away those regions which have defected from the Empire. When he has finished the audience sees the rough outline of modern Austria, but Radosin can only think in terms of the past:

> Radosin: Sieben Völker stehen mit uns um den Tisch – und
> jeder davon hat für das Ganze geblutet, wie das
> Ganze für ihn . . . wir waren doch mehr schon als *eine*
> Nation – eins sind wir aus sieben gewesen – ihr wollt

aus der hellen Wohnung aurück in den Zuchtstall.

Sokal: – Aber es sind *unsre* Ställe, Herr Oberst.[10]

Unable to survive the collapse of the world as he has interpreted it, Radosin commits suicide, his death symptomatic of the inner weakness of the Empire's political structure. His brother officers pay their last respects in a moving epitaph to an age that is gone; as each drops a handful of soil into the grave he expresses his new-found identity. In burying the past the officers proclaim the future:

Erde aus Ungarn – Erde aus Polen – Erde aus Kärnten – Slove-nische Erde – Tschechische Erde – Römische Erde . . .

until finally it is the turn of the Jewish medical officer, Dr. Grün:

mit einem Zögern, aber nicht lächerlich, eher rührend Erde – aus – Erde aus Österreich.[11]

Ironically, since scarcely two decades later this New Austria was to embrace the protagonists of a new form of 'racial hygiene', it is a Jew who first declares his allegiance to this new state – the point can scarcely have been lost on post-1945 audiences; while the others look back, blinkered by the past, he has no past loyalties and can only look forward. Unfettered by historical preconceptions, but in dire need of a spiritual home, Grün effectively accepts the validity of Radosin's idealism, stripped of its geographical overtones. More ominously for the future of these new states, Zierowitz, a fiery nationalist defector from the imperial idea, can see what has gone wrong, but is himself powerless to move with the times. In his words there is more than an echo of the wishful thinking symptomatic of Hapsburg nostalgia; the concept of 'Maß' in particular, with its overtones of order and cohesion, is particularly revealing:

Freilich in diesem Reich, das nun aus ist, da war noch ein Maß dagewesen, das für uns alle gereicht haben könnte, wenn man dort nicht zurückgeschaut hätte, statt vor.[12]

Csokor's play ends with the new nationalists departing for their new homelands, it does not show their arrival, nor does it do more than hint at the problematic future they will face bereft of the protective shelter of superior authority. For the audiences in Austria after 1945 this was a most convenient caesura, it allowed them to indulge their national identity without requiring them to subject this emotion to critical scrutiny. *3. November 1918* manifests the strengths and weaknesses of the Austrian condition. The search for continuity, the desire to reaffirm values which were once held to be paramount leads the modern writer and his audience from political reality towards an investigation of metaphysical values of general relevance, towards history or towards a combination of both aspects. If historical themes are not to become mere pageantry their relevance to the world in which they are received must be apparent. In *3. November 1918*, and more particularly in the reception it received from audiences in Austria after 1945 it is hard to escape the conclusion that historicism represented an aesthetically pleasing and conveniently less obtrusive means of avoiding direct confrontation with the present. The 'Heimkehrer' who paraded before the Viennese public after 1945 were returning home from the 1914–18 conflict, not, as in Germany, from the Nazi war-machine. One possible explanation for this may be the commonly held feeling, tantamount to a myth in its own right, and one that had been beatified by the terms of the Moscow Memorandum, that, having been dragged into the conflict against her will, Austria did not have to purge herself of collective guilt and, as a consequence, there was not the terrible gulf between the individual returning home to find himself at odds with society and the society which regarded those returning as manifestations of a past it would sooner forget.

This does not mean that Austrian literature ignored the effects of National Socialism, rather that it tended to consider moral implications on a general plane rather than in a contemporary setting. Fritz Hochwälder's drama *Meier Helmbrecht* (1946) reworked a medieval theme to comment on the brutality of the Nazi era as a whole and its effect on individuals and communities in particular, but of necessity the play does not draw a direct equation. Similarly Jesuit Paraguay (*Das Heilige Experiment* – The Holy Experiment, 1943) and revolutionary France (*Der öffentliche Ankläger* – The Public Prosecutor, 1948) are a direct response to Höchwälder's experiences of National Socialism. In both cases the author felt the need for an historical perspective to provide the focus for the present and it was not until the 1960s that Hochwälder dealt directly with the Nazi era in *Der Himbeerpflücker* (The Raspberry-picker, 1964) and *Der Befehl* (The Order, 1966/67) and by then of course he

30

was once more dealing in historical reconstruction. Saiko's novels submerge political considerations under a preoccupation with psychological implications; even when the setting is the civil disturbances in Austria in the 1930s (*Der Mann im Schilf*, The Man in the Reeds, 1955) the emphasis is on the inner world of the protagonist, and although the setting for Saiko's first novel *Auf dem Floß* (On the Raft, publ. 1948) is Austria in the years immediately after World War I, the world in which the novel moves is anachronistically feudal and nineteenth century in spirit and totally unrepresentative of the social and political attitudes of the First Republic.

Saiko's concern is not history but psychology, he creates his idiosyncratic world to allow the sub-conscious ebb and flow of the psyche unhindered expression. Deliberately eschewing direct and literal contact with reality Saiko nonetheless creates a powerful panorama of psychological truths. He expresses this primary concern in his essay *Der Roman heute und morgen* (The Novel today and tomorrow) where he defines the central preoccupation of modern literature as:

> Die Erweiterung des Aussagbaren im Vor und Unbewußten, des Irrationalen, die Gestaltung jener in der Regel nicht wahrgehabten Kräfte und Einstellungen, die dem Gebiet des Animistischen und Magischen angehören, die im tiefsten Seelenleben verankert und von da aus wirksam sind. . . . Die Aufgabe des Künstlers aber ist es zu zeigen, wie dieses 'Agens der Tiefe', wie die untergründigen hintergründigen Mächte durch die oberste Konventionsschicht hindurchbrechen und zum Konflikt mit deren Instanzen die wesenhaften und bewegenden Ursachen beisteuern.[13]

Saiko's 'magic realism' combines science and inspiration, analysis and metaphysical speculation returning again and again to the world of myth. In his work, however, this is not the local myth of Hapsburg identity; instead Saiko is able to imbue the milieu and events of his work with an awareness of forces which are universal.

Saiko's involvement with psychology is echoed in the works of Manès Sperber (b. 1905), a former student of the Viennese Alfred Adler. Sperber's major work, the trilogy *Wie eine Träne im Ozean* (publ. 1961) (*Der verbrannte Dornbusch*, 1949; *Tiefer als der Abgrund*, 1950; *Die verlorene Bucht*, 1955 (Like a Tear in the Ocean – The Burned Thornbush: Deeper than the Pit: The Lost Bay) was described by Walther Karsch as a literary document of the tragic fate of the European intellectual. Sperber's political leanings, (he left the communist party in protest against Stalin's show trials in the 1930s) ensure that his work is firmly rooted in social awareness, and the three novels which form *Wie eine Träne im Ozean* take a retrospective look at the years 1931–1945 with nine European countries as their setting. Sperber takes as his theme those communists whose attempts to change the world fail because the ideals in which they believe are perverted and abused by those they called their comrades. Sperber's keen eye for the discrepancy between illusion and reality is reflected in his belief in life as a series of revolutionary upheavals, as a constant state of flux, in which the successful revolution immediately sparks off its successor at the moment of fulfilment. It is a clear repudiation of the stasis of 'Ordnung' so beloved by many of his fellow-countrymen.

Sperber is insistent that he is not writing a political novel; indeed with his psychological background it is no surprise to find his work highly intellectual in tone and determinedly receptive to parable:

. . . Ich (habe) keine Gewißheiten zu bieten, sondern (mache) nur Fragen spruchreif; Charaktere, Situationen, Handlungen . . . Ereignisse, Erlebnisse und Erfahrungen (werden) hier nur dann behandelt, wenn sie in sich ein Gleichnis bergen.

. . . Das Dunkel eines Augenblickes trennt eine Szene von der anderen: Das Licht wandert dorthin, wo die Handlung es braucht. Was wie eine Episode aussieht, wird sich 300 Seiten später als ein höchst bedeutungsreicher Teil der Haupthandlung enthüllen; der Mann, der zuerst die zentrale Figur zu sein scheint, wird langsam zu einer Nebenfigur. Der Vordergrund tritt häufig zurück, der Hintergrund wird zum Zentrum der Handlung, ehe ihn das Dunkel wieder einhüllt.

. . . Dieser trilogische Roman hat nur scheinbar ein Ende, ihm fehlt überhaupt eine tröstliche Moral. Wie so viele andere Schriftsteller vor ihm, hat der Autor seinen Lesern nur eines angeboten – mit ihm seine Einsamkeit zu teilen. Vielleicht ist dies die einzige Form der Gemeinschaft, in der jene zueinanderfinden, die aus der gleichen Quelle den Mut schöpfen müssen, ohne Illusionen zu leben.[14]

Reich-Ranicki[15] disputes Sperber's claim that his novel uses politics as its raw material rather than its theme, arguing that *Wie eine Träne im Ozean* is a political novel, a handbook which highlights the workings of communism and the fascination it exerts every bit as much as it expresses the tragic fate of those who fight for the ideals they believe to be right. Be this as it may, the extracts from the *Vorwort* to the trilogy quoted above are sufficient indication of the intellectual and psychological tendencies which sustain the work. The association of apparently unconnected ideas, the apparent shifting of emphases, the insecurity of knowledge and above all the overwhelming sense of isolation reflect the author's preoccupation with an inner world transcending the limits of the world of 'reality' in which his characters move. By concentrating on the 'inner world' Sperber derives the strength to support his belief in the progress of mankind, for in the light of his psychoanalytical experience he is all too aware that it is only in the nakedness of the inner self that illusion and self-deceit can be swept aside and ultimate truth prevail.

The characteristic feature of this, the transitional generation of modern Austrian writers, is their abandonment of the explicitly Hapsburg milieu and its replacement by a keen awareness of monolithic domination of whatever kind. The Austrian preoccupation with language, from Hofmannsthal's despairing Chandos Letter onwards, suggests increasing despair as to the validity of the world in which the writers move. Sigmund Freud's analytical techniques and his illustration of the uncertainties of linguistic usage, the flawed channel of communication between the mind and the lips and the overriding domination of the conscious by the subconscious intensified this awareness. Karl Kraus' response was to posit an ideal of language, seeking a medium in which it was impossible to be grammatical and hypocritical and untruthful at the same time, while Ödön von Horváth's *Bildungsjargon*, an educated jargon consisting of cliché, platitude and received generalizations, represents a more negative communication of these fears. In 1914 Kraus could argue that there came a time when all good writers must stand up and be seen to be remaining silent – a particularly pertinent comment in view of the many illustrious Austrian literati who found employment during the First World War in the citation department of the Austrian War Office if not in direct propaganda work, but the silence with which his successors greeted the horrors of 1939–45 seems far less positive.

33

The personal record of many of these writers shows that their silence was not indifference but the consequence of an increasing introspection. The legacy of the Hapsburg years had conditioned the individual to disregard the possibility of change; disbelief in such a possibility bred pessimism and introspection, and self-analysis seemed the only available course of action. This literary parallel to the political *Lagermentalität* is the social aspect of a tendency in which the possibility of communication is denied and where the individual feels obliged to recreate a new totality around fixed points which he himself establishes. Gütersloh's 'total novel': *Sonne und Mond*, ein historischer Roman aus der Gegenwart,[16] a search for meaningful correspondences in an a-political context, is a direct echo of the trauma of political collapse. The 'historical present' combining as it does distance from reality with a spiritual appeal to the contemporary reader, and establishing landmarks which are spiritual and inward rather than objective is one escape, aestheticism is another. The sinologist Peter Kien in Canetti's novel *Die Blendung* (The Delusion, publ. 1935) turns away from the world to his world of books. His research articles, understood by barely a handful of other scholars, epitomize Canetti's despair at the possibility of effective 'rational' communication. Kien's inevitable defeat by the forces at large in this sordid world owes more to his weakness than their strength. His brother Georg, it should also be noted, has exchanged a successful career in gynaecology for an equally successful psychiatric practice. While Georg Kien is still very much of the world it is undeniably a world which he can fashion and interpret in response to his own preconceptions. The brain has usurped the womb and relegated it to incidental importance.

Peter Kien's response to the challenge of the world is indicted as a form of aesthetic escapism. The bankruptcy of his approach is highlighted in the conflagration which consumes him and his library, an event inspired by Canetti's own response to the burning of the Vienna Palace of Justice in 1927. Not every reader will sense this equation, however, and it is a characteristic of this generation that its exploration of the depths of inner psychology frequently disregards the social and political context in which the inner and outer worlds meet. The Austrian search for depth, for inner meaning, can all too readily lead to concern with patterns of existence rather than existence itself. Such wilful myopia is indeed the target of Heimito von Doderer's concept of

Apperzeptionsverweigerung by which the author criticizes a refusal to 'apperceive', that is to open the mind to i⁺s full potential and respond to all the stimuli that are in the atmosphere. The *Apperzeptionsverweigerer* thinks in preconceived patterns, drawing an artificial distinction between inner and outer worlds. As a consequence he sees life in terms of his private prejudices and obsessions; for him perhaps only 'dicke Damen'[17] are beautiful, or, conditioned by a lifetime in the civil service, he continues to think speak and act by the tenets of the *Dienstpragmatik*, the civil service code, even after his retirement.

The mythologizing of such personal fixations must, at least in part, reflect the influence of Sigmund Freud whose studies of the individual psyche gave the writer licence to create and study private myths, exchanging the external domination of the Hapsburg myth for a psychological extrapolation of inner preoccupations. This tendency is already evident in Kafka's work. His two 'Hapsburg' novels, *Das Schloß* and *Der Prozeß*, (The Castle; The Trial) while clearly products of a first-hand awareness of imperial bureaucratic practice, dispense with an overt Hapsburg background and centre their attention on an individual who is caught up in the workings of his own personal myth. Josef K. carries his trial with him wherever he goes; the court appears unexpectedly from behind a closed door at opposite ends of town, and in *Das Schloß* K., in claiming employment by the Castle, challenges the very existence of such a supreme authority. Indeed the Castle, as depicted by Kafka, in the opening pages of the novel, can be seen as nothing less than a product of collective suggestibility:

> Es war weder eine alte Ritterburg noch ein neuer Prunkbau, sondern eine ausgedehnte Anlage, die aus wenigen zweistöckigen, aber aus vielen eng aneinander stehenden niedrigen Bauten bestand; hätte man nicht gewußt, daß es ein Schloß sei, hätte man es für ein Städtchen halten können.[18]

The transitional generation of post-war writers combines an awareness of the dangers of such collective myths with a freedom from the Austro-Hungarian obsession. After all, the bureaucratic obscurantism prior to 1914 fades into insignificance for those who have weathered the executive decisions and linguistic euphemisms of mass murder and political tyranny after 1933. Even so, it seems that this is a generation unable to shed its past completely; the monolithic imperial presence had gone, but the writers of this generation are still obsessed by the power of the Idea. Years of political sterility had bred an exaggerated respect for the power and validity of literature as such, and it had come to exist in its own right and was not measured by the yardstick of the market place. The most basic conflicts are, as a consequence, frequently raised to an allegorical or universal level as if the answers cannot be found by looking at contemporary society. Like Doderer's ex-civil servant Julius Zihal in *Die erleuchteten Fenster* (The Illuminated Windows, 1951) the Austrian writer of this generation seems to prefer a telescope and a carefully-controlled pattern of observation in which he may choose his subject-matter.

This traditional 'positive' approach is perhaps best exemplified in the work of Max Mell (1882–1971). Mell's strong Christian beliefs, which had sustained him during the Nazi era, were expressed in the pre-war Christian *Festspiele* with which his name is so often associated: *Das Apostelspiel*, (The Apostles, 1923), *Das Schutzengelspiel*, (The Guardian Angel, 1923) and *Das Nachfolge' Christispiel* (The Imitation of Christ, 1927). In the darkening days of the 1930s Mell outlined his conception of the role of literature in troubled times, an account that is revealing in its attitude to social relevance:

Dieses Element im Dichterischen, das Ordnende, scheint mir heute vor allem beansprucht zu werden; es ist ihr größtes: aber was sonst als das Größte könnte dieser Zeit zu Hilfe kommen? . . . Denn außerhalb der künstlerischen Weltdeutung ist das Chaos.[19]

Creative writing, then, is an antidote to reality, it is to provide the sense of order and cohesion lacking in everyday existence. From here it is but a short step to an aesthetically biased view of the world which transcends the mundane to seek its own justification on a universal level. The temptation to see the world, not as it is, but according to one's own principles is hard to resist; the spectre of Doderer's *Apperzeptionsverweigerung* is not far away.

As Heinz Kindermann notes, the essence of Mell's work is the invocation of powers of healing and order to resolve contemporary chaos – it is an ambitious, if not unrealistic, undertaking. Mell concentrates on individual strengths and weaknesses in order to project a world that is self-sufficient and in balance and he attempts this by means of artistic vision: 'Der Dramatiker muß ein größeres Ganzes vor sich sehen, eine Gemeinschaft,'[20] Kindermann seems almost mesmerized by this prospect:

Der [Gemeinschaft] aber vermag der Dramatiker nur zu dienen, wenn er den Schritt vom Bloß-Heutigen nicht nur vorausschauend ins Morgen, sondern ins Dauernde, ins Gültige wagt.[21]

The elevated gaze which rightly looks beyond the short term can so readily come to terms with a 'größeres Ganzes' whose validity and permanence is self-supporting simply because it does avoid the present reality. The crucial distinction between Mell and Hochwälder, for example, is that while Hochwälder shares Mell's sense of tradition and concern with individual and spiritual dilemma he is able to transcend and adapt the inward-looking aspects of Mell's approach and establish a discernible relationship to the concerns of contemporary society. Like Mell Hochwälder turns to historical themes, but they are directly concerned with the uncomfortable fact that in any clash between idealism and *Realpolitik* it is the latter which will emerge victorious. Mell does not attempt to disguise the ascendancy of power politics, but in focusing his attention on the spiritual response he lays himself open to the charge of moral dilettantism.

During the war years the Nazis sanctioned Mell's dramatisation of the Nibelung theme (although his other work was not acceptable). Mell's readiness to write and have his work performed within the Nazi sphere of influence gives some indication of his attitude to political events, but his treatment of this legend should not be seen as an act of ideological faith. Mell's concern was to underline the essential unity of myth and religion as an irrational and mystical force, beyond the power of reason and yet of paramount sociological importance. The weakness of his work after 1945 is that it tended to exist in a vacuum, apparently unscathed by events of which the author as an individual was very much aware.

Mell's best known post-war work is his historical drama *Jeanne d'Arc* (1955). It contains all the *minutiae* which a twentieth-century public have learned to associate with political show-trials – acts of expediency rather than justice, and the dilemma of political complicity – and yet the play remains encapsulated in fifteenth-century France and is apparently unwilling to consider the implications of anything but the individual crisis of his leading characters. Joan of Arc's supreme Christian confidence takes her very much out of the realm of the normal – as was to be expected – for Mell saw in Joan a timeless symbol of his conviction that Evil must be seen to triumph for Good to conquer in the end. This comforting belief, testimony of the 'größeres Ganzes' to which Mell's work is devoted, may strike a less committed ear as complacent, coming as it does so soon after the political events of the recent past.

The major figure in the play is not Joan herself, but her English custodian Peter Manuel, a man of this world with a healthy disbelief in saints, witches or anything he cannot explain. He is certain of one thing however, and that is that in this world of evil God is far away and retreating yet further. Manuel's despair as Joan burns at the stake and her God fails to rescue her turns into a desperate desire to be able to believe and acquire some protective shield from the horrors of existence. His final words at the close of the play confirm the psychological bias which has pertained throughout:

Es ist ein grausamer Boden, auf den wir ins Leben gesetzt werden. Ein Trost ist: er kann es nicht hindern, daß auf ihm die Heiligen wachsen.[22]

For Mell the story of Joan of Arc becomes a document of individual faith and divine ordinance; the shadow of Brecht's variants on the same theme and of Hochwälder's ability to select historical themes with a clear relevance to contemporary society underlines the limitations of Mell's approach. Mell embraces the 'größeres Ganzes' where Hochwälder exposes its paralysing effect on individual activity and responsibility. *Menschwerdung*, Heimito von Doderer's doctrine of spiritual regeneration also readily assumes the semblance of a carefully-contrived escape from a social impasse. The conveniently optimistic belief that human qualities can reassert themselves is less than convincing from a post-Nazi perspective or when seen in comparison to the soulless landscapes of, say, Kafka's works. Unlike Mell Doderer sought to give his canvas a sounder base and attempted to combine his vision with the precise topography of Vienna. Ironically, his efforts merely laid him open to the charge that he presented a photographic image which glossed over unpleasant aspects below the surface. It must be said in this respect, that this may have been the attraction of such a methodology for Doderer.

If the generation for whom National Socialism was a watershed have a weakness it is in their readiness to deal with existential problems with little or no regard for common-or-garden existence. The epitome of the divorce between literature and politics in Austrian writing immediately after the war must surely be the so-called 'Brecht-boycott' – a campaign which successfully prevented Brecht's works from performance on the Viennese stage until the 1960s. The boycott was upheld and sustained by the particular efforts of Hans Weigel and Friedrich Torberg, and although never completely effective, it kept the 'communist menace' at arm's length for an unconscionable time.

The boycott was justified by its supporters in a piece of special pleading which, reduced to its essence, ran as follows: to allow Brecht a forum for his 'propaganda' was the first stage of a process which would culminate in audiences deciding that communism itself could scarcely be such a bad thing if it produced writers who could write such good plays. It was not the plays themselves to which exception was taken, they were acknowledged to be good, it was the message they contained. To the outsider this amusing literary squabble seems very petty, but it centres on a widely-held belief that literature 'was above all that'. A greater irony is the absurd sight of a cultural tradition so steeped in historical drama as a means of propaganda with such expert practitioners in its ranks as Bruckner and Grillparzer effectively denying its own birthright by refusing to extend the same privilege to a fellow-writer. The deliberately historical or allegorical setting for so many of Brecht's plays ought to protect their message and not allow it to be diluted or diminished by unnecesary detail; *Leben des Galilei, Mutter Courage, Der kaukasische Kreidekreis* and *Der gute Mensch von Sezuan* (Galileo Galilei; Mother Courage; The Caucasian Chalk Circle; The Good Woman of Sezuan) all embrace a vision that is as cohesive as Mell's 'größeres Ganzes'. The only essential difference is that Mell's was black and Brecht's was red.

The Brecht boycott represents the last vestiges of the pre-war *Lagermentalität* and was eventually overwhelmed by a shift in public opinion, but side by side with this 'official' boycott, it is salutary to recall that the Viennese public had imposed its own 'unofficial' boycott on another writer who also seemed to challenge the principles on which its society was based.

Ödön von Horváth's *Geschichten aus dem Wiener Wald*, performed in Vienna in 1948 had to wait until 1968 to gain any public acceptance, but when popularity did come it came in a veritable spate of Horváth productions and variants as if a new literary industry had been born. By the 1960s, of course, Horváth had been safely dead for nearly thirty years. It is this fact that makes his modernity all the more striking, for if any one of the pre-war writers has a close affinity to the younger post-war generation it must be Horváth. He does not retreat into aestheticism, religiosity or psychology but attacks a social malaise in that most unliterary form, the *Volksstück*. Anti-cerebral and instinctive in its appeal, it is an emphatic rejection of literary escapism and a determined critique of society.

Horváth uses the *Volksstück* to destroy the carefully nurtured collective image of 'Old Vienna', and he paints a devastatingly frank picture of a society dominated by the *Kleinbürger* and concerned only with its own self-preservation. He counterpoints this interpretation with an ironical introduction of all the paraphenalia of uncritical nostalgia – the world of Johann Strauss's waltzes and the wine, women and song of light operetta – a montage which obliged his audiences to look again at 'their tradition' in a new and less flattering light. His iconoclasm cost Horváth access to the stage for some twenty years, but by taking drama back to the popular level, by replacing intellectual and thinking characters by the intellectually-limited *Kleinbürger* whose cultural pretensions were expressed in cliché and platitude Horváth paved the way for writers like Bauer and Handke in Austria and Kroetz and Sperr in Bavaria.

Both Horváth and Hochwälder draw on the *Volksstück* as a reflection of a vital and immediate element of the Austrian cultural tradition. While Horváth recreates the genre in a modern idiom, Hochwälder looks back to the mood and flavour of Nestroy in his attempts to give the positive features of the Austrian talent for introspection a meaningful social context. Both writers, however, are united in their rejection of intellectual rationalization which they condemn as a search for sanctuary from the world as it is. When such attempts to withdraw from the world do not actually end in disaster, both writers show how close to the brink such rationalization and retreat into an inner world have brought the individual and the society of which he is a part. For Hochwälder as for Horváth collectivity bred danger; Hochwälder revealed the psychological repercussions, Horváth attacked its social manifestations. In their response to and adaptation of this most Austrian of forms, Hochwälder and Horváth epitomize the combination of continuity and change so characteristic of a generation bisected by the age of National Socialism.

NOTES

1. 'At the moment there are only two authors writing in Austria – Lernet and Holenia'. The comment comes from a lecture given in 1948.
2. 'Those who went into exile did not bring a new literature back with them, and nothing has emerged from the rubble here. Even those who sought refuge with the victors have discovered that they too have lost the war. . . . For writers in German, like ourselves, the standard-bearers are the great names of the past – Kafka, Musil and Broch. There are no great names writing in our language any more. The signposts read: Joyce and Malraux, Camus and Sartre, Wilder and Gide and Proust. What's left is Zuckmayer.'

   'Vom Sinn der Literatur in dieser Zeit', a lecture given to a meeting of modern authors and composers in St Veit an der Glan on 11 October 1952. A typescript of the paper is held in the *Dokumentationsstelle für neuere österreichische Literatur*, Vienna.
3. 'Austria was born five minutes before Austria collapsed, on 12 February 1938. . . . It was then that a sense of positive identity with Austria was felt for the first time, and I believe that these four weeks from February to March 1938 were crucial. Without them the tremendous influx of all that was Austrian back into Austria after 1945 would have been impossible. . . . Emigration and exile and the resultant quasi-abstract preoccupation with Austria created a concept of Austria which could not be destroyed . . .'

   From an interview and discussion between Weigel and Professor Viktor Suchy, Director of the *Dokumentationsstelle für neuere österreichische Literatur*, Vienna. Their discussion is one of the many valuable tapes available to scholars (Ref. 042 A1–044 B1).
4. 'Kakanien' is derived from the German initials for 'imperial and royal': k.u.k. or k.k. One of the many niceties of the Hapsburg era was the subtle constitutional distinction between the two. In addition the sound 'kaka' would be familiar to all German readers as a reminder of their early toilet training! In Musil's novel the word 'Kakanien' represents a critical attitude to the Empire with all its absurdities, paradoxes and self-delusions. cf. Claudio Magris, *Der habsburgische Mythos in der österreichischen Literatur*, Salzburg, 1966.
5. 'Tarockanien' was a far less critical concept. Herzmanovsky-Orlando (1877–1954) is the quintessential literary dilettante. He wrote to please and indulge himself and his nostalgic and rose-coloured view of

history was not generally available until after his death. His editor Friedrich Torberg has recently been taken to task on the grounds that his edition of Herzmanovsky-Orlando's works has tended to do violence to the original.

6. 'in an Empire that is built on individuals, not on nations and boundaries', *3. November 1918*, Act Three. References to this work are taken from *Dichtung aus Österreich*, Drama, ed. by H. Kindermann and M. Dietrich, Vienna and Munich, 1966, pp. 589–615, where the play is reproduced in full. This reference is p. 615.

7. 'The old, so-called k.u.k. army German with its light touch of dialect, coloured in each case by the particular national allegiance of the speaker.' ibid. p. 589.

8. 'For the further away from home they were, the more they became true Greeks, not Athenians or Spartans or Thebans.'
ibid. Act One, p. 596.

9. 'A fatherland that unites nations' ibid. Act Two, p. 597.

10. 'There are seven nations standing round this table – and each of us has shed blood for the greater cause as the cause has bled for each of us. . . . We were much more than *one* nation – we were *one* forged from *seven*, and now you want to leave this splendid mansion and go back to the breeding-stables?' 'But colonel they are *our* stables!'
ibid. Act Two, pp. 604:605.

11. 'Soil from Hungary – soil from Poland – soil from Carinthia – Slovenian soil – Czech soil – Roman soil – . . .
(*he hesitates, but the effect is moving, not comic*)
soil – from — soil from Austria!'
ibid. Act Three, p. 607.

12. 'It's true, this Empire which has gone now, offered each of us all that we needed, and it would have been enough if we hadn't kept looking over our shoulders rather than to the future.' ibid. Act Three, p. 612.

13. 'to extend the range of what is predicable in the pre- and sub-conscious, the range of the irrational, to give shape and form to those forces and attitudes which are not generally perceived but which, as part of the realm of animism and magic, are rooted at the very heart of the psyche from where their influence beams out . . . It is the artist's task to show how this '*agens* from the inner depths', how these subterranean and complicated forces pierce the outermost layer of convention and furnish the essential motor energy for the conflict with the instances of convention.'
Quoted in: Heinz Rieder, 'George Saiko', in: *Literatur und Kritik*, 7 (1972), 577–85. This passage is from p. 577.

14. 'I can offer no certainties, all I can do is pose the questions; Characters, situations, actions . . . events, experiences, all these appear here only if they are contain a parable beneath the surface.
. . . A moment's darkness is all that separates one scene from the next. The spotlight moves wherever the action demands. What at first appears no more than an episode is revealed some 300 pages later as one of the most significant elements of the main action; the man, who at first sight, appears to be the central figure, is gradually seen to be of

much less importance. The foreground frequently recedes, allowing the focus of attention to shift to the background, until once again, the darkness returns and shrouds it from our view.

. . . This trilogy only seems to have a conclusion, there is no hint of a comforting moral at all. Like so many writers before him, the author has offered his readers one thing only – a share in his solitude. Perhaps this is the only sense of community there is nowadays, a communion of those who must draw their strength from the same spring in order to face up to the prospect of a life without illusions.'

Manès Sperber, *Wie eine Träne im Ozean*, Romantrilogie, Europaverlag, Vienna, 1976, p. 5.

15. Marcel Reich-Ranicki, *Deutsche Literatur in West und Ost*, Munich, 1966 pp. 257–62.

16. '*Sun and Moon*, a historical novel from the present.' cf. the chapter on the total novel below.

17. 'fat ladies'. The reference is to Doderer's novel *Die Dämonen* and the character Kajetan von Schlaggenberg whose taste in women is on the grand scale.

18. 'It was neither an old medieval fortress nor a new mansion, but a rambling construction made up of a series of tightly-packed low buildings with the occasional two-storey structure here and there; if you hadn't known it was a castle, you might have thought it was a small town.'

Franz Kafka, *Das Schloß*, ed. Max Brod, New York, 1946, p. 18

19. 'This aspect of writing, the creation of order, is, it seems to me of particular relevance today; indeed it is the prime function of writing, because in today's circumstances nothing less than the highest effort will prevail. . . . . Beyond the interpretation of the world provided by the artist lies chaos.'

Quoted in the Programme to '*Jeanne d'Arc*', Vereinigte Bühnen Graz, Steiermark, 1969/70, p. 10.

20. 'The dramatist must have in front of him the vision of a greater unity, a community'. ibid. p. 10.

21. 'The dramatist can only serve this community if he is prepared to risk exchanging the merely topical and looking beyond what tomorrow may bring to what is permanent and valid.' ibid. p. 10.

22. 'The world into which we are born is a fearsome place, but at least we have this to comfort us: it cannot prevent saints from growing up alongside us as well'.

Jeanne d'Arc in *Die Heilige Johanna*, Theater der Jahrhunderte, ed. by Joachim Schondorff, Langen-Müller, Munich and Vienna, 1964, pp. 341–91. This quotation p. 391.

Shadows of the Past:
The Drama of Fritz Hochwälder

Alan Best

When *Das Heilige Experiment* (The Holy Experiment), written in exile in Switzerland in 1941/2, was performed at the re-opening of the Burgtheater in Vienna in 1947, it was greeted with unanimous acclaim from all political and religious persuasions, a sure sign of Hochwälder's *rapport* with the mood and sensibilities of Austria immediately after the National Socialist era. Since 1947 the Austrian literary and theatrical scene has progressed, but Hochwälder himself has gone his own way and today, although a name to be mentioned with respect, he stands alone, aloof, embattled and perhaps embittered when he compares the very luke-warm reception accorded to his recent play *Lazaretti oder Der Säbeltiger* (Lazaretti or The Sabre-toothed Tiger, 1975) to the attention paid to the experiments and ploys of contemporary theatre which he has so caustically dismissed. Hochwälder's stated determination to write plays which an audience will *want* to go and see, plays which will entertain an audience, and above all plays which while giving the audience food for thought will not bore it cannot be faulted in theory; in practice, as *Lazaretti* shows, good intentions are not enough. Having criticized his contemporaries so sharply, Hochwälder can scarcely complain if he is hoist with his own petard.

Hochwälder stands outside the main current of Austrian life both geographically and spiritually. Having chosen exile in Switzerland in 1938, he has lived there ever since, and despite statements of how Austrian and Viennese he feels himself to be, the tradition to which he lays claim seems very much that of the First Republic rather than the Second. His support for such younger Austrians as Wolfgang Bauer derives from their reinvigoration of the *Volksstück*, a tradition central to Hochwälder's own drama. Hochwälder traces a line of descent from Raimund and Nestroy via Ödön von Horváth to himself and believes that the *Volksstück* embodies a living tradition and one particularly suited to the contemporary world. The public which properly seeks entertainment in the theatre must also, according to Hochwälder, be encouraged to recognize themselves in what they see on the stage, and the dramatist must make his audience consciously strip off the masks of self-pretence and complacency and look at the truth:

Die Tradition, der ich mich zugehörig fühle, ist die des Wiener Volkstheaters. Und nichts, keine Zeitwidrigkeit, kein Exodus, kann eine Tradition, die man einmal in sich aufgenommen hat, verdräggen und ersetzen. Die Wiener Luft hat mir Unschätzbares gegeben: Klarheit des Gedankens, Sinn für Form, Theaterblut. Freilich, ich bezeichne mich nicht unbedingt als 'Schriftsteller', mit Vergnügen bleibe ich Analphabet, um auf meine Weise Stücke auf die Bretter zu stellen – unliterarisch, unprätentiös, volkstümlich.[1]

Yet for all Hochwälder's evocation of Raimund and Nestroy, for all his subtle use of the stock characters, situations and techniques of the *Volkstheater* in plays as diverse as *Das Heilige Experiment* and *Der Himbeerpflücker* (The Raspberry-picker, 1964), despite his use of dialect, 'sprechende Namen', cases of mistaken identity and twists in the course of events that more properly belong to the *Märchen*, Hochwälder is always searching for that most Austrian of qualities 'die Tiefe', the depth of inner meaning which will justify and enhance the superficial level on which the action takes place. Unpretentious and unliterary he may claim to be, but Hochwälder is first and foremost a moralist.

Hochwälder's plays are very much in the old tradition. They have a well-defined plot, recognizable – even archetypal – characters who are readily understood, and a clear thread of development, and if very little happens in a play by Hochwälder this is principally due to the author's cynical view that the individual can never escape his own fate. If in *Huis Clos* Hell is other people, for Hochwälder's characters it is the *alter ego* of themselves which they are obliged to see; trapped in a web of their own making they can only watch the noose threatening to tighten around their necks and, if by some chance they escape there is no suggestion of individual merit. The judge Smalejus in *Die Herberge*, (The Refuge, 1958) summarizes Hochwälder's feelings when he asks:

45

'Der Blinde, der im Irrtum Wahrheit findet, . . . – handelt der gerecht?'[2]

The axis of Hochwälder's plays is the conflict between Power and Justice, that is between the demands of the Ideal and the limitations of Reality. In *Das Heilige Experiment* this takes the form of the confrontation between the Jesuit State in Paraguay and the Spanish throne, in *Der öffentliche Ankläger* (The Public Prosecutor, 1947/8) it is represented in an inverted form by the situation of the Public Prosecutor Fouquier-Tinville. In the Huguenot drama *Donadieu* (1953) it is the conflict between a personal cause and the general good, while in *Der Himbeerpflücker* there is no such conflict because the 'good Nazis' of Bad Brauning, lacking any capacity for conscience, survive because they have thereby the means of avoiding a direct conflict. Inspector Mittermayer in *Der Befehl* (The Order, 1966/7) finds this conflict in the suppressed regions of his subconscious while in Hochwälder's recent play, *Lazaretti*, the battleground of his dramatic world is neatly summarized in two comments, the first from the early moments of the play, the second from the close:

> Wir sollten uns eingestehen, daß das Niedrige, Gemeine, schlechthin Böse in uns allen schläft und jederzeit zum Ausbruch kommen kann.[3]
> Will niemand einsehn, daß die schlimmste Verfolgung in uns selbst ist?[4]

Lazaretti is an old man's play for old men. Both its protagonists Peter Camenisch and Victor Lazaretti are in their sixties and spend most of the play looking over their shoulders at a long departed youth; they are rivals on the academic front, Camenisch being pressed for his latest work (as yet unwritten) and Lazaretti, pursued relentlessly by forces he senses but which no-one else can, seeking sanctuary with his erstwhile mentor for himself and for his own completed manuscript. Lazaretti's solution to the contemporary problem of urban terrorism, around which the play revolves, is to propose the foundation of an international society which will unite all young and idealistic people and enable them to intervene where necessary and use force against the merchants of force. Lazaretti believes that man is basically evil and corrupt, but by the end of the play, like most of Hochwälder's characters, he finds his most cherished theories put to the test. If his premise is false, then his life's work is useless if not downright dangerous and will become a bible for social destruction; if, on the other hand man is pre-ordained to disappear from the face of the earth like the now extinct sabre-toothed tiger of the play's title, then Lazaretti's efforts have been a waste of time. He has built his work into a protective wall about himself, has created an illusion of security and now fears to watch it crumble. If mankind *is* destined to become extinct then the sole means Lazaretti recognizes as capable of bringing man to an awareness of *mores* – that is force – is superfluous if not ridiculous. His retreat into a sanatorium, which allows his 'friend' Camenisch to pass Lazaretti's work off as his own, represents the only escape from a reality which is too daunting to accept.

In one way or another, all of Hochwälder's characters find that an abyss has opened up between the world and themselves, in some way things are no longer what they were, and the individual has to come to terms with this 'new reality' whether this is external and concrete or internal and psychological. When the normal no longer pertains the individual is thrown back on his own self-reliance, but Hochwälder portrays individuals who are subject to the ordinance of a powerful, impersonal will, an authority to which they have sujugated themselves entirely. The crisis in Hochwälder's plays comes with the inevitable discovery that this protective authority is not all-embracing. Despite all appearances to the contrary it is eventually shown to be inherently destructive.

Hochwälder's own fate during the Nazi era naturally inclines him to the position of the outsider, the exile, the man with a cause and, because he is an Austrian, to the relationship between the individual and 'Ordnung', that most Austrian of concepts. The Pater Provincial in *Das Heilige Experiment* and the Nazi Steißhäuptl in *Der Himbeerpflücker* are in this latter respect in well-nigh identical situations; though they are set in different historical eras they share a common fate – the collapse of their ideal world. The Pater Provincial must preside over the destruction of his dream – the Jesuit state in Paraguay, while Steißhäuptl has already seen his dream – the Thousand-Year Reich, shattered. He day-dreams nostalgically of the days of a close-knit brotherhood, a sense of purpose, security and order:

Was war man damals, und was ist man jetzt? – Reich, aber vom Idealen her betrachtet, ein Dreck! Ortsgruppenleiter! – Wenn ich dran denk, kommt mir die Gegenwart wie ein böser Traum vor, damals hat das Erwartungsfrohe geherrscht, das Aufopferungsvolle – damals haben wir den Alltag vergessen, nein: er hat uns vergessen. . . .[5]

This indeed was the aim of the Jesuits in Paraguay. Seeing reality around them they created a latter-day Paradise in which the greatest punishment was expulsion. They were so successful in fact that the Paraguayan Indios in Hochwälder's play know of no better existence than life within the Jesuit reductions. For their part the Nazis of Bad Brauning knew no letter life than the 'Blut and Ehre' of the SS. It is a chilling and unexpected comparison, but the retrospective light which *Der Himbeerpflücker* casts on *Das Heilige Experiment* (which was, after all, written during the Third Reich's most successful period) turns the Jesuit drama from a question of conscience into a study of the evils of individual reliance on external support. It was the temptations of 'Ordnung' that led Europe from the uncertainties of the Weimar Republic to the holocaust of National Socialism. It is the seductive appeal of 'Ordnung' which Hochwälder depicts as causing the downfall of the thousands of Indios who were converted by the Jesuits and shepherded into the safety of the reductions.

By the 1970s *Das Heilige Experiment* had lost the immediate appeal it held in the late 1940s and 1950s. It had become conventional, if comfortable, wisdom that the individual must follow his conscience above all else, but since this was never the real nub of the play, the furore raised by Hochhuth's *Der Stellvertreter* (The Representative) cannot detract from Hochwälder's play. His Jesuit drama sets out to remind its audience that there is no such thing as 'The Truth'. Over *Das Heilige Experiment* as over Austro-Hungary and the post-Imperial myths of its glory there hangs the shadow of a hierarchy whose morality is dubious and whose latent totalitarianism pernicious. Hochwälder uses historical situations to highlight individual contemporary problems. The Jesuit state becomes the paradigm of the role of conscience, but the heart of the play is the price which the individual has to pay to find the security of an easy conscience.

Das Heilige Experiment does not discuss the rights and wrongs of State versus Church, for there *is* no right in this play. The falsity of the accusations laid against the Society of Jesus is immaterial, the

48

fault of which the Jesuits are never accused, but of which they *are* guilty, is that they and those under their pastoral care have ceased to rely on individual judgement, and have become dominated by a hierarchical machine. The comforting concept of an Order, the oath of total and unquestioning obedience to his Superior which every Jesuit makes, has an unholy echo in Nazi Germany. The strength the individual gains from membership of such an Order, a strength which the Jesuits in Hochwälder's play put forward as a self-justification in their conversions of the Paraguayan Indios, has reduced the Indios to little more than puppets. The Jesuits are everything to the Indios and the reductions have become island paradises. The Ideal State is indeed attracting converts to Christianity, but on the basis that material advantage and the all-embracing, all-providing religion that will feed and clothe them is worth more than the pleasures of polygamy. Although the eighteenth-century Jesuits have not declared independence from Spain they have nonetheless withdrawn from the real world and created a state within a state. This oblique reminder of the 'Lagermentalität' of the First Republic, of withdrawal into inward-looking camps and of antagonism to political adversaries is the almost inevitable result of the Jesuits' laudable attempts to create God's world on earth. It cannot be done, and in the attempt the Jesuits have deprived the individual of his crucial obligation: to act as an individual.

It is this conflict which so attracts Hochwälder, and the debate the Pater Provincial conducts with himself as he tries to decide whether or not to obey the instructions brought by the special Jesuit envoy is not, as he thinks, between conscience and duty, but between his duty to the Spanish throne and the Jesuit Order on the one hand, and his duty to the Jesuit state in Paraguay on the other. This is a crucial distinction, for the Pater Provincial's obligation to Spain and the Order is as a subordinate, and in any conflict his role will be that of the individual, while he himself is Authority vis à vis the Jesuit State and the Indios. The Pater Provincial reflects the illusory and essentially protective nature of the Idea, of Authority, of 'Ordnung'. Everything he has done has been in vain. The Jesuits are indeed supreme in Paraguay, but they have allowed their idealism to blind them to the fact that they are a microcosm not the macrocosm. They are part of the real world and are forced to a belated and painful recognition of this fact.

On his death-bed, the Pater Provincial claims that Pater Oros was right to rebel and that the Jesuits should have resisted the orders received from Rome to quit Paraguay, but this outburst is not the voice of conscience in triumph, but that of a man no longer of this world who can afford the luxury of idealism; political machinations count for nothing now. The Pater Provincial condemns Oros thus: 'Du hast das Gehorsamsgelübde gebrochen . . . der Provincial verdammt dich,'[6] but the apparent certainty and assurance of this impersonally-phrased rebuke, coming as it does from within the security of a system, the Jesuit hierarchy, is proved to be illusory. The Pater Provincial hears the same promptings in his own heart and recognizes that he has been driven into an impossible situation.

At the end of the fourth act he tore down the map of Paraguay, the cause of the wounds inflicted on him by his own rebellious Indios: 'Diese . . . hat . . . es getan! Mein . . . eigenes . . . Werk. . . . Dieser Staat – Der Antichrist!!'[7] Part of the map remains on the wall, that part containing the image of St. Francis Xaver, whose example the Jesuits believe they have followed, but who was strong enough to work on his own as an individual. St Francis' end was one of loneliness and self-reliance, he was marooned on an island waiting for a boat to ferry him on, he is indeed the example to emulate, but with the best of intentions the Jesuits chose to reflect St Francis' zeal in their own manner, one which allowed them to escape the misery and fear of self-reliance, the testing doubts of true Christianity. The Jesuits in Paraguay had the luxury of security and they drew their Christian strength from what they created. As the Provincial belatedly realizes, they have been worshipping a graven image and it is the innocent, simple Indios who must pay the price for the Jesuits' reluctance or inability to stand alone.

Of all the Patres portrayed in the play Hochwälder's use of Pater Oros is the most successful. The Patres, and indeed the other lesser characters, derive from the tradition of the *Volksstück*; Pater Hundertpfund, the Superior, a benevolently despotic schoolmaster; Peter Clarke, the procurator, an Englishman imbued with the spirit of fair play and good business sense; Mynheer Cornelis, the choleric Dutch tea-buyer; the viperous prelate of Buenos Aires; the members of the investigating commission; each is a cameo characterization that throws the grimmer struggle into lighter relief while at the same time providing a firm infrastructure on which the philosophical element of the play can be founded. Ladislaus Oros, a former soldier who has served with distinction before offering his talents to the Society of Jesus, has built up a well-drilled fighting force of thirty thousand men. There is no *need* for this force in the Jesuit state, but Authority, in this case a Royal Privilege, has made provision for such a force and so it has been set up.

Oros is an archetypal disciple of the Idea, and far from being a revolutionary priest is a reactionary. He explicitly embodies those who have chosen to serve God in an earthly way and is an extreme example of the attitude that has overtaken all the Patres. Unable to shed his background (he still wears his spurs beneath his Jesuit cloth) he has exchanged one military campaign for another, and is thus enabled to help himself as he serves Christ. The Jesuit Order grants Oros the reassurance in the face of death which no other army could, and, significantly, when the religious cause Oros has espoused is threatened, he reacts as the soldier and the man of action he is. The other Patres lament and debate, Oros organizes the revolt. Even his reproach to the Provincial has a military tinge, he accuses him of deserting the flag. Once the protective order crumbles, individuals such as Oros, thrown back on their own resources, desperately search for an alternative shield. Should they fail to find one, their whole world collapses.

The 'normal' world has been turned upside down in *Das Heilige Experiment*. Hochwälder presents moral right, justice and true Christian charity as seductions. *Realpolitik* wins the day, but only because the Jesuits chose to confront the politicians on a political level. Hochwälder shows that the spirit of Christ is indestructible, but the shadow Christ casts over those who serve Him in their way rather than in His is used here as a starting point in the sequence of studies into the interaction of individual needs and social requirements that constitute Hochwälder's dramatic oeuvre.

Of Hochwälder's first dramatic phase, the historical plays *Der öffentliche Ankläger* (1947/48) and *Donadieu* (1953) are the best known companions to his Jesuit drama. Set in Revolutionary and Huguenot France respectively, both works centre on the aspirations of an individual brought to a reckoning with the force which has hitherto been his mainstay. Where the Pater Provincial was suborned by the idealism of his cause, Fouquier-Tinville the Public Prosecutor and instrument of the Prairial Laws was seduced into total and unquestioning subservience by the ultimate Either-Or: co-operation or decapitation. From his position of personal weakness Fouquier-Tinville has been able to create a position of strength through his espousal of the Cause. He rightly describes himself as a slave of his position, for he found security in the breath-taking momentum of the revolutionary and Prairial treadmill, but now that this is slowing down the Public Prosecutor feels the need for a new patron:

> Gib mir ein gutes Gesetz und maßvolle Befehle – und du hast in mir einen gewissenhaften Beamten, der keinen Finger breit davon abweicht! Gib mir blutige Befehle und ich werde zum Satan.[8]

The Pater Provincial's exclusive belief in his cause is echoed in Fouquier-Tinville's desperate support of the Thermidor government. This has all the fervour of the committed idealist, and for the same reason. If that handhold goes, the whole basis of his existence is lost. Fouquier-Tinville is a monster, but it was the machine which has made him such. He deserves to die, and it is ironically fitting that he should be charged with securing the execution of one last unnamed victim before the Prairial Laws which he has so ably administered are repealed and should find, too late, that he has engineered his own downfall. The individual in Hochwälder's world may seem to be destroyed by events, but these events have invariably been set in motion by some act on the part of that same individual. Hochwälder's cynicism is maintained to the end of the play, for, when this intriguingly tangled plot has been unravelled and evil personified has been destroyed, the play closes with Teresia Tallien and her husband locked in an atmosphere of mutual hostility and fear. They have engineered Fouquier-Tinville's downfall, the Terror is over, but little has changed.

Fouquier-Tinville's dedicated service to a worthless ideal echoes the Nazi bureaucrat who spent his day signing death-warrants; both may plead duty as their excuse, but Hochwälder does not merely condemn in this play. His study of the public prosecutor shows him to be a man with feelings who would like to be humane, but who has been destroyed by the machine he serves. He has been robbed of any capacity for individual thought. The greater historical distance of the French Revolution allows the moral dilemmas posed by the Third Reich to be considered more dispassionately. Both the Jesuit drama and the Revolutionary piece also gain from Hochwälder's judicious use of verbal and situational humour, a licence he could not have allowed himself in a study of the perils of totalitarianism written in the 1940s.

The individual is shown locked in the web of the past, from which there is no escape. In *Donadieu* Hochwälder internalizes the 'Order' which affords protection, depicting a Huguenot noble living on the fires of hatred and a desire for revenge. Donadieu is ultimately forced to emerge from behind his castle walls and face the real world. His castle, so long a bastion of freedom, is shown to have become a prison for a mind trapped by the past and Donadieu is obliged to tear down this illusory protection as the price that must be paid if his religion is to be allowed to survive. He must live uncomfortably in the world as it is and not seek an alternative. There can be no 'happy end' in Hochwälder's work. Evil conquers again and again and his historical plays together with a cynical reworking of the legend of *Esther* (1940) and the medieval *Meier Helmbrecht* (1946) merely highlight the irrelevance and dangers of individual subservience to abstract beliefs.

The second phase in Hochwälder's dramatic development marks a shift in emphasis from historical plays to allegorical and legendary settings. Two plays, *Donnerstag* (Thursday, 1959) a modern mystery play complete with all the trimmings of the Austrian Magic Theatre, and *1003* (1964) combine to provide question and answer as to the fate of man. In *Donnerstag* the architect Niklaus Pomfrit enters into an agreement with Underdevil Wondrak of Belial Incorporated by which he will gain understanding of the meaning to the world; in *1003* the writer Ulrich Valmont, alone and listening to tape recordings of his own voice, is visited by Pomfrit (under the alias Bloner). Since his entry into Belial Incorporated Pomfrit has become

unangreifbar, unverwundbar, unüberwindlich, – ein moderner Alberich, den nichts berührt und nichts mehr trifft, wie einst im Märchen der Mann mit dem kalten Herzen.[9]

It is this security which Hochwälder's characters all seek for themselves, a security unattainable in reality, and it is in a realistic, if allegorical setting that both *Die Herberge* (1954/55) and *Der Unschuldige* (Innocent, 1958) are set.

Hochwälder believed that, together with *Der öffentliche Ankläger* and *Das Heilige Experiment*, it would be for *Die*

Herberge that he would be remembered. It seems an unlikely choice, but it indicates the considerations Hochwälder is trying to raise in his work. Of all his plays *Die Herberge* is consistently closest to the *Volksstück*. It has a village-inn as its setting, a no-man's-land on the way from one town to the next surrounded by forest. The play is peopled with a rich assortment of types and characters who would be equally at home in a play by Nestroy. Here too is a self-contained community about to suffer considerable upheaval, for the 'traveller's rest' of the title proves to be anything but a haven for the money-lender Berullis. Indeed one of the neater ironies of Hochwälder's work lies in the titles of his plays: The Holy Experiment has unholy consequences; the public prosecutor is tried and condemned *in camera*, and the innocence of Christian, the central character of *Der Unschuldige* is not beyond reasonable doubt.

The money-lender Berullis, on his way to another extortionate piece of business, decides to spend a night at the inn which forms the focal point of *Die Herberge* and is robbed of a box containing a thousand gold pieces. After raising hue and cry it transpires that the thief is the son of a man Berullis himself cheated out of an identical amount many years previously. This ironic situation, a spectre rising from the past to threaten an individual who has long since developed beyond the context of that now historical moment is a motif that will dominate the rest of Hochwälder's work and marks Hochwälder's concern to probe the workings of the mind, and particularly of conscience. The shock of self-recognition, the trauma of coming to terms with an identity one did not even suspect in oneself underlines Hochwälder's dramatic message: no-one is safe from such a moment of unmasking. Historical set-pieces on a grand scale where such a moment of realization is subservient to the main events give way to a study of Everyman in his many guises.

Berullis has dedicated his life to making money in order to keep at a distance an emotional void which would otherwise be intolerable. Staschia, the landlord's daughter reawakens Berullis' sense of being human and with it his capacity to feel guilt. Both Berullis and his man-servant Andusj are shadows of their real selves. Andusj has committed a crime and attempts to bury all memory of what he has done by attaching himself, body and soul, to the money-lender on whom he is totally reliant. When Berullis changes, Andusj cannot continue in this way and confesses to his crime – his essential sense of security and protection has lapsed.

Here, with a vengeance but in a non-political context, is the dilemma of 'Vergangenheitsbewältigung' on an existential level. Hochwälder shows both the tragedy of the man condemned never to escape his past and the irrelevance of 'justice' in such a context. If a man like Berullis can continue his extortionate trade there is no merit to human justice, on the other hand if the individual's conscience is truly awakened justice becomes superfluous. What is it then that protects the individual from himself? The judge, summoned to hear Berullis' accusations, has one answer:

> . . . Wer denkt, schätzt die Welt ein, wie sie ist. Wer die Welt einschätzt, wie sie ist, weiß: bloß Ordnung hält sie in ihrer Bahn. Nichts außer Ordnung schützt den Menschen vor den Menschen. Da es keine Gerechtigkeit gibt, muß Ordnung herrschen[10] . . .

Yet, as the earlier plays have shown, the seductive power of precisely such an 'Ordnung' is as disruptive as it is corrective. The short answer is that in Hochwälder's view the individual can trust neither himself nor those about him. If justice is done it is either by chance or it begs the question. Christian in *Der Unschuldige* may not be responsible for the corpse found in his garden, but by the end of the play he and those about him have learnt that he is certainly capable of murder. Hochwälder's discomfitting belief that each of us has a potential skeleton in the cupboard is, perhaps, the major shift in emphasis from the early plays, which tended to concentrate on special cases in particular situations.

The third progression in Hochwälder's work is reflected in two plays directly linked to the National Socialist era. Both were inspired by external stimuli rather than an initial inner prompting, but both *Der Himbeerpflücker* (1964) and *Der Befehl* (1965ff.) must be accounted two of his most successful plays. The events in each play relate the situations of contemporary Austrians when obliged to reconsider their activities during the National Socialist era and both works complement each other neatly. *Der Himbeerpflücker* presents a study of unrepentant hard-core Nazis in the flourishing, and aptly-named town of Bad Brauning while *Der Befehl* (of which there are two versions, a television screenplay and a revised and improved version for the theatre) traces the fortunes of a former military policeman in occupied Holland whose model record then and since seem to make him the ideal choice to hunt down a brutal Nazi child-murderer. Hochwälder's dramatic concern, to unnerve his audience, to shake their self-convictions, is fully realized, for while the Nazis of Bad Brauning are no better than they ought to be, the modest, conscientious Inspektor Mittermayer who is the central character of *Der Befehl* stands revealed at the end of that play as the very monster he was ordered to hunt down. There is no pretence to Mittermayer, he *is* the most decent of men; how then could he be what he transpires? It is the impossibility of knowing, the trauma of uncertainty, which Hochwälder invokes in an intensified re-working of his original theme: the individual morally destroyed by the comforting reassurance of 'Ordnung'.

Described by its author as a 'böser Schwank über eine aktuelle Sache'[11] *Der Himbeerpflücker* borrows on the basic *Volksstück* device of the comedy of mistaken identity and weaves both comic and macabre variations to that theme. The characters have the life, vitality and self-satisfaction to be utterly credible, while their dialogue, embroidered with the clichés and slogans of a bygone age, reveals how firmly and desperately they are wedded to the past. The 'Raspberry-picker' is the cover-name given to an SS official from the nearby concentration camp who relaxed by sending inmates into the hills to pick raspberries so that he could pick them off from a distance with his rifle. His sudden disappearance in 1945, leaving the then *Ortsgruppenleiter* Steißhäuptl (now the mayor of Bad Brauning) to dispose of the chests of gold fillings etc. extracted from the camp inmates, is the basis on which the mayor's post-war prosperity is based. Steißhäuptl is also the landlord 'Zum weißen Lamm', a widower with a daughter, Sieglinde, and feared in his household for his rigid moral principles. His nostalgia for the past is characteristic: 'Man hat damals gehofft aus heißem Herzen – und dann war alles aus, ein Traum aus Blut und Treue'.[12] The collapse and defeat of National Socialism in 1945, the expulsion from the paradise of certainty and community is a situation which encapsulates each of Hochwälder's central characters as their carefully constructed order of things falls about them. The ironic difference here is that as *Der Himbeerpflücker* is so closely rooted in reality its characters are not, in the final resort, obliged to change. Steißhäuptl may panic, but he shows none of the remorse or fundamental shift in attitude that overtook the money-lender Berullis. Berullis after all was safely set in the context of a 'dramatic legend' where such moral shifts may be possible. The reality is markedly grimmer.

The 'Himbeerpflücker' who so disturbs the peace in Bad Brauning is, however, not the real SS man but a petty criminal on the run. Alexander Kerz, who arrives at 'The White Lamb' with his girl, seeks a room 'and no questions asked'. However, in the true tradition of the *Volksstück*, the local Nazis consistently misinterpret Kerz's every statement and gesture to fit their own preconceptions. Hochwälder uses their respect and enthusiasm for the man in whom they claim to see all that was great and good of former days to expose the Nazi era for the petty criminal adventure it represented for so many. The attitude shown by the Nazis to Kerz, this *Herrenmensch*, who in fact cannot stand the sight of blood, expresses their own need to dream, to escape from themselves. The unlikely correlation of Kerz, whom the audience sees as anything but heroic, with Nazi glory, underlines the delusive power of the 'Ordnung' and its capacity to transform reality into the realm of wish-fulfilment. Hochwälder's presentation allows the Nazis to recognize and hail a criminal as the apogee of all that they dream. He needs make no further comment.

The power conferred on an individual by the aura of an appropriate 'Ordnung' is neatly satirized in the character of Zagl, the factotum of the inn. In the presence of what he believes to be the spirit of 'the good old days' Zagl becomes a 'New Man' and is transformed from male dormant to male dominant, blossoming for a brief spell until with the discovery of the true state of affairs, he subsides once more into hen-pecked subservience. When Kerz's girl, Grappina, disillusioned because he cannot live up to her aspirations, denounces her boy-friend and makes off with the booty Hochwälder assembles a grotesque realignment of forces. Now that the affair is no longer political but 'criminal', the chief of police who was brow-beaten into silent acquiescence by hints about certain past events, re-discovers the 'Ordnung' which allows him to function, and Kerz is arrested. The power of illusion and capacity for self-deception, the secure foundation on which weak personalities hope to build their future, ensure that the Steißhäuptls of this world will survive and flourish. The *Volksstück* element of the play allows Hochwälder to expose such aspirations ironically, and through comedy, to deflate them and reveal them in their true and unflattering perspective. Even so, the crisis of self-recognition, the most destructive force in

Hochwälder's dramaturgy, never seriously threatens to disturb the peace of mind enjoyed by Steißhäuptl and his associates. Their lack of human understanding is in sharp contrast to the self-doubts and questionings suffered by Inspektor Mittermayer, Steißhäuptl's less fortunate comrade-in-arms, in *Der Befehl*.

As his name suggests, Mittermayer represents the 'decent', average man. Like Max Frisch's Biedermann he is to be representative, an Everyman who must learn the truth about himself which his mind has suppressed and which, more importantly, no-one who first met him after 1945 can credit. It is this dichotomy which Hochwälder uses to illustrate the vulnerability of the individual will in the context of 'Ordnung'. Mittermayer is a latter-day Oedipus, condemned by his own absolute response to a sense of order, and more particularly to the suggestiveness of the word 'Befehl'. Indeed the play opens with his wife criticizing him for this very fault: 'Für dich existiert nichts als Befehl, Gehorsam, Dienst'.[13] The fate that is to catch up with the inspector is thus writ large from the start.

Mittermayer's dedication is both his strength and his fatal weakness. Within the bounds of 'Ordnung', that is within the framework of the post-war Austrian police service, his efficiency is a by-word; 'excommunicated', as he was after the *Anschluß* for his anti-Nazi views, Mittermayer faced a bleak future for he had made the police force his whole life. Similarly, Mittermayer fears the prospect of early retirement, a very real threat since his health is poor, but his anxiety derives not from financial grounds but because, like the Cross to the Jesuit, the police force is his only support. In Mittermayer's present attachment to the service, the elision of his individual will and corporate authority in earlier times is suggested.

The stimulus for Mittermayer's investigation into past events is not conscience but political expediency. The request to track down the child-murderer comes from the girl's father, whose present position as part of a delegation with whom the Austrians wish to keep on good terms ensures a response. De Goede, the father, asks for information – he wants to see the man responsible for his daughter's death so that he can see for himself what such a man looks like, but the Austrians turn this request for *knowledge* into an act of vengeance and self-justification. Justice will be done, but at the same time it will be used to protect the reputation of the state and its servants, who must be shown to be above such acts at all –

political – costs.

In *Der Himbeerpflücker* Hochwälder presented a monster masquerading as an affable citizen, but in *Der Befehl* he reminds his audience that no-one can deny the monster within himself. Chillingly, Hochwälder takes the cliché of the mild-mannered 'good citizen' with a black past and twists it to his own ends. Apologists for the SS who argue that bygones should be bygones, as well as those who thirst after vengeance for crimes committed years in the past, are both stopped dead in their tracks by this device. Ironically, it is the argument put forward by the Nazi apologists which at first sight seems to gain the greater support from the play – surely, what Mittermayer has done since the war must expunge his aberrations during it? For Hochwälder however, the urge of conscience is supreme; he is determined to turn the individual in on himself and force him, and the audience, to examine the inner self and to expose the duality of human nature and the sheer impossibility of *knowing* how things stand. The essence of Hochwälder's work and the focal point of his criticism of contemporary Austrian society is to be found in its emphasis of the insecurity and instability of the seemingly impregnable. It is Hochwälder's sustaining thesis that none of us really know ourselves; the spectre of the Jekyll and Hyde within us all, revealed in a manner which is quite clearly aiming for catharsis stresses both Hochwälder's modernity and his links to the traditional theatre. When De Goede meets Mittermayer before the investigation begins, he comments 'Der erste Blick in ein Gesicht trügt nie'[14] – and this to the murderer of his child. This is more than bitter irony, it is tragic confirmation of a motif that has run just below the surface in all Hochwälder's work: there is no sanctuary for the decent man, furthermore, there may not even be such a thing as a 'decent man'.

Mittermayer represents the world at large, he is a reminder that the aura of respectability can be both reality *and* façade. He stumbles towards the truth about himself, coming to a horrified awareness in an orgy of alcohol, transformed in his drunken state to the brutal vicious animal he once was in Amsterdam. When his assistant Dwornik, who has been pursuing enquiries of his own, confronts Mittermayer with the truth and begs him to help the Dutchman to come to terms with *his* past, the inspector finds the courage to assume individual responsibility:

Mittermayer: Ich war es, und ich bin es.

Dwornik:	Es war die Zeit.
Mittermayer:	Es waren die Menschen.[15]

Faced with the truth about himself Mittermayer is utterly lost and virtually commits suicide by approaching a vicious criminal who shoots him down. Suddenly society has found another victim, the witch-hunt changes direction leaving the personal tragedy unresolved. It is left to Dwornik to explain matters to De Goede and to close with play with the unsettling conclusion:

> Manchmal bleibt einem nichts übrig, als sich zu bekreuzigen – nicht vor den andern, nein: vor sich selbst. – Und es sollten sich viele auf diese Weise bekreuzigen.[16]

There is no optimism in Hochwälder's view of the world and perhaps one of the most Austrian traits in his work is its combination of mordant scepticism bordering on despair combined with a faculty for lightness of touch and a persistent faith in the necessity of meeting life on its own terms. Throughout his career Hochwälder has explored the relationship between the individual and the society whose protection he seeks. Be this Jesuit, National Socialist or the Second Republic, Hochwälder deftly varies the contexts in which this relationship is seen. One of the most striking features of his drama is its combination of thematic consistency within an apparently developing social framework. There is no escape for the individual suborned by the delusion of security; Hochwälder's characters, and by implication society at large, can escape neither their own true nature nor the realities of the past. Caught in a vortex that is of his own making, Hochwälder's 'hero' inhabits a world that combines the implacability of Kafka with the mellow astringency of Nestroy.

NOTES

1. Fritz Hochwälder, 'Über mein Theater', rev. version, in: *Der Befehl*, Stiasny Bücherei Vol. 170, Graz 1967, pp. 88–107. This extract p. 99. 'I feel very much a part of the traditional Viennese popular theatre. Once you have lived and breathed in the atmosphere of such a tradition, nothing, neither the perversity of the times, nor a general exodus, can suppress or supplant its influence. I cannot say how much I owe to Vienna – I learnt to think clearly and discovered a sense for form and I got the theatre in my blood. I make no claims to be a

"writer", I am a happy analphabet writing for the theatre in the way I want to write: my plays are unliterary, they are unpretentious, but they are popular.'

2. Fritz Hochwälder, *Dramen*, Graz 1975, 2 vols. *Die Herberge*, Vol. 2. Unless otherwise stated references to the text are to this edition, indicated thus: *Dramen, 1975* followed by volume number and page reference.
   Act III, p. 137: 'If a blind man accidentally stumbles on the truth – do you call that justice?'

3. Fritz Hochwälder, *Lazaretti oder Der Säbeltiger*, Graz 1975. Act I, p. 7: 'We must face facts. We are all mean, petty and downright evil underneath the surface. Sooner or later the truth oozes out.'

4. ibid. Act III, p. 58: 'Won't we ever learn? We persecute ourselves much better than anyone else ever could.'

5. *Dramen*, 1975, *Der Himbeerpflücker*, Vol. 2. Act I, p. 234: 'Those were the days – just look at me now! Rich enough, but without ideals I'm a nobody! Ortsgruppenleiter!! Just thinking about it makes today seem like a bad dream. In those days we had something to look forward to, something that made the sacrifices worthwhile. We didn't worry about everyday matters, no, all that was left far behind . . .'

6. *Dramen*, 1975 *Das Heilige Experiment*, Vol. 1. Act V Scene 3, p. 138: 'You have broken your oath of obedience . . . as your Provincial I pronounce you damned.'

7. ibid Act IV Scene 7, p. 135: 'This . . . is . . . the cause! My . . . own . . . work. . . . This state – the anti-Christ!!'

8. *Dramen*, 1975, *Der öffentliche Ankläger*, Vol. 1. Act I, Scene 6, p. 267: 'Give me a good law and reasonable directives and I am your obedient and conscientious servant. So far and no farther! Order blood shed and I'm the Devil himself.'

9. Fritz Hochwälder, 'Über mein Theater', in *Der Befehl*, Stiasny Bücherei Vol. 170, Graz 1967, p. 103:
   '. . . unassailable, invulnerable, invincible, a modern Alberich. Nothing can harm him, nothing will move him. He's like the man in the fairy-tale: his heart is frozen solid.'

10. *Dramen*, 1975, *Die Herberge*, Vol. 2. Act II, p. 101; 103: 'Anyone with half a brain takes the world as he finds it and it doesn't take much to realize that it's order that keeps it turning. Only one thing protects man from his neighbour – and that's order. . . . Since there is no such thing as justice we have to make do with order.'

11. Conversation with Dieter Hasselblatt, 12 May 1971 on Hochwälder's 60th birthday. Dokumentationsstelle für neuere österreichische Literatur/Tape 1051 A1: 'a wicked farce on a topical theme.'

12. *Dramen*, 1975, *Der Himbeerpflücker*, Vol. 2. Act I, p. 232: 'We were full of hope in those days – and suddenly there was nothing left, just a dream of blood and loyalty.'

13. *Dramen*, 1975, *Der Befehl*, Vol. 2. Act I, Scene 1, p. 281: 'Order, Obey, Serve – that's all you know.'

14. ibid. Act I Scene 2, p. 286: 'When you meet someone for the first time, look him in the eye. That will tell you all you need to know.'

15. ibid. Act III Scene 2, p. 331: Mittermayer: It was me then and it's me now. Dwornik: It was the way things were then. Mittermayer: It was the way *we* were.

16. ibid. Act III Scene 4, p. 336: 'Sometimes all you can do is cross yourself and pray: 'Deliver us from evil' – the evil that is within us. There are a great many who should be doing just that.'

The 'total novel': Heimito von Doderer and Albert Paris Gütersloh

Peter Pabisch and Alan Best

The major part of the novelistic work of Heimito von Doderer and Albert Paris Gütersloh reflects the turbulent history of twentieth-century Austria as seen from the vantage point of the years following World War Two. In their novels a new image of Austria is projected: that of a nation looking, in the manner of the Roman god Janus, back upon the past and at the same time forward into the future. It has often been said that the situation in Austria under the Hapsburg Monarchy, that sprawling, multi-cultural mosaic of people and countries, was never serious but always hopeless. It was precisely this static condition, this quasi-comfortable, quiet desperation in which the people felt no oppression but saw no prospect of change, that provided the tragi-comic milieu which proved such a fertile breeding ground for modern Austrian literature.

Among the traditional genres, the most powerful category of prose writing is clearly the monumental novel, which, as Doderer himself once said, distinguishes itself from the other genres like a cathedral silhouetted against the skyline of a medieval city. Doderer's own gigantic novels, *Die Strudlhofstiege, oder Melzer und die Tiefe der Jahre* (The Strudlhof Steps, or Melzer and the Depth of Years, 1951) (912 pages) and *Die Dämonen: Nach der Chronik des Sektionrates Geyrenhoff*, (The Demons: From The Chronicle of 'Sektionsrat' Geyrenhoff 1956) (1,347 pages), the second and third parts of his 'Viennese trilogy' and Gütersloh's *Sonne und Mond* (Sun and Moon, 1962) provide a daunting prospect for any student of literary architecture. Doderer is by far the better known author today, but his intellectual affinity with Gütersloh is both striking and significant, and it is Gütersloh who acted as the catalyst for Doderer's own creative development.

Above all Gütersloh was an instigator of new trends in Austrian art after 1945, in particular the Viennese art school of phantastic realism; he was a life-long idol for Doderer, who fashioned his own concept of the 'total novel' after Gütersloh's theories, without ever wholly subordinating his own ideas to those of Gütersloh. Gütersloh lived mostly in Vienna and its immediate vicinity. He worked not only as a painter and author, but also as a stage setter, director and even as an actor until his work was deemed 'entartet' by the National Socialists and he was forbidden to write or paint. After 1945 his support for modern art intensified and he tried to bridge the gap between pre-war modern artists and the post-war generation. His own beginnings reach back to expressionism, even to *Jugendstil* and *Art Nouveau*. He was, beside Egon Schiele, one of the most gifted students of Gustav Klimt and a member of the artistic circle of Klimt's followers.

Gütersloh considered art and painting to be his principal profession, and taught in these fields from 1929 onwards, but he never neglected his literary interests. By 1909 he had written *Die tanzende Törin* (The Dancing Fool) while working as a stage-setter and director under Max Reinhardt in Berlin. This expressionistic novel was written in two versions, the longer of which appeared in Berlin in 1911, while the shorter version was published in Munich in 1913. This second version was republished by Langen-Müller in 1973. Doderer read the second version while a prisoner-of-war in Russia in 1920. It was a rather singular introduction to Gütersloh's work: even today, only a few persons beside Doderer have read the novel, which, charged with typical expressionistic antipathy for bourgeois morality, provides a study of the tribulations of youth.

Ruth, the daughter of a prosperous banker, is under pressure from her parents to marry 'respectably', but she herself is vehemently opposed to such a prospect and attempts to thwart their plans by pretending to have lost her virginity. Her outraged parents expel her from home, and she goes to Vienna to become a dancer but without success and eventually finds herself in the gutter in Amsterdam. Shaken by her experience, Ruth begins to have grave self-doubts, and, gradually, out of desperation and defensiveness, her character turns cynical, scornful, and aggressive, so much so that one of her admirers, a blind man, is driven to suicide because of her. Despite its portrayal of bourgeois decadence and doom, the novel fairly glows with the fervour of a young generation which has created a new era of art. It is picturesque, it is erotic: in its sentence structure it often resembles *Sekundenstil*, although Gütersloh avoids the dispassionate and apparently objective descriptions of literary naturalism and the work is written in a narrative style which

Gütersloh was later to abandon as he searched to develop and perfect the alogical pattern of the 'total novel' as he conceived it.

In 1930 Doderer published his extensive and illustrated study of Gütersloh, *Der Fall Gütersloh: Ein Schicksal und seine Deutung*, (The Case of Gütersloh: A Destiny and its Meaning) thus bringing Gütersloh's name to the attention of a (slightly) wider circle. The study was republished after the war and until the 1960s remained the only detailed treatment of Gütersloh the painter and author, establishing Doderer as the pre-eminent authority on the man and his work. In a lengthy three chapter introduction, Doderer detailed the dual talents of the man whom he regarded as his teacher and spiritual mentor, and *Der Fall Gütersloh* is biography with a difference, revealing Doderer's own preoccupations as he himself developed his novelistic skills. Indeed, although their relationship cooled for a while as a consequence of Doderer's flirtations with the Nazis in the 1930's, Doderer maintained the relationship throughout his lifetime. It was a very one-sided affair: Doderer was the admirer, Gütersloh the admired. He wrote enthusiastically to Gütersloh in 1946 of his unceasing preoccupation with his 'master', adding 'One can almost say that I am thinking of you behind your back',[1] and when he edited an anthology of Gütersloh's works in 1963, his choice of title was well-nigh predictable: *Gewaltig staunt der Mensch*, (Man is truly amazed).

Doderer seems to have been almost obsessively convinced that it was his mission to introduce Gütersloh to a discerning public. He wrote on one occasion that he could scarcely wait 'bis der Hörbereich für meine Rede über Sie geschaffen sein wird'.[2] There is little doubt that Doderer's studies of Gütersloh formed a crucial element in his own evolution as a novelist, not least by providing him with a means of disentangling himself from the web of theoretical confusion into which he occasionally strayed.

By the time of the *Anschluß* in 1938 Gütersloh had gained national and international recognition, had completed four novels and published numerous essays in journals and newspapers. Among these latter were his ironic and philosophical meditations on daily events, published in the *Wiener Zeitung* from 1932 to 1936 and published in 1970 under the title *Miniaturen der Schöpfung* (Miniatures of Creation). Gütersloh's work up to 1938 reveals him as a creator of new art and literature constantly striving to further his development. His literature moves gradually away from expressionism and the narrative format of his first novel until he adopts a monological style, intellectual and abstract, which reaches its climax after the war in his principal literary work, the novel *Sonne und Mond* (1962).

Gütersloh had begun the novel in 1935, writing not so much for the reader as for himself and his own conception of the function of language; it is upon this attitude that he bases his concept of the 'total novel', an attempt to replace epic breadth by epic depth, an accumulation of concepts, stimuli and ideas in an achronological pattern which has its own centre of gravity and natural laws. The narrator in *Sonne und Mond* informs the reader of this process and of the challenge it represents:

> Wir finden einen Augenblick schön, in ihm einen noch schöneren und so fort – bei gleichzeitiger Zusammenziehung der mathematischen Zeit bis auf Null und sofortiger Ausdehnung derselben unter Null ins ziemlich Unendliche, so daß eine negative Zeit entsteht, in der, wie wir glauben, auch all das geschieht, was in den Welträumen geschieht: das viel mehr als blitzschnelle Fallen des Lichtstrahls oder die Flucht fernster Sternhaufen fort von unserem Universum in ein anderes – , und so läßt dieses Darstellen unsere Gestalten wie angeschnittene Torten stehen oder wie ihrer Fassaden beraubte Häuser.[3]

As Trommler[4] notes, in conquering time the narrator conquers reality, and his universality, his capacity for embracing an awareness of all experience is immanent and potential in every phrase or statement, every metaphor and image.

The reader is warned, at the beginning of the third chapter of *Sonne und Mond*, that the so-called narration is on the brink of jumping ahead erratically, with no regard for logical context:

> Weil aber noch etliche Abschweifungen folgen sollen, tut der Leser gut, schon jetzt an sie sich zu gewöhnen und nicht zu verlangen, daß schnurgerade fortgefahren werde.[5]

Indeed a virtually impenetrable thicket of thoughts and ideas is interwined with the very simple plot which Gütersloh satirically recounts in the beginning, and to which he returns at the novel's conclusion some 800 pages later. Baron Enguerrand wills his family estate to his nephew, 'dem ohne Aufenthalt durch die fünf Erdteile schweifenden Grafen Lunarin.'[6] After the baron's death Lunarin returns briefly and engages the farmer, Till Adelseher, as the temporary manager of his property during his absence. Adelseher proves so competent that Lunarin, upon his second return at the end of the novel, gives the castle to Adelseher. Considered in terms of rudimentary symbolism, this change in ownership reflects the transition from feudalism to democracy as viewed in the mirror of Austrian history. The intent of this peaceful changeover is to ensure that the former servants do not destroy their own inheritance, but care for it as their own from now on. The 'Dame' in Lunarin's company, however, expresses doubts as to the future and cannot bring herself to regard Adelseher as anything other than a peasant.

In the novel Gütersloh soars intellectually above realms of thought in all philosophical directions; he illuminates each realm from a central, focal position and links them together in a network of his own idiosyncracy:

> Wir haben, wie der Leuchturm, den Kopf voll Augen und drehen uns um uns selbst, sehen alles und bleiben am Platze.[7]

His treatment of language is reminiscent of the 'l'art pour l'art' attitude of the French symbolists. Gütersloh sees language as a material that creates its own art, just as colours 'build' a painting or bright silk threads make a Gobelin tapestry. Thus he creates with language a phantastic reality rather than a mere copy of reality, dispensing with a plot as such. It follows that the traditional interaction of schematic construction and free play of language is absent in such a language-bound work as Sonne und Mond, as it is also, for example, in Musil's Der Mann ohne Eigenschaften. As Trommler somewhat ironically notes: 'Die "Krise des Romans", das ist eine Krise der "Universalität".'[8]

The more deeply one enters into the symbolic world of Sonne und Mond (a title deliberately representative of Adelseher and Lunarin), the more Gütersloh's literary topos retreats from outer historical reality towards psychological and problematical considerations.

It was Thomas Mann who argued that the narrative underwent a process of intensification and refinement as the prose novel gradually cast its epic skin;[9] Mann saw this as an essentially nineteenth-century phenomenon. While not a direct heir to the tradition of the Bildungs- or Entwicklungsroman, Doderer's genuflection towards Dostoewsky in naming his chronicle of Sektionsrat Geyrenhoff Die

Dämonen shows a conscious sense of obligation to the European tradition of the realistic novel. In his theoretical study of the novel, *Grundlagen und Funktion des Romans* (The Basis and Function of the Novel, 1958), written to 'clear his mind' after the enervations of the Viennese trilogy, Doderer declared that form was the means by which the novel became a genuine linguistic creation (*Sprachkunstwerk*).[10] The literary issue of this theoretical exercise and of his subsequent encounter with Gütersloh's *Sonne und Mond* was his novel *Die Merowinger oder Die totale Familie* (The Merovingians, or The Total Family, 1962), his most mature novel from the point of view of clear critical language, and a delightful satire full of word-play and irony concerning a decadent family of the Viennese nobility. Doderer's concern for the primacy of form, he even went so far as to draw (on his father's drawing-board) elaborate diagrams showing the schema of his plot, with graph-like lines representing the rise and fall of the level of tension at various points in the novel, and with page numbers indicated corresponding to the appearance of the novel's characters on various occasions,[11] distinguishes him from Gütersloh, who did not believe that a novel needed a conclusion, other than one brought about by sheer fatigue or by the death of the author.[12]

Doderer could never accept such a view. He was, above all a narrator, a story-teller with a fine sense for the descriptive force of language. He sought to portray a 'fictitious external reality' and refused to be limited by what he called the relative shallowness of psychological patterns. For him the novel is a means of documenting the vividness ('Anschaulichkeit') of his age, and his own historical studies inevitably condition this documentation.

Doderer's work presents the reader with a colourful scenario and a wealth of figures in the settings of Austria, Austria-Hungary, and, predominantly, Vienna. It is a scenario of epic breadth and proportions, but it is not conceived as a mirror of reality but as a honeycombed storehouse from whence the novelist can derive his inspiration. The raw material thus extracted is then dependent on language for its effect, and must achieve more than a mere literal transmission of ideas on to the written page:

> Sprache und Sprach-Objekt müssen weit getrennt bleiben. Wächst die Sprache an ihrem Objekte fest, dann verfällt sie der Mitteilung. Sie muß frei beweglich bleiben und mit ihrem Gegenstande spielen wie der Springbrunnen mit dem Ball.[13]

68

In accepting this principle Doderer displays the essential difference between his own literary view and Gütersloh's conception of the 'total' novel. He is critical of the lack of intent to narrate on the part of both Gütersloh and Musil; whereas in the monological, more introverted techniques of these two authors the language tends to follow its own course Doderer's own works are moulded to a predeterminate form. Doderer was conscious of the musical structure of his works and indeed called nine of his novellas 'divertimenti' and likened his novels to Beethoven's symphonies. The whole range of his work reveals his determination to maintain a sense of structure and thus ensure that the reader, like a voyager on a ship watching the last land-fall slip over the horizon, can put his trust in the narrator in the knowledge that all is under control and a course charted.[14] There is much travelling and sight-seeing in Doderer's work but no great suggestion of a clearly-defined destination or final resolution to his plots.

Doderer fears becoming a mere story-teller, and thus accepts Gütersloh's principles to a limited extent. Yet where Gütersloh creates language for its own sake devoid of any intellectual or artistic function Doderer cannot easily dismiss the world of objects. He formulated his beliefs in 1941:

> Der totale Roman ist der geometrische Ort aller Punkte, die sich gleich weit entfernt befinden von der Kunst, der Wissenschaft und vom Leben tel qu'il est.[15]

And even after the experience of *Sonne und Mond*, as late in fact as 1965, shortly before his death Doderer still defined the art of the novel as follows:

> Die Kunst des Romans besteht darin, außervernünftige Zusammenhänge entdecken zu können, welche schließlich auch das Vernünftige mit einschließen. Von da her muß der Roman durchaus 'verständlich' sein, mindestens aber einer großen Zahl von Lesern so erscheinen, die ihn garnicht verstehen.[16]

This formula may perhaps contain the secret of the monumental character of Doderer's work. By 'durchaus "verständlich"' Doderer is emphasizing the view that the novelist must consider the reader, as if expecting the reader's comment or reaction. At the same time he respects Gütersloh's principles in the phrase 'außer-vernünftige Zusammenhänge', and concedes the independence of the creative phantasy of the author and the necessity of granting the author creative scope. In his *Neunzehn Lebensläufe* (Nineteen curricula vitae), published to honour his seventieth birthday, Doderer reiterates this ambivalent principle. In these biographies he strays into the world of constructive phantasy and abandons the mode of autobiographical presentation. They do not pertain to Doderer and the empirical world; rather 'der Mensch ist universal gemeint'[17] and, in Doderer's terminology 'apperceived' from a spiritual distance.

Where Gütersloh's was in many respects a life governed by calm rationality, religio-philosophical wisdom and gradual evolutionary development, Doderer's was a series of mishaps, mistakes and remorse over his own shortcomings. Doderer's spiritual development through the 1930s and 1940s is directly reflected in his literary work, not least in his acute awareness of the demonology of the inner mind and the deadening fabric of political and social ideologies. We may never know precisely why Doderer joined the illegal Austrian Nazi party in 1933, but five years later he burned his membership card in the presence of friends as a symbolic dissociation from the movement and its ideology. Two years later, in 1940, he was converted to Catholicism, the act of an individual striving to regain and enhance his sense of humanity. Ironically Doderer's name remained on the list of Nazi party members, since the party did not officially recognize resignations and in the post-Nazi purge after the war Doderer was forbidden to publish until 1948.

Doderer began work on his exhaustive novel *Die Dämonen* in 1931 some four years before Gütersloh embarked on *Sonne und Mond*. Originally Doderer called the work *Die Dämonen der Ostmark* (The Demons of the Eastern March), but his gradual disillusion with the implications of National Socialism in particular and all ideology in general is best seen in the first of the three novels of the 'Viennese trilogy' *Die erleuchteten Fenster oder Die Menschwerdung des Amtsrates Julius Zihal* (The Illuminated Windows or The Humanization of 'Amtsrat' Julius Zihal). Although published in 1951 this highly-readable, and by Doderer's standards, concise novel (191 pages) was begun in 1939 and must reflect the psychological and spiritual catharsis and liberation of its author.

In his search for a universal concept of mankind Doderer sought to establish a means whereby the individual could express his own essential individuality. His essay *Sexualität und totaler Staat* (Sexuality and the Totalitarian State) written in 1948 and revised in 1951 provides a theoretical gloss which is an invaluable aid to an understanding of his novels. With the shadow of National Socialism still looming large, Doderer declared: 'Der totale Staat ist konsolidierte Apperzeptionsverweigerung: somit eine zweite Wirklichkeit.'[18] 'Apperception' for Doderer involves a capacity on the part of the individual to open his or her mind and senses to all the stimuli and phenomena to which he or she is exposed; this is in distinction to mere 'perception' which represents a purely mechanical contact with the external world. Any ideology, be it political or social, will necessarily channel the thoughts and ideas of its adherents, they will tend to perceive the world about them in less 'universal' and more blinkered terms, and will act according to received ideas rather than their own personal motivation. Ideology and life are for Doderer in constant and inevitable opposition.

The increasing passivity and tendency to categorize life is seen by Doderer as an affront to humanity and a retreat into what he calls the:

> Pseudologischen, in einem pseudologischen Raum . . . dessen Koordinatensystem im Handumdrehen erstellt ist.
>
> Der Pseudologe vernebelt sich selbst. Bei ihm wird eine zweite Welt errichtet, und keineswegs wird in der ersten, wie sie nun einmal ist, verblieben.[19]

Those who have fallen victim to such an outlook on life are branded 'Apperzeptionsverweigerer' because they have created, often unwittingly and as a direct consequence of the social circumstances and ethos in which they move, a psychological bolt-hole from which they must be tempted. The only answer to the 'Apperzeptionsverweigerer', but it is always successful, is to make him face up to reality:

> Die Apperzeptions-Verweigerung schützt einen konsolidierten pseudologischen Raum vor der Wiederherstellung des analogischen Grundzustandes.[20]

This 'modern manifestation of stupidity' as Doderer terms it, is grotesquely and humorously caricatured in the person of the Amts-

71

rat Julius Zihal. Now a retired civil-servant Zihal cannot shake off the practices and attitudes of a lifetime of bureaucratic activity, perhaps the most insidious ideology of them all. He lives in his own world and when he begins to notice what is happening behind the illuminated windows of the appartment block opposite his own, and some of the scenes include sexually titillating glimpses, he reacts with all the fervour and thoroughness of the dedicated civil servant. He acquires a spy-glass and a notebook and like some medieval astronomer begins to quarter 'his' heavens, carefully regulating his observations and noting what he has seen. Zihal is no Peeping-Tom, he conducts his nocturnal sightings with increasing seriousness and they become a second life, to the extent that they cause him to reorganise his 'normal' day-to-day existence. Zihal acquires better optical instruments and as he becomes more sophisticated recreates his own total environment, the 'Objektstotalität' which is all-embracing. He is cocooned in a projection of his own fantasy, in the second reality to which Doderer referred.

The novel is a satirical assault on the perversion inherent in all forms of ideology; it is more grotesque and humorous in Zihal's case because the Amtsrat's bureaucratic tendencies and his sexual instincts have become intertwined. Zihal's working life has been the embodiment of *Apperzeptionsverweigerung*, indeed even after his retirement he constantly measures his actions by reference to the civil servants' code of practice, and it was this tendency to role-playing and rote-functioning which Doderer wished to expose. The mechanistic links to the external world which constitute perception are compared in *Sexualität und totaler Staat* with the molecular and chemical synthesis which characterizes apperception. Doderer does not claim that the blinkered, aggressive sexuality of modern society is the basis of all 'pseudology' but he does insist that it is a particularly significant indicator:

> Der Sexualakt stellt, unter diesem Winkel gesehen, einen der intensivsten Fälle der Apperzeption überhaupt dar, eine der mächtigsten Klammern und zugleich Brücken zwischen innen und außen . . . und das heißt hier nichts anderes als: Wirklichkeit.[21]

Zihal's nocturnal foragings with his telescope however, reflect a pseudo-sexuality, they are the essence of *Apperzeptionsverweigerung* and he himself is constitutionally incapable of any other attitude. This too is inevitable. He is isolated, withdrawn and psychologically incomplete. As Doderer argues:

> Die Apperzeptions-Verweigerung ist eine spontan auftretende krampfartige Bewegung der Seele. Sie schließt den Sack des pseudologischen Raumes – wie mit einem elastischen Ring. Was nun folgt ist eine Art invertierter Apperzeption: der Zwang zur Vereinzelung des Einzelnen im Einzelsten.[22]

Zihal's *Menschwerdung*, his release from life by the dead paragraphs of the civil servants' code, comes in a relationship he forges with a female postal official Rosl Oplatek. Ironically, their relationship is sealed when he presents her with the opera glasses he first used for his nocturnal observations.

Zihal's situation, escape from the second reality to the genuine or first reality of human relationships and his consequent 'humanization' is set against a rather light-hearted background. His *erotica more geometrico* reflecting the dehumanized world of the bureaucrat allows the reader to savour the humour of his incongruous behaviour.

In *Die Dämonen* the novelist Kajetan von Schlaggenberg is an archetypal *Apperzeptionsverweigerer*. His taste is for 'DD' (i.e. Dicke Damen), he has constructed his whole attitude on this predilection and has eyes for nothing else. Nonetheless Doderer is at pains to insist that the second reality is a transitional stage, ultimately transcended by exposure to the sheer weight of facts and realities. Like Doderer himself his characters are seduced into an *Apperzeptionsverweigerung*, they embark on an 'Umweg' until they manage to bring the inner and outer world together in some form of harmony and eventually are humanized and enabled to see reality as it is. This is essentially an ethical achievement and underlines Doderer's profound morality; it cannot, however, escape the reader's notice that the author is indulging in some rather desperate optimism and perhaps convincing himself thereby that the society he depicts is not in need of radical change. While it is unfair to label *Die Dämonen* a defence of the bourgeoisie and of conservative nobility, i.e. the social register to which Doderer himself felt most closely drawn,[23] it must be said that his optimistic belief in the capacity of 'Menschwerdung' to achieve the co-incidence of inner and outer realities suggests a reluctance to attack the structure of society itself. Literature, for Doderer, was not an instrument of

73

social change, or at least not directly: 'Wenn der Mensch . . . seine Hoffnung auf eine Veränderung der äußeren Umstände setzt, dann ist er in den Weg der Schwäche eingebogen.'[24] Any reconciliation of inner awareness and outer reality, any achievement of the 'Deckung' of these two realities, is best achieved, according to Doderer through a psychological awakening on the part of the individual. The function of literature is to service this process; it should not concern itself with social engineering. Such insistence on the individual psyche is typically Austrian and wholly admirable, where it can be challenged is that it tends to concentrate on individual symptoms and ignore the disease itself. It is much easier to arrive at optimistic conclusions if one concentrates on individual aspects and any author who deliberately chooses a historical canvas for his work, as in the 'Viennese trilogy' but does not drive his conclusions beyond individual cases runs the risk of being dismissed as irrelevant.

The Viennese trilogy portrays life in a fictitious Viennese society from the end of the monarchy in 1918 to the burning down of the Palace of Justice in 1927, an event which Doderer considers marks the fall of the First Austrian Republic. True to his conception of the total novel, themes lose their importance and are subsumed in a complex presentation of what passes for reality. The characters too, and there are over 130 in the trilogy, are not so much individually drawn as presented as an integrated group in the collective scene, with certain figures emerging more strongly to catch and hold the reader's attention. Mary K., who loses a leg when run over by a tram, gains a new self-assurance and attitude to life; the former Lt. Melzer, also in *Die Strudlhofstiege*, who shakes off the trauma of his wartime experiences and the young historian René von Stangeler are three cases in point. Stangeler is closely linked to Doderer himself, and his role underlines two crucial elements in his work: a strong autobiographical strain and the role of memory. Both these features, it should be noted, stemming from a personalized approach to society and shifting the emphasis towards an individual rather than a social preoccupation. Doderer creates a personal distance from the events he portrayed; the flight of stairs helped crystallize his memories of Vienna in the 1940s while he was on active service. This 'Gedächtnis-Distanz', the filtering of social, historical and personal experience through the skein of memory gives such such extensive works as *Die Strudlhofstiege* and *Die Dämonen* a sense of simultaneity, totality, of apperception if you will.

The novelist, Doderer wrote, must apperceive, but he must also come to terms with what he finds:

Die Apperzeption verbindet chemisch mit dem Objekt, die Sprache trennt und befreit uns davon, wenn sie es bewältigt.[25]

In the *Groß-Symbol* of the flight of steps Doderer affirms both the capacity for apperception and its implication:

Die Gegenwart ist nur ein kleines brennendes Lichtlein, das flackert: wahre Erhellung aber kommt stetig aus dem Vergangenen.[26]

The steps offer, in addition, the possibility of ascending and descending from one temporal or spatial level to the next; they symbolize a non-fanatical compromise with life. Again Doderer's critics would claim that he fails to put such true enlightenment to effective use, merely illuminating individual success and choosing to ignore the wider social spectrum.

Doderer is pre-eminently a realistic writer, indeed the nature of his work precludes any other approach. The broad, detailed canvas, the historical and topographical detail leads to a multitude of characters, episodes and incidents. The counterpoint of autobiography and objective observation of the constituent episodes as they coalesce to a choate structure emphasise Doderer's conviction that there is no direct approach that will resolve the problems of contemporary life. His highly metaphorical, associative and even additive technique is like the working of a richly-coloured tapestry; the individual threads lose all significance save as a vivid part of the finished image. Critics tend to agree as to Doderer's pre-eminence as a technician and master of the novel form; where they diverge, those who would challenge his stature do so on the grounds that his failure to criticise society as it is has reduced the significance of his work to precisely that of an illustrative, and interesting, historical tapestry. Claudio Magris suggested that Doderer's work was a search for order in chaos and for a bridge over the abyss,[27] and it is true that all Doderer's novels reflect the traumatic ideological upheavals of his and his country's recent past. Yet it would be wrong to concentrate on such concepts as 'Menschwerdung' or to dwell on the political or a-political nature of his work to the detriment of a consideration of what Doderer hoped to achieve in his efforts to create a 'total novel'.

The background against which both he and Gütersloh wrote is a significant factor, as significant in its way as the 'werkimmanenten' elements. Both authors witnessed the founding of the Second Republic and the charting of a new political face to Europe and their response to these events colours their literary perspective. As Trommler concludes his study of the modern Austrian novel:

> Angesichts der perfekten Kommunikationsmittel des Zeitalters eröffnet der Roman eine andere Dimension des Wirklichen. Er muß absehen vom Erzählen, um etwas erzählen zu können. Er sucht nicht mehr das Sagbare zu sagen, sondern das Unsagbare einzugrenzen.[28]

For these novelists, the direct route was no longer viable. In their own way both attempted to use language to create a new focal point and reference. The total novel, complete in itself and to itself, epitomizes the paradox that the shortest route and the direct statement can no longer effectively express the implications of contemporary life.

NOTES

1. H. v. Doderer, *Tangenten: Tagebuch eines Schriftstellers*: 1940–1950 Munich, 1964 pp. 420–21.
2. 'when conditions are right for receiving my account of your works'. ibid. p. 421.
3. Albert Paris Gütersloh, *Sonne und Mond: Ein historischer Roman aus der Gegenwart*, Munich, 1962, p. 89: 'We are struck by the beauty of a particular instant, and within that instant we find one that is even more beautiful and so on, so that mathematical time ceases to count and is reduced to zero, and below zero it immediately expands into relative infinity, creating, as it were, a negative time which, as we believe, records everything, including everything that takes place across the face of creation: the ray of light passing faster than lightning or the disappearance of distant galaxies from the edge of our universe into another – and this manner of presentation means that our characters seem like cakes which have been cut or houses whose facade has been torn down.'
4. Frank Trommler, *Roman und Wirklichkeit: Eine Ortsbestimmung am Beispiel von Musil, Broch, Roth, Doderer und Gütersloh*, Stuttgart 1966, p. 155.

5. *Sonne und Mond* p. 69: 'Because there will be several digressions in what follows, the reader will do well to accustom himself to them at this point, and not demand absolute continuity.'

6. *Sonne und Mond* p. 7: 'To Count Lunarin, who is currently roaming non-stop across the five continents.'

7. *Sonne und Mond* p. 69: Like the lighthouse, our head is filled with eyes; and we rotate slowly around, seeing everything and yet staying where we are.

8. Trommler op. cit. p. 149: 'The "crisis of the novel" is a crisis of "universality"'.

9. Thomas Mann, 'Die Kunst des Romans' (1939), quoted in *Theorie und Technik des Romans im 20. Jahrhundert*, ed. by Hartmut Steinecke, Tübingen, 1972, p. 10. The original reads: Als der Prosa-Roman sich vom Epos ablöste, trat die Erzählung einen Weg zur Verinnerlichung und Verfeinerung an, der lang war und an dessen Beginn diese Tendenz noch gar nicht zu ahnen war.

10. Quoted in Steinecke op. cit. p. 83. The original reads: Das bedeutet die Priorität der Form vor den Inhalten: in der Tat wird erst durch sie der Roman zum eigentlichen Sprachkunstwerk.

11. cf. *Die zeitgenössische Literatur Österreichs*, ed. by Hilde Spiel, Zurich and Munich, 1976, p. 168. A colour illustration of the plan for chapter 11 of the third part of *Die Dämonen*.

12. Cf. Steinecke op. cit. p. 110: A.P. Gütersloh, 'Der innere Erdteil. Aus den "Wörterbüchern"' (1966).

13. H. v. Doderer, *Repertorium: Ein Begreifbuch von höheren und niederen Lebens-Sachen*, Munich, 1969, p. 233: 'Language and object must remain widely separated. Language firmly attached to its object is reduced to the role of sheer communication. It needs to move freely and play with its object as a fountain balances a ball on top of a jet of water.'

14. Doderer, *Repertorium* p. 202. The original reads: mit unbestimmt sich wegwendender Küste im Sonnenglast . . . (übernimmt) der Kapitän für große Fahrt unser Schiff: es ist der Romancier. (1957)

15. Doderer, *Repertorium* p. 202: 'The total novel is the geometric centre of all points located equidistant from art, science and life-as-it-is.'

16. Doderer, *Repertorium* p. 200: 'The art of the novel consists in the ability to discover extra-rational connections which ultimately embrace the rational as well. And from this point on the novel must be wholly 'understandable; or at least it must appear so to a large number of readers who do not in fact understand it at all.'

17. Doderer, *Tangenten* p. 18: 'Man is seen on a universal scale.'

18. Doderer, 'Sexualität und totaler Staat', in *Die Wiederkehr der Drachen*, Aufsätze/Traktate/Reden, ed. W. Schmidt-Dengler, Munich, 1970, pp. 275–98.
p. 293: 'The totalitarian state is consolidated refusal to apperceive, and consequently a second reality.'

19. ibid. p. 277: 'a retreat into the pseudological, a pseudological region whose system of co-ordinates is established at a moment's notice. The pseudologist mystifies himself. He creates a second world, totally

abandoning the first, the world as it really is.'

20. ibid. p. 282. 'A refusal to apperceive protects a consolidated pseudological region from the re-establishment of the analogical condition which is its basis.'
21. ibid. p. 281. 'Seen from this aspect the sexual act represents one of the most deep-rooted instances of apperception imaginable; it is at one and the same time one of the most powerful clamps and bridges between the inner and the outer . . . and in this case that means just one thing: reality.'
22. ibid. p. 294: 'The refusal to apperceive is a spontaneous cramp-like mental reaction. It seals the sac of the pseudological region as if with an elastic ring. The consequence is a form of inverted apperception: a compulsive isolation of the individual in ever-increasing and deepening preoccupation with minutiae.'
23. Cf. C.E. Williams, 'Heimito von Doderer' in *The Broken Eagle*, London, 1974, pp. 132–147.
24. Doderer, *Tangenten*, p. 250: 'Those who set any store in a shift in external factors have already taken the first steps down the road of weakness.'
25. Doderer, *Repertorium*, p. 27. 'Apperception binds us chemically with our objects; language separates and frees us from them, if it can sufficiently assert itself.'
26. ibid. pp. 94–95: 'The present is only a small burning light that flickers: true enlightenment shines steadily from what has gone before.'
27. Claudio Magris, *Der habsburgische Mythos in der österreichischen Literatur*, Salzburg, 1966, p. 302.
28. Trommler, *Roman und Wirklichkeit*, p. 167:
'In an age when the means of communication function perfectly the novel provides a different dimension to reality. The novel discounts narrative in order to have something to narrate, and it no longer seeks to say what can be said but to define the limits of what cannot be said.'

The authors gratefully acknowledge the assistance of Darwin Kahler Wheat (The University of New Mexico) in translating this article from the German.

Elias Canetti:
The Intellectual as King Canute

David Turner

In that most Austrian of stories, *Der arme Spielmann* (The Poor Musician), Grillparzer depicted the attempt of one man – part saint, part fool – to avoid contact with 'sordid' everyday life, including sex and commercialism, and to assert the independence and supremacy of the inner world of 'Geist'. He also depicted the failure of the attempt: the metaphorical flood, symbol of the mass against which the hero determinedly sets his face, becomes in the end a literal flood that engulfs him. The same basic theme, which was to be reworked in later generations, for example in Hofmannsthal's *Märchen der 672. Nacht* (Tale of the 672nd Night), now in the context of late nineteenth-century aestheticism, appears again in the twentieth century as the central focus of Elias Canetti's only novel and most widely read work, *Die Blendung* (The Delusion). Indeed, it is a paradigm of Canetti's entire work as a writer and thinker. For here is a man who, although acutely aware of the most disturbing manifestations of political and economic life in twentieth-century Germany and Austria – two world wars, massive inflation, the seduction of the masses, the brutal exercise of power – as well as of the pernicious effects of individual human egoism and monomania, has become suspicious of action and has chosen instead to rely on his intellectual and moral powers to counter such intractable realities. To some extent of course his background and upbringing have made him a homeless outsider. He has done much of his writing in a foreign country (England) and all of it in a language (German) which was not his mother tongue; and this had inevitably led to a strange mixture of involvement in and detachment from those realities. Yet over and above that, it is as though Canetti has wanted to demonstrate the power of mind over matter, to halt the tide of even political events by the sheer force of the intellect.

The paradox is that long before the publication of the work which, more than any other, was to express the unshakable tenacity of that will, the study *Masse und Macht* (Crowds and Power), his imaginative works, notably *Die Blendung* and the play *Die Befristeten* (Their Days are Numbered), had already called the possibility of success into question. But this should come as no surprise from a man whose whole attitude to human nature is summed up in a paradox: 'Es gibt wenig Schlechtes, was ich vom Menschen wie der Menschheit nicht zu sagen hätte. Und doch ist mein Stolz auf sie noch immer so groß, daß ich nur eines wirklich hasse: ihren Feind, den Tod.'[1]

In his novel, first published in 1935 and later revised, Canetti follows the basic pattern set by Grillparzer's story, but pushes matters to much greater extremes of both intensity and extensity, in that, on the one hand, the protagonist's attempt to preserve his inner world from contamination by the realities that surround him is pursued with an unprecedented, obsessive force and, on the other, the background against which he is set is made up almost entirely of other individuals whose admittedly very different aims are subject to the same single-minded compulsion. The result is a picture of chaos, a free-for-all between *idées fixes* which are equal in intensity and differ only in direction, a plot which contains more double-crossings than a spy-thriller, a rapid succession of ironies deriving from the thwarting of so many designs.

The philologist Peter Kien represents the world of pure intellect, where books have taken the place of people, the written word in its apparently clear and immovable content has supplanted the messy involvement of the spoken word, and where truth can shine out unhindered by such complicating factors as people and everyday objects. Women in particular pose a threat to this world and are the objects of hatred and fear, while sex, which entails the most intimate human contact, is the ultimate horror.

In a novel full of ironies it is the central irony that this intellectual recluse should be tempted out of his isolation and become entangled in the most squalid manner with the world he so despises, exposed to its most predatory representatives. He is first caught at his weakest point, when he observes the care with which his housekeeper Therese handles his books and falsely assumes an intellectual curiosity. Thereafter, the sexual fiasco of his wedding night and the solid domestic furniture which she introduces into the inner sanctum of his library mark only the first of many humiliations and exploitations to which he is increasingly subjected, until his mind is overwhelmed and he finally sets fire to his precious library and is himself engulfed by the flames. There have been brave attempts to put some positive construction on his end, to see it as a modern variant of Goethe's mystical 'Stirb und werde' (Die to be reborn) or as a return from isolation to an all-embracing unity.[2] But what the novel convincingly depicts is the defeat, the mental disintegration of the hero, brought about not only by the exploitation of those around him, but by his own refusal to acknowledge all that within himself which links him with other human beings, by his self-imposed isolation, by the denial of any personal mutability, of what his brother calls 'the mass within the individual'. He dies moreover without the enlightenment that comes to the young aesthete of Hofmannsthal's *Märchen*, who comes to hate his premature death so much that 'he hated his life because it had brought him to this point'. Kien dies rather in delusion, resembling nothing so much as those paranoiac rulers whom Canetti will later describe in his study of crowds and power: taking his troops (i.e. books) with him into death so that none should survive his defeat or pass into the control of another.[3]

Of the three most important figures who are variously ranged against Kien his housekeeper and subsequent wife, Therese, is dominated by lust for money, while her undoubted sexual appetite is to be regarded as the chief means to this end; Benedikt Pfaff, the former policeman, now caretaker of the house where Kien has his appartment, seeks power over others by naked terror and brute force; and Fischerle, the hunchbacked dwarf, who is no less keen than Therese to lay his hands on Kien's money, is governed by the 'higher' motive of seeking to establish himself as world chess champion.

Behind the individual *idées fixes* of these three it is not difficult to detect the common search for domination, nor to relate them to some of the manifestations of power discussed subsequently in *Masse und Macht*. What is only too easy to overlook, however, is that the representative of pure 'Geist', who has many of the attributes of the *ingénu*, careless of money and doomed to destruction at the hands of his more cunning fellows, is scarcely less preoccupied with the exercise of power. And it is not only in death that he betrays characteristics of the paranoiac ruler; they are there from the beginning in his attempt to build a protective space around himself; they are revealed in his mobilization of an army of books against the arch-enemy Therese; they are present too in that sense of uniqueness with which he justifies to himself his supposed killing of her. Altogether his relationship with Therese represents a

81

constantly-shifting power struggle, described in terms of victory and defeat. And what emerges most forcibly from all this, what is perhaps the most compelling lesson of the whole novel, is the fundamental impotence and self-contradiction of the intellectual ivory tower. Kien's victories are either imaginary or of such a purely intellectual kind as to have no force whatsoever in the world of real power. And in effect he implicitly acknowledges the powerlessness of his mental armoury: when Therese begins to extend her domestic domain and encroach too palpably on his intellectual reserve, he has little hesitation in enlisting the muscle of Pfaff to try and get rid of her. 'Geist' cannot divorce itself from the everyday realities of life; even as it seeks to assert its power, it betrays its impotence in isolation; and in the very attempt to free itself from its mortal enemy, matter, it must needs make use of the enemy's weapons. Nor should Kien's usual carelessness in financial matters, in such stark contrast to the crass materialism of those around him, blind us to the simple fact that this is only possible because he has inherited money for which he has not had to work.[4]

That Kien's undoubted achievements as a scholar are bought at a price accounts in part for the title Canetti eventually chose for his novel.[5] The title denotes, first, the blinkered concentration of his existence, which requires not only a library without windows on to the world, but ultimately also the practice of closing his eyes quite literally to everything that does not belong to his academic work, thereby attempting to overcome the categories of time, space, and matter altogether. The title also relates, however, to a blindness which affects all the characters equally and is less of a self-imposed condition than a simple consequence of their monomania. They are so possessed by their egocentric purpose, so locked in their private vision, that they cannot grasp the reality of their situation and are particularly susceptible to illusions, never more so than when they imagine they can see through their opponent. The culmination of this collective blindness occurs in a scene at the police station, a setting where, ideally, truth should be brought to light. In a masterly passage of comic writing Kien confesses to the murder of his wife even as she stands, a supposed hallucination, in front of him, while she believes he is admitting to the murder of an earlier wife and so imagines she has discovered the secret of his early morning activities, and the caretaker Pfaff construes the confession as a sly means of bringing his own act of brutal murder to the attention of the police. This travesty of an investigation, in which each person is blinded by his own obsession, is under the theoretical control of an officer whose proud but empty boast is: 'Mir macht keiner was vor' (You can't fool me).

Critics have not been slow to recognize in *Die Blendung* a reflection of that theme which has so fascinated the modern Austrian (though not only Austrian) mind: the problem of language. But it is important to note crucial differences from what Hofmannsthal describes in his 'Chandos Letter' or Musil depicts as part of the confusions of his young Törless. There the problem lies in language itself, in the deceptive ease with which it masks the problematic nature of things and our uncertain understanding of them, or in its inadequacy as a rational medium to deal with the irrational, emotional, intuitive areas of life. In the case of Canetti the problem lies rather with the people who use language; in his novel, as also to a large extent in his first two plays, the characters are so blinded by their own *idée fixe* that their patterns of speech have become fossilized and they themselves have become incapable of conducting a dialogue. The conversations of *Die Blendung* are typically therefore a series of juxtaposed monologues.[6]

The blindness of the characters also finds a concrete counterpart in the locations of the novel. The atmosphere is as claustrophobic as a Kafka novel, and that not merely because we rarely move out of doors and only once, as we follow the hero's brother, leave the confines of a city we assume to be Vienna (although in its presentation of a chaotic society full of possessed people it is also modelled on the Berlin Canetti got to know in the nineteen-twenties).[7] The atmosphere is still more a result of the way in which the four main characters inhabit confined spaces even within the interiors available to them: Kien his windowless library; Therese her kitchen, that powerhouse of the material basis of life; Pfaff the small cabinet from which he keeps a tyrannical eye on all who seek entrance to Ehrlichstraße 24; Fischerle the space under the bed on which his wife prostitutes herself, the space from which he also offers her customers a game of chess!

Canetti clearly has considerable gifts as a comic writer. His exposure of monomaniacal absurdity, his ability to create sheer Bedlam, provoke irresistible laughter. Repeatedly, however, even as we laugh at the characters, a chill horror overtakes us. Its chief source is the grotesque distortion of humanity we are being made to witness. For just as the inanimate objects of this world can assume a life of their own in the imagination of the characters, so also the characters themselves can be debased into animals or reduced to one exaggerated attribute: Therese to her stiff blue skirt, Pfaff to his naked fist. Although we may be tempted to dismiss such phenomena as the products of distorted, subjective vision, there is no escaping the implications, horrific as well as comic, of the things the characters do, the perverse tenacity with which they pursue their aim, the disproportionate effort they devote to its fulfilment, and the mental and even physical contortions they perform along the way. Moreover, even the subjective vision of the characters cannot in practice be dismissed so easily by the reader. And this is an important consequence of Canetti's narrative method, which deliberately renounces the possibility of a unified, authoritative stance in favour of a multiplicity of perspectives, not for the sake of experiment, but as a natural expression of the fragmented world of conflicting monomanias he is depicting. No one perspective is binding; and as we enter in turn the private world of the main characters, we adjust our understanding accordingly. But for the time being we are subjected to the full force of each individual conviction, which is frequently magnified by the way in which the narrator adopts the vocabulary of the particular character and, more especially, by his habit of presenting their fantasies with all the seriousness and immediacy of real events. The novel nowhere attempts to provide a resolution of these discordant private visions; and the perspective with which it closes is insane as well as private. That *Die Blendung* thus denies us the consoling sense of some universal order or harmony that remains intact may be related to Canetti's concern to do full justice to the reality of a world that seemed to have fallen apart.[8]

Whether in general, however, he is able to persuade us that his novel presents a valid and recognizable picture of the world, however partial, foreshortened, or caricatured, is open to question. When he records that one of the most important influences on the writing of the novel was the burning of the Viennese Palace of Justice in 1927, a mass response – in which he himself felt caught up – to the brutal murder of a group of workers in the Burgenland,[9] some engagement with contemporary social and political reality would seem to be involved. Yet it is hard to find. Although there may be some link with Kien's act of incendiarism as a mass experience,[10] it would be absurd to understand the destruction of this ivory-tower scholar and his esoteric library as a meaningful commentary on the actions of those workers. It is possible to see the

ironic description of the Theresianum, the vast building which performs the function of state pawnshop, as a criticism of institutionalized exploitation of the poor and of a national scale of values
according to which the luxuries are placed first, necessities second,
and works of the intellect last of all; but the force of the criticism is
reduced by our growing realization that it is being presented from
the idiosyncratic point of view of the scholar Kien. The novel may
provide flashes of insight into the mentality of fascism – in the
descriptions of the brutal tyranny of Pfaff or the readiness of the
crowd at the Theresianum to fasten on a scapegoat – but no
sustained correspondence emerges; Canetti has not attempted a
more coherent political allegory such as we find in Thomas Mann's
Doktor Faustus.

Much of the difficulty in relating the fictional world to that of the
reality we know may be traced, however, to the author's manner of
presentation. Distortion and exaggeration are legitimate weapons
of the satirical artist, but when taken beyond certain limits they can
defeat their object. In *Die Blendung* it is probably less a matter of
individual extravagance than of collective exaggeration. Stefan
Zweig, on whom Canetti has spent only a few contemptuous
words,[11] was similarly fascinated by monomania and loved to depict
it in his stories. Leaving aside his different conception of the
phenomenon as a blind, demonic, instinctive force which, typically,
breaks through the civilized surface of life, it is instructive to note
how he used his favourite framework technique to isolate the
exceptional quality of his central characters, yet at the same time
provide a sympathetic bridge between them and the reader. In *Die
Blendung*, by contrast, Canetti has renounced the possibility of a
consistent, reliable narrator to provide a context, a standard by
which to measure the monomaniacal hero; the background is popu-
lated by other monomaniacs. Although this may be seen as part of
the modernity of the novel, it also entails the danger of blunting the
satirical edge, since the alternatives presented are equally horrify-
ing. In such a world of physical and mental freaks freakishness
becomes the norm. There may admittedly be something of the satirical aim which Canetti was later to discuss in connection with Swift:
that is, the attempt to define the limits of what is human, terrifying
people into an awareness of those limits. But it is doubtful whether
things work out like this in practice. For despite the sensation of
horror the reader can all-too easily shrug his shoulders at a fictional
world in which he fails to perceive an image, however distorted, of

his own world.

The world of *Die Blendung* is not, however, entirely made up of monomaniacal freaks. With the appearance of the protagonist's brother, Georg Kien, a breath of something like normality comes into the novel. And it is not for nothing that he is presented as a literal outsider, who has to travel in from abroad. He seems altogether more sympathetic and humane than the rest, having renounced 'Macht', having abandoned a lucrative position as a successful gynaecologist in favour of psychiatric medicine, where, in the sharpest contrast to the others, who are locked in their own private world, he seeks to enter into the mentality of each of his patients. At several points his views echo those of Canetti himself, especially when he talks of the necessity for man to acknowledge the 'mass within himself'. His creator has indeed spoken of him as representing the positive side of the mass.[12] Yet, for all the insight he brings into the novel as an internal commentator, his position remains dubious. Although he manages to extricate his brother from his immediate enemies, he fails to assess his mental state adequately and leaves him to his suicide – a considerable failure of judgement for a psychiatrist. Furthermore, the experience which seems to govern his present life, the encounter with a human 'gorilla', a man whom he regards as having renounced the stereotypes of conventional life – like Musil's 'man without qualities' – and discovered its authentic, primitive basis, can only be seen as a dangerous foundation on which to build any meaningful society in the modern world. In the end it seems appropriate that the voice of Georg Kien should take its place structurally as one of the many perspectives offered. The voice of humanity crying in the wilderness is drowned by the howl of the jackals and their demented victim.

Twentieth-century literature has often been concerned with cultural disintegration, the collapse of traditional values, former certainties, and nowhere more so than in Austria, where the end of a centuries-old dynasty and the fragmentation of a vast, multinational empire provided its most telling visible symbol, so that for a writer like Joseph Roth the nostalgic hankering after universalism and traditional values could take the form of a desire to restore the Hapsburg monarchy. If Canetti had been able to complete his original plan to write a series of eight novels, each having as its central character a man possessed by a different monomania, we might have possessed an extensive documentation of this cultural disintegration, such as we find, for example, in Broch's trilogy *Die Schlaf-wandler* (The Sleep Walkers), most explicitly in the passages interwoven into the third novel which appear under the heading 'Zerfall der Werte' (The Collapse of Values). In spite of its structure and presentation the novel which alone remains of Canetti's original project is unable to achieve this: the scholar Peter Kien is certainly alienated from the rest of the world, but those around him do not embody, even negatively, a wide range of cultural values, but only an all-too similar crude egoism. What has gone is not an ancient culture, but the capacity for human love and understanding.

A similar sense of rampant egoism and a denial of any consoling ideals or compensating values also pervade the three plays which Canetti has written and still acknowledges. They are experimental plays in the sense that they conduct experiments with the human condition, by asking the question: 'What would life be like if . . .?' The characters emerge therefore, even more markedly than those of Horváth, like clearly profiled puppets, lacking development, manipulated by the author and placed in a series of situations that perform the function of laboratory tests. Our interest is directed to their various attitudes and responses and not, for example, to any dramatic clash of personality. They elicit no sympathetic identification; instead, by virtue of their egocentric nature and the author's widespread use of such traditional devices as catch-phrases and 'sprechende Namen', they maintain a distance that encourages detached observation.

Since all three plays are to a large extent demonstration pieces, most of those who appear on the long lists of *dramatis personae* clearly serve an illustrative purpose, representing the widest possible variety of responses to the experimental question posed. And it is here that Canetti displays his greatest skill: in giving linguistic life to such a wide range of figures, especially so in the two earlier plays, where his fine ear for Viennese dialect comes into its own. The theoretical background to this gift, which owes much to the linguistic satire of Karl Kraus, is the concept of what Canetti has called the 'akustische Maske', the distinctive linguistic profile – based on pitch, speed of delivery, and a nuclear vocabulary of some five hundred words – which marks off each person from the rest. And the practical skill, which, as in *Die Blendung*, also establishes the individual's limited vision, his stereotyped responses, often even his *idée fixe*, undoubtedly owes much to the author's own conscious eavesdropping on the conversations of others in public places such as cafés.

Each play is built around a single idea, an idea basically so simple that it might have been expressed in the form of an aphorism.[13] And it is no surprise to find that Canetti's *Aufzeichnungen* (Notes) abound in such aphoristically expressed hypotheses, which question the norms of human life. Any one of them might have been expanded into a play; and some of them even come close to the situations tested in the plays we already have. In *Die Hochzeit* (The Wedding Feast), written between 1931 and 1932 but first performed in 1965, the question posed is essentially that which is central to the tradition of the morality play, including its modern revivals in Hofmannsthal: what would happen if we were suddenly faced with death? Here, however, it is not a solitary individual but a whole society, symbolized by the varied inhabitants of a block of flats, which is put to the test. It is an effete, predatory, sexually lax society, bearing all the marks of a modern *fin de siècle*, enjoying a 'high time' (the original meaning of 'Hochzeit'), looking to its inheritance, the house, to provide solutions without attempting to contribute anything to it; and it is presented by Canetti with such satirical pungency that the scandal caused by its first performance can only be construed as a combination of obtuseness and misplaced moral fervour.[14] Erich Fried relates the play to the nineteen-thirties, under the threat of the Second World War,[15] but it might equally well reflect the doomed world of pre-1914 Vienna. As long as the threat of an earthquake remains theoretical, part of an idle game, the 'immoral', frivolous surface prevails, but as soon as it becomes real – and the heart of the play is reached – the pitiful essence of the characters is laid bare: many return to the security of conventional behaviour; some foolishly refuse to take the catastrophe seriously; while others speculate commercially on the ruin that will follow. It is characteristic of Canetti that in adopting some of the conventions of the morality play he stops short of any firm advocacy of positive, lasting values. When the admonitory figure of the dying Frau Kokosch is finally permitted to speak, having been silenced for so long, she utters no words of wisdom, but only domestic banalities. And the last word is left to a parrot!

In the *Komödie der Eitelkeit* (Comedy of Vanity), written between 1933 and 1934 but not published in book form until 1950, we might suppose the central idea to be man's inability to live without some degree of vanity. For we are transported here to a world where photographs and mirrors, those symbols of human vanity, have been outlawed, but where men find ready substitutes and prohibition follows its customary course, increasing the fascination of what it seeks to destroy and begetting an underworld of black-marketeering and mirror-brothels. We are also shown how philanthropic acts and political involvement in even the worthiest of causes can be, and perhaps always are, an indirect means of self-flattery. But over and above these satirical points, which are scored with relative ease, over and above the incidental comments the play makes on the workings of a totalitarian state, fanaticism, and mass psychology, Canetti reveals a yet more profound insight into human nature: that we cannot live without some form of image of ourselves, whether it be an ideal, a fantasy, the flattery of others, the impression we make on them, or simply the reflection that comes from conversation with them. Without some 'mirror' our sense of identity is lost. At the end of the play therefore the self-hood celebrated by the crowd comes not through the pseudo-Nietzschean self-confidence proclaimed by Heinrich Föhn, but through the re-instatement of the mirror. It is moreover – and this is the gloomy irony of the conclusion – a dangerously egocentric self-hood, easily manipulated by the demagogic Föhn, who is himself seeking only self-glorification. Once again the seemingly positive values of the piece are ultimately called into question and founder on what Canetti seems to regard as the fundamental human weakness: egoism.

In *Die Befristeten*, at which Canetti worked during the early nineteen-fifties, the focus of interest is again death, or – more precisely – our attitude to death. He explores that strange mixture of certainty and uncertainty that follows from the fact that we do not know when our appointed hour will come, but does so negatively, by creating a futuristic world in which this no longer obtains. Here people are known not by name, but by a number which denotes the span supposedly allotted to them. Whether this clinical world of certainties leads to greater happiness is the question posed by the play. Certainly it helps to bestow a mental and social calm and forms an apparently solid basis for planning ahead. But it is unable to banish fear of the moment of death itself; and the very knowledge of the appointed hour can produce an intolerable mental burden. It instils a glowing confidence into many, but in doing so establishes an unfeeling hierarchy in which those who are to live longest enjoy a position of privilege and a sense of superiority in survival, that dangerous attitude which Canetti will later explore, notably in connection with the study of power. The calm surface of life in the play is maintained only because the individual accepts outward conformity, but is otherwise locked in his own egocentric world, shunning all compassion, the very quality which, as Canetti argues elsewhere, makes us human.[16] Compassion, we are led to conclude, depends on the common fears and uncertainties of the 'old' order. Moreover, this very calm presupposes, indeed embodies, to an unusual degree that acceptance of death which the author universally and strenuously resists.

The smooth surface of this world is in fact ruffled in the play itself by the questioning mind of a sceptic and searcher after truth, who, acting to some degree at least as the author's spokesman, unmasks its whole basis as a piece of official deception. And from the moment when tradition has to defend itself the play begins incidentally to shed light on the workings of both an authoritarian state and zealous religious orthodoxy, as well as on mass psychology. Although the doubter seems to gain a victory, the play as a whole follows the pattern of the earlier ones in turning its back on easy, comforting solutions. Instead, just as in Kafka's *Das Schloß* or *In der Strafkolonie* (In the Penal Colony), the questioning of the sceptical outsider is itself questioned. Those whom he has freed from the oppression of superstition submit themselves to a new superstition, a new orthodoxy: that they will not die at all. In enjoying their new freedom they rob others of their freedom. Canetti's avowed intention was to show that truth cannot be divorced from responsibility,[17] but what he has managed to do is to cast doubt on the course of all forms of revolution, however just their original premises.

While the two earlier plays still move largely in the orbit of *Die Blendung*, with its strong Viennese flavour, it is also true that, even from the time of the *Komödie der Eitelkeit*, Canetti was formulating with increasing insistence some of the issues that were to be central to his monumental study *Masse und Macht*. Among the most important of these are: death and man's attitude towards it; the pervasive and potentially dangerous urge to outlive others; the behaviour and psychology of crowds; the effects of authority and, specifically, of commands.

Masse und Macht occupied Canetti's attention for some thirty-five years. It grew out of experiences of crowd behaviour during the years following the first world war: mass protests against inflation, demonstrations after the assassination of Walter Rathenau, the burning of the Palace of Justice mentioned earlier, even the sounds of the crowds at football matches.[18] But it was not until the nineteen-thirties that he came to realize that any account of crowds would be incomplete if it did not also include a study of the complementary phenomenon of power. That the book did not appear until 1960 bears witness to the foresight of Broch, who warned the author as long ago as 1933 that it would be a life's work – but who himself proceeded to work on a study of mass psychology. It is also, like the vast bibliography it includes, a testimony to the high seriousness of Canetti's purpose.

His method is to try and illuminate his twin subjects from various angles: historical, anthropological, and ethnographical; mythological and folkloristic; ethological and psychological, even psychiatric. Transitions from one to the other are often spare or even absent, so that the reader is left to fill out many gaps in the argument, while, as in the plays, ready-made solutions of whatever social, political, psychological, or religious persuasion are avoided. The result is that what may seem to some an integrated approach will appear to others merely eclectic and inconclusive.

Much of the work is taken up with classification and description: with distinctions, for example, between 'open' crowds, which constantly need to grow and fear nothing so much as their own collapse, and 'closed' crowds, which seek permanence in self-limitation; with disinctions according to the speed of formation and dispersal of the crowd; with distinctions according to the motivating force behind the mass (flight, pursuit of a victim or enemy, prohibition experienced in common, the overthrow of an old order, a shared celebration); with discussions of those features of the natural world (fire, sea, river, forest, corn, wind, sand) which, through myth and dream, have come to impress themselves on the human consciousness as symbols of particular facets of the mass; with the isolation of those mass symbols which belong in a special way to individual nations (the sea to England as a symbol of what has to be mastered, a source of change and danger; the army or its natural equivalent, the forest, to Germany as a symbol of that upright, steadfast, well-regulated mass in which the individual may lose himself); or with an examination of the ways in which power relationships are expressed by posture (sitting, standing, kneeling, and so forth).

Interesting as these descriptive sections are, Canetti is at his most fascinating when dealing with those areas which touch, explicitly or implicitly, on the realities of recent history. Here, as he examines

91

crucial aspects of his subject, he has some memorable and stimulating observations on the psychology of both mass experience and dictatorship. Explaining the galvanizing effect of the name 'Versailles' on the German mentality, he argues that the army was the decisive factor in the sense of national unity after the Franco-Prussian war and that, although the army was a closed mass, the First World War provided the opportunity for the whole German people to become an open mass, full of an enthusiasm which embraced even the supposedly international Social Democrats. The outbreak of war in 1914 also begat National Socialism, because it was then that Hitler experienced himself for the only time as a mass. And his subsequent life was an attempt to recreate that experience from outside: Germany was to become again what it was then, to be unified in the consciousness of its military impetus. But Hitler would never have succeeded if the Treaty of Versailles, in robbing Germany of its army, had not thereby robbed it of its 'closed' mass. For it is a law of masses that if a 'closed' mass is thwarted, it forms itself into an 'open' mass, in this case the party, which could embrace all, including women and children.

Studying the characteristics of masses has also led Canetti to trace a development from the inflation of the nineteen-twenties to the later persecution of the Jews. He sees a close relation between man and his money. And what happens in a period of rapid inflation is that, just as the individual character of each unit is lost and the clear hierarchy of the coins collapses as the mass increases, so too individual people lose their identity and self-confidence, while the nation as a whole feels itself devalued. In this situation the natural desire is to discover something that is even more worthless, that can be thrown away like money or stamped on like vermin. The Jews, because of their traditional associations with money, met the requirement ideally.

Equally compelling in their relevance to some of the more gruesome aspects of recent history are those passages where Canetti deals with power as it is exercised in its clearest and most extreme form: by absolute rulers and dictators ('Machthaber'), whose inner mechanism is here laid bare and explained. The importance of knowledge is revealed in the dictator's need to preserve his own secrets but penetrate those of everyone else and in the function of questions and questioning in the practice of power. His desire to inhabit spacious rooms and keep others at a distance is shown to betray a sense of threat which, the more active it becomes, requires more and more executions, since the only safe subjects are dead ones. His subjects indeed, the mass on which his power feeds, are regarded as inferiors, pests which may be exterminated in millions. And if this sounds like paranoia, it is no accident. For Canetti draws close parallels, amounting virtually to identification, between the dictator and the paranoiac and devotes considerable space in this study of crowds and power to the hallucinations of a famous psychiatric patient.

Death, the central issue for Canetti, looms large throughout the work. It forms the background to that pleasurable sense of superiority in survival ('Überleben') which affects us all even as we mourn, but which appears in its starkest form in the behaviour of the ruler, as the ultimate token of power. As commander-in-chief on the field of battle his power lies not only in disposing over the lives of thousands of men, but finally in surviving a great mass of dead, as though he himself were personally responsible for their death. And when at other times he orders the execution of subjects he is not merely eliminating real or imaginary traitors, but enjoying the pernicious power of survival. In this respect too the ruler feeds on the mass, since the larger the number of dead, of those whom he has survived, the greater will be his sense of invulnerability and uniqueness ('Einzigkeit').

Death also plays its part in the crucial question of commands ('Befehle'). For behind every command there stands ultimately the threat of death from a superior power. In the one who receives it, Canetti argues, the command leaves behind a 'sting', which may be stored up for years unless he can rid himself of it by passing it on to an inferior. Only if a command is received collectively, in a mass where it affects all equally, does it not leave behind a sting. Yet no one needs a mass more than the individual who is full of stings, the accumulated burden of the commands received. And revolution is seen therefore as a mass formation created from those who suffer from similar stings, from which they seek to free themselves, directing their action against any who represent the commands they have received. For the ruler who issues a command it is an assertion of power, which gives him a sense of victory; yet even in his success he is left with the threat of recoil, which grows into what Canetti calls 'Befehlsangst', the fear that the inferior will one day take his revenge. And with that we again approach the realm of paranoia.

Considering the time and effort which went into the writing of *Masse und Macht* it is not surprising that many of its central ideas have coloured Canetti's other writing too. We have already noted, for example, the characteristics of the paranoiac ruler in the protagonist of *Die Blendung* and some of the manifestations of the search for power and superiority in the other characters; we have observed the exercise of institutionalized power (especially in prohibitions), various patterns of crowd behaviour, and the centrality of death in the plays, and the role of the 'Überleben' motif in the social hierarchy of *Die Befristeten*. The pervasiveness of these ideas is even more pronounced, however, in a volume entitled *Das Gewissen der Worte* (The Conscience of Words), which gathers together essays and talks from as far apart as 1936 and 1974. One piece, 'Macht und Überleben' (Power and Survival), has direct links with the larger work; another, sparked off by the memoirs of Hitler's architect Albert Speer, is principally concerned with Hitler himself, the largely unseen presence behind the whole of *Masse und Macht*: with his quest for permanence, invulnerability, and survival in the sense of outliving all others or, if he should fail, taking his entire people with him into death; with his grandiose architectural schemes, buildings designed to accommodate his masses or, more properly, allow them to expand, intended to outdo in size all his historical rivals and so assert his superiority and somehow extend his own life. Even where we might not expect it, however, the same basic ideas are an insistent presence. When Canetti records how he first came under the spell of Karl Kraus but later resisted his dominance, he speaks not only in terms of the satirist's ability to incite an intellectual witchhunt, 'eine Hetzmasse aus Intellektuellen', but also of his stifling dictatorship in matters of taste. In Confucius he sees a man who avoided the exercise of power, even feared contamination by it, and whose attitude to death was such that he refused to answer questions about the time after death, seeking thereby to diminish the desire to survive, which Canetti regards as one of the most delicate problems even today. Of his beloved Kafka, whose letters to Felice Bauer provoked Canetti to write his longest and most absorbing essay, he says that, although he was an expert in power, he himself remained powerless, seeking constantly to escape from its domain; his only weapons against it were silence and the attempts to transform himself into something small; the freedom he asserted was that of the weak man who finds salvation in failures rather than victories. And in a shorter piece, 'Dr. Hachiyas Tagebuch aus Hiroschima', in which Canetti praises the honesty of a man whose diary records his first bewildered reactions to the

94

dropping of the atomic bomb, he again brings out the importance of 'Überleben', especially in the writer's sense of having outlived his friends and relatives, which is present even as he mourns their loss.

Psychological illumination is clearly Canetti's great strength – and here the influence of Freud is surely greater than he openly acknowledges. But psychological illumination is also a severely limiting factor. This is barely noticeable in the essays of *Das Gewissen der Worte*, many of which have some biographical starting-point: diaries, memoirs, letters. But in the more ambitious *Masse und Macht* the restriction is painfully obvious. Although he provides valuable new insights into the psychology of the dictator, of crowd behaviour, of power relationships within hierarchical structures, although there is much suggestive force in his juxtapositions of ancient myth and modern psychology or of the customs of primitive peoples and the workings of modern states, his conclusions must remain partial. For he has chosen to treat a subject of considerable social, political, and economic import without any of the methods and arguments of the sociologist, political scientist, or economist. His avowed aim has been to think through everything himself and so overcome the specialisms of others with a universalism or synthesis of his own.[19] But it has proved a problematic undertaking; in deciding what secondary help to use and what to ignore he has acted with an arbitrary selectivity. *Masse und Macht* represents the 'observations of a non-political man', to use a phrase of Thomas Mann. In this Canetti could be said to be conforming to an Austrian pattern, whereby judgement of social and political issues is made according to criteria which could be aesthetic (Musil), metaphysical and cultural (Roth), or psychological (Freud, Stefan Zweig). Another way of putting it would be to say that, notwithstanding Canetti's much broader concerns, there is in the end too much of Peter Kien in his creator, too much of the intellectual's fear of involvement with the sordid facts of life, to permit the confrontation with contemporary political reality which the origins of the work seemed to promise. And the concluding proposal, that the way to attack power, which may manifest itself in contemporary political or industrial structures in both East and West, is to look the command straight in the eye and find some way of robbing it of its sting, is a feeble anti-climax, as impotent a gesture as the chalk line which Grillparzer's poor musician draws across his room to keep an unpleasant reality at bay.

NOTES

1. 'I've had a great deal of bad to say about both individuals and mankind in general; but I'm still sufficiently proud of them to hate one thing only: their enemy, death.' Elias Canetti, *Die gerettete Zunge: Geschichte einer Jugend*, Munich, 1977, p. 14.
2. Dieter Dissinger, *Vereinzelung und Massenwahn: Elias Canettis Roman 'Die Blendung'*, Bonn, 1971. Quoted from a review by Manfred Moser in *Literatur und Kritik*, 65 (1972), 313. See also Dieter Dissinger, 'Der Roman *Die Blendung'*, *Text und Kritik*, 28 (1970), p. 33.
3. Cf. especially 'Hitler nach Speer', in *Das Gewissen der Worte: Essays*, Munich, n.d. (1976?), p. 174. In an earlier chapter of *Die Blendung* entitled 'Mobilmachung' Kien is described haranguing his books as though they were his army.
4. Annemarie Auer, 'Ein Genie und sein Sonderling – Elias Canetti und *Die Blendung'*, *Sinn und Form*, 21 (1969), pp. 967 and 979. Cf. also Claudio Magris, 'Die rasenden Elektronen', in *Canetti lesen: Erfahrungen mit seinen Büchern*, ed. Herbert G. Göpfert, Munich, 1975 (= Reihe Hanser 188), p. 45.
5. An earlier title was *Kant fängt Feuer*. See Canetti, 'Das erste Buch: *Die Blendung'*, in *Das Gewissen der Worte*, p. 222.
6. In an essay on Karl Kraus dating from 1965 Canetti writes: 'Ich begriff, daß Menschen zwar zueinander sprechen, aber sich nicht verstehen; daß ihre Worte Stöße sind, die an den Worten der anderen abprallen; daß es keine größere Illusion gibt als die Meinung, Sprache sei ein Mittel der Kommunikation zwischen Menschen.' 'Karl Kraus, Schule des Widerstands', *Das Gewissen der Worte*, p. 45.
7. Cf. 'Das erste Buch', *Das Gewissen der Worte*, pp. 227–229.
8. ibid., p. 229.
9. ibid., pp. 224–225.
10. Cf. Manfred Durzak, *Gespräche über den Roman: Formbestimmungen und Analysen*, Frankfurt/Main, 1976, pp. 92–93.
11. ibid., pp. 88–89.
12. ibid., p. 99.
13. Günter Rühle, quoted by Peter Laemmle, 'Macht und Ohnmacht des Ohrenzeugen', in *Canetti lesen*, p. 48.
14. Cf. Peter Laemmle, loc. cit., pp. 60–61.
15. Erich Fried, in the introduction to his selection of Canetti's writings, *Welt im Kopf*, Graz and Vienna, 1962 (= Stiasny Bücherei 102), p. 12.
16. 'Hitler nach Speer', *Das Gewissen der Worte*, p. 179.
17. *Die Provinz des Menschen: Aufzeichnungen 1942–1972*, Munich, 1973, pp. 242–243.
18. Cf. Peter Laemmle, 'Macht und Ohnmacht des Ohrenzeugen', in *Canetti lesen*, pp. 51–52.
19. Cf. *Die Provinz des Menschen*, p. 49.

George Saiko: Worlds Within World

C. E. Williams

In a passage characterizing modernist fiction, David Lodge notes that its emphasis on introspection, analysis or reverie inevitably reduces the scope and significance of external events which are central to the traditional realist novel; that a modernist novel often lacks exposition or internal logical connections, instead casting the reader into situations which he gradually comes to understand by inference and association; that it abandons the device of an omniscient and intrusive narrator, handles the sequence of time with notable freedom and inventiveness, and adopts the repetition, variation or contrast of images, motifs or typological allusions as a structural principle in place of an architectonic ordering by plot and action, causality and chronology.

In George Saiko's first novel *Auf dem Floß* (On the Raft), which was completed in 1938 but not published for another decade, these formal features are fully exemplified. In his second major novel *Der Mann im Schilf* (The Man in the Reeds) (1955) many of them are still present, though in a significantly modified manner. Yet the underlying themes of these works, and in the earlier novel even the choice of characters and milieu, are an extension of older preoccupations in Austrian literature. Saiko stands at a point of transition where a traditional *Weltbild* is challenged and discredited, but where certain ethical values connected with it are finally reaffirmed. The revolutionary modernism of his fictional techniques is not harnessed to a revolutionary or anarchistic ideology, to absurdist despair or existentialist self assertion, but to an undramatic pragmatic humanism whose roots lie in the Austrian Enlightenment.

The contrast between modernism and traditionalism is most marked in his first novel. It is informed by an explicit distrust of commonplace surface reality and the language of conventional discourse. The linear progression of events is disrupted and even transcended – as Thomas Mann had envisaged – by a highly orga-

97

nized system of leitmotifs and internal echoes which establish analogies between nominally discrete experiences or situations, now linked by associations of which at times only the reader can be aware. The narrative point of view shifts back and forth between the characters in the *style indirecte libre*, the sparing interventions of the third person narrator outweighed by the account of unspoken thoughts and feelings. The technique not only focusses our attention on the workings of consciousness but also emphasises the dissociation between the inner and the outer life. Desire silently anticipates reality or writes an alternative scenario, the imagination remedies past mistakes and recovers – for a while – what has been lost. Intuitive insights, unformulated apprehensions strive for expression against the inadequacy and lack of differentiation of discursive language: though instead of resorting to allusive, multi-layered imagery in the symbolist manner, Saiko prefers a dauntingly abstract idiom.

Similarly characters scrutinise one another for a glimpse of something which mere speech does not reveal; or they ponder words which say more or less than intended. The combined effect of these techniques is a 'desubstantiation' of reality, a process fed by two not entirely unconnected sources, traditional Austrian inwardness and depth psychology. Saiko explodes the conventions of the closed form, thereby challenging our very perception of the empirical world and its illusion of factuality. Nevertheless his narrative is still structured by meaningful patterns of experience.

One such pattern is that of contrast and parallelism, most noticeable in the configuration of the women characters. Alexander, the Prince on whose estate the novel is set, is confronted by two opposing figures. On the one hand there is Marischka, an exotic gipsy girl, the embodiment of dark sensuality and primitive drives. Her demonic sexuality is reminiscent not only of a cultural archetype but more specifically of such Austrian variants on the theme as Hofmannsthal's gipsy girl in *Der Turm* (The Tower) or the alluvial Frieda in Kafka's *Das Schloß* or Musil's Grigia. On the other hand there is Mary Countess Tremblaye who offers the promise of erotic fulfilment without the associations of illicit, humiliating animality. Marischka plunges her aristocratic lover into a frenzied ambivalence of repulsion and fascination, estranging him from the daylight world and the rational self. She represents an unredeemed impersonal sexuality which puts his maleness on trial and devours it. The roots of Alexander's conflict lie in childhood experience: Mary is a substitute for the mother from whose warmth and intimacy he felt excluded as a boy. He fears that in losing Mary he is being condemned to repeat the pattern of deprivation. For his friend and rival Eugen, Mary represents a similar synthesis; he too oscillates between the attractions of a wittily intellectual spirit (Nietzsche's 'Socratic' principle, perhaps) and an overwhelming sensuality, realizing that in the perfect partner they must complement one another. In the end Alexander looks to Mary's daughter Gise as the agent of his fulfilment, after we have been treated to a somewhat tedious exploration of child psychology and sibling rivalry in the relationship between Mary's adolescent children. In all this, Freudian insights are invoked in an attempt to give fresh life to what is in effect a tired dualism.

The triangular relationships belong to a fictional stock-cupboard which the nineteenth century had already ransacked – especially if we remember that the polarity of the two women corresponds to differences of social class. The triteness of the sexual plot is off-set, however, by the memorable characterisation of Marischka, who takes on almost mythic proportions as an alien, destructive force, avenging herself on a culture which seeks to exploit and domesticate her. Her pagan gods, her black magic, her animistic communion with natural objects, her hetaerism and her indestructibility point to a survival of that ancient matriarchy which Bachofen deemed to have preceded the ascendancy of the male. She seems bent on subverting and counteracting the patriarchal domination, a motif to be found also in Broch's *Bergroman* (Mountain Novel) and – in satirical vein – in Gerhart Fritsch's *Fasching*. The propriety of demonizing this gipsy girl in the years of Hitler's racial hygiene is open to question; but to raise the problem is merely to emphasise the archaic unreality of the novel's social ambience.

Alexander faces another pattern of contrast or parallelism in his relationship with his brother, a Catholic bishop, and Eugen, a Russian emigré. Fraternal conflict is common to both of Saiko's novels, particularly the notion of the younger brother (in this case Alexander) attempting to assert or prove himself in defiance of an elder brother's condescending superiority and scorn. The Prince is haunted by a sense of insecurity which is partly social – having inherited the estate by default, thanks to his brother's voluntary renunciation, he secretly fears an equally fortuitous disinheritance and *déclassement* – and partly psychological – when they were boys, his brother was assimilated to the father's world of which

99

Alexander could never feel an entirely integral part. Alexander's failure to attain emotional satisfaction in adulthood derives from such unresolved childhood tensions. Again, however, the Freudianism sustains a familiar dialectic – this time, one which goes back to eighteenth century literature.

The Bishop combines asceticism and moral absolutism with a keen sense of social decorum, while Alexander cultivates philosophical relativism and a measure of social eccentricity. Both positions are subjected to critical scrutiny: true freedom, what Saiko's contemporary and friend Doderer called 'Menschwerdung', is shown to be indeed dependent upon fulfilling moral and social responsibilities, but equally upon learning to live with the predicaments and paradoxes inherent in the modern world, instead of escaping into the ontological security of traditional orthodoxy. Yet the fact that Alexander's particular duty should take the form of assuring the continuation of the family line through a socially desirable marriage demonstrates the paradoxical survival of a conservative social ethos that belies the ostensible radicalism of Saiko's novel.

On the other hand the feudal world of the novel is not presented uncritically. Alexander is an aristocrat who has weathered the collapse of the Hapsburg Empire with his power and influence undiminished, but his social redundancy is manifest. On his estate he is a mere figure-head, humoured by long-suffering servants who still feel some respect for what he represents. The estate itself runs at a deficit and is shored up only by income from tenants who are more efficient than he, and from industrial investments. The feudal way of life, as he is only too aware, is living on borrowed time. We are repeatedly reminded of the disparity between the Prince's elevated status and his human shortcomings. For all his worldly airs and liberated attitudes, he is a dependent, insecure and immature figure. He has surrounded himself with inanimate relics designed to glorify their owner and to reflect his originality, intrepidity and masculinity, much as Imre von Gyurkicz surrounds himself with military 'emblems' in Doderer's *Dämonen*. The reification of reality, conveyed by the leitmotif of the glass showcase, is a ploy to render it frozen and harmless, capable of being manipulated at Alexander's will. (Yet insofar as the suspended existence retains its potential power or provides a crystallisation of wish-fulfilment or private fears, it can continue to exert an animistic influence and perpetuate the dependence of the beholder: both the Prince and

Joschko experience this while Marischka and the maliciously destructive Imre fear it.)

The Prince's prize specimen is his Slovak coachman Joschko, whose legendary strength is matched only by his loyalty and respect towards his master. This profoundly unrebellious, forbearing, naive soul is a noteworthy addition to the line of 'treue Diener' who have their special place in the 'Hapsburg myth'. Here, however, his faithfulness merely throws into relief the callous egotism of his master. For reasons of his own, Alexander constantly forces Joschko into a mould that is at odds with his true self. Joschko's suffering at the hands of Marischka results from the Prince's attempt to dispose of her by marrying her off to his domestic Hercules. Slowly poisoned by the gipsy, Joschko undergoes a martyrdom that culminates in Alexander's bizarre plan to have his body stuffed and mounted, so that he may serve the Prince's purpose more reliably than he seemed able to do in life. Though Joschko is spared this ultimate indignity, the paternalism vaunted by the Hapsburg myth makers stands utterly dishonoured and discredited.

Indeed the criticism of the social order which the Prince represents is unsparing. The local nobility fritters away its debt-ridden existence in embittered squabbling, dubious marriages and scandalous financial enterprises. The flotsam of the Empire have suddenly discovered the 'Idea' which ostensibly justified Hapsburg rule and proclaim the need to hearken to the 'voice of the people' where once they were sufficiently self-confident to dispense with any ideological superstructure. The Prince reflects with ironic envy upon the certitudes of an earlier generation in contrast to the doubts and upheavals of his own age – yet those same men are seen to have ruined Mary's family by their profligacy.

In the course of the novel we follow Alexander's gradual maturation, a process of self-discovery which completes his estrangement from the decaying aristocratic world in which he lives. Evasion and dependence make way for commitment, a painfully acquired self-reliance, and an acknowledgement of guilt. The inconsequentiality of the outcome, which amounts to a reinforcement of the status quo, is thus all the more striking. Alexander's *Menschwerdung* does not lift entirely the veil of 'false consciousness'. A disturbing degree of moral confusion attends this conclusion, in that the martyrdom of Joschko and the emotional self-laceration of the young girl Gise are nonchalantly accepted as the price of Alexander's emancipation. The past, with all its suffering, errors and defeats, is made good again, the moral account balanced. Such sublime egotism is mercifully absent from the denouement of *Der Mann im Schilf* which likewise ends at the moment of moral decision: there the pain that redeems the protagonist is not so easily transcended nor the sting of finality so readily removed.

In the contrasting figure of the Prince's Russian friend we see an aristocrat who has been socially and ideologically dispossessed by the Revolution and thrown back on his own human resources. True, he too has a history of weakness and cowardice, evasion and dependence, but these have been purged by suffering and moral commitment. The graphic account of his near-execution in a freezing Russian prison yard anticipates the resurrection motif in *Der Mann im Schilf* and conveys the traumatic sense of stark mortality and miraculous rebirth with which Dostoevsky invested a similar incident. It is here that the image of the raft conjured up in the novel's title is first mentioned in the text; it recurs in a key exchange between Eugen and Alexander about the religious meaning of existence.

Alexander realises that without a point of metaphysical reference man becomes a prey to *Angst*, passenger on a raft drifting helplessly into the unknown. He offers a familiar outline of progressive cultural decline from a universal Christian cosmogony via liberalism and rationalism to the modern cult of collectivism, power politics and nationalism which spells the ruin of Europe. (A similar diagnosis can be found in the writing of Werfel, Roth and Broch in the thirties.) While Eugen agrees about the evils of nationalism – a warning repeated by a character in *Der Mann im Schilf* and rooted in Saiko's strongly Austrian sense of the destructiveness of the militant nation state – he leaps to the defence of reason, fragile and defective though it may be. If he too is a partner on the raft, he is determined to influence its course through the application of active reason. The question of whether life is contingent or providentially determined – it is intimated – is fallacious: where God reveals himself in absence and silence, metaphysical protest and submission alike are the echo of his voice. The problem with this paradoxical religiosity is that it seems superfluous to what is in effect a wholly immanent view of life. But it provides an answer of sorts to the questionings of Gise, as she tries to reconcile a conventional faith with her growing awareness of evil, pain, ugliness and the realm of the 'dark god'.

Saiko's second novel *Der Mann im Schilf* recognizably extends the theme and technique of his first book, yet achieves a closer integration of the two. In one respect the result is a greater degree of social and moral realism. In July 1934 an Austrian intellectual returns to a rain-soaked Salzburg landscape in the company of an English archaeologist and his wife after an unsuccessful expedition to Crete. They are caught up in the abortive Nazi putsch, as a consequence of which the protagonist's brother and fiancée die. The novel ends with the preparations of the original party to leave Austria again. In a work where the emphasis lies firmly on analysis and interpretation rather than incident, the image of the exile or outsider is one of the structuring motifs that coordinate our response to the narrative. It is not merely that Robert on returning to his homeland is bemusedly confronted with a new reality: he remains thereafter a spiritual exile, estranged and isolated. In contrast with traditional associations, however, his exile was not a search for penance and purification but a self-imposed flight from decision, responsibility and commitment. Passion and compromise turned his exotic asylum into a dystopia and the Robert who returns is an embittered figure who has squandered his energies, achieved little, and lived an arid, narrow existence. The novel is among other things a study of his alienated consciousness.

If the other major theme of the book is to illuminate the socio-political crisis that grips Austria, this is not because Saiko is now preoccupied with the historicity of events. His dominant interest continues to lie in the motivation and reactions of his characters. In a sense the particular political context is unimportant, for Saiko desires to explore the representative nature of what we are witnessing, the self-destruction of the *zoon politikon*. However, the choice of Austrian politics at this juncture is scarcely fortuitous. What Saiko exposes are the noisome duplicities, the tangled ramifications, the viciousness and futile waste, the confused loyalties and conflicting aspirations which were endemic in the Austrian dilemma after 1918. And although the ending of the novel may be politically inconclusive, it contains the seeds of events to come, revealed at a point where our powers of discernment are not yet threatened by direct emotional involvement, where in Doderer's words our eyes are not yet stupefied by horror. (It must be added that Saiko's analysis of the Austrian catastrophe is far more ruthless and abrasive than Doderer's.)

Thus Saiko forcibly reminds us of the inability of the citizens to identify with the Austrian Republic, a state which to them lacks political credibility – particularly when the conflict with Nazi Germany cuts across their instinctive tribal loyalties. Their anomie is intensified by a legacy of the Imperial past. Among the peasants of the Salzburg mountains there prevails a centuries-old distrust of central government in Vienna and its various exploitative devices. By savagely crushing any open insurrection in the past, the authorities have encouraged the growth of a devious, sullen or servile acquiescence married to a surreptitious self-defence against the predacity of the State.

The debunking of yet another facet of the 'Hapsburg myth' is a by-product of Saiko's disillusioning exposure of the cynicism of this peasant world with its outbursts of brutality and frustration, its violent hatred of authority and outsiders, its animal lusts and pagan superstitions. His realism corrects the affirmative tendency of *Auf dem Floß* and anticipates the critical *Heimatliteratur* of Hans Lebert and Thomas Bernhard. The image of the faithful, upright and conscientious Austrian public servant is implicitly belied by a gallery of politicians and bureaucrats who are thoroughly venal and corrupt, who trim their sails to the political wind most likely to prevail, and withal obey the two commandments of civil service success: never commit yourself, and never offend your superior. Political action is invariably shown to be a displacement activity, political ideas to be a rationalisation of psychological need. In this inability to contemplate the objective force of political ideas or to allow the possibility of disinterested commitment, Saiko succumbs to a feature of the very tradition of which elsewhere he is so sceptical – the psychological reductionism which characterizes much Austrian thinking about politics. Yet even if his analysis cannot be accepted as a total explanation, it is peculiarly appropriate to a situation as bereft of ideological conviction as that of Austria between Hitler and Mussolini, where as we see even the peasants who support the Nazis are driven by a fickle opportunism that owns no loyalty except self-interest.

The unmasking of political motives culminates in the confrontation between Robert's brother, a former Rittmeister and now a disenchanted Party member, and the conspiratorial Ministerialrat Mostbaumer who eventually liquidates him. The former, though not squeamish, desperately needs to fill the emptiness of his existence with a sense of communality and to find a moral justification for his actions. With their reprehensible self-seeking and misguided terrorism, his fellow *Illegalen* are, he feels, prejudicing the future of the cause. Mostbaumer, who personifies the amoral cult of action and political egotism, retaliates by killing the Rittmeister in a deliberate test of nerve, a deed which ultimately springs from suppurating memories of personal humiliation quite unconnected with his victim. (The murder seems to echo the fatal opposition of Esch and Huguenau in Broch's *Schlafwandler* trilogy.) Yet, like other political agents in the novel, he shows himself reluctant to shoulder responsibility for his actions. The clandestine Nazis prefer to regard themselves as executors of a higher authority which justifies their criminality by invoking the demands of 'necessity' or 'history'. The Führer cult, of which in fact we see little enough in the novel, is explained in just these terms, as a religious surrogate; the Führer is the final arbiter of what is right, the repository of the law, the justification of sacrifice and heroism – within modest and well-rewarded limits. This dimension is cogently explored in J.P. Stern's study of Hitler's leadership.

Those who are unwilling to accept responsibility for their actions cast around for a scape-goat: the eponymous man in the reeds, a wounded fugitive who is being hunted by the government forces. The scapegoat motif, prefigured in the role of Joschko, is another of the structuring images of the narrative. There are intriguing parallels between the man in the reeds and the 'wild man' of Central European folk-lore, a young man who impersonated the tree spirit by covering himself with leaves and moss, and was hunted through the woods and streets of his village before being figuratively assassinated. In a nineteenth-century Bohemian version attributed by Frazer to a town some fifty miles from Saiko's birthplace, a straw effigy was then carried on a stretcher and cast into water by the local executioner. If we discount the pantheism, what is significant about the 'wild man' is that he shares with the exile or stranger the experience of social estrangement and ostracization, an analogy which underlines the importance of the fugitive for Robert.

In goading him to help the fugitive escape, Hanna, his fiancée, forces Robert to override his natural distrust of demonstrative, binding actions. It is for her a means of breaking out of a circle of futility and helplessness rather than an explicitly political gesture. In fact, her motives are anti-political, since the man in the reeds represents for her all those who are abused, exploited and sacrificed by unscrupulous politicians. The alarums and excursions ensuing from the various efforts to rescue or capture the lone fugitive do not entirely dispel a suspicion that he may not, or may no longer exist. His symbolic role is thereby merely heightened. To the ritualistic search for a scapegoat on the socio-political level is added his peculiar significance for the two estranged lovers, Hanna and Robert, who sense in him a kindred soul adrift in a hostile element. The reedbeds convey that sense of disorientation, impenetrability and treacherously shifting ground that haunts Robert, the returning exile, and indeed epitomise the bleak existential view of the novel as a whole. The lovers' rescue attempt is synonymous with an endeavour to find and liberate their own selves and to reconstitute their relationship. The 'man in the reeds' marks the point at which the private and political arcs of the novel intersect.

The notion of self-discovery, however, proves to be inseparable from association with death. Robert remembers an incident when he narrowly escaped drowning and experienced a feeling of extinction and rebirth (like Eugen in *Auf dem Floß*). In his relationship with Hanna he has an opportunity to slough off his old self and make a new beginning.

The ending of the novel points up the poignant ambiguity surrounding the image of regeneration. Hanna is shot while driving the 'man in the reeds' to safety; all that is found in the van is an empty roll of sailcloth, a symbolic shroud from which the fugitive seems to have escaped. This ambiguity is consistent with the ritualistic drama of the scapegoat figure. The 'wild man' of folk-lore was resurrected in a more youthful, vigorous form after his blood had been shed on the ground or over the onlookers: here in the novel it is in fact Hanna who is said to look as if someone had poured blood over her, while the fugitive and, by extension, Robert undergo a rebirth. In committing himself to the rescue attempt, Robert attains to a sense of religious awe. They are all subsumed in God, he reflects, their deaths but a minor adjustment to a cosmos which is ever-changing, yet ever the same – a transition barely noticeable to that unthinkable idea which men call God. Yet Robert's resignation is tempered by a bitter awareness of the finality of death.

On the one hand we have Hanna's sacrifice and Robert's numb grief; on the other, there is the discarded shroud, the vanished fugitive. Robert is left with a barely articulated glimpse of understanding, a token of rebirth, and a challenge to justify his humanly redeemed existence – which may in the very process of redemption have lost its sole possibility of richness and fulfilment, just as the 'man in the reeds' may have been rescued only to perish in the holocaust to come. The exile or stranger, the fugitive and scapegoat are images of exposure, isolation, deprivation and danger. The ominous, enervating sound of the reeds is all-pervading. To be born anew is to be restored to the world in all its complexity and pain, not to experience some glorious transfiguration. In its openness and ambivalence, the conclusion of *Der Mann im Schilf* remains true to a tragic vision of life which Saiko's earlier novel had tried to transcend through obsolete notions of *Bildung* and social obligation.

The modernist techniques that were such a prominent feature of *Auf dem Floß* are here employed with restraint. They do not dissolve the empirical world but underpin it. Much of the narrative is devoted to a quest for the well-springs of motivation or to attempts to capture the inchoate, volatile substance of emotional response. The compulsive power of the inner life is again attested by the peremptory invasion of the conscious mind by traumatic images from the past, triggered off by an association of ideas or personal symbols. Saiko knew his Joyce and Faulkner, to say nothing of Freud. But he felt that the novel, in addition to illumining the recesses of the psyche, should prevent us from succumbing to solipsistic irrationalism by offering us a meaningful, coherent interpretation of the world. Like Freud he exposed the unconscious in order to try and diminish the threat it posed. It is this moral purpose that links Saiko to a nineteenth century tradition, despite his aesthetic modernism. Among modern Austrian prose writers, it is Hermann Broch with whom he has the greatest affinity.

Saiko's literary achievement is considerable, but not without flaws. His imagination and intelligence are fettered by hackneyed relationships to which no amount of subtle psychologising can lend vitality or human significance. A fatal banality lurks in the background of *Der Mann im Schilf*, in the clichéd pattern of the forsaken fiancée, Robert's affair with his employer's wife, the complaisant but unpredictable husband, the exotic mediterranean lover and a triple variation on the theme of the eternal triangle. Novelettish features are also discernible in *Auf dem Floß*. Saiko's creative range is limited, while his psychologism tends to reduce character to case history. His moral seriousness demands respect, as does his determined demythologizing of Austria's image of herself, long before this became part of the radical chic of the sixties. At the last, however, his art fails to enrich or deepen our perception of the world. If it appeals to our intelligence, it lacks creative excitement.

Ödön Von Horváth:
The *Volksstück* Revived

Alan Best

The Austrian première of Ödön von Horváth's *Volksstück, Geschichten aus dem Wiener Wald* (Tales from the Vienna Woods, 1931) took place in Vienna in December 1948, some ten years after the author's death. The play was not well received:

> Das Volkstheater spielt (weiß der Teufel weshalb) die zwölf Bilder von Ödön von Horváth 'Geschichten aus dem Wiener Wald'. Erste Unverfrorenheit: diese peinliche Panoptikum ein 'Volksstück' zu nennen. Zweite: diese Verunglimpfung Wiens grad den Wienern vorzusetzen. Dritte: ein ausgesucht hochqualifiziertes Darsteller-Team auf solch disqualifizierten Spielplatz zu treiben, der ein ausgemacht antihumanitärer Sumpf ist.[1]

Hans Jungbauer's production had clearly been everything Horváth could have wished; he himself had anticipated such objections to his work in a radio discussion with Willi Cronauer in 1932:

> Man wirft mir vor, ich sei zu derb, zu ekelhaft, zu unheimlich, zu zynisch . . . und man übersieht dabei, daß ich doch kein anderes Bestreben habe, als die Welt so zu schildern, wie sie halt leider ist. . . . Der Widerwille eines Teiles des Publikums beruht wohl darauf, daß dieser Teil sich in den Personen auf der Bühne selbst erkennt – und es gibt natürlich Menschen, die über sich selbst nicht lachen können – und besonders nicht über mehr oder minder bewußtes, höchst privates Triebleben.[2]

'Know thyself' ('Erkenne dich selbst'), a watchword of Horváth's drama, is the key to the provocation he caused. The audience his work so successfully outraged in 1948 could forgive Horváth many things, but being right was not one of them. Vienna wished to wipe the slate clean and make a fresh start; the Viennese felt they had

suffered and in suffering had emerged reborn. Their nostalgic longing for the 'good old days' before the nightmare of the war was now
being ruthlessly undermined by a pertinent reminder that those
times were themselves an illusion. Johann Strauss, the Wiener
Wald, the Heurige, even the hallowed tradition of the *Volksstück*
and 'their' Nestroy were being taken in vain. A whole society and its
way of life was being pilloried and having survived assault from outside, Vienna in 1948 was particularly resentful of such an attack
from within.

The readiness of the *Bürger* to create and then inhabit a world of
illusion and half-truth, to discover a protective 'Ordnung' and ordinance which served to justify an essentially exploitative way of
life was anathema to Horváth and he sought to expose it at every
turn.

Twenty years later, when the Volkstheater revived *Geschichten
aus dem Wiener Wald*, audiences responded more positively.
Twenty years of consolidation enabled the bourgeoisie to feel more
secure and self-assured, it came to terms with the play as 'social
history' in the confidence that times had changed and that yesterday's problems had little contemporary relevance. Despite the
powerful example of Qualtinger's *Herr Karl*[3], or perhaps because
of it, Horváth's play barely ruffled a few feathers, only a nagging
doubt remained that things might not have changed for the better,
and that was only half-expressed:

Ein großer Abend, auf Horváths Weise eine Dokumentation.
Um eine Dichtung zu sein, müßte dieses Stück etwas vom
anderen Österreich, vom Österreich der Nichtspießer, zeigen
oder wenigstens spüren lassen. Es müßte uns rückahnen
lassen, daß damals der Ausweg aus dem Labyrinth solcher
Österreicherei schon offenstand.[4]

For Horváth, however, there *was* no escape from the labyrinth. He
saw life as an unending conflict between the individual and his environment, a conflict that was generic in any capitalist society:

Dieses ewige Schlachten, bei dem es zu keinem Frieden kommen
soll – höchstens, daß mal ein Individuum für einige Momente
die Illusion des Waffenstillstandes genießt. . . . Dieser aussichts-
lose Kampf des Individuums (basiert) auf bestialischen Trieben,
also (darf) die heroische und feige Art des Kampfes nur als ein

109

Formproblem der Bestialität, die bekanntlich weder gut ist noch böse, betrachtet werden.[5]

Antagonism, exploitation and an almost feudal disregard for human decency are the characteristics of the society Horváth depicts and exposes. Fear and insecurity are endemic to this world, fear heightened by the uncertain economic situation of the 1920s and 1930s with its prospects of massive unemployment, its political unrest and a virtually unrelieved struggle for personal survival. In such a climate those who had anything to lose held desperately to it, and their materialistic outlook extended over their whole way of life. The archetype of such an attitude, for Horváth at least, was the *Kleinbürger*, the petty bourgeois. Restricted in his intellectual horizon, but with some cultural pretensions, fearful for his pension or his nest-egg and jealous of the encroaching proletariat mass beneath him, the *Kleinbürger* nonetheless epitomized society most clearly and it is the *Kleinbürger* whom Horváth selects as 'Volk':

Nun besteht aber Deutschland, wie alle übrigen europäischen Staaten zu neunzig Prozent aus vollendeten oder verhinderten Kleinbürgern, auf alle Fälle aus Kleinbürgern. Will ich also das Volk schildern, darf ich natürlich nicht nur die zehn Prozent schildern, sondern als treuer Chronist meiner Zeit, die große Masse! Das ganze Deutschland muß es sein.[6]

Following in the footsteps of Nestroy and the *Lokalstück*, that more or less realistic comedy of Austrian life, Horváth, an acute observer, chronicles the significant characteristics of the *Kleinbürger* and assembles these features in a *montage* of contrast, contradiction and interrelated comment. He presents this species through the medium of a modernized and suitably adapted *Volksstück* because his concern is to strip away all pretension and reveal the true nature of existence in this social sphere. The down-to-earth, rude vigour of the 'Volk' allows him to create in a twentieth-century idiom 'ein wahrhaftiges Volkstheater . . . das an die Instinkte und nicht an den Intellekt des Volkes appelliert.'[7]

The apparent simplicity and objectivity of the 'Volksstück' – the telling of a simple tale – throws the full weight of impact on to the dialogue. Horváth's itinerant upbringing meant that he approached the German language as an outsider and listened to it with an outsider's ear. As a consequence his characters speak a

110

language that is immediately recognisable and yet geographically elusive; it is the language of a social class whose pretensions are about to be exploded. Apart from the essential South German/ Austrian colour to Horváth's plays, a feature basic both to the saccharine emotionalism and the speed at which his characters think and speak, he was at pains to deny that dialect had any part in his works and insisted that his characters should avail themselves of a *Hochdeutsch* which the audience would recognize as affected and contrived. Horváth's characters shelter behind the protective camouflage of what he terms a *Bildungsjargon* (educated clap-trap), which is sufficiently at odds with their natural and instinctive manner of speaking to reveal the conventional pleasantry, the pretty compliment or the correct turn of phrase as indicators of an artificial way of life. The language of Horváth's plays is, as a consequence, clichéd, banal, hackneyed and over-ripe. His characters have grown up in a cultural and moral ghetto and have been conditioned to follow norms laid down by an impersonal and shadowy authority, namely tradition. They are on the one hand too weak or too narrow-minded to challenge such authority and yet on the other frequently shrewd enough to invoke the weight of this 'authority' where they see it is to their own advantage. Horváth's characters, then, live at secondhand and this alienation finds direct expression in their attempts at communication, for while they are anything other than inarticulate they display a remarkable talent for engaging in divergent monologues:

Es hat sich nun durch das Kleinbürgertum eine Zersetzung der eigentlichen Dialekte gebildet, nämlich durch den Bildungsjargon. Um einen heutigen Menschen realistisch schildern zu können, muß ich also den Bildungsjargon sprechen lassen. Der Bildungsjargon (und seine Ursachen) fordern aber natürlich zur Kritik heraus – und so entsteht der Dialog des neuen Volksstückes, und damit der Mensch, und damit erst die dramatische Handlung – eine Synthese aus Ernst und Ironie.[8]

The closed order of the *Kleinbürger*, with its moral hypocrisy and disingenuous espousal of tradition represents a labyrinth in which genuine human emotion cannot hope to prosper. As in the world of business, survival means concealing one's weak points and exploiting those one has discovered in others, and the products of this order are caught in a vicious circle for every chance exposure to and stimulation of such essentially individual feelings as love or affection sets them against the social norm as embodied by those who can conceal their own aggressive egotism behind the *mores* and practices which are generally accepted. In presenting characters who converse in inverted commas and think in terms of financial accounts Horváth directly challenges the greater part of his society and the principles on which it is based.

In Horváth's hands the *Volksstück* becomes a deliberately aggressive idiom. He does not believe in man's innate goodness and concentrates on his sexuality as evidence of the essential conflict for social survival. Consequently, Horváth's deployment of the traditional features of the *Volksstück*: comedy, verbal juggling and legerdemain, stock figures, dual situations, folk-songs and musical accompaniment are used against rather than with the grain. They serve not to reflect the vitality of the instincts, as in the traditional *Volksstück*, but to provide an insistent refrain lamenting the lost innocence of twentieth-century man. Indeed one of the most significant aspects of Horváth's presentation is its recurrent emphasis on the conflict *within* the individual, the conflict between instinct and intellect. In the defensively derivative habitat of the *Kleinbürger* listening to the promptings of one's instincts is tantamount to revolution and a challenge to society; the irony is that in such a situation the intellect is unable to cope with such a response and leaves the individual vulnerable to the first recognizable stimulus to appear.

Elisabeth, the central figure in Horváth's 'dance of death', the ironically named *Glaube Liebe Hoffnung* (Faith, Hope, Charity, 1932), falls foul of society's code, but compounds that felony by allowing her heart to rule her head. Her desperate need to be loved encourages her to conceal her 'criminal' past from her new lover who is a policeman. In all her actions she lives for the day, hoping that tomorrow will bring a turn for the better. Elisabeth faces prison if she does not pay off a fine for working as a traveller in ladies underpinnings without a licence, and she is constantly obliged to beg or misappropriate money from various sources to keep away from the attentions of the police. Her inevitable failure and suicide leaves scarcely a ripple; society ignores her passing as it ignored her dilemma.

In a draft to the play, which he later discarded as superfluous, Horváth showed Elisabeth accepting a lift from a young student so as to save herself the train fare to her next destination. The car breaks down and the young man announces that they will have to

112

shelter from the impending storm. Elisabeth tries to talk herself out of giving in to what she knows will follow: 'Bitte nicht, Elisabeth – hernach bist du immer zwei Tage lang erledigt'[9] but the combination of the setting, the dialogue and the context prove too much for her. After they have finished the young man confesses that the car didn't break down at all: 'Alles Berechnung. Ich habe es berechnet und du hast es erwartet.'[10] He is correct: the right words in the right context are irresistible. Elisabeth, like so many products of the petty bourgeoisie cannot but be a creature of habit with Pavlovian responses to stimuli, her social situation is built on reactions to suggestions and requirements which come from outside sources; Horváth's commentary on this social malaise is to provide the seduction with an appropriately clichéd musical background, beginning with the 'March of the Siamese Guard,' modulating to a pianissimo rendition of 'The Rustle of Spring' while the couple make love. This ironic combination of martial and romantic music, a device frequently repeated in Horváth's plays catches the duality of the Austrian dream. Elisabeth's discomfiture is completed when the student's car refuses to start; the sheer pettiness which is sufficient to destroy her is a measure of her inner weakness and vulnerability.

Horváth's antipathy towards National Socialism and indeed all manifestations of Fascism is scarcely surprising; the National Socialists were perhaps *the* political party to which the *Kleinbürger* felt drawn. Horváth's most overt reckoning came in the 'Schauspiel' *Sladek der schwarze Reichswehrmann* (Sladek of the Black 'Reichswehr', 1929), a study in gullibility and double-dealing for which the Nazis never forgave him, but Horváth returned to the threat posed by National Socialism to a free society in the 'Volksstück' *Italienische Nacht* (An Italian Evening, 1930). The Italian evening, a regular social event in the small south German town where the play is set, represents a declaration of faith in the spirit of the republic by 'enlightened' local society, in this case the Liberals and Communists. On this occasion however, the evening coincides with a gathering of Nazis (the play is set circa 1930), a hint of the wider political challenge to come. There are, however, no committed politicians in this provincial backwater; there is a Communist agitator, who is in favour of doing something rather than talking, but he comes from Magdeburg and is viewed with suspicion as an outsider by the local party members. The prime concern of these citizens, whatever their political affiliation, is personal security,

113

and this Horváth underlines through a range of sexual allusion. He neatly exploits the no-man's-land of sexual encounter with its cross-currents of conscious and subconscious activity. His characters have learnt their political lines by rote and the unwitting hypocrisy of their situation is revealed as blatantly sexual acts become subsumed into social and political convention. In the post-Freudian era such elision is ripe for exploitation and ironic comment and Horváth mixes sexual and political elements to this end. Martin, the leader of the local Communists, is upbraided by Betz for insisting that sexual relations should not cut across party lines. Horváth has Betz juggle a series of half-learnt and earnestly applied concepts:

Ich glaub, du übersiehst etwas sehr Wichtiges bei deiner Beurteilung der politischen Weltlage, nämlich das Liebesleben in der Natur. Ich habe mich in der letzten Zeit mit den Werken von Professor Freud befaßt, kann ich dir sagen. Du darfst doch nicht vergessen, daß um unser Ich herum Aggressionstriebe gruppiert sind, die mit unserem Eros in einem ewigen Kampfe liegen, und die sich zum Beispiel als Selbstmordtriebe äußern, oder auch als Sadismus, Masochismus, Lustmord. . . . Ich kann dir sagen, daß unsere Aggressionstriebe eine direkt überragende Rolle bei der Verwirklichung des Sozialismus spielen, nämlich als Hemmung.[11]

Unwittingly Betz has made a vital link; socialism requires the individual to relinquish some of his individualism for the common good, but the *Kleinbürger* dare not prejudice his position, for if he is not dominant he feels subservient. Martin angrily rejects Betz's thesis because he interprets it as an accusation of hypocrisy whereas the audience can see it for what it really is, a reflection that for all his political commitment Martin too needs a social order where values are consistent and predictable. To this extent he does stand in contrast to the 'Stadtrat,' a leading light in the ranks of republicanism, who rules over his wife like an oriental despot. He is the archetypal *Kleinbürger*; his political activities – liberal republicanism – are belied by the reactionary conservatism of his marital activities. He would rather leave his wife at home, for her presence by his side reminds him of the balancing act he is constantly required to perform. In the event this is the occasion on which he tries his wife's patience too sorely and she rounds on him with a devastating venom which leaves him speechless:

114

Oh du unmöglicher Mann! Draußen Prolet, drinnen Kapitalist! Die Herren hier sollen dich nur mal genau kennenlernen! Mich beutet er aus, mich! Dreißig Jahr, dreißig Jahr! (*Sie weint*)[12]

Her accusation exposes the *Kleinbürger's* capacity to profess one set of values and practise another and yet when her husband stands on the brink of public humiliation it is Adele herself who puts to flight the bullying Nazi major before he can achieve a minor but effective political coup. Adele defends her husband with a momentum of energy which proves irresistable and yet it is ironic that in defending her husband Adele is assuring the continuation of her own role as private chattel. Through her Horváth shows the pervasive nature of the petty bourgeois ethos; in defending herself, Adele unwittingly defends the social hypocrisy of the *Kleinbürger*.

The ultimate comment on the underlying egocentricity and self-assertiveness of the *Kleinbürger* comes from the 'Wirt'. His political steadfastness has been well-illustrated since his establishment is used by the Fascists in the afternoon and the Republicans in the evening. As the Italian evening draws to its close the 'Wirt' is somewhat the worse for drink and in this maudlin state reveals the only successful basis of the *Kleinbürger's* survival:

(*plötzlich verträumt*) Ich denk jetzt an meinen Abort. Siehst, früher da waren nur so erotische Sprüch' an der Wand dringestanden, hernach im Krieg lauter patriotische und jetzt lauter politische – glaubs mir: solangs nicht wieder erotisch werden, solang wird das deutsche Volk nicht wieder gesunden[13]

Even so, such an overt recognition of sexual, that is animal, motivation can only be confessed through graffiti; in public the *Kleinbürger* claims to be motivated by higher concerns. Karl, the musician, whose political allegiance is to the left, reserves the right to be sexually independent and attaches himself to the politically indifferent Leni. Karl's avowed independence is a charade, for his search for a partner who will bolster his own ego has to be concealed behind a socially acceptable, that is political, façade:

Karl: Ich bin nämlich nicht so veranlagt, daß ich eine Blume einfach nur so abbrech, am Wegrand. Ich muß auch menschlich einen Kontakt haben und das geht bei mir

115

über die Politik.

Leni: Geh, das glaubens doch selber nicht!

Karl: Doch! Ich könnt zum Beispiel nie mit einer Frau auf die Dauer harmonieren, die da eine andere Weltanschauung hätt.

Leni: Ihr Männer habt alle eine ähnliche Weltanschauung. (*Stille*)[14]

Leni's response deflates Karl's self-indulgent posturing and indicates the dubious nature of political activity in this play. The stage-direction is a crucial part of this unmasking process: 'Bitte achten Sie genau auf die Pausen im Dialog, die ich mit "Stille" bezeichne', Horváth wrote in the *Gebrauchsanweisung*, 'hier kämpft das Bewußtsein oder Unterbewußtsein miteinander, und das muß sichtbar werden.'[15] The dramatic caesura, allowing the hollowness or weight of what has been said to make itself felt, stripping the cliché of its protective veneer, is Horváth's equivalent to Brecht's technique of *Verfremdung*; working from within the play it represents the momentary lapse of the mental screen which protects the individual from a vision of his real self, a vision which the audience immediately see repressed as the characters continue a moment later as if nothing had happened. Nowhere is the wilful refusal of the *Kleinbürger* to face up to reality better illustrated.

The validity of Leni's comment is all the more evident since the audience has only just seen Karl with Anna, Martin's girl. She has been sent on the 'politischen Strich' to pick up a Fascist and discover what the Fascists are planning. Karl's high-flown belief in the dignity of man was belied by his actions; despite his political protestations Karl is a *Kleinbürger* at heart, as Horváth illustrates:

Es hat doch keinen Sinn, als Vieh durch das Leben zu laufen und immer nur an die Befriedigung seiner niederen Instinkte zu denken.
(*Er legt seinen Arm unwillkürlich um ihre Taille, ohne zu wissen, was er tut. Anna nimmt seine Hand langsam fort von dort und sieht ihm lang an. Karl wird sich bewußt, was er getan hat. Stille.*
Tückisch) Aber komisch finde ich das doch von Martin.[16]

When Anna finds her Fascist, in front of the statue of the Kaiser which two overenthusiastic Communists have painted red, Horváth shows how both sides of the political fence are linked. The Fascist's political anger at Jewish influence rouses him to feverish sexual activity, and his fury at the desecration of his political ideal is given sexual expression:

Der Faschist: Es wird Zeit, daß wir uns wieder mal die Hosen anziehen und merken, daß wir Zimbern und Teutonen sind! (*Er wirft sich auf sie*)
Anna: Nicht! Nein! (*Sie wehrt sich*)
(*Jetzt fällt das Licht auf das Denkmal und man sieht nun seine Majestät mit dem roten Kopf*)
Der Faschist: (*läßt ab von Anna, heiser*) Was? – Nein, diese Schändung – diese Schändung – Der Gott, der Eisen wachsen ließ! –Rache! – Gott steh uns bei! Deutschland erwache!
(*In der Ferne das Hakenkreuzlied*)[17]

The apoplectic stream of slogans at the moment of intense sexual and political emotion reveals the extent to which the *Kleinbürger* is a prisoner of his own conventions. By drawing a series of variations, half-echoes and inner dissonances Horváth allows the outer action of his *Volksstücke* to proceed unchecked while ensuring that his audience recognize the underlying criticism. All the characters are tarred with the same brush; the Pyrrhic victory of the forces of republicanism over the forces of reaction in *Italienische Nacht* is all-too clear, the 'Stadtrat's' closing speech neatly echoes Horváth's pessimism:

Stadtrat: Na also! Von einer akuten Bedrohung der demokratischen Republik kann natürlich keineswegs gesprochen werden. Solange es einen republikanischen Schutzverband gibt . . . solange kann die Republik ruhig schlafen.
Martin: Gute Nacht![18]

The creation of a dominant and unifying tone is an essential feature of Horváth's style. The overt sexual-political interaction of *Italienische Nacht* is replaced by a less strident note in his most famous play *Geschichten aus dem Wiener Wald*. Here the tone is that of 'Gay Vienna' set against the three-four time signature of the waltz king. Indeed the fourth scene of the play is evocatively en-

117

titled 'An der schönen blauen Donau' suggesting the comfortable backcloth of illusion against which Marianne's tragedy is played out; it is here by the romantic Danube that Marianne first speaks to the feckless Alfred who represents her dream of true love and offers hope of an escape from the predictability of marriage to her fiancé Oskar, her next-door neighbour and local butcher. Alfred and Marianne meet to the strains of a Strauss waltz played on a portable gramophone and it is clear from Horváth's stage directions that they have both allowed themselves to be transported by the setting and the music, picking up the unspoken romantic cue 'we were fated to meet here' and allowing fantasy to become 'reality'. Their meeting is almost a parody of the less romantic and decidedly sexual encounter between Marianne's father, the 'Zauberkönig' and Alfred's mistress the ageing Valerie which the audience has witnessed in the previous scene. While Alfred and Marianne indulge their romantic longings the audience can set their clichés against those of an elder generation and draw its own conclusions.

The tone of *Geschichten aus dem Wiener Wald* is stylized and affected; as in the *Volksstück* tradition the characters are larger than life and coarsely drawn, for they are representatives of a social situation and lack the personal capacity to achieve tragic stature in themselves. Their dialogue is similarly affected and grandiose as they strive to maintain the position they feel is due to them in society. Firmly entrenched in a world of fixed values and expectations the *Kleinbürger* has acquired a language of independent means, a manner of expression whose currency is generally recognized by his fellows and behind which he may consciously or unconsciously conceal his own personal inadequacy. The individual in Horváth's drama is trapped as much by the language of social intercourse as by the physical manifestations of the *Kleinbürgertum*. Occasionally, a character like Marianne in the *Wiener Wald* or Elisabeth in *Glaube Liebe Hoffnung* show their awareness of their imprisonment and try to turn it to their advantage, but they only come to grief; all they can achieve is to exchange one socially acceptable role for another, Marianne discards the role of dutiful daughter to become the romantic heroine raising her man to a new level of existence only to find herself once more rummaging in laundry baskets for lost suspenders, Elisabeth escapes from the world of corsets and suspender belts to play the role of loving wife creating a home for her man but must watch the dream collapse in the face of 'public respectability'. The successful individual in Horváth's plays is the one whose role is beyond challenge and such a role depends on establishing for oneself a niche in the hierarchy of bourgeois conventionality. Alfred's complaint at the end of *Geschichten aus dem Wiener Wald* when he learns that the son Marianne bore him, the cause of all her misery, has died reveals this preoccupation: 'So ohne Kinder hört man eigentlich auf. Man setzt sich nicht fort und stirbt aus! Schad!'[19] This essentially hierarchical interpretation, male-dominated and sexually motivated, is the fulcrum of activity in the world of the *Kleinbürger*. When Marianne is no longer there to find the 'Zauberkönig's' lost suspenders and support him in his own image his world crumbles, he loses interest in his shop and stands revealed as weak and vulnerable. Marianne exercises the same function for Alfred, as the direct echo of lost suspenders ironically underlines.

The veneer of respectability concealing the predatory nature of human relations is well-nigh transparent in *Geschichten aus dem Wiener Wald*; behind the unexceptional façade of the 'Quiet Street in the Eighth District' lurks a brutality and animal viciousness. Oskar cannot kiss Marianne without biting her, he demonstrates his skill in ju-jitsu at their engagement party by throwing her to the ground and it is Oskar who half-throttles his bride-to-be at the end of the play to prevent her attacking the 'Großmutter' who has done away with her child. Oskar's sentimental melancholy, when set against the violence and slaughter epitomized by the carcasses of the butcher's shop, emphasizes society's ambivalence as does Horváth's alternation of martial music and the romantic lilt of the Viennese waltz. The very setting of the 'Stille Straße' is an ironic comment on contemporary society for between them the butcher's shop, the 'Zauberkönig's' magic and doll's hospital cum toyshop and Valerie's 'Tabaktrafik' combine the three most dominant features of the *Kleinbürgertum*. The dressed carcasses reflect aggression, violence and exploitation; the 'Zauberkönig's' wares pretence, façade and sleight of hand; and the 'Tabaktrafik' self-indulgence, vicarious experience and the preservation of illusion and idyll – namely picture postcards, the lottery and tobacco. As with the opening scene of the play, Horváth's technique is to allow a *tableau vivant* to run in mime and create a mood which he can then expose as false. The illusion of order and respectability, dominant preoccupations of this stratum of society, are indicated by the figure of the butcher in a clean apron in the doorway of his shop and the young girl emerging with her purchases and peeping into the

119

window of the toyshop next-door. The musical accompaniment, 'Tales from the Vienna Woods' played on a well-worn piano by a less than accomplished pianist both completes the illusion and is the first stage in its exposure.

The violence scarcely concealed behind this façade emerges with Havlitschek, Oskar's assistant, a giant of a man. His hands and apron are covered with blood and he is in a towering rage threatening all forms of brutality against the young girl, who has had the temerity to cast aspersions on his 'Blutwurst'. Only the exaggerated compliments paid his sausage-making by the 'Rittmeister' manage to calm him; once the conventions are ignored the violent reality is clear, again and again Horváth shows the world of the *Kleinbürger* closing ranks to avoid or make good such lapses in 'good manners'. The various civilities are bracketed by the piano accompaniment, giving the characters the effect of being figures on a musical box. Horváth uses the music to comment on the essential falsity of the scene and to show Marianne in contrast to the others. Not until the end of Scene Two is music played while Marianne is on-stage, whereas it is used consistently to counterpoint the dialogue between the other more clearly recognizable members of the *Kleinbürgertum*. When Marianne sees Alfred for the first time she is arranging the shop window and her response to his flirting through the glass is sudden, she lets down the shop-blind – 'und der Walzer bricht wieder ab, mitten im Takt. Alfred erblickt Valerie. Stille.'[20] The artificial environment is thus shown to have added Marianne to its list of victims! Her attraction to Alfred makes her vulnerable to the falsity of the illusion he represents.

The musical accompaniment to this meeting, *In lauschiger Nacht*, recurs in the following scene, the engagement party in the Wiener Wald, and as such is characteristic of Horváth's use of musical repetition for ironic effect and social comment. Marianne, for example, sings *Das Lied von der Wachau* as her audition piece for the baroness 'with international connections' and the song is heard again when the 'Zauberkönig' and his friends are enjoying themselves at the 'Heurige.' Its recurrence at this stage reminds the audience of the extent to which Marianne's idealized view of the world has been shattered and stands in stark contrast to the job Marianne's audition secured. The cabaret performance at Maxim's presents a neat caricature of the *Kleinbürger*'s approach to life. It begins with the waltz *Wiener Blut* to which a number of girls in traditional Viennese costume dance. Their performance is ecstatically received and the orchestra then plays a march. The second number, to the strains of the 'Blue Danube' consists of three half-naked girls representing Danube water-sprites. This is followed by the march *Fridericus rex* to which three wholly naked girls enact a representation of the Zeppelin, bringing the audience to its feet to acclaim this achievement by singing the first verse of the *Deutschlandlied*. This progression, in which the underlying sexual motivation emerges from behind socially acceptable images reaches its conclusion in the final number. Entitled 'The Pursuit of Happiness' and set to Schumann's *Träumerei*, it consists of a group of naked girls struggling to reach a golden sphere on which stands 'happiness': 'Das Glück ist ebenfalls unbekleidet und heißt Marianne.'[21] The 'Zauberkönig' who has not been slow to applaud the appearance of naked beauties in the earlier scenes is beside himself with shock when he recognizes Marianne. The poise and 'savoir faire' the audience has come to associate with his appearance crumbles away; and indeed he is so shaken that he reverts to dialect, one of the few occasions when the pretentiousness of the *Kleinbürgertum* is swept aside. Father and daughter confront each other in a devastatingly frank exchange from which neither can recover, except by pretending that it never happened:

Zauberkonig: Laß dein Mutterl aus dem Spiel, bitt ich mir aus! Wenn sie dich so gesehen hätt, so nacket auf dem Podium herumstehen – dich den Blicken der Allgemeinheit preisgeben – Ja, schämst dich denn gar nicht mehr? Pfui Teufel!
Marianne: Nein, das kann ich mir nicht leisten, daß ich mich schäm.
Stille
Die Musik in der Bar ist nun verstummt.[22]

From this point on things go from bad to worse for Marianne, until, drained by the exigencies of social hypocrisy, she finally agrees to fulfil her father's wishes and marry Oskar. Her last defiant gesture before she allows herself to be sacrificed on the altar of respectability and the convenience of others represents a rare moment of genuine emotion. Horváth underlines this by having Marianne too speak in dialect. Her defiance is, however, meaningless; as the audience soon learn, Leopold, her child is dead. There could be no better illustration of the vicious circle into which

121

Marianne has been drawn:

Marianne: (*wendet sich langsam der Puppenklinik zu – legt die Hand auf die Klinke und dreht sich dann nochmals Valerie Alfred und Oskar zu:*) Ich möcht jetzt nur noch was sagen. Es ist mir nämlich zu guter Letzt scheißwurscht – und das, was ich da tu, tu ich nur wegen dem kleinen Leopold, der doch nichts dafür kann. – (*Sie öffnet die Tür und das Glockenspiel erklingt, als wäre nichts geschehen*).[23]

Nothing has changed, Marianne's trials have left scarcely a trace in the world of the *Kleinbürger*, in a few months' time she will be the only one to even think of them. Horváth's 'happy ends', like those of Nestroy, are manifestly contrived; Oskar will marry Marianne – and the 'Zauberkönig' will live happily ever after and the clichéd motto to *Kasimir und Karoline* (Kasimir and Karoline, 1932) – 'Love lasts forever' – ('Und die Liebe höret nimmer auf') is starkly belied by the ease with which Karoline discards one man at the Munich 'Oktoberfest' and ends the play with another. What she fails to realize is that 'Oberleutnant' Schürzinger, a tailor with a keen eye for his own advantage, exploits her from the moment they meet. Their relationship is shown to be emotionally sterile before it has had time to develop beyond sexual attraction.

In structure *Kasimir und Karoline* is markedly different to *Geschichten aus dem Wiener Wald*, consisting of a linear sequence of 117 scenes of varying length, moulded into a coherent unit by a carefully orchestrated pattern of echo and variation. The Munich 'Oktoberfest,' the setting for the play, allows the *Kleinbürger* the opportunity to relax and be himself. From the men who stand at the foot of the slide to look up the girls' skirts as they slide down, to the vicarious voyeurism offered by the circus freaks and the predatory nature of the sexual skirmishes mounted by Rauch and Speer, Horváth's insistent reminder of the aggression and exploitation that is second nature to the *Kleinbürger* is evident throughout. The fairground music and sounds that are the constant backcloth to the dialogue are augmented by a use of specific tunes as in the *Wiener Wald*. Once again the Zeppelin makes an appearance, floating away to the strains of the 'Radetzkymarsch' on a piano, the music breaking off in mid-bar so that Karoline and Schürzinger can pick up their conversation as if it had never been broken off. Since they are, as it were, conversing by numbers, the content of what they say is secondary.

The disparity between words and actions is interlaced between Horváth's cynical comment on the bestial nature of the *Kleinbürger*'s activities. Juanita, the Gorilla-girl in the side-show of freaks, performs by singing the Barcarole from *The Tales of Hoffmann* and as she sings of love, Schürzinger is seen to put his arm round Karoline's waist and draw her to him. Everyone is having a good time and Kasimir's bleak future as one of the many unemployed is not allowed to interfere with the general enjoyment. Indeed Kasimir has become an uncomfortable reminder to others of the grim economic reality beyond the fairground, a reality they would rather forget. Without a job and with no prospects of employment, Kasimir's increasing isolation underlines the wilful myopia of the *Kleinbürger*. It is not that they cannot see reality, for Karoline herself recognizes and accepts the void that awaits her, but true to her petty bourgeois upbringing she stylizes reality to make it more acceptable:

Man hat halt oft so eine Sehnsucht in sich – aber dann kehrt man zurück mit gebrochenen Flügeln und das Leben geht weiter, als wär man nie dabei gewesen – [24]

Karoline is clearly talking from repeated personal experience, and like the class she represents, she hasn't learnt from her suffering. Kasimir, for his part, finds consolation with Erna, a former serving-girl. They too have no illusions as to the bleak future that awaits them beyond the fairground, and in the penultimate scene of the play Horváth presents an implicit reckoning with the oppressive nature of the *Kleinbürger*. Even now when genuine emotion is struggling to surface, it is in the form of a wry exchange epitomizing society's impersonal features. Kasimir and Erna can only declare their feelings for each other through 'proverbs', any attempt at direct communication ends in failure:

Kasimir: Träume sind Schäume.
    Erna: Solange wir uns nicht aufhängen, werden wir nicht verhungern.
    (*Stille*)
Kasimir: Du, Erna –
    Erna: Was?

Kasimir: Nichts.
        (*Stille*)[25]

Horváth's contribution to modern drama, a resurgence of interest in the *Volksstück* as a form of contemporary social criticism,
bore fruit in the generation of young writers who came to the fore in
the 1960s. Wolfgang Bauer, Franz Xaver Kroetz and Martin Sperr,
sharing Horváth's experience of the Austro-Bavarian region owe
their predecessor a considerable debt. The emphases have
changed, but so have the preoccupations and concerns of society
and the Volk; nonetheless the use of language as an expression of
alienation, the closed world of everyday situations facing the ordinary man presented on stage in language and terms that derive from
the real world rather than an inward-looking artistic clique, all this
owes much to Horváth's *Volksstücke* of the 1930s. If his work now
seems stylized and mellow in comparison to the brutal directness of
his successors this can only be a reflection of the extent to which the
Kleinbürger still holds sway.

NOTES

1. 'God knows why, but the Volkstheater is presenting "Tales from the
   Vienna Woods" in twelve scenes by Ödön von Horváth. As if it
   weren't insult enough to dub this miserable panopticum a "folk-play",
   they choose to lay this calumny of Vienna before the Viennese and rub
   salt in the wound by engaging the best actors they can find to wallow in
   this anti-humanitarian swamp.'
       Österreichische Zeitung, 1948. Quoted in *Materialien zu Ödön
   von Horváths 'Geschichten aus dem Wiener Wald'*, ed. Traugott
   Krischke, Suhrkamp, Frankfurt, 1972, p. 141.
2. 'They say I'm too crude, too disgusting, too weird, too cynical . . . and
   they just don't see that my only aim is to show the world as it really
   is. . . . I annoy people because they recognize themselves in the
   characters on stage – and of course some people just cannot laugh at
   themselves, especially when what they are shown are their own highly
   personal instincts, of which they are often only half-aware themselves.'
       Ödön von Horváth, *Gesammelte Werke*, Band I Volksstücke,
   Schauspiele, Frankfurt/Main Suhrkamp, 1970 p. 13.
3. H. Qualtinger and C. Merz, *Der Herr Karl*, a cabaret monologue with
   Qualtinger as the bigoted warehouseman who reflects on the changing
   fortunes of his life and unwittingly exposes the moral vacuity of the
   little man who changes course with every shift of the political wind and

ends up no better off than he was when he began. The play was first performed in 1961 and rapidly acquired legendary status. (cf. *Der Herr Karl and weiteres Heiteres*, rororo No. 0607).

4. 'A superb evening, a documentary à la Horváth. But to be a creative work there needed to be some indication of the other Austria, the Austria of the non-philistines, or at least a hint of it. The audience must be allowed to sense that the way out of the labyrinth of that sort of Austrianism was already signposted.'

E.T. Kauer 'Schauspiel aus Zwischen-Österreich', Volksstimme, Vienna, 1968. Quoted in: *Materialien zu Geschichten aus dem Wiener Wald*, p. 163.

5. 'It's ceaseless slaughter, there's no hope of peace – except that now and again someone somewhere enjoys a few moments which seem like an armistice. . . . The individual struggles on hopelessly driven by his animal instincts, and so the only way to regard this heroic and cowardly sort of in-fighting is as a study of the form this bestiality takes, since such bestiality, as everyone knows, cannot be seen in terms of good or bad.'

Ödön von Horváth, 'Randbemerkung' (i.e. Introduction) to *Glaube Liebe Hoffnung, Gesammelte Werke* I p. 328.

6. 'Like every other European country Germany consists of some 90% complete or incomplete petty bourgeois, but certainly of petty bourgeois. If I want to portray the people I cannot deal with the other 10%, I'm a serious observer of my times so I have to look at the majority. It has to be all Germany.'

Ödön von Horváth, 'Gebrauchsanweisung', *Gesammelte Werke*, Vol. IV p. 662.

7. 'a genuine popular theatre . . . which appeals to people's instincts and not to their intellect.' 'Gebrauchsanweisung', ibid. p. 662.

8. 'Thanks to the petty bourgeoisie genuine dialects have disappeared, and the reason for that is cultural jargon. If I want one of my characters to speak realistically today then I have to make him use this cultural jargon. Cultural jargon (and its causes) inevitably provokes criticism and so we arrive at the dialogue used in the new folk-play, and as a result the character of such a play and finally the dramatic action – a synthesis of seriousness and irony!'

'Gebrauchsanweisung', ibid. pp. 662–3.

9. 'Don't do it Elizabeth – you know you're no good for anything for at least two days if you do – '

Discarded Scene 33, quoted in *Gesammelte Werke* IV, p. 292.

10. 'All according to plan. I planned it this way and you knew what was coming.' Discarded Scene 36, quoted in *Gesammelte Werke* IV, p. 293.

11. 'It seems to me that your assessment of the world political scene is incomplete – what about sex? I've spent a lot of time recently reading Professor Freud, I can tell you, and what you must realize is that our ego is surrounded by aggressive instincts all of which are constantly in conflict with our eros. That's what gives us suicidal tendencies or makes us sadists or masochists or sex-murderers. . . . I can tell you this, our aggressive instincts are a direct and dominant factor in the

realization of our socialist aims – they act against them.'

Ödön von Horváth, *Italienische Nacht*, Zweites Bild, *Gesammelte Werke*, Vol. I p. 112.

12. 'You're impossible! Proletarian in public and a capitalist at heart! If only your friends here knew what you were really like! I'm the one he exploits, me! Thirty years, thirty years!' (*She bursts into tears*)

Italienische Nacht, Siebentes Bild, *Gesammelte Werke*, Vol. I p. 152.

13. (*Suddenly dreamy*)' Look at our loo. Once there was nothing but sex on the walls, then along came the war and everyone started writing patriotic slogans – now its all political. Believe me, the German people will never be strong again until we get back to sex –'

Italienische Nacht, Siebentes Bild, *Gesammelte Werke*, Vol. I pp 148–9.

14. *Karl*: I'm not like that, I can't just pluck a flower from the wayside as I go by. I need to feel involved and for me that means politics.

Leni: Get away with you, you don't even believe that yourself!

Karl: Oh yes. I could never ever feel really in tune with a woman who was looking for something different in life.

Leni: We all know what you men are looking for.

(*Silence*)

Italienische Nacht, Drittes Bild, *Gesammelte Werke*, Vol. I, p. 119.

15. 'It is important to pay particular attention to the pauses in the dialogue which are marked "Silence", this is where the conscious or subconscious are in conflict and the audience must realize that.'

'Gebrauchsanweisung', *Gesammelte Werke*, Vol. IV, p. 664.

16. 'There's more to life than living like an animal and thinking of nothing but sexual pleasure' (*Without realizing what he is doing he automatically puts his arm round her waist. Anna deliberately takes his hand away and gives him a long look. Karl realizes what he has done. Silence.*

Maliciously) I still think its a funny thing for Martin to do.

Italienische Nacht, Drittes Bild, *Gesammelte Werke*, Vol. I, pp. 117–8.

17. *The Fascist*: It's high time we got our trousers on again and remembered we are Teutons and Tsimbers! (*He throws himself on top of her*)

Anna: No! Stop! (*She tries to fend him off*)

(*At this point the light falls on the statue revealing His Majesty with his head painted red*)

The Fascist: (*lets Anna go, hoarsely*) What's this? – It's sacrilege, it's an obscenity – The God who made us hard as iron! – Revenge! – God be with us! Germany awake!

(*In the distance the Song of the Swastika*).

Italienische Nacht, Viertes Bild, *Gesammelte Werke*, Vol. I p. 124.

18. *Stadtrat*: There we are then. There's no question of a serious threat to our democratic republic. As long as we have the association for the defence of the republic . . . we republicans can sleep undisturbed.

Martin: And good night to you, too!

Italienische Nacht, Siebentes Bild, *Gesammelte Werke*, Vol. I, p. 156.

19. 'Without children there's no point in going on. There's no one to follow you, you become extinct! It's a shame!'
    Geschichten aus dem Wiener Wald, Dritter Teil, IV Draußen in der Wachau,
    Gesammelte Werke, Vol. I, pp. 250–1.
20. 'and once again the waltz breaks off in mid-beat. Alfred catches sight of Valerie. Silence.'
    ibid. Erster Teil, II Stille Straße im achten Bezirk, *Gesammelte Werke*, Vol. I, p. 173.
21. 'Happiness is also naked and is called Marianne!'
    ibid. Dritter Teil, I Beim Heurigen, *Gesammelte Werke*, Vol. I p. 228.
22. *Zauberkönig*: Don't you bring your mother into this, I won't have it. If she'd been able to see you like that, standing on the stage with your clothes off and letting everyone see what you're made of – aren't you ashamed of yourself? It's disgusting!
    Marianne: No, I can't afford to be ashamed of myself.
    Silence
    The music in the bar has stopped now.
    ibid. pp. 231–2.
23. *Marianne*: (*turns slowly towards the dolls' hospital, puts her hand on the door handle and then turns back again to face Valerie, Alfred and Oskar*) There's just one thing I want to say. I don't give a fart – the only reason I'm doing it is for little Leopold, he can't help it. –
    (*She opens the door and the musical bells ring as if nothing has happened*)
    ibid. Dritter Teil, III, Und abermals in der stillen Straße im achten Bezirk, *Gesammelte Werke* Vol. I p. 247.
24. 'Often you feel this deep longing inside you – but then you come back with your wings broken and life goes on just the same as if you'd never been there at all.!'
    Kasimir und Karoline, Scene 114, Gesammelte Werke, Vol. I, p. 322.
25. *Kasimir*: Dreams are mere shadows.
    Erna: As long as we don't hang ourselves we'll not starve to death.
    (*Silence*)
    Kasimir: Erna –
    Erna: What?
    Kasimir: Nothing.
    (*Silence*)
    ibid. Scene 116, *Gesammelte Werke*, Vol. I p. 323.

III The Innovator in a Suspect World

Alan Best

The creative impotence which Hofmannsthal's Lord Chandos so eloquently expressed in his famous 'Letter' as he struggled to come to terms with a world in which he could neither think nor speak coherently[1] has a disturbing parallel in the literature written in Germany and Austria after 1945. The new generation of writers began to experiment with and taste the pleasures of what was, for them, a new-found freedom to say what they wanted in the manner they chose. It soon transpired, however, that 'freedom' was not enough, for in addition to the many practical obstacles standing between creation and publication (obstacles to some extent overcome by enlightened encouragement from such established figures as Otto Basil and Hans Weigel and by the emergence of numerous, if often ephemeral, literary journals) the greatest obstacle of all was the very medium of their creative inspiration.

In attempting to communicate their grief and pain, their hopes and beliefs many writers found themselves obliged to use words and phrases which had become tainted and discredited, words that still carried the stench of the concentration-camp and the swastika in every syllable. Some words, of course, were readily identifiable with the malpractices and policies of National Socialism and were avoided by everyone ('ausrotten', 'Lebensraum' etc.) but for the sensitive and creative ear it seemed that the whole language had been defiled by exposure to the lips of the totalitarian authorities and their hangers-on and to the very air in which they were spoken. For those who felt this way it was impossible to listen to a children's choir singing *Silent Night* without recalling the less happy and less innocent context of drunken concentration camp guards singing the same words on Christmas Eve. Paul Celan formulated the creative void which stemmed from the years 1933–45 and the dilemma facing the poet after Auschwitz in a speech delivered in 1958:

Die Sprache blieb unverloren, ja, trotz allem. Aber sie mußte nun hindurchgehen durch ihre eigenen Antwortlosigkeiten, hindurchgehen durch furchtbares Verstummen, hindurchgehen durch die tausend Finsternisse todbringender Rede. Sie ging hindurch und gab keine Wörter her für das, was geschah; aber sie ging durch dieses Geschehen. Ging hindurch und durfte wieder zutage treten, 'angereichert' von all dem.

In dieser Sprache habe ich, in jenen Jahren und in den Jahren nachher, Gedichte zu schreiben versucht: um zu sprechen, um mich zu orientieren, um zu erkunden, wo ich mich befand und wohin es mit mir wollte, um mir Wirklichkeit zu entwerfen.[2]

Language, then, was to become a dominant preoccupation for many writers in the post-war era. Having thrown off political tyranny the writers felt constrained by the echoes which still lingered in society's means of dialogue and communication and sought to break through to a new approach which would bring a sense of identity, purpose and reality and allow for a new start. Indeed one of the most serious charges laid by Erich Fried against the Federal Republic's response to the left-wing extra-parliamentary opposition is that it is Fascist in both deed and word:

Diese Gesetze (gehen) sowohl ihrer Sprachform als ihrem Inhalt nach nicht auf gute deutsche Rechtstradition, sondern vielmehr auf Hitlers berühmten Volksgerichtspräsidenten Roland Freisler zurück.[3]

For Fried there is a direct equation between the language of the Nazi era and the mind which resorts to such phraseology. He sees a society which has failed to purge itself of its past and so he uses its linguistic practices to make his point.

The 'enrichment' of which Celan speaks must then be countered if the German language is again to become an appropriate medium for the poet's message, but, as Fried's poetry shows, a direct approach can only use the language of yesterday. Where Fried deliberately employs a simple every-day style to attack society in its own terms, other writers, less politically motivated, eschewed the frontal assault for an eliptical arabesque of words and images whose effect and unsullied meaning derived from a sequence of fleeting and interacting moments of contact. *Sprachgitter*, (The Grid of Language), the title of a collection of Celan's poems, indicates the poet's awareness of the difficulties of direct communication in the changed conditions after 1945. Communication was possible but difficult. Language had to pass through a grille which, while allowing communication, changed and broke up the words as they passed from one side to the other, emerging ultimately as 'zwei Mundvoll Schweigen', two mouthfuls of silence. The indirect approach which such barriers make necessary, is best epitomized in a poem from the collection *Mohn und Gedächtnis* (Poppy and Memory). 'Corona' is both an exhortation to mankind and an affirmation of the power of love to create new order and meaning in an apparently alien and sterile world, and the key to the poem lies in its title.

The poet takes the image of the sun hanging in the sky, to all intents and purposes a vivid overgrown orange, solid and static, and reminds the reader that such a view of the sun is an illusion. Scientists know this and at times of the eclipse of the sun by the moon we are all able to see the shafts of light and energy which reveal the sun's true nature. The corona is evidence that we cannot rely on the seemingly empirical evidence of our eyes, it is a reminder to look with fresh eyes at everything around us, to examine the interrelationship of objects and of images and act according to the spirit of what these things have to tell us in their own non-verbal language, what they illustrate by their very existence. 'Corona' appeals to man to regain his harmony with nature, to create order out of chaos by the act of love, in itself an affirmation of the possibility of creativity and an example (in plastic terms) of the harmony achieved by two bodies lovingly entwined. The language of love, the language of dreams, the language of the mind stimulated beyond the norm by opiates, these are not logical verbalizations but intuitive apperceptions from which a residual truth can be gleaned and applied in the everyday world.

Yet despite all the difficulties and obstacles facing the poet, for many language remained the sacred torch which must not be laid aside. Christine Busta, a devout Catholic, stresses such devotional obligations in her use of the phrase 'Hinknien am Beichtstuhl der Sprache'.[4] Her work displays a deceptive easiness and accessibility, and many of her poems were in fact written for children, but the poet uses her images and metaphors to enhance the superficial picture and bridge a deeply-felt schism between her vision of the world and her capacity to communicate what she feels; without falling victim to dogmatic or artificial procedures she experiments with language both as a tool and as a play-thing, delighting in the various

130

effects language can be made to achieve. Behind the playfulness, nevertheless, is a clear awareness of what such experimentation represents:

> Die Welt ist fremd genug. Wahrscheinlich verfremdet jeder von uns, aber ich mach's nicht vorsätzlich, es ist manchmal einfach notwendig, daß ich bewußt und willentlich verfremde. . . . Die Verfremdung ist für mich etwas Natürliches. . . .[5]

'Verfremdung' as practised by Christine Busta is more akin to a form of paraphrase, and her predilection for biblical texts which she chooses to render accessible for our time stems from her sense of personal vulnerability. By responding to such external stimuli the poet can shelter behind the safety of an impersonal third party: 'Es ist eher manchmal der Wille da, nicht so sehr Ich zu sagen, obwohl es für mich fast unvermeidlich ist.'[6] The contradiction and the tension between the lyrical 'Ich' and the poetic mask is one of the most telling features of her work, as she seeks out a viable means of communication and affirmation of mankind:

> Die Kreatur wird in der Liebe verewigt
> Um Gottes willen, sag du.[7]

The desperate need to feel that there is an audience 'on the other side of the poem', that it is possible to communicate intimately with someone else, to use the familiar 'du' preoccupies the writers discussed in this section. Celan described poetry as a 'Flaschenpost', that is, a letter sealed in a bottle and thrown into the sea to be carried by the winds and the tide. The poet hopes his message will be washed up on some distant shore or plucked out of the water by a passing sailor, he believes that communication is possible, but never underestimates its hazardous nature. For such devoutly Christian writers as Busta and Christine Lavant the uncertain dialogue and indistinct relationship between man and God provides a double paradigm for man's increased sense of desolation and solitude and for the promise of 'safe arrival'. Both writers are confident that the tribulations of man's journey through life and the misery and pain of life on this world will be rewarded by the greater harmony of the after-life and yet both Busta and Lavant conceal their despair at the present behind a landscape of village-life and natural cycles.

131

In Lavant's case escape is also sought in a world of dreams and much sought-after release through death, but she subsumes her personal isolation in a metaphorical range of imagery and transfuses it with the traditional and familiar imagery of Christian belief. For her too, these Christian trappings, although offering comfort and the promise of the life to come, are of no immediate practical relevance in this life. They are stars in the firmament offering later hope and a sense of direction now, a reminder to the poet that her faith will be rewarded:

> Fragt nicht, was die Nacht durchschneidet,
> denn es ist ja meine Nacht
> und mein großer Pfauenschrei
> und ganz innen drin die Zunge
> mit der Botschaft nur für mich.[8]

The encapsulated and self-contained world of Lavant and Busta, the world of parable and accessible metaphor gives their poems a direct appeal and an immediacy notably lacking in the work of their younger counterparts, Aichinger, Bachmann and Celan, and yet the motivation and the response is well-nigh identical. For Busta and Lavant the Christian faith is an immediate illustration of the need to draw hope from present fear, to sense promise from latent chaos. The Christian tradition is a personal and deeply-felt confession for both Lavant and Busta. Those who share their faith can find their own sense of direction by virtue of the familiar landmarks of metaphor and symbol.

A new and more demanding approach to life was presented in 1946 by Ilse Aichinger in her polemic *Aufruf zum Mißtrauen* (Appeal for Scepticism), published in *Der Plan*. Here and in other programmatic pieces Aichinger can be seen to speak for her generation as a whole in rejecting the role which her elders seemed all too ready to thrust upon the rising generation. Aichinger and her peers saw no reason why they should take up a mantle of collective poetic responsibility and represent the new Austria, indeed, they found themselves unable to accept anything 'collective.' They were determined to be nobody's ambassadors except their own, and Aichinger's appeal for a critical revaluation of the world and the individual's own role in that world reflects their new scepticism, uncertainty and doubt as to the social and moral foundations of this 'new society'. For Aichinger such scepticism is the *sine qua non* of a valid existence. Its absence in 1938 had devastating consequences, what is needed is an innoculation so that a resistance to such manifestations can be built up. There is to be no looking the other way, no more closing one's eyes to reality. Everything must be placed in doubt, not least the individual doubter:

> *Sich selbst müssen Sie mißtrauen!* . . . Uns selbst müssen wir mißtrauen. . . . Trauen wir dem Gott in allen, die uns begegnen, und mißtrauen wir der Schlange in unserem Herzen! Werden wir mißtrauisch gegen uns selbst, um vertrauenswürdiger zu sein![9]

The ambivalent fluctuation between doubt and hope characterizes Aichinger's work. She and the other writers who share her views are constantly exploring, seeking new paths forward, attempting to hack their way through a jungle labyrinth of fraud, emptiness and cant. For them, the primary means of progress is language and they regard the poet as an architect of the future, whose bricks and mortar are the words and images of communication. Indeed they see the world as dependant on the poet's skill and echo Wittgenstein's belief: 'Die Grenzen meiner Sprache bedeuten die Grenze meiner Welt.'[10] It is little wonder that, faced with the unwelcome realization that language was proving inadequate for the poet's mission, so many post-war writers should regard the world as suspect and alien. Aichinger, for example, is so conscious of the constraints on her use of language that she crystallizes the tensions between creator and medium in an image of two companions on a journey. Her essay *Meine Sprache und Ich* (My Language and I, 1968) considers the growing alienation between language and speaker. Language is given its own separate identity, it no longer seems part of the poet but an alter ego: 'Meine Sprache und Ich, wir reden nicht miteinander, wir haben uns nichts zu sagen.'[11] The essay begins just short of a frontier post, a deliberate reminder of the *Grenzsituation* discomfiting the poet, and language is refusing to continue their common journey: 'Sie folgte mir widerwillig, nicht weiter als hierher. Wir könnten ebensogut Zöllner sein.'[12] Meaning, significance have become dutiable articles, to be scrutinized before clearance, but by shifting the nature of the image Aichinger is able to show that it is the means of communication, not the individual who is under threat. Searching for documents of legitimation the 'Ich' refuses to allow language to speak for her 'Meine Sprache ist ihnen verdächtig, nicht ich'[13] and resolves to help smuggle this

133

'refugee' to safety and the capacity to speak once more with confidence and truth:

> Die Unterhaltung allein wird ihr helfen, das Gespräch über sie, die Beobachtungen, die sich wiederholen. Man wird mit der Zeit nichts mehr von ihr wollen. Und ich werde das meinige dazutun. Ich werde hier und dort einen Satz einflechten, der sie unverdächtig macht.[14]

Aichinger's ever-increasing hermeticism derives directly from the sense of estrangement and the loss of faith in language as a means of direct communication. Her work places a heavy burden on the reader through its obscurity and self-indulgent imagery and yet what she creates is an unvarnished and unretouched kinetic reality in a world of shifting referents. The short story *Spiegelgeschichte* (Reverse Sequence) takes the reader into a world where chronology is reversed. A young woman lies dying and relives her whole life in her mind's eye, from grave to cradle. Within the context of the story this 'absurd' situation is totally acceptable and the intrusions from those gathered round the death-bed are seen as irrelevant. The logic of the 'normal' world is effectively, but implicitly questioned. Aichinger's scepticism, bordering as it frequently does on nihilism, is equally effective in her novel *Die größere Hoffnung* (The Greater Hope, 1948) where the reader is never allowed to forget that the central figure, the child Ellen, has no future. The explosive dénouement is a convenient and almost irrelevant intrusion of the outer world into the inner emptiness. Aichinger's language is characterized by its capacity to evoke a clear and telling silence, it is a silence that acknowledges the abuses to which open communication is vulnerable. She forges links which are arbitrary, for their unifying logic is personal and internal. The meaning is clear to the writer, who offers them to the public with no concessions. Association of such ideas defies logic and is the mark of an order of things that is wholly introspective and egocentric. It is for the reader to complete the image, to give of himself, to try and make something of the silences that ensue. Aichinger's silences provoke questions, and the questions demand answers. The reader is taken on trust to engage in a private, whispered dialogue. The passage *Schlechte Wörter* (Bad Words, 1976) is unequivocal in its refusal to be anything but oblique:

> Niemand kann von mir verlangen, daß ich Zusammenhänge her-

stelle, solange sie vermeidbar sind. Ich bin nicht wahllos wie das Leben, für da mir auch die bessere Bezeichnung eben entflohen ist. Lassen wir es *Leben* heißen, vielleicht verdient es nichts Besseres. *Leben* ist kein besonderes Wort und *sterben* auch nicht. Beide sind angreifbar, überdecken statt zu definieren. Vielleicht weiß ich warum. Definieren grenzt an Unterhöhlen und setzt dem Zugriff der Träume aus.[15]

The intellectual hide and seek which Aichinger's work provokes launches the reader on a voyage of discovery and exploration in a world of confusion, but it is a world in which the hope of understanding can be sensed behind the next word and the succeeding image. Celan, too, stressed the need to search and the mystery of silence:

> Lippe wußte. Lippe weiß.
> Lippe schweigt es zu Ende.[16]

Celan regards poems as the only means of orientation left to man in a world which is 'überflogen von Sternen, die Menschenwerk sind'[17] and laments the 'starke Neigung zum Verstummen'[18] which such a condition creates. For Celan poetry became ever more difficult as he seemed to lose faith in the capacity of his words to seek out the counterpart, the addressee, the reader who could complete the work.

For Ingeborg Bachmann such a sense of isolation and silence was a direct consequence of social malaise. Social influences and cultural impulses have made the individual a 'zum Schweigen gebrachtes *Ich aus Schweigen*'[19] incapable of communication, incapable of individual action. Much of her prose work has a Kafkan timbre, not only in the more obvious echoes of *Das 30. Jahr* (The Thirtieth Year), where an individual is obliged to take stock and discover that the world is not as he had envisaged it. The two short narratives *Alles* (Everything) and *Ein Wildermuth* (A Wildermuth, 1956/57) encapsulate the central scepticism and doubt that underpin the poetry of her generation. Bachmann isolates the 'naive' individual, the person 'ohne Arg', the man or woman who has yet to respond to the 'Aufruf zum Mißtrauen', shakes him from his protective cocoon and sends him out into the world with new eyes. The central figure of *Das 30. Jahr* is described thus:

Er wäre gerne mit einer neuen Sprache wiedergekehrt, die

getaugt hätte, das erfahrene Geheimnis auszudrücken[20]

but this new awareness is incapable of transmission and the individual is left with a vision of a new reality but the knowledge that he cannot pass it on. Both here and in *Alles* enlightenment comes to one who then suffers the agonies and frustrations of verbal impotence. The father-to-be in *Alles* realises that he must save his child from the normal routine and teach it to go its own way. The Kafkan flash of insight which accompanies the news that he has started a new life shatters the old world and makes its preoccupations seem hollow:

> Ich kam auf Gedanken, unvermutet, wie man auf Minen kommt, von solcher Sprengkraft, daß ich hätte zurückschrecken müssen, aber ich ging weiter, ohne Sinn für die Gefahr. . . . Ich sah mich mit einemmal in anderen Zusammenhängen, mich und das Kind, das zu einem bestimmten Zeitpunkt, Anfang oder Mitte November, an die Reihe kommen sollte mit seinem Leben genauso wie einst ich, genau wie alle vor mir.[21]

As the story develops so its relevance to Bachmann's situation as a poet becomes clear: it is a paradigm for the creative dilemma. The insight is there, but the means of communication which will enable the poet to show an alternative approach are inadequate.

Against the 'natural' background of expectant parenthood Bachmann illustrates the gulf that opens up between the old and the new realizations. Both parents-to-be become wholly child-orientated, the mother in the traditional way, but the father becomes obsessed by the need to bring the child up properly, and, as the child grows from infancy to the first hesitant attempts at verbal communication the dilemma becomes acute. Now is the moment of truth, the moment when things can be explained or will be lost forever:

> Alles ist eine Frage der Sprache und nicht nur dieser einen deutschen Sprache, die mit anderen geschaffen wurde in Babel, um die Welt zu verwirren. Denn darunter schwelt noch eine Sprache, die reicht bis in die Gesten und Blicke, das Abwickeln der Gedanken und den Gang der Gefühle, und in ihr ist schon all unser Unglück. Alles war eine Frage, ob ich das Kind bewahren konnte vor unserer Sprache, bis es eine neue begründet hatte und eine neue Zeit einleiten konnte.[22]

136

Yet, for all his awareness of the direction he should guide his child, the father discovers that the direct, but non-verbal language of the world about his child, the language of the leaves, the rivers, the trees and all the rest, is inaccessible and tantalisingly elusive. As the father mournfully puts it:

Ich war neu geboren, aber er war es nicht! Ich war es ja, ich war der erste Mensch und habe alles verspielt, hab nichts getan.[23]

Caught in this vicious circle the father loses all interest in his son, who becomes an object of indifference to him; even the news that the child has fallen to his death during a school outing fails to rouse the father, so taken up has he become with what he regards as his failure to open up a new form of insight and release mankind from the cul-de-sac of social conformity.

Bachmann uses the central figure of the father to echo the cruel dilemma of the modern age. The vision is perceived, the goal is clear, but the way is impassable. The individual may pierce the veil, but is increasingly isolated by his realization that he cannot communicate what he has discovered. The world in which he moves and the world in which he thinks have become estranged, and the two are linked by silences and despairing monologues.

There could scarcely be a greater contrast between the poetry of Celan and Bachmann on the one hand and that of Erich Fried on the other, and yet all three share the same distrust of an approach which reflects the beliefs and manners of general society. However, where Bachmann and Celan retreat into metaphor and imagery which eschews the every day, Fried deliberately applies the sullied and sordid language of everyday usage to hoist society with its own petard. His use of verbatim extracts of newspaper articles and advertisements in his poetry (as in *Tiermarkt-Ankauf*, Animals Wanted), his deliberate and choice use of puns and of direct and graphic language serves to expose society's inadequacies. He too despairs of finding an attentive listener to his work, but unlike Celan or Bachmann for whom such despair led to deliberate ambiguity and elusiveness, Fried meets his public head on. The journalistic cliché, the deliberate banality of the political slogan turn society's language back against itself. The primary colouring of such polemics as *und Vietnam und* (And Vietnam and) emphasize Fried's determination to penetrate the mind of the casual and complacent reader and arouse him to political consciousness. Fried is very much a political poet, and hence reliant on an immediate effect, but behind the first response he has carefully hidden a secondary implication which the unwary reader finds it impossible to avoid. Fried's response to Adorno's concern for poetry after Auschwitz is typically presented. Not for Fried the macabre invocations of Celan's *Todesfuge* (Death Fugue); *Fragen nach der Poesie seit Auschwitz* (Questions about Poetry after Auschwitz) manages to suggest, in the most poetic way, that Auschwitz is no great milestone on its own and that latter-day atrocities are still being perpetrated world-wide. Only the poets, says Fried, know what happened to poetry:

> das wissen nur lyrische Dichter
> die unentwegten
> Rufer zum Vogelschutz
> in der bald wieder heilen Welt.[24]

There is, however, something forlorn about this image; despite its suggestion that the future is secure, the preservation of wild-life and endangered species is not one of society's most noticeable concerns.

Fried too reflects on society's failure to learn the lessons of National Socialism; his silences reflect both his disillusion and the fear of what the future may hold in such a society – *Anpassung* (Adaptation):

> Gestern fing ich an
> sprechen zu lernen
> Heute lerne ich schweigen
> Morgen höre ich
> zu lernen auf.[25]

As an 'engagierter Dichter' Fried exists in the political arena, cutting through the Gordian knot of linguistic complexities, and revealing the identity of repressive politics and traditional patterns of speech. His work is dominated by the same two concepts that so preoccupied the other writers of this section, 'Angst' and 'Zweifel', fear and doubt. Fried's poem of that name is an effective assessment of their common cause:

Zweifle nicht
an dem
der dir sagt
er hat Angst

aber hab Angst
vor dem
der dir sagt
er kennt keinen Zweifel.[26]

To succeed, to move forward, the innovator needs the eye of the sceptic and the faith of the committed. The discomfiture of fear, the anxiety that forces the individual forward is set against the complacency that is the bane of social and political life. Positive, questioning doubt forces each individual to ask questions; it is implicit in Fried's work that those who do so have declared themselves at odds with the *status quo* and the political and social conservatism it represents. As such he welcomes the dissenting adult into his camp, for only with scepticism is there any prospect of a new, alternative and tolerant society in which the individual may once again be himself and live at one with the world about him.

NOTES

1. Hugo von Hofmannsthal, *Ein Brief*, 1902.
2. 'In spite of everything, however, language survived. But it had to live through its own inability to give answers, through fearful periods of speechlessness and the thousand black moments of words that meant death. Language lived through all this and could find no words to describe what was happening; but it lived through all that went on, and, eventually could surface once more 'enriched' by what it had experienced. This is the language in which I have tried to write my poems, both during those years and after; poems in which I have been speaking in order to get my bearings, in order to discover where I was and where I was supposed to be heading, in order to map out my own reality.'

   Paul Celan, *Ansprache anläßlich der Entgegennahme des Literaturpreises der Freien Hansestadt Bremen.*
   Reproduced in: Paul Celan, *Ausgewählte Gedichte*, edition suhrkamp 262, Frankfurt, 1968, p. 128.
3. 'These laws, both in their terminology and their content, have nothing in common with the sound tradition of German law; in fact they are much closer to those of Roland Freisler, the notorious president of

Hitler's People's Court.'

Erich Fried, *So kam ich unter die Deutschen*, Hamburg, 1977, p. 111.

4. 'To kneel down at the confessional of language'. The phrase is by Weinheber.
5. 'The world is strange enough. I think we all tend to distance ourselves from what we see but I do not do it purposely, it is just that sometimes I feel I have no alternative but to distance myself consciously and deliberately from what I see. It is something that comes quite naturally to me.'

Taken from a conversation between Christina Busta and Viktor Suchy, held on tape in the *Dokumentationsstelle für neure österreichische Literatur*. Ref. 199 A1, dated June 24 1968.

6. 'Sometimes I feel the urge not to say 'I' so much, although I find it well-nigh impossible to use any other form.' ibid.
7. 'Love perpetuates all creatures, for God's sake, say you.' ibid. This is a question from 'Unverlangter Text für einen Reiseprojekt'. From the collection *Salzgärten*, Salzburg, 1975.
8. 'Do not ask what pierces the night, for it is my night, and mine the great peacock's cry and at its centre the tongue which carries the message that is meant for me alone.'

Christine Lavant, 'Fragt nicht, was die Nacht durchschneidet', quoted in: *Zwischenbilanz*, ed. W. Weiss and S. Schmid, Salzburg, 1976, p. 189.

9. 'Be suspicious of yourselves! We must be suspicious of ourselves. . . . Let us put our trust in the God who is in everyone we meet and distrust the serpent in our own hearts! We must be wary of ourselves so that we may show ourselves more worthy of the confidence that is placed in us.'
Ilse Aichinger, 'Aufruf zum Mißtrauen,' *Der Plan*, 1946, p. 588.

10. 'The limits of my language signify the limits of my world.'
11. 'My language and I no longer speak to one another, we have nothing to say.'

Ilse Aichinger, *Meine Sprache und Ich*, reproduced in: Ilse Aichinger, *Dialoge, Erzählungen, Gedichte*, Reclam 7939, Stuttgart, 1971, pp. 3–6. This extract p. 4.

12. 'She followed me reluctantly, but has refused to go any further than here. We could just as easily be customs officials.' ibid. p. 5.
13. 'My language is what they find suspicious, not me.! ibid. p. 5.
14. 'Merely talking will help her, conversations about her, comments which are repeated over and over. Gradually no-one will worry about her any more. And I will play my part – I'll put in a word or two here and there so that she doesn't arouse suspicion any more.' ibid. p. 6.
15. 'No-one can make me produce links if they can be avoided. I have a choice unlike life, for which I cannot find a better description at the moment. So, let us call it *Life*, perhaps it doesn't deserve anything better. There is nothing special about the world *Life*, nor *dying* for that matter. Both can be accused of concealing rather than defining, and I think I know why. To define something is tantamount to undermining it and makes it impossible to grasp one's dreams.'

Ilse Aichinger, *Schlechte Wörter*, Frankfurt, 1976, p. 8.

16. 'Lip knew. Lip knows.
    Lip says nothing – and it is over.'
    Paul Celan, *In Mundhöhe*.

17. 'under a panoply of stars which are of man's making.'
    Paul Celan, *Ausgewählte Gedichte*, p. 129.

18. 'the strong tendency to be rendered speechless'.
    Paul Celan, *Der Meridian*, (Speech delivered on receipt of the Georg Büchner Prize), quoted in *Ausgewählte Gedichte* pp. 133–48. This extract p. 143.

19. 'an *I of silences* reduced to silence'.
    Ingeborg Bachmann, *Das dreißigste Jahr*, in: *Werke*, Munich, 1978, vol. 2, p. 102.

20. 'He would have gladly returned with a new language, one which would have been capable of conveying the secret he had learned.'
    Bachmann, ibid. p. 108.

21. 'I came across thoughts, unexpectedly, much as you encounter mines, of such explosive power that I ought to have been frightened into going back, but I went on with no thought for the dangers involved. . . . All at once I saw myself in different circumstances, I saw myself and this child which, at a predetermined time, early or mid-November, would in its turn begin its life just as I had and just as everyone else had before me.'
    Bachmann, *Alles, Werke*, vol. 2, p. 139.

22. 'It is all a question of language and not merely this one German language which was created with all the others in Babel in order to confuse the world. Under the surface another language is smouldering, a language which extends as far as gestures and looks, the unravelling of thoughts and the course of feelings, and it is this language which contains all our misfortune. It all came down to the same question, could I protect the child from our language, until it had established a new one and could usher in a new era.'
    Bachmann, ibid. p. 143.

23. 'I had been born again, but he had not! It was I who was the new Adam and I had wasted my chance and done nothing.'
    Bachmann, ibid. p. 149.

24. 'Only those who write poetry know that, those stubborn campaigners for the protection of wild birds in a world that will soon be whole again!'.
    Erich Fried, *100 Gedichte ohne Vaterland*, Berlin, 1978. [This volume was published simultaneously in English by John Calder. The poems were translated into English by Stuart Hood.] This extract p. 58.

25. 'Yesterday I began to learn to speak, today I am learning to be silent, tomorrow I shall stop learning'.
    ibid. p. 68.

26. 'You need not doubt a person who tells you he is afraid – but watch out for the person who tells you he has no doubts'.
    ibid. p. 89.

Paul Celan and
the Metaphorical Poets

Rex Last

It is more than a little misleading to write in terms of the 'metaphorical poets', as if they were either a tightly-knit group or even as a looser association of writers like the Gruppe 47; the term is, however, little more than a generalization which seeks to describe (with moderate success) one particular direction which Austrian literature, and poetry especially, has taken since the Second World War.

What links the four most important names associated with metaphorical poetry is a preoccupation with language as a paradoxical phenomenon; as both the means of communication and at the same time a limitation on the possibilities of communication itself. It has also been pointed out more than once – and rather tritely – that three of the principal metaphorical poets are poetesses; but there is nothing particularly 'feminine' about their poetry, nor should one express surprise that the conditions of contemporary society are at last permitting the creative powers of the distaff side to assume their proper place in the cultural scene.

The least substantial of the poets to be considered here is Christine Busta, but she, too, is preoccupied with reaching out to and beyond the limits of language. In the course of her speech of thanks on her receipt of the Austrian State Prize of 1969, she underlined that it was the function of the creative artist to grasp what she termed 'the unheard, which strives to become audible in the loving and suffering encounter between spirit and matter'. This does not, however, signify that we are about to confront the intense religious doubts and tortured self-questionings which we shall encounter in the works of Christine Lavant; on the contrary, Busta is confident in her Catholic faith, which is one of the strongest pillars of the Austrian cultural tradition. And in many respects, her poetry can be regarded as an act of Christian witness.

Her verses have more than a suggestion of the old-fashioned about them, and this is largely conditioned by her predilection for traditional, much-exploited metaphors in an endeavour to infuse new life into them and express her untypically positive view of the world – the natural world, that is: civilization and its ills are the object of her criticism. The poem 'Vögel' (Birds) from the collection *Lampe und Delphin* (Lamp and Dolphin) demonstrates her skill in handling metaphor:

Deine Augen sind Vögel in schattigen Nestern.
Als ich die Rinde des Baumes berührte,
flogen sie auf und mir zu.

Nun wohnen sie mir im Herzen.
Tief im glühenden Laub meines Mittags.
Schlaf und Gehör ist nun mein Leben
allen geheimsten Vogelliedern.[1]

These lines demonstrate that, for Busta as for all of these poets, the metaphor is not merely an associative technical device; it acquires in their hands a separate identity and significance which permit it to assume an entirely new linguistic rôle: the 'eyes' of the poem just cited are not 'real' eyes, nor is the natural setting that of the 'real' external physical world. The 'eyes', 'birds', and the rest are, rather, metaphorical neologisms which seek to encode the surreal and inner world of the spirit through the medium of familiar, but inevitably inadequate, words. To stand a phrase on its head, the metaphorical poets are seeking to pour old wine into new bottles; and it is the observation of their attempts to achieve an impossible communicative goal which lends their poetry its difficulty and renders it so fascinating to the reader (particularly one who recognizes the strong links with the French Symbolist poets).

Busta's metaphorical world, dominated as it is by concepts denoting the things of nature, has been rather glibly related back to Stifter's 'sanftes Gesetz' (gentle law) of nature; but this fails to take into account the less positive, more searching tone of her more recent work, as the very title of her latest collection, *Salzgärten* (Saltings), indicates. Here she reveals her compassion for the sufferings that form an inevitable part of life:

und es bleibt uns allein der Schmerz, der immer, immer
in uns forttönt bis zum letzten Stern.[2]

Despite this, even in the collection's title poem the pain is mellowed both by the brilliance of the metaphorical encapsulation of her positive faith, and by the very faith itself that hope of renewal should never be allowed to fade, even in the most unlikely of circumstances:

> Über vertrocknenden
> Wasserbeeten
> blüht unsichtbar
> die Phönixblume
> aus der weißen
> Asche der See.[3]

By contrast, the metaphorical realms inhabited by Christine Lavant are infused with a real sense of personal and private suffering: when she writes of a 'Botschaft des Elends' (message of wretchedness), it is to her own misery that she is referring in her intense and autobiographical verses. Her antithetical explorations of self-accusation and of personal guilt (which have been irrelevantly dubbed 'Baroque' simply because they *are* antithetical) are constantly ploughing the same furrow, and this leads to a measure of monotony in her work.

Here the salt is of tears almost corroding the eyes which, in their turn, are not the doorway to a magic inner world but to a private hell of suffering:

> Brich nur weiter das gelobte Brot!
> Es ist durch und durch schon angesäuert
> von dem Salz, das meine Augen scheuert
> und die Schale anzufüllen droht.[4]

The 'bowl' to which reference is made is the beggar's bowl ('Bettlerschale') of the collection's title, the empty bowl of the anguished individual seeking in vain for a response and for human contact. Whereas Busta finds positive renewal, for Lavant there is only the prospect of continued suffering. The opening poem of the collection *Der Pfauenschrei* speaks of continuing night, of unending suffering, and of a 'Botschaft' (message) designed solely for herself.

Selbst wenn morgen dann die Sonne
ganz erschöpft und fast verwachsen
mit der Fegefeuerknospe
rasten will, wird sie vertrieben –
denn es ist ja meine Knospe
auf dem Rücken meines Steines
und für meine nächste Nacht.[5]

Of the trio of lady metaphorical poets, Ingeborg Bachmann has proven the most successful as well as the most substantial. She, too, concentrates on the limits of our understanding; in a speech of thanks to one of the many important literary prizes she received in her lifetime, she spoke in these terms of the function of the poet: 'We extend our possibilities in the interplay between the impossible and the possible.' And it is this endeavour to extend the range of human awareness and understanding of all facets of human existence that infuses her entire work.

Bachmann stands accused by some of her critics as in many respects a victim of her own success: paradoxically, the argument goes, she may well have branched out into different areas of literary creation had she not been successful in penning attractive and accessible poetry in her first collection *Die gestundete Zeit* (Time deferred) (1953). The source of her popularity is her willingness to confront the prickly issues of the immediate historical past and the uncomfortable facts of the present in unpretentious and powerful language, through which shines a remarkably intelligent and penetrating mind.

That the critical accusation is groundless is amply demonstrated by the inner consistency of her work (which includes poetry, much fêted radio plays, short stories, and a novel, *Malina*, 1971); in all of her writings she pursues the same potentially esoteric and conceptually demanding themes, regardless of the excessive praise she has received in some quarters (notably by the critical fraternity within Austria itself), as well as of the isolated voices in the enemy camp who have inexplicably branded much of her later work as 'kitsch'.

Her educational background, culminating in a dissertation on the critical reception of Martin Heidegger's philosophy of Existentialism, helped to lay the principal foundations for her preoccupation with the nature of reality and the potential for its explication within the limitations of language. If Heidegger is the source of her existential involvement, Bachmann owes her methodological

145

approach to creativity to Wittgenstein, especially in the context of a world-picture comprised of images which cannot aspire to achieving a complete understanding of the truth about the nature of existence, since we are of necessity obliged to operate within the boundaries of that reality, and within the limitations of language; these constraints render us incapable of objectivizing or comprehending the full essence of our existence on this planet.

One immediate consequence that flows from this stance is that, once again, the imagery in her poetry should be regarded neither as illustrations nor as ornamentation, but rather as interrelating elements in a complex totality operating on the outer boundaries of meaning. To cite Wittgenstein, as has Bachmann: 'The limits of my language signify the limits of my world.'

Departure and flight are key themes in her poetry, and parallel the iterative processes noted in the case of Busta and Lavant. Her symbolic journey is an exploration of the relationship between the self and the world beyond the self, through the imperfect medium of language. The exploration is not one which offers a prospect of a positive outcome:

> Ärmlich brennt das Licht der Lupinen.
> Dein Blick spürt im Nebel:
> die auf Widerruf gestundete Zeit
> wird sichtbar am Horizont.
> . . .
> Lösch die Lupinen!
>
> Es kommen härtere Tage.[6]

Her searchings, replete with references to ships and the sea, to autumn and to the lonely and disoriented wanderer, reveal that individual existence may indeed have no ultimate significance, but despite that what we create out of our existence may indeed live on:

> Nur Sinken um uns von Gestirnen. Abglanz und Schweigen.
> Doch das Lied überm Staub danach
> wird uns übersteigen.[7]

But the figure who towers above all the other metaphorical poets is that of Paul Celan, born under the name of Antschel, a Rumanian Jew best known for one single much-anthologized poem 'Todesfuge' (Fugue of Death), which, as has frequently been pointed out, is somewhat untypical of his work at large, in that it is rhythmical, fluent and relatively accessible: image succeeds image in bold and fluent patterns which contrast strikingly with the sparse and almost inscrutable verses of the more mature Celan. In one very significant respect, however, 'Todesfuge' is typical of Celan; namely, in its obsessive preoccupation with the Jewish race and its persecution throughout the ages.

Celan's parents were interned in a concentration camp, where they met their deaths; but although Celan himself managed to escape, the experiences of the war left an indelible scar on him and constitute one of the dominant themes of his poetry, which also owes a great deal to the rich variety of cultural traditions to which Celan was exposed by virtue of his origins and the situations into which fate brought him. As Prawer aptly expresses it:

> Out of his experience of exile and horror, out of his wanderings in German, Jewish, Slav and French cultural and ethnic regions, Paul Celan has managed to fashion a German poetry whose compelling force has been acknowledged even by those who are most disturbed by its occasional preciosity and its sometimes all-too-wilful obscurity.[8]

It is this compelling force, this obsessiveness which communicates itself irresistibly to the reader, even though the meaning may remain elusive to the point of inscrutability.

His first important book of poems, *Mohn und Gedächtnis* (Poppy and Memory), appeared in 1952; as its title suggests, it is preoccupied with the painful past and with an attempt to come to terms with it. Celan is concerned with his own past experiences, and too with a sense of guilt about what happened to his parents; but he reaches out far beyond his personal sufferings to consider the fate of the Jews under National Socialism and, too, the broader issue of the relationship between Judaism and Christianity. The incantatory tone of the collection is established in the opening poem, 'Ein Lied in der Wüste' (A Song in the Wilderness):

> Denn tot sind die Engel und blind ward der Herr in der Gegend von Akra,
> und keiner ist, der mir betreue im Schlaf die zur Ruhe hier gingen.[9]

The language is intense and difficult, the associations largely biblical and Jewish, but often of such obscurity that critics are forced to admit defeat and dub them 'surreal'.

The pessimism of this collection is further heightened by the celebrated 'Todesfuge', about which a great deal of critical ink has been spilled. The poem, which concerns the sufferings of the Jews in a Nazi concentration camp, but which some observers regard as partly a love poem, is deliberately couched in a highly stylized mode; it is in essence an attempt – and a highly successful one – to translate into poetic terms the musical form of the fugue. A number of independent images are established and then repeated with variations in order and emphasis up to a climactic point, after which the poem fades away on a dying cadence.

'Todesfuge' also parallels a device from the visual arts: it is a kind of poetic collage, in which graphic images are juxtaposed in a series of 'pictures' without any attempt to fuse them together; in addition, most of the individual images contain their own internal contradictions: the prisoners drink 'black milk'; they are made to dig 'a grave in the sky'; the camp commandant (or one of the guards; his exact identity is not specified) splits into two contradictory people, the gentle lover who writes home and the vicious warder; and the golden-haired representative of German womanhood, Margarete, is set against the ashen-haired Sulamith. Only at the climactic point of the poem is there an end-rhyme, stressing both the inevitability of death and destruction, and also the key significance of colours to the poem:

> der Tod ist ein Meister aus Deutschland sein Auge ist blau
> er trifft dich mit bleierner Kugel er trifft dich genau[10]

Only when the colours refer to the Germans are they used in their normal application: blue eyes, golden hair, leaden bullet – the references to colour in the context of the Jews are, however, distorted: black milk, and ashen hair for Sulamith. These two latter are also distorted biblical borrowings: milk is a symbol for purity in the Old Testament and Shulamite is raven-haired. Beyond this, the whole poem represents a negation of the promises of the Lord to the people of Israel. Not least among the bitterly distorted images is that of the smoke of the crematorium chimney rising into the sky like incense; instead of the Jews sacrificing to their God and the

148

sweet smoke ascending like a prayer, they themselves are victims on the altar of the Third Reich.

This incantatory, hypnotic fugue of death is one of the pinnacles of twentieth-century German poetry, and as such has, not surprisingly, attracted an excess of exegetic endeavour; but it is not the precise meaning of the less obvious images that hold the key to the poem (the snakes, for example, with which the commandant 'plays'), but rather the overall impact of repetition and variation with its unusual rhythmical patterns and bleak message to the victims of oppression.

Towards the end of *Mohn und Gedächtnis*, there is a suggestion that Celan is beginning to move away from the intense bleakness of 'Todesfuge'; and this incipient optimism moves cautiously forward in his next collection, appropriately entitled *Von Schwelle zu Schwelle* (From Threshold to Threshold; 1955), although it is clear that his starting point is such that he has no choice but to take a positive direction:

> Nun aber schrumpft der Ort, wo du stehst:
> Wohin jetzt, Schattenentblößter, wohin?
> Steige. Taste empor.
> Dünner wirst du, unkenntlicher, feiner!
> Feiner: ein Faden,
> an dem er herabwill, der Stern:
> um unten zu schwimmen, unten,
> wo er sich schimmern sieht: in der Dünung
> wandernder Worte.[11]

The lines grope their way towards a dimly-seen awareness of the possibility of attaining a new synthesis, of being able to command the all-embracing but extremely elusive forces of language in order to reflect the infinite. Equally, they indicate a shift in emphasis away from personal issues into the direction of recognizing his broader mission as a poet.

But his message, as the lines just quoted will readily demonstrate, is far from unambiguous, since what he is trying to grasp and convey is so complex, remote, and far beyond the confines of rationalistic thought patterns. His poetry, in essence, operates on the brink of silence, on the outer limits of significance. In 'Stimmen' (Voices), the first poem of his most celebrated collection *Sprachgitter* (The Grid of Language; 1959), half-perceived voices speak of the Jewish past, of death, and finally no voice speaks of a suffering that will never cease.

The imagery is compressed and oblique, the language sparse and unwilling to yield up its secrets:

> *Stimmen* vom Nesselweg her:
>
> Komm auf den Händen zu uns.
> Wer mit der Lampe allein ist,
> hat nur die Hand, draus zu lesen.[12]

Here the voices speak of the *via dolorosa* of Jewry, of the nettle-grown path which has marked the hands of all those who have passed along it and who now, in solitary bereavement and anguish, cast their eyes on the scars and can yet feel the searing pain which derives not only from the specific sufferings of individuals in the concentration camps, but also from the centuries of persecution which have burdened the Jews since the death of Christ.

Not surprisingly, the motif of the tear appears time and again, in the first instance as a recollection of Jewish guilt in the voice of Jacob:

> Die Tränen.
> Die Tränen im Bruderaug.
> Eine blieb hängen, wuchs.
> Wir wohnen darin.[13]

The theme of guilt is carried through to a stanza which deals with the voices in the Ark, and to those outside, sinking, doomed to perish in the Flood for their sins. Ultimately, there is no voice to speak, only the resinous secretion of a plant, oozing 'large as an eye' its own unending grief:

> ein
> Fruchtblatt, augengroß, tief
> geritzt; es
> hängt, will nicht
> vernarben.[14]

These key themes of the tear-brimming eye and of silence are also central to an understanding of the title poem of the collection:

150

> Iris, Schwimmerin, traumlos und trüb:
> der Himmel, herzgrau, muß nah sein.
> . . .
> Die Fliesen. Darauf,
> dicht beieinander, die beiden
> herzgrauen Lachen:
> zwei
> Mundvoll Schweigen.[15]

The eye's search for heaven fails, dimmed with tears, and ends downcast, making two pools of water, two mouthfuls of silence. In its endeavours to attain a measure of comprehension of the world beyond the self, the eye had tried to penetrate through the 'bars' of its lashes (a not untypical juxtaposition of a round shape and a straight line in Celan's poetry); but, in a refutation of Gottfried Benn's confident view of the power of the word, Celan takes over his notion of 'Gitter' (grid) and transposes it to the eye which peers out into the world, employing the cilia of its lid (again the image is Benn's) as sensory organs. However, all that transpires is greyness and silence; there is no flash of illumination, no insight into the self or the world beyond, as lines from the poem that comes after 'Sprachgitter' obsessively underline:

> Augen weltblind,
> Augen im Sterbegeklüft,
> Augen Augen.[16]

This immensely difficult and painstaking search characterizes the whole of *Sprachgitter*, as the title of the collection, with its ramifying and ambiguous sweep of connotations, implies. It has been variously interpreted in terms of the two-way flow of significances through the grid of language (rather like Bachmann's concept of language) which both filters and inhibits the flow of concepts and their expression; or as the grille through which the members of a closed order communicate with the outside world (a kind of parallel to Rilke's 'schmale Leier', narrow lyre); and it has also been accorded a variety of more exotic and less plausible connotations.

In his next collection, *Die Niemandsrose* (Nobody's Rose), Celan concentrates his attention once again on Judaism. It is no coincidence that the volume is dedicated to the Russian Jewish poet Osip

151

Mandelstam. Once again, the title – as happens so frequently with Celan – contains an inner contradiction, the nature of which becomes clear in the poem 'Psalm', which contains within itself the title of the collection:

> Gelobt seist du, Niemand.
> Dir zulieb wollen
> wir blühn.
> Dir
> entgegen.[17]

Once more, as these lines demonstrate, negation within a religious frame of reference plays a prominent rôle. The psalm is directed not, as one might reasonably expect, at the God of the Jews, but at 'no one'. Like the rose, man grows and blossoms and fades in the service of a deity who remains unknown to him. The precise significance of the 'no one' – and this should come as no surprise to the Celan reader – is caught up in an inextricable web of complexities. It has been pointed out that, in the Old Testament, the rose is identified with Israel; but now, after all the sufferings of the Jewish people, the rose is no longer God's but nobody's; and it is therefore only appropriate that psalms should now be directed not towards God, but to this no one.

Given such a bleak assessment of the present spiritual condition of the Jews, it is almost inevitable that Celan should return to the concentration camp motifs of 'Todesfuge', and, indeed the collection *Niemandsrose* opens with lines that develop the motif of 'digging' a grave in the sky:

> Sie gruben und hörten nichts mehr;
> wir wurden nicht weise, erfanden kein Lied,
> erdachten sich keinerlei Sprache.
> Sie gruben.
> . . .
> Ich grabe, du gräbst, und es gräbt auch der Wurm,
> und das Singende dort sagt: Sie graben.[18]

Their digging leads to the unearthing of no positive solutions; its meaninglessness as an activity is reflected in the poem's recitation of the present tense of the verb. Meaning has shrunk back into the word, the supposed bearer of significances.

This drift into silence is reflected also in the poem 'Mandorla', which depicts an almond-shaped glory from whose centre the expected figure of Christ is absent. Once again God has vanished, leaving nothing in His place.

Only in the collection *Fadensonnen* (Thread-suns, 1968) are there to be found some strains of optimism, in poems relating to the 1967 Arab-Israeli war; but, in general, Celan's later poetry becomes ever more obscure, lacking in inner unity, a fact which seems to indicate that he has given up all hope of even searching, let alone identifying a goal. And in 1970, Celan drowned in the river Seine. It is presumed that he took his own life.

What characterizes the poetry of all four of these so-called metaphorical poets (who should really, as has been amply made evident, be dubbed 'Neo-Symbolists', if it is felt necessary to affix a label to them) is a search through the inner eye (an image which occurs time and again in their work, as we have seen) for an explication of the nature of existence, for a 'someone' or 'something' beyond the apparent emptiness and meaninglessness of life. In more general poetic terms, they have done a notable service to contemporary poetry by demonstrating that the way forward for poetry as a means of literary expression does not necessarily lie through the abandonment of traditional lyrical forms and modes of expression, even though our contemporary perception and awareness of the nature of reality has been so radically transformed.

NOTES

1. 'Your eyes are birds in shady nests.
   When I touched the tree's bark
   they flew up and towards me.

   Now they dwell in my heart.
   Deep in the glowing foliage of my noon.
   Sleep and hearing my life is now
   to all the most secret songs of birds.'

   Lampe und Delphin, p. 15
2. 'and all that remains for us is the pain, which ever, ever resounds on within us until the last star.'

   Salzgärten, p. 35
3. 'Over the drying
   water beds

blooms invisible
the phoenix flower
out of the white
ash of the sea.'

Salzgärten, p. 83

4. 'Just break on the promised bread!
It is soured through and through
from the salt, which scoured my eyes
and threatens to fill the bowl.'

Die Betterlerschale, p. 5

5. 'Even when in the morning now the sun
quite exhausted and almost over grown
seeks to rest with the purgatorial
bud, it is driven away –
for you see it is my bud
on the back of my stone
and for my next night.'

Der Pfauenschrei, p. 5

6. 'Wretchedly burns the lupins' light.
Your gaze detects in the mist:
Time deferred for recantation
appears on the horizon.

. . .

Put out the lupins!
Harder days are coming.'

Die gestundete Zeit, (Werke, I p. 37)

7 'Only the sinking of stars about us. Fading glow and silence.
But the song of the dust to come
will be too much for us.'

Anrufung des großen Bären, (Werke, I. p. 147)

8. 'Paul Celan', in B Keith-Smith (ed.), *Essays on Contemporary German Literature*, London, 1966, p. 162.

9 'For dead are the angels and blind became the Lord in the regions of Akra,
and none there is to watch over for me, in sleep, those who went to rest there.'

Mohn und Gedächtnis, p. 7

10. 'Death is a master from Germany his eye is blue
he strikes you with the lead ball he strikes you true'

Mohn und Gedächtnis, p. 38

11. 'But now the place where you stand is shrinking:
Where to now, man shorn of shadow, where?
Climb. Grope upwards.
You become thinner, less recognisable, finer!
Finer: a thread
down which the star seeks to come:
to swim down below, down below,
where it can see itself shimmering: in the swell of wandering words.'

Von Schwelle zu Schwelle, p. 59

154

12. '*Voices* from the nettle path this way:

Come on your hands to us.
He who is alone with the lamp,
only has his hand to read from it.'

Sprachgitter, p. 7

13. 'Tears.
Tears in a brother's eye.
One stayed suspended, grew.
We dwell within it.'

Sprachgitter, p. 8

14. 'a
Carpel, large as an eye, deeply
fissured; it
hangs there and will not
scar.'

Sprachgitter, p. 9

15. 'Iris, swimmer, dreamless and clouded:
the sky, heart-grey, must be near.
. . .
The flagstones. On them,
close together, the two
heart-grey pools:
two
mouthfuls of silence.'

Sprachgitter, p. 28

16. 'Eyes, world-blind,
eyes in the abyss of death,
eyes eyes.'

Sprachgitter, p. 29

17. 'Praised be thou, No one.
For thy sake
we will bloom.
Towards
you.'

Die Niemandsrose, p. 23

18. 'They dug and heard nothing more;
they did not become wise, discovered no song,
thought out no language for themselves.
They dug.
. . .
I dig, thou diggest, and the worm digs too,
and the singing there says: They dug.'

Die Niemandsrose, p. 9

Ilse Aichinger:
The Sceptical Narrator

Hans Wolfschütz

Ilse Aichinger has won many literary prizes and gained numerous distinctions, she has enjoyed considerable enlightened critical attention and yet, for all that, she still stands on the sidelines of the contemporary literary scene in the German-speaking sphere. She contributed much in the immediate post-war years in the struggle to re-establish a literature worthy of that name but even so she took no part in the ensuing 'literary miracle'. Her role was that of a pathfinder, marking out a course which many of the younger Austrian writers were to tread with considerable success, but in any consideration of the Austrian pre-eminence in the literary world of the 1960s and 1970s her name scarcely merits more than the occasional mention. There is nothing spectacular or eye-catching about Aichinger's life and work; she has made her home in a village on the Austrian-Bavarian border, where, since the death of her husband Günter Eich, she leads a life of seclusion. Her writing is equally concerned with withdrawal and solitude, and may be said to have a frontier of its own, living an uncomfortable existence at the boundaries of the expressible world. Nonetheless there is none of the mystifying aura in her life which surrounds the defensive existences of Thomas Bernhard or Peter Handke and their associated scandals and rumours. Aichinger's literature is devoid of all direct, tangible relation to recognizable reality and free of fashionable attitudinizing; her work is too difficult and too inaccessible for it ever to become a proving-ground for the making and unmaking of critical reputations in the popular field; it places too many unexpected demands on the reader for her ever to reach a wide public. Even now, some thirty years after the publication of her first work, the novel *Die größere Hoffnung* (The Greater Hope, 1948), Aichinger is something of an unknown quantity in the contemporary literary scene and is likely to remain such.

Aichinger's original choice of profession, medicine, was closed to her during the Third Reich as a half-Jewess and when in 1945 she could begin to study, she found it impossible to continue. Her original desire to help and heal others was overwhelmed by the sheer weight of her own personal experiences of persecution and alienation and the need to come to terms with her memories and find her own salvation. So, like so many other Austrian writers, she turned to creative writing as a means of self-help and personal rehabilitation in the face of a hostile, threatening environment. Her early experiences – the destruction of middle-class values and a sense of security and her life as a 'racially-impure' outcast – can be seen in all her work. While she has clearly distanced herself from the autobiographical elements so near the surface in *Die größere Hoffnung*, certain basic situations – threat, retreat and above all self-restriction in isolation – are common to all her works, and give her literary *oeuvre* an unmistakable unity and perspective.

The 'Sicht der Entfremdung'[1], the alienated vision, so characteristic of Aichinger, has its roots in a deep-seated scepticism and suspicion of all that is familiar and customary, and it is scarcely by chance that her first literary publication should bear the title *Aufruf zum Mißtrauen*. This quasi-manifesto of 1946 derives its *engagement* and its note of impassioned pleading from the author's early disillusion at the developments in the world about her. Aichinger shared the concern of so many of her colleagues at the growing tendency in society to dispense with self-criticism and to push the memories of the perils and torments of the recent past to one side in an unseemly haste to return to the well-worn tracks of security and familiarity. Her aims, expressed not only here in this appeal, but in her work as a whole, were to counter this tendency:

Und wir beruhigen uns wieder. Aber wir sollen uns nicht beruhigen![2]

Her demand for critical alertness derives from her belief that the outer liberation of 1945 has failed to achieve a return to truth which, for her, is above all evident in the dilemma of the individual tentatively seeking his own role after the horrors of collective ideology. The threat which Aichinger knows is more than a purely external, historically- and politically-definable phenomenon in the third person; she regards the catastrophic events of the twentieth century as a catastrophe in the first person, a failure to detect what she calls the 'Schlange in unserem Herzen', the serpent in our hearts:

Aber keiner sicherte sich gegen sich selbst. So wuchs die Bestie unbewacht und unbeobachtet durch die Generationen. Wir haben sie erfahren! Wir haben sie erlitten, um uns, an uns und vielleicht auch in uns![3]

The 'frozen, lonely I', so frequently depicted by Borchert and others in the immediate post-war years, can no longer be seen as the ultimate guarantee of an unambiguous confrontation with the world. Indeed, for Aichinger the only way to the secrets of the world lies through self-examination and self-scrutiny; it follows then, that the central thesis of her manifesto is not an appeal for the re-evaluation of social and political conditions but for critical introspection:

Sich selbst müssen Sie mißtrauen! Ja? Haben Sie richtig verstanden? Uns selbst müssen wir mißtrauen! Der Klarheit unserer Absichten, der Tiefe unserer Gedanken, der Güte unserer Taten! Unserer eigenen Wahrhaftigkeit müssen wir mißtrauen! Schwingt nicht schon wieder Lüge darin? Ist sie nicht gläsern vor Lieblosigkeit? Unserer eigenen Liebe! Ist sie nicht angefault von Selbstsucht? Unserer eigenen Ehre! Ist sie nicht brüchig vor Hochmut?[4]

Aichinger's exhortations that we should discover the alien element in ourselves, that we should turn back from the securities and certainties of the world we know and peer into the abyss of our own existence should not be interpreted as the expression of some psychological curiosity that has become the means to its own end; the descent she propounds with all its torments and self-dissections has more mythical and religious connotations – it is the way of suffering and despair whose goal is the hope of a new and more meaningful relationship with reality:

Die glauben zu sein, sind nicht. Nur die zweifeln an sich, dürfen landen, nur die gelitten haben . . .[5]

The mystic vision of a definite 'landing', set as it is in direct contrast to the awareness of the loss of reality, characterizes Aichinger's writing from the onset. Her work is teleological, though, with the exception of the early works, the goal so full of hope becomes ever more distant without actually disappearing. Aichinger is increasingly dominated by a restless quest that shows an ever-growing preoccupation with its own searching and which recognizes creative exploration as an activity that is both dangerous and highly problematic.

Thus the confrontation with the self is not least a confrontation with language as the medium of one's veracity. For Aichinger, as with so many other authors of her generation, this was a direct result of her experiences of the wilful abuse and degradation to which National Socialists had exposed her mother tongue:

> Der Sinn war schon immer in Gefahr gewesen, nun aber drohte er zu ertrinken, und die Wörter blieben wie kleine verlassene Häuser steil und steif und sinnlos zu beiden Seiten des roten Flusses.[6]

But where others, for example Wolfgang Borchert, attempt to reclaim these dead ruins by means of an everyday language that has been stripped of all flourishes and decorations and so by-pass the need for a critical reflection of language, Aichinger chooses a heightened form of linguistic alienation; the only alternative as she sees it would be total silence, a 'solution' she rejects most strongly in *Die größere Hoffnung*. Here, the old man who so vehemently turns on the group of Jewish children who have decided not to use German any more, must be seen as speaking for Aichinger herself. He tells the children not to forget German but to re-learn it:

> Und ihr wollt das Deutsche verlernen? Ich helfe euch nicht dazu. Aber ich helfe euch, es neu zu erlernen, vorsichtig, behutsam, wie man ein Licht anzündet in einem dunklen Haus . . .[7]

Language can only be re-lit after it has been dimmed, it must first be hermetically sealed off from the false brightness with which it is surrounded. Only after the empty shells of words have been cleansed of their direct objective correlations and the corruption of their pragmatic meaning can they gain a new and deeper significance in the subjectivity of poetic formulation:

> Vielleicht sehe ich meine Aufgabe als Autorin überhaupt darin, die Sprache von ihrem Mitteilungscharakter zu befreien und wieder zu sich selbst zu bringen: so, daß sie wieder mitteilen kann.[8]

Aichinger's poetic application of language in which she frees herself from the need to copy and turns instead to a bold, often unexpected sequence of metaphors stands in direct contrast to the meagre, grammatically and stylistically compacted neo-realism which is so characteristic a feature of the immediate post-war era in West Germany. Her sense of alienation either dissolves all recognizable social reference or, as in her later work, chooses not to seek any such reference at all.

Aichinger's emphasis on the inner rather than the outer world is particularly evident in her treatment of historical time in the one work which has a clear relationship with the world of facts and figures. *Die größere Hoffnung*, her only novel to date, is set in Vienna in the last days of National Socialism and has as its background the horrors of war and the persecution of Jews. For Aichinger, however, it is not the time itself that is important but the reactions to the threats which this era posed. Thus she concentrates her attention on the restricted world of the experiences undergone by the girl Ellen, whose young mind transforms reality into a series of phantastic and nightmarish visions of horror. There is no description of reality; story-line and epic breath are replaced in this most 'unnovelistic' novel by a lyrical flow, by an associative sequence of variable metaphors ranging from original and paradoxical coinings of striking poetic intensity to some trite expressionistic borrowings. The result is a dream-like world in which inanimate objects come to life and human beings are reduced to impersonal horror-figures.

Aichinger has turned a political phenomenon into a natural sequence whose guiding stars are threat and suffering; she does not refer to the National Socialists by name, but like Alfred Andersch in his novel *Sansibar oder der letzte Grund* (Sansibar, or the Final Reason, 1952) she calls them merely 'the others', reducing them to a hostile, faceless mass. The Nazis appear as a manifestation of evil as such, taking their place on the 'street of guilt' which has been man's lot since his expulsion from Paradise. The events of this novel are universal and ubiquitous; they take place 'zu keiner Stunde' – 'in no time' (this is the title of a later collection of Aichinger's dialogues). *Die Größere Hoffnung* must be reckoned one of the earliest attempts to come to terms with the Nazi past but with a particularly Austrian flavour: analysis of historical reality has been superseded by poetic transfiguration.

The novel is given its unity by the theme of existential transformation which holds the flood of images together and gives them

160

purpose. The ten loosely-linked chapters each present variations on a common event: the collapse of an illusory security and headlong fall into the 'Grauen der Verlassenheit', the horror of abandonment, the death-filled consciousness of reality. Each chapter marks a staging-post in the martyrdom of the half-Jew Ellen as she progresses from her illusory 'great hope' to the 'greater hope' which will at the same time mark her death.

The novel begins with Ellen's attempt to escape Nazi persecution by joining her Jewish mother in the freedom of the United States. This is the only direct link in the whole work between freedom and its realization in a social and political context, but for Aichinger it represents a flight avoiding confrontation with the self, with fear or with suffering, and the Statue of Liberty paradoxically becomes a symbol of an unreal, romantic freedom, a 'blue' vision not unlike the dream of 'Sansibar' in Andersch's novel. Ellen's attempts to emigrate fail and she is forced to leave the dream world of her 'great hope' and to adopt as her creed the advice of the consul who denies her a visa:

Wer sich nicht selbst das Visum gibt, bleibt immer gefangen. Nur wer sich selbst das Visum gibt, wird frei.[9]

However, before Ellen has learnt to appreciate this existentialist concept of freedom herself she must first undergo a series of experiences each of which brings her a stage nearer this goal. She begins by accepting her own state of racial undesirability and joins up with a group of persecuted Jewish children. She believes she has found her identity by voluntarily sewing the Star of David on her clothes and sharing their pilgrimage to death but even this decision, coloured as it is with a mystic longing for death, is no more than an expression of her flight into a 'großes Spiel', a great game, as the title of the central, sixth chapter indicates. Ellen is not allowed on the transport taking her friends to the concentration camp and, rejected yet again, she must face up to the inferno of the adult world on her own. Only now, shorn of the protection of a group and in total isolation can she find her own directives, her 'eigene Vorschriften', only now, as Andersch puts it, can she act 'im eigenen Auftrag', on her own account. So, with a mysterious message of peace she makes her way in the turmoil of battle during the last days of the war to the 'Bridges'. The bridges have been long since blown or mined, and it is a landmine which kills Ellen, but she is able to pass on the message she carries. The 'greater hope', the message which Aichinger gives to her reader, is enshrined in Ellen's journey into herself which gives her a vision of a new future beyond the immediacy of death:

> '. . . die Brücke steht nicht mehr!'
> 'Wir bauen sie neu!'
> 'Wie soll sie heißen?'
> 'Die größere Hoffnung, unsere Hoffnung.'[10]

It is not only in these final words that Aichinger's own doubts contained in *Aufruf zum Mißtrauen* of 1946 seem to be resolved; in fact, all through the novel the reader is able to sense, not least in the beguiling beauty of its language, an undercurrent of consolation which stands in marked contrast to the horrors of the experienced world. As K.H. Kramberg noted on the reissue of the novel, Aichinger

> (macht) aus dem gräßlichsten Massenmord der Geschichte einen quasi sakralen Vollzug. Hinter dem Henker erscheint der Messias, aus dem Hakenkreuz wird das Kruzifix des Erlösers.[11]

If *Die größere Hoffnung* may be said to fail then it is a failure symptomatic of the inability of a young generation of writers after 1945 to cope with the plethora of experiences which bear down on them unmercifully. Their sheer presence produces such helplessness and disorientation that despite frequent professions of a new beginning so many writers found themselves following paths which others had marked out. In Austria in particular, where 1945 had never been considered a tabula rasa, there was a wave of familiarization with and reclamation of the philosophical and literary ideas which had been denied those within the confines of the National Socialist realm. In Aichinger's case this is evident in the existentialist pattern which determines the inner action of the novel in such a way that the author's own experience is almost wholly transcended. It is also evident in her language, but here Aichinger has not only adapted but, with some exceptions, made her own the stylistic features of Expressionism to which she had been drawn.[12] The strength of *Die größere Hoffnung* is, then, to be found more in the subtle linguistic presentation of individual moments and it is not surprising that in her later work Aichinger turned almost exclusively to shorter literary forms. Her efforts to filter out all but the essential, her search for the individual word in her quest that cautiously and circumspectly seeks out a new language is much more suited to short pieces of prose or lyric than to the epic breath of the novel form.

Aichinger's early narrative pieces are for the most part parables; they may not directly proclaim their message and they tend to leave it to the reader to interpret events for himself, but they nonetheless guide him towards a particular solution. *Der Gefesselte* (The Bound Man), perhaps the best known and most conventional of her parables, begins with the 'improbable event' of a man who wakes up one morning to find himself bound and fettered. The parallels to Kafka cannot be ignored; like Kafka in *Die Verwandlung*, Aichinger has translated a metaphorical image of imprisonment into the actual state, but she also reduces the original image by accepting this loss of freedom *a priori* as a precondition which is not even questioned. Kafka leaves his reader to puzzle out for himself what sort of a world it is that can cause such restrictions on the individual, Aichinger does not even consider it a question worth asking. We are given no clue as to the source of these fetters and when they are later cut through by the wife of his employer, a circus-director, this is seen less as an external intervention than as a reflection of a development that has already taken place in the mind of the central character.

Whereas in *Die größere Hoffnung* a hostile, if faceless world at large provided the background for loss of liberty, in *Der Gefesselte* the centre of attention is solely directed towards the amount of 'play' – i.e. the possibility of self-assertion – which the restriction allows. The narrative traces the development of this most unpromethean bound man to his career as a contortionist who spends a glorious summer as the star of a travelling circus and reaches his peak in autumn with a successful contest with a wolf:

In einer Bewegung, die dem Sturz eines großen Vogels glich – und er wußte jetzt sicher, daß Fliegen nur in einer ganz bestimmten Art der Fesselung möglich war –, warf er sich auf ihn und brachte ihn zum Fallen. Wie in einem leichten Rausch fühlte er, daß er die tödliche Überlegenheit der freien Glieder verloren hatte, die Menschen unterliegen läßt.[13]

This intoxicating lightness in which the bound man feels himself the animal's equal represents a moment of transition. He loses the almost divine freedom of movement, (in which there is more than an echo of the grace of Kleist's mechanical puppet), in the very moment in which he no longer regards his fetters as an impediment. When, then, his fetters are cut away against his will and his movements seem to lose all sense of purpose, he can only defend himself against the wolf in a second confrontation with a pistol, and the reader sees the paradox in Aichinger's concept of freedom, a freedom which is only possible in the awareness of imprisonment and by the individual's acceptance of its impenetrable laws.

Such a paradoxical relationship between imprisonment and freedom (or between resignation and mystic visions of redemption) is particularly evident in the narrative piece *Rede unter dem Galgen* which was indeed the original title of Aichinger's first prose collection, published in Austria in 1952. In this narrative a condemned man, pardoned against his will and released from the gallows to return to life, compares his situation to the mysterious connection between the rising and the setting of the sun:

> Schon kriecht die Sonne das Gebälk hinunter und drängt sich zwischen euch und macht sich billig, fällt tief und tiefer, steigt, fällt und will sich wehren, steigt höher und fällt durch ihr eigenes Steigen nur immer tiefer über euch, bis sie am hohen Mittag erst erkennt, daß nur ihr eigener Fall sie wieder aus dem Staub reißt, daß sie erst sinken muß, um über ihre eigenen Schatten den Himmel wieder zu erreichen . . .[14]

There is no possibility of attempting to counter the overwhelming forces which control the movement of the sun, and indeed any such attempt must lead to hopeless defeat. Only when the individual gains true insight, which moment comes with the acceptance of the authority of an order of things that is in itself absurd, can he sense order for himself and the possibility of attaining the unattainable – only then can he 'jump over his own shadow'.

The central figure of this narrative rebels, following the image of the sun, against the order imposed on him – he is a fire-raiser. His moment of recognition, his 'high noon' is the gallows. Here, high above everyone else and face to face with death, he has become someone 'den ihr nicht mehr täuschen könnt', someone proof against all deceptions. And yet, or perhaps because he is aware of the way the world is, the fire-raiser finally conforms to the senselessness of its laws:

164

habt keine Angst, daß ich noch einmal Feuer an eure Ernte lege –
sie wird zu Licht und Asche auch ohne mich! Ich will es ruhig
erwarten.
Ich will den Hafer im Sand der Ebbe säen und in verbrannte
Scheunen ernten, und ich will Burgen bauen, der Flut zum Fraß
. . . ich will den Himmel ernten, der verheißen ist.[15]

In declining all attempts to change things in any way, in his willingness to sit back and wait, the fire-raiser adopts an attitude which in
its religious overtones of forthcoming salvation also recalls the
Austrian tradition of the sublimation of individual aspirations
under the auspices of some higher order. The belief in a unified and
structured world evident in this tradition has, however, given way
in Aichinger's work to a different credo: the certainty of individual
alienation. The fire-raiser in this narrative re-enters life with a
scepticism that strips away the illusion that order is a natural state of
affairs. It is an awareness of the absurd nature of the world that
turns resignation and fatalism into triumphant defiance and transforms self-sacrifice into self-assertion.

This self-assertion is expressed in the narrative form itself. In *Der
Gefesselte* the distance of the epic past tense and the third person
narrative allow for a symbolic pattern of events that has causal-
chronological properties reflecting an inner development; the
action, such as it is, in *Rede unter dem Galgen* and *Spiegelgeschichte*
(Reverse sequence) is contained in the subjective transformations
of a narrator who expresses him- or herself directly in the narrative
present. Things happen to these speakers, and yet the meaning of
these events is not contained in a parable-like interpretation of
external happenings but, on the contrary, in the process of unmasking and revelation of what they indicate. Both of these narratives
take the form of a sceptical address directed against those who
determine the real time-sequence or who claim to recognize it. The
fire-raiser, speaking under the direct shadow of death, consistently
challenges the validity both of his executioner and of the crowd
gathered to watch him hang, and ultimately of the messenger who
brings his reprieve. It is this confrontation with representatives of
the world, and that alone, which enables the narrative 'I' to find its
own essence, to discover life for itself.

The extent to which such 'reverse narrative' represents resistance
and self-assertion may be seen in the structure of *Spiegelgeschichte*.

Aichinger was awarded the Prize of the 'Group 47' in 1952 for this 'story', which is well-nigh guaranteed to wrong-foot any reader used to traditional narrative logic. *Spiegelgeschichte* is an account of the memories of a girl who is about to die, tracing her life from the threshold of the grave to the cradle and her entry into the world. What in traditional terms would be the 'real' action of the story, the dying girl's transition from the onset of her last moments of resistance to her final collapse and death, is constantly brought to the reader's eye through a series of interpolations which interrupt the inner action (the process of memory reaching ever further into the mind), and it is this inner action which provides the focal point of the story. The mirror-like reversal of the normal sequence of cause and effect destroys the 'natural' appearance of a human life and exposes the falsity inherent in that state of psychological acclimatization which passes for 'reality'.

In *Spiegelgeschichte* the narrative 'I' seeks to define itself, however negatively and perversely, by reference to the world of facts and figures, but this is a trait increasingly absent from Aichinger's later texts, whose narrators are no longer placed in the context of 'realistic' events to which they react. The arc of action becomes more and more introspective with little external reference. The narrative which had taken the form of a dialogue or disputation with the laws of the external world has been replaced by a self-contained monologue – a form wholly typical of Aichinger's work of the 1960s.

The author's retreat to a world bound by her own existence is well-shown in the collection *Wo ich wohne* (Where I Live, 1963). The title-story takes as its theme the irreversible chasm that separates the individual from the world about him and the inevitable transition this entails: a movement from dialogue to monologue. Unlike the other narratives of this collection *Wo ich wohne* retains a clear-cut 'plot' of symbolic nature, for the narrator's home sinks storey by storey down into the cellar in a manner reminiscent of the image of the setting sun in *Rede unter dem Galgen*, but without revealing the existence of any laws of a manifestly absurd world or offering the prospect of self-assertive defiance. The mystical overlay of the previous narratives with their message of the 'forlorn hope' which translates descent into ascent is totally lacking. The narrative 'I' has become more circumspect and no longer seeks to emulate the fire-raiser in his desire to 'reap heavens' nor the dying girl who set the vision of a new beginning against her imminent death. The 'I' of this text barely whispers and is much less sure of itself; indeed it only speaks to itself in the knowledge that what is happening concerns itself and no-one else:

> Nebenan höre ich die Atemzüge des Studenten, der bei mir wohnt; er ist Schiffsbaustudent, und er atmet tief und gleichmäßig. Er hat keine Ahnung von dem, was geschehen ist. Er hat keine Ahnung, und ich liege hier wach. Ich frage mich, ob ich ihn morgen fragen werde. Er geht wenig aus, und wahrscheinlich ist er zu Hause gewesen, während ich im Konzert war. Er müßte es wissen. Vielleicht frage ich auch die Aufräumefrau.
>
> Nein. Ich werde es nicht tun. Wie sollte ich denn jemanden fragen, der mich nicht fragt?[16]

If nobody asks any questions there can be neither answer nor explanation. With this realization of the unsuspecting nature and lack of communicative fluency in a world that has become a prisoner of the old-established ways the narrative 'I' cannot even begin to think in terms of protest; it remains transfixed by its own helplessness and vulnerability, finding some fleeting consolation in the fact that up to now the narrower 'world' of its own home has at least stayed the same. But here too things have changed: the windows are now half their original size and offer a much more restricted view, and if the descent should continue, as the narrative 'I' fears, and reach the canal and beyond then even this view will disappear and be shut out.

Most of the other texts of this collection and of the subsequent collection *Eliza Eliza* (1965) place the descent, which in *Wo ich wohne* still retained a link with familiar surroundings, at a point where there are no reassuringly familiar points of reference. The windows of *Wo ich wohne* are turned in *Mein Vater aus Stroh* (My Father's made of Straw) to one small broken pane in a coach-house and in *Die Maus* (The Mouse) they are no more than slits allowing the occasional shafts of light into a narrow room. The narrators, like the mouse are 'undiscoverable' or can only be reached with great difficulty. They always seem to be speaking from the far side of a bridge which they have no intention of crossing (*Mein grüner Esel*, My Green Ass), or from a room which bears all the signs of a hasty departure of old friends:

> Und nun ist niemand mehr hier, und von selbst kann ich mich

nicht umwenden, um zu sehen, ob Hut und Schal noch am Bett-
knauf hängen . . .
So aber liege ich halb aufrecht, die seidenen Kleider verknüllt
unter dem grauen Tuch, und bei offenen Schränken, die Koffer
sind fort. (*Die Puppe*, The Doll)[17]

There is more than a hint of Beckett's foreshortened characters in
these incarcerated narrators with their physical disability and vulnerability (the mouse always evading pursuit, and the readily-
combustible parent), with their inability and reluctance to raise
their eyes beyond their own preoccupations. The 'I' in *Die
Ankunft* (The Arrival), having arrived at a strange place on his journey resolutely declines anything with an idyllic overtone: an invitation to take a walk through the vineyards, to spend some time with
his brother, children laughing (in *Die Maus* Aichinger wrote 'Alles
Gelächter vollzieht sich ohne mich' – 'If people laugh it has nothing
to do with me'). The 'I' shuts himself away in the confines of the
room he has been allocated and allows the few meagre objects to
'direct' his life:

Wie bestürzend, hier zu Hause zu sein, an diesem unbekannten
Ort, und hier das Obst schon lange geerntet zu haben und es wei-
terzuernten, mit Kindern und Kindeskindern, mit Leitern und
Körben.[18]

The revelation of the pure present, the fusion of past and future experience so that there are 'keine anderen Orte mehr', 'no other
places anymore', is described as a disturbing experience; it brings
nothing liberating or relaxing in its manifestations. The narrator is
not one of the carefree tourists who like 'Liedersänger auf den Ter-
rassen . . . für immer bei ihrer Schönheit bleiben, bei den
gedrechselten Himmeln, beim Jubel ihrer Harfen'.[19] Any rejoicing
he does has come from a deep-seated sense of vulnerability and is
half-choked by his realization that his heavens are bearing down on
him:

Wie viele Himmel senken sich heute zu mir herab und nehmen
mir noch einmal den Atem, ehe sie ihn mir lassen . . .[20]

This fear of the final 'breathlessness' is perhaps the most
characteristic element in the lives of the narrators of these texts, for

each has to learn to live without the features and aspects which they had hitherto taken for granted:

> Ich habe meinen Holzfahrschein verloren, wie ich weiterkommen soll, weiß ich nicht.[21]

The 'I' of *Holzfahrscheine* (Wood-tickets) finds himself in a strange region and discovers that all the 'usual' guarantees of protection and safe passage to his idyllic destination (towards the 'fishponds and the shinier chapels') have lost their power – 'das ist jetzt alles dahin'. Now all he has is a sense of disorientation, of uncertainty and, inevitably, a growing fear and anxiety. Nonetheless like the narrators in the other texts he attempts to learn from his experience and rejects the temptations and wishful thinking which suggest the paths and directions that mattered earlier; in fact, he turns his loss into a positive experience:

> mit wenigen Worten: ich werde nicht am Kirchstrand baden. Nichts wird mir lieb und wert werden, nicht einmal eine Gewohnheit, kein Spiel wird für mich spielen. Mein Verlust wird sich als etwas Unerfindliches herausstellen: als etwas, das Findigkeit mir niemals gewährt hätte . . .[22]

It is the same way of sorrow and tribulation which Aichinger's young heroine Ellen trod in *Die größere Hoffnung*, but with a crucial difference. No-one is building bridges any more, nor is there any hope of salvation and redemption in the future. *Holzfahrscheine* ends with what may be called the 'lesser hope' – 'Sehen wir weiter' – 'let's keep on looking'.

The narrator in *Die Maus* is no less ruled by this determination to embrace the unknown, to live with fear and restriction in a place which for him could be a trap or a refuge. The light which penetrates his tiny room and the paces which he hears do suggest that a way out is possible, but the narrator takes pains to ward off all temptations to escape and utterly rejects any attempt to free him from his present situation:

> Fast alles führt zu weit. Bleiben wir deshalb an dem Ort, an dem ich bin . . .[23]

His rejection of the connecting thread to the real world is not, however, a denial of the world at large; all Aichinger's narrators can be seen in the same light as the 'straw-father':

> er hält sich in der Remise, er hält sich auf dem Eis und ist von der Welt nicht abzubringen.[24]

The all-embracing uncertainty of the ice which robs the coach-house of any suggestion that it might be a homely and idyllic refuge from the 'good old times' is, in fact, seen as the pre-condition for a new approach to the world, an approach which may reveal a splinter of reality that is more authentic than the reality that has been lost. It is for this precise reason that the narrator in *Die Maus* has no intention of looking for a way out:

> So bin ich hier und horche, meine Ohren sind scharf und tasten mit dem Holz zugleich die Eisfelder ab, ich kontrolliere nichts, ich bin zugegen. Das ist auch ein Vorteil meiner Lage. Alle anderen kommen leicht in den Verdacht, sie möchten etwas kontrollieren, in die Hand bekommen, sich über etwas setzen. Aber ich nicht. Ich höre das Eis so beteiligt wie unbeteiligt brechen, diese Waage halte ich, solange ich hier bin. Und ich bevorzuge nichts, keine Tummelplätze, keine höhenumstandenen Bäche, keine Schwärmer, ich bin allem gleich gut.[25]

By concentrating on collecting and registering all the sensations which the 'icefield' make on him, he feels he may be able to free the world of all the value-judgements, categories and projections which have weighed it down and to establish a more restricted reality, but one which is less distorted and dissembling than its predecessor. This is not merely a decision to renounce greater knowledge of the world but a disavowal of individual wishes and preferences; it is a conscious attempt not to seek self-knowledge and self-realization:

> ich will keinen Spiegel, keine Glasscheibe und nicht einmal eine finstere Handvoll Wasser, die mir mein Bild zurückwirft. Wer weiß, vielleicht besteht mein Jubel darin, daß ich unauffindbar bin.[26]

The purely meditative, self-oblivious approach to the world allows the narrator to enjoy his modicum of happiness. It is a 'wunschloses Glück', a wish-free happiness, to twist the title of a narrative by

170

Peter Handke.

The narrator of *Mein grüner Esel* does not even begin to conceive the temptations to discover an escape which beset the mouse. He is too distanced from what appears to him as a dead, desolate, decaying world on the other side of the bridge with its shut-down power-station, boarded-up windows and a street which leads in a 'Weltrichtung', a world-direction, 'mit der ich ohnehin nie etwas anfangen konnte'.[27] Even so his eyes (with the mouse it was hearing and feeling) are always on the bridge: but the ass which appears and vanishes on the bridge with equal rapidity is more akin to some mystical vision than to any recognizable reality; the narrator knows as little about where it came from or where it is going as he does about its origins and background. Wallmann regards it as representing 'das ein wenig grotesk anmutende Zeichen für die Realität außerhalb des Realen'[28], a reality which despite its utter lack of any sense of security is nonetheless more genuine than the desolate world that has been left behind. Even so the narrator never intends to achieve a closer relationship with this animal, not from any aversion, but because of his determination not to fall into the 'old mistakes' all over again. Thus he approaches the ass on a purely linguistic level, by means of hypotheses, suppositions and questions all raised by the animal's mysterious appearances. But even this tentative relationship is fragile, for there is no certainty that the ass will appear. It is described as unreliable, having already failed to manifest itself on two occasions, and the narrator is more than a little afraid that one day it will fail to appear altogether. If this were to happen, he would no longer have the 'Luft zum Atem', the air to breathe which the ass's presence guarantees, and being deprived of that he would not even be able to ask himself the questions for which there are no answers.

Thus the threat of 'breathlessness' which on a purely existential level is the result of a deliberate rejection of the normal sources of breath, (the rejection of the 'fresh breezes' which the mouse refuses to allow to reach him), is directly linked to the danger posed by loss of linguistic capacity. As is characteristic of Austrian modernism after the turn of the century the crisis of reality is sensed as a crisis of language. When they lose contact with the world Aichinger's narrators also lose the fluency which allows words to convey objects. The narrative *Meine Sprache und ich* (My Language and I, first published 1968) whose theme is the relationship between language, the 'I' and the world, begins with the recognition that language does not reveal the world to the 'I' but merely encloses it:

> Sie reicht nicht weit. Rund um, rund um mich herum, immer rund um und so fort.[29]

Language is like a room which has been sound-proofed to keep the sound out; it can be both protection to the individual in his refuge, or the wall which keeps a prisoner in his cell, and, while protecting the 'I' from too immediate an intrusion by objects, it also prevents him from gaining contact with the world outside. It is a very similar pattern to that provided by Peter Handke in *Kaspar* which also appeared in 1968, although Handke does not interpret man's linguistic existence as some solipsistic self-incarceration but rather as his enrolment in the ranks of a clearly-defined social order. Whilst Kaspar can only react to the closed order in which he finds himself with a gesture of anarchy, Aichinger still senses a way out – retreat into the private world of the individual himself. Thus she withdraws her language from public commerce and retires into the distance of a remote sphere all her own.

In *Erinnerungen für Samuel Greenberg* (Memories for Samuel Greenberg) Aichinger writes 'Ich war ein Sprößling, eine Form des Geredes' but she concludes this narrative with the words 'Aber es nützt nichts, wir müssen auf Reisen gehen. Wir müssen fort.'[30] In *Meine Sprache und ich* language is presented as a travelling-companion for the narrator on his journey across the frontier of the real world; just over the border (rather like the mouse or the narrator in *Mein grüner Esel* who remain within sight and sound of the world) language and narrator pause for breath:

> Da sitze ich dann mit meiner Sprache, nur drei Meter von denen entfernt, die so reden. Aber wir sind durch, wir haben passiert, wir können uns niederlassen, wenn wir atemlos sind.[31]

As this struggle for breath shows, the journey has not been accomplished without loss and suffering:

> Meine Sprache hatte früher einen lila Schal, aber er ist weg. Ich fürchte, daß wir uns hier die Gesundheit verderben. Wenn meine Sprache die Stimme verliert, hat sie einen Grund mehr, das Gespräch mit mir sein zu lassen.[32]

Any words spoken here at the extremities of the world are uttered under the shadow of imminent speechlessness. All of Aichinger's narrators struggle for breath like the couple in *Alte Liebe* who speak 'mit einem Windstoß um Atem kämpfend'[33]; they wrest a language from the silence about them, a language which follows traditional patterns of grammar but has dispensed with all accepted patterns of meaning. The images which such a language creates clearly refer to something, but it is no longer possible to decipher this 'something' or translate it into rational concepts. Poetic transformation of language was ever a guiding principle in Aichinger's work, and in the narratives of the 1960s and 1970s it seems to have reached its zenith, for the metaphors and symbols of the earlier texts have now acquired a wholly independent existence of their own:

> Es wäre verfehlt, in dieser Sprache nach einem Hintersinn zu fahnden, der sich in Chiffren präsentierte, für die man einen Code ermitteln müßte. Auch wird weder eine geträumte noch eine phantasierte Welt vorgeführt, sondern die Sprache zielt ernstlich und unmittelbar auf Wirklichkeit, allerdings nicht auf eine solche, die sich in ruhender Objektivität und Distanz einem Betrachter gegenüber befindet. Welt ist überhaupt nicht gegeben, ist auf keine Weise feststellbar.[34]

There is no room for logical development in the poetic world which such a language creates. It is a world dominated by the improbable, the incongruous, the fragmentary and by the arbitrary shifts from one set of images to another. Aichinger's later texts have little in common with the traditional short-story narrative form; they are neither parables, since they defy all parabolic meaning, nor are they fairy-tales since they lack the internal logic of fairy-tale events and can by no yardstick be considered fables since they are devoid of the confidence and knowledge which characterizes a didactic approach. The more accessible pieces such as *Die Maus, Die Puppe* or *Mein grüner Esel* do at least offer the reader a chance to find his bearings; despite the absence of some externally identifiable action there are remnants of a fictitious world, some remote location where a voice can be heard speaking. Even so it is a voice which, while clearly identifiable as 'I', cannot be conceived of in human terms.

In the later texts the clearly definable personal perspective has disappeared. Language is no longer linked to a particular psychological awareness and the images exist in their own right and enjoy a purely associative sequence. Such narratives cannot be confined within the concept of the everyday; on the contrary, the reader, denied all chance of referring back to his own world is obliged to move onward into Aichinger's poetic world and free himself from the ice-pack of his compacted linguistic practices by discovering new horizons in himself. Only when he has ceased to be a passive recipient of traditional meanings and has made himself an explorer, a fellow-poet and creator, can he write the stories which the author denies him.

Der Querbalken (The Cross-beam) marks the transition from narrative that retains structured perspectives to a world of imagery that has its own rules and conventions:

> Ich wollte mich auf einem Querbalken niederlassen. Ich wollte wissen, was ein Querbalken ist, aber niemand sagt es mir.[35]

This first-person narrative opens in a manner reminiscent of the earlier texts, not least when the cross-beam is described as an object 'der dem Halt dienen sollte, vielleicht der Rettung'.[36] We seem to learn something of the private existence of this 'I', something of his quest for a safe place which, like the green ass can give him 'air to breathe'. But *Der Querbalken* lacks the possessive attribute of *Mein grüner Esel* or *Mein Vater aus Stroh* and so by the second sentence of the piece the accent has shifted from the 'I' to the object itself; the subjective dilemma gives ground to attempts to define the cross-beam itself. The narrator looks outside his own problems in much the same way as the mouse sought to escape any reflective surface which could pick up its own image: 'Was ist ein Querbalken? Nicht, was ist er mir, sondern, was ist er?'[37] Any search for the real nature of an object is bound to fail when it comes to giving that object a name; it is a process the narrator desperately fears, for it makes him increasingly aware of the unbridgeable gulf between word and object, name and essence. The answers he discovers and records in wide-ranging, complex and often purely intuitive images can only be the 'Ersatzantworten' to which Wolfgang Hildesheimer refers in his analysis of the work.[38] The narrator gains but negative insights and is left at the end of the narrative with the same question with which he began.

Aichinger's most recent narratives were published with some poems and a radio play in a collection with the characteristic title

174

schlechte Wörter (Bad Words, 1976). Almost without exception they are concerned with the question of putting names to aspects of reality and thus follow the pattern set by *Der Querbalken*. The narrative *Flecken* (Spots), for example, discusses a specific phenomenon, although now the unifying first-person perspective is abandoned. The spots in question have appeared on some arm-chairs:

> Wir haben jetzt Flecken auf unseren Sesseln. Es sieht aus, als hätte jemand Milch darüber geschüttet. Diese Flecken sind zu bedenken.[39]

There has been a change, perhaps disturbing or annoying but in any case unexpected, and this change sets in motion a train of thought. The narrative which follows throws up a sequence of assertions, conclusions, hints, hypotheses and questions which interact one with another, which come together and contradict each other. Statements are made and retracted and the result is a linguistic condition of permanent uncertainty, underlaid by a series of interpolated comments which question the very validity and purpose of any attempt to express reality in language:

> Nicht zu bedenken . . . In Worten nicht bildbar . . . Mit niemandem zu erörtern, nicht aufzuschließen . . .[40]

By the end of the narrative the reader has perhaps made some progress towards these spots but he cannot hope to find their true essence by means of words. Language can only bow to their superiority:

> Die Flecken siegen. Sie siegen auch.[41]

If then, as Aichinger writes in the narrative *Schlechte Wörter*, nothing can escape its 'unzutreffenden Umkreis', its inapplicable context, the poet is faced with the crucial decision as to whether there is any point in saying anything; but whenever Aichinger questions the validity of creative writing as she does, for example, in *Wisconsin und Apfelreis* (Wisconsin and Apple pudding) – 'Soll man wieder beginnen, die alten rührseligen Geschichten zu erzählen?'[42] – or, as in *Der Querbalken*, when she explicitly renounces language as a medium – 'Ich will ihn nicht mehr benennen'[43] – she immediately counters this negativism with an impassioned plea to continue despite all, to fight on against the silence of a grotesque death-mask:

> Aber die erzählt ja nichts mehr. Die hat aufgehört . . . Den Mund hat sie auch offen stehen lassen, halb offen, das sieht hirnrissig aus, das darf sie nicht . . . sie soll weiter erzählen . . . zerr sie an den verqueren Strähnen, kneif sie in die Wangen, aber sag ihr, sie soll weiter erzählen. Sie soll weiter erzählen.[44]

Aichinger, in her own modest way, continues with her writing, knowing that the signs she points to may well prove of little help ('unzutreffende Bezeichnungen') and that the words she uses may be inadequate or 'schlecht'. Her hope is that some of her burning scepticism of language may impart itself to the reader and that as a consequence he may come to realize that received patterns of meaning are no more permanent than the pieces of a jigsaw puzzle and can and should be broken up and taken apart. Thus her writing may be seen as a contribution to the infiltration and exposure of a world that suffers from a surfeit of linguistic interpretation. Aichinger's work is an acquired taste and only those few who have the courage to accompany her into her own hermetic world can grasp its true flavour.

NOTES

1. Ilse Aichinger, 'Die Sicht der Entfremdung. Über Berichte und Geschichten von Ernst Schnabel', in: *Frankfurter Hefte*, 9 (1954), 56–60.
2. 'And we calm down again. But we shouldn't calm down'.
   Ilse Aichinger, 'Aufruf zum Mißtrauen', in: *Plan*, 1 (1946), No. 7, 588.
3. 'But no-one sought of seeking protection against himself and so the beast could grow from generation to generation and no-one paid it any attention. We have met it face to face! We have suffered at its hands – around us and perhaps in us as well.'
   Aichinger, *Aufruf zum Mißtrauen*, op. cit.
4. '*You must be suspicious of yourself!* Have you understood what I am saying? We must all be suspicious of ourselves! We cannot place any reliance on knowing what we have in mind, on our ability to think profound thoughts or perform good works. We must be suspicious of our own integrity for is it not ridden with lies from the start and glazed by the absence of love? And what of our own love? It is rotten with selfishness! And our honour? It crumbles away with our arrogance'.
   Aichinger, *Aufruf zum Mißtrauen*, op. cit.
5. 'Those who think they exist have no being. Only those who doubt

themselves are allowed to land, only those who have suffered . . .'
Ilse Aichinger, *Die größere Hoffnung*, Frankfurt/M., 1966, p. 67.

6. 'There always was a threat to meaning but now it is on the verge of drowning and the words are like small abandoned houses, standing steep and stiff and without meaning on the banks of the red-flowing river'.
Aichinger, *Die größere Hoffnung*, p. 70.

7. 'So you want to forget all the German you have learnt? Well, I won't help you do that, but I will help you to learn it from the beginning again, cautiously and carefully as if you were lighting a candle in a dark house . . .'
Aichinger, *Die größere Hoffnung*, p. 78.

8. 'It may be that as a writer I feel obliged to relieve language of its role as a communicator and bring it back to its senses: then it will be able to communicate once more'.
This quotation is taken from an interview with Ilse Aichinger published in: *Die Presse*, 14/15.6.1975.

9. 'You have to issue your own visa to be free; those who cannot will always be prisoners'.
Aichinger, *Die größere Hoffnung*, p. 14.

10. '. . . the bridge isn't there any more!'
'We'll build it again!'
'What shall we call it?'
'The greater hope, our hope.'
Aichinger, *Die größere Hoffnung*, p. 237.

11. 'Aichinger has given the most horrific example of mass murder in history an almost sacral fulfilment. The messiah can be seen in the executioner's shadow and the swastika has been transformed into the redeemer's crucifix'.
K.H. Kramberg, 'Ellen und die fremde Macht', in: *Süddeutsche Zeitung*, 26.2.1977.

12. Cf. Urs Widmer, *1945 oder die 'NEUE SPRACHE'*, Düsseldorf, 1964, (=*Wirkendes Wort*, Schriftenreihe, vol. 2), pp. 110f.

13. 'He threw himself on the wolf like a bird swooping on its prey and cast it to the ground, and as he did so he realized that you could only fly if you were bound in a very particular way. As though in a slight intoxication he felt that he had lost the fatal superiority of his free limbs which is the cause of man's downfall'.
Ilse Aichinger, *Der Gefesselte*. Quoted from the collection *Nachricht vom Tag* (Frankfurt/M., 1970, (=Fischer Bücherei 1140).) which contains most of Aichinger's narratives of the 1950s and 1960s. This quotation p. 15.

14. 'The sun is beginning to sink down the scaffold and feel its way amongst you and making itself comfortable, going lower and lower; it rises, falls, tries to resist, rises a little and then by its very upward movement sinks even lower amongst you until at noon it realizes that only its own descent will drag it away from the dust and that it has to sink in order to rise back up into the sky over its own shadow . . .'
Aichinger, 'Rede unter dem Galgen', in: *Nachricht vom Tag*, p. 63.

15. 'You need not worry, I am not going to set fire to your harvest any more – it will be flames and ashes without my help! I can bide my time. I want to sow oats in the sand at low tide and gather the harvest in burnt-out barns, I want to build castles so that the tide can eat them away . . . I want to reap the heaven that is promised'.
   Aichinger, 'Rede unter dem Galgen', in: *Nachricht vom Tag*, p. 65.

16. 'I can hear the student who lives in my flat breathing in the next room; he is studying naval architecture and breathes deeply and evenly. He has no conception of what has happened. He has no idea at all while I lie awake here. I wonder if I ought to ask him tomorrow. He doesn't go out much and he may well have been at home while I was at the concert. He ought to know. Perhaps I'll ask the cleaning lady as well.
   No. I won't do that. How could I ask questions of someone who doesn't ask me anything?'
   Aichinger, 'Wo ich wohne', in: *Nachricht vom Tag*, p. 67.

17. 'And now there is nobody left and I can't turn myself round to see if there is still a hat and scarf hanging on the bed-post . . .
   So here I lie, half propped-up, silk clothes crumpled under a grey blanket, and the wardrobes are open and the cases have gone'.
   Aichinger, 'Die Puppe', in: *Nachricht vom Tag*, pp. 78f.

18. 'How disturbing to be here at home in this unknown place, to have finished picking the fruit a long time ago and yet to go on picking it with children and children's children, with ladders and baskets'.
   Aichinger, 'Die Ankunft', in: *Nachricht vom Tag*, p. 85.

19. 'minstrels on the terraces who are forever singing of beauty, of exquisitely wrought heavens and whose harps are always rejoicing'.
   Aichinger, 'Die Ankunft', in: *Nachricht vom Tag*, p. 85.

20. 'How many heavens seem to descend on me today, taking my breath away once more before they let me breathe again . . .'
   Aichinger, 'Die Ankunft', in: *Nachricht vom Tag*, pp. 85f.

21. 'I have lost my wood-ticket. I just don't know how I can get any further'.
   Aichinger, 'Holzfahrscheine', in: *Nachricht vom Tag*, p. 87.

22. 'To put it briefly: I will not go bathing on the church beach. I will not want anything, I will not like anything – not even the things I used to do. There will be no games played for me. I know that what I have lost will turn out to be something indefinable – and no amount of ingenuity would have gained it for me . . .'
   Aichinger, 'Holzfahrscheine', in: *Nachricht vom Tag*, p. 91.

23. 'Almost everything goes too far. That's why I think we should stay here, where I am . . .'
   Aichinger, 'Die Maus', in: *Nachricht vom Tag*, p. 81.

24. 'He holds out inside the coach-house, he sticks firmly to the ice and he won't be distracted from the world'.
   Aichinger, 'Mein Vater aus Stroh', in: *Nachricht vom Tag*, p. 96.

25. 'So here I am, listening. I have sharp ears and as they sound out the wood they sound out the ice-fields as well. I am not checking. I am just here. That is one of the advantages of my position. Everyone else can

so easily be suspected of wanting to keep a check on something, to take hold of it, to have it under their control. Not I. I listen to the ice-breaking and it does not move me one way or the other, and so long as I am here I can keep this in balance. I have got no favourites, no play-grounds, no shady streams, no fanatics – I am the same to all'.

Aichinger, 'Die Maus', in: *Nachricht vom Tag*, p. 82.

26. 'I don't want a mirror, a piece of glass and not even a dark handful of water which will reflect my image. Who knows, perhaps I am rejoicing because no one can find me'.

Aichinger, 'Die Maus', in: *Nachricht vom Tag*, p. 83.

27. 'a world-direction I have never much cared for anyhow'.

Aichinger, 'Mein grüner Esel', in: *Nachricht vom Tag*, p. 74.

28. 'a slightly grotesque sign for the reality outside the real'.

Jürgen P. Wallmann, 'Ilse Aichinger und ihre Dichtung', in: *Universitas*, 28 (1973), 41–45. This quotation p. 42.

29. 'It doesn't go far. Round, round me and round and round'.

Aichinger, 'Meine Sprache und ich', in: Ilse Aichinger, *Dialoge, Erzählungen, Gedichte*, Stuttgart, 1971, (=Reclam 7939), p. 3.

30. 'I was a young shoot, a form of speech . . . But it doesn't help, we have to travel. We have to go away'.

Aichinger, 'Erinnerungen für Samuel Greenberg', in: *Nachricht vom Tag,* pp. 177f.

31. 'Here I sit with my language, just three meters away from people who speak like that. But we are on the other side and we can pause for a while if we run out of breath'.

Aichinger, 'Meine Sprache und ich', in: *Dialoge, Erzählungen, Gedichte*, p. 3.

32. 'My language used to have a lilac scarf, but that's gone now. I don't think the air here is very good for us. If my language loses her voice, she has another reason not to talk to me any more'.

Aichinger, 'Meine Sprache und ich', in: *Dialoge, Erzählungen, Gedichte*, p. 5.

33. 'struggling for breath with a gust of wind'.

Aichinger, 'Alte Liebe', in: *Nachricht vom Tag*, p. 101.

34. 'It would be a mistake to search for some hidden meaning in this language as if it were a cypher for which one had to provide the key. The world it presents is neither dreamed nor imagined, its language is concerned with reality, but with a reality that cannot be seen in any objective or measureable relationship with its observer. There is no world as such, it cannot be grasped'.

Werner Eggers, 'Ilse Aichinger', in: Dietrich Weber (ed.), *Deutsche Literatur seit 1945. In Einzeldarstellungen*, vol. I, Stuttgart, 1968, (=Kröners Taschenausgabe 382), pp. 221–238. This quotation pp. 226f.

35. 'I wanted to sit down on a cross-beam. I wanted to know what a cross-beam is, but no-one will tell me'.

Aichinger, 'Der Querbalken', in: *Nachricht vom Tag*, p. 142.

36. 'which should act as a support, perhaps as a means of salvation'.

Aichinger, 'Der Querbalken', in: *Nachricht vom Tag*, p. 142.

37. 'What is a cross-beam? Not what is it to me, but what is it?'
    Aichinger, 'Der Querbalken', in: *Nachricht vom Tag*, p. 145.
38. 'surrogate answers'.
    Wolfgang Hildesheimer, 'Das absurde Ich', in: Wolfgang Hildeshei-
    mer, *Interpretationen. James Joyce, Georg Büchner, Zwei Frank-
    furter Vorlesungen*, Frankfurt/M., 1969, (= edition suhrkamp 297),
    pp. 84–110. This quotation p. 96.
39. 'Now we have got spots on our chairs. It looks as if someone had
    spilled milk over them. These spots need thinking about'.
    Aichinger, 'Flecken', in: Ilse Aichinger, *schlechte Wörter*, Frank-
    furt/M., 1976, p. 11.
40. 'Cannot be thought about . . . cannot be put into words . . . imposs-
    ible to discuss with anyone, impenetrable'.
    Aichinger, 'Flecken', in: *schlechte Wörter*, p. 13.
41. 'The spots win. They too win'
    Aichinger, 'Flecken', in: *schlechte Wörter*, p. 14.
42. 'Ought we really start telling the old sentimental tales over again?'
    Aichinger, 'Wisconsin und Apfelreis', in: *schlechte Wörter*, p. 59.
43. 'I have decided not to give it a name any more'.
    Aichinger, 'Der Querbalken', in: *Nachricht vom Tag,* p. 145.
44. 'But she doesn't tell us anything now. She has stopped . . . Her mouth
    is still open, half-open; that looks moronic, she shouldn't be like that,
    she should go on telling us things . . . pull at her tangled hair, pinch her
    cheeks, but tell her to go on talking to us. She has got to keep talking to
    us'.
    Aichinger, 'Wisconsin und Apfelreis', in: *schlechte Wörter*, p. 62.

Erich Fried: Poetry and Politics

Rex Last

Erich Fried lives in London, his home for many years now, as a full-time writer and translator. Perhaps he is most widely known as a political poet, and also in relation to his engagement on behalf of the student leader Rudi Dutschke, but he does not fit into the image that this suggests of a radical leftist blindly espousing every revolutionary cause that chances along, good or bad. Fried's stance is essentially critical; he challenges persecution and injustice from whatever quarter, from the American war in Vietnam to Israeli treatment of the Palestinians. On one occasion, he even goes so far as to accuse the English of cherishing fonder illusions of being the master race than ever blighted the Germans.

If anything, Fried might be accused of being too provocative and too negative, of indiscriminate iconoclasm. It is all too easy to destroy, runs the cliché; putting forward positive proposals for beneficial change in personal attitudes and in society at large is quite a different matter. But the negative elements in his work form an essential part of his world view, and his provocations derive directly from his keen, almost ruthless intelligence and penetrating insight into any situation to which he directs his attention.

Fried refuses to be pigeon-holed into a neat category. In an age in which poets are almost invariably prefaced by some descriptor like 'concrete', 'Neo-Dadaist', 'experimental', and the like, Fried exploits many kinds of poetic form, from concrete poetry at one extreme to traditional lyricism at the other. His chief concern is with the practice of his craft, with stirring the reader's attention, sharing with him his thoughts and experiences, and challenging him to think and feel differently, to see old issues in a new light, to re-examine received ideas and confront the realities of contemporary life. But, for all his political indignations, genuine though they undoubtedly are, Fried is essentially that very old-fashioned animal, a creative artist first and foremost.

Not the least significant of the principal threads that run through Fried's work is his preoccupation with Nazism and the Second World War, which dates back to his experiences in his native Vienna and his enforced exile from Austria. He was born in 1921, and brought up in the Austrian capital; in 1938 his parents were arrested and interned; a month later, his father was released, dying from injuries received during interrogation by the Gestapo; and when his mother was released after serving thirteen months of a five year sentence, she and her son fled to England. Finding himself in a foreign country without means of support, Fried turned his hand to a variety of different jobs, but it was clear that his main talents lay in the sphere of creative writing, and from 1946 onwards he concentrated his attentions on poetry, prose, translating and freelance journalistic work.

The long shadow of Nazism and the Second World War which falls across his work is most sharply reflected in his most substantial venture into prose to date, the novel *Ein Soldat und ein Mädchen* (A Soldier and a Girl),[1] which, although published in 1960, was many years in the making, having been begun as far back as 1946. It may seem strange that a writer of such confident fluency – on his own admission, he composes his Shakespeare translations 'at speed' in order not to lose sight of the drama as a whole – should require such a lengthy period of gestation. Fried himself draws attention to this fact in the postscript he wrote to the novel. *Ein Soldat und ein Mädchen*, he admits, meant more to him than anything else he had hitherto put down on paper, yet at the same time it proved exceedingly difficult to write, not least because he was wrestling with emotions and attitudes which had not resolved themselves within his own mind, and indeed even the finished novel has much of the air of the 'workshop' about it.

Ein Soldat und ein Mädchen does not consist of one homogenous, smoothly developing narrative strand: it is deliberately disjointed, not least because the narrative technique of the first part is such that the narrator-cum-author (fact and fiction are merged together) keeps intervening with his own observations, at times indicating how difficult it had been to continue writing from such-and-such a point, lending the whole a sense of incompleteness, of one's having been invited to a housewarming before the plasterers have come or the roof has been tiled, and observing the craftsmen at work rather than admiring the finished construction. (This fact has not prevented some critics from attacking the work on these very grounds.) As a result, the reader both becomes caught up in the sense of immediacy conveyed by the feelings of the soldier whose bizarre lot is being depicted and also somewhat uncomfortable, sensing that he is intruding, witnessing an intensely private situation in which the presence of an outsider is almost unwelcome.

The novel concerns an ex-German Jew become GI who finds himself in Germany just after the end of the war, experiencing all the discomfiture and restlessness of an army man in a huge organization which has outlived its primary objective – inflicting defeat on the Nazis – and which carries on functioning, uncomfortably aware of its irrelevance in a situation in which constructive as opposed to destructive actions have to be taken. The GI is part of the guard at a prison where Helga, a beautiful Nazi camp warder, is under sentence of death. In reply to the conventional question as to what her last wish might be, she states that she wants to spend her last night with a soldier, 'that one', the central figure of the narrative.

A welter of confused and conflicting emotions floods through him. He is expected to engage in an act of love with a woman who symbolises all that he has hated with such vehemence and has as a soldier actively sought to destroy; and yet, at the same time, hatred merges into fascination, with a sense that in some strange manner she is a martyr figure, and their coming together a symbolic reconciliation, the enactment of some bizarre *ius ultimae noctis*. This foreshadows one of Fried's principal preoccupations as a poet, namely, pleading the cause of reconciliation between people and peoples, breaking a link in the chain of aggression and counter-aggression which has wrought such devastation in this century.

Ein Soldat und ein Mädchen is lyrical in tone rather than epic, but, characteristically of Fried, the emotion is not left to feed on itself, and the reader is not permitted to lapse into passive identification with the characters; he is encouraged to think as a result of feeling, and to think hard. Fried is operating on a moral rather than party political level, presenting difficult questions rather than glib solutions, not the least of which is a quite literal attempt to make the reader see people from the other side, and also to confront him with the unanswerable fact of death, which here, exceptionally, comes for Helga at an entirely predictable moment.

The theme of war and the issues it generates is also pursued by Fried throughout his poetry, two volumes of which – *und Vietnam und* (and Vietnam and)[2] and *Höre, Israel!* (Hear, o Israel!)[3] – are specifically concerned with contemporary conflict situations.

To borrow a term from Brechtian dramaturgy, much of Fried's poetry is 'epic' in the sense that it is not merely a self-contained entity, developing internally on the basis of an initial emotional impulse. Reaction to an event or situation external to the poem is a key feature of Fried's poetry. As was the case with Ein *Soldat und ein Mädchen*, Fried permits and encourages on the one hand appreciation on an emotional and aesthetic level and, on the other, rational 'alienation'. The two work in harness to achieve at times remarkable effects, as in this deceptively simply parabolic miniature from *und Vietnam und*:

Weiße Hände
rotes Haar
blaue Augen

Weiße Steine
rotes Blut
blaue Lippen

Weiße Knochen
roter Sand
blauer Himmel[4]

The poem is classical in its clarity and balance. Employing the colours of the United States flag, Fried depicts in deliberately depersonalized terms three stages in the career of a white American soldier in Vietnam. He first is shown as a new arrival, an 'all-American guy', pampered by the best that civilization can offer, with his white hands and clear, open, blue eyes; then he witnesses the slaughter of Vietnamese citizens; and, finally, he himself meets his death, lying with bleached bones in a desert which is partly of his own making. (Or, as Erich Fried points out in a letter to me, the blood could be wholly that of the Vietnamese. The ambiguity is deliberate.) The title of the poem is 'Einbürgerung', which signifies the process of naturalization, of becoming a 'Bürger' or citizen, that is to say, of coming to share the fate of the citizens of a devastated country which has become the American soldier's land by adoption.

Fried, it must be stressed, is not just attacking the Americans simply because they are Americans (however fashionable a target they may be of radical opprobrium). He is no simplistic politicizing poet; his anger is directed against all warmongers, and his sympathies are engaged on behalf of all those who suffer, all who are caught in the crossfire of military conflict. One moment he can be castigating Christendom for persecuting the Jews under the ironic title 'Fortschritt' (Progress):

> Nach neunzehn Jahrhunderten
> wurde in Rom verkündet
> daß Israel nicht Kollektivschuld
> am Tode Christi trägt
>
> Nun werden auch
> die toten Juden erklären:
> Wir wurden niemals erschlagen
> von Christenhand[5]

But, a few pages later, he turns against Israel in another typically pointed antithetical statement:

> Eure Sehnsucht war
> wie die anderen Völker zu werden
> die euch mordeten
> Nun seid ihr geworden wie sie[6]

This poem bears the same title – 'Höre, Israel!' – as the collection devoted to the Israeli-Palestinian conflict, and is reprinted there in a greatly expanded version.

In the introduction, he sets out his position:

Zionist war ich nie, religiös nur kurze Zeit als Kind . . . aber das Schicksal der Juden ist mir keineswegs gleichgültig. Ich hoffe sogar, auch ohne jüdisches Volksbewußtsein oder israelisches Nationalgefühl, sozusagen nebenher, ein besserer Jude zu sein als jene Chauvinisten und Zionisten, die, was immer ihre Absicht sein mag, in Wirklichkeit 'ihr Volk' immer tiefer in eine Lage hineintreiben, die schließlich zu einer Katastrophe für die Juden im

185

heutigen Israel führen könnte.[7]

Fried regards the relationship between cultural or ethnic groups in terms of a Darwinian struggle in which one side acts the role of the oppressor, the other the oppressed, one in which, when the roles are reversed, the erstwhile victims so readily embrace their new superiority, and become worse than their tormentors ever were:

> Und fast alle Menschen
> denen fast alles angetan wurde
> sagten dann mit fast versagender Stimme:
> 'Der Tag wird kommen
>
> Der Tag an dem wir fast allen
> fast alles antun werden
> was sie uns angetan haben'[8]

This is why the Vietnam poems bear the odd title 'and Vietnam and', stressing the fact that the Indo-China war is just one link in an apparently unending chain of such situations.

The final section of *Höre, Israel!* concerns a specific illustration of this phenomenon. It is called 'Nach Fürstenfeldbruck' (After Fürstenfeldbruck), and demonstrates that no one nation or race has cornered the market in persecution, and that a sense of justice, like a sense of injustice, can so readily cause violation of the law. The sixteenth-century horse dealer Michael Kohlhaas, in the story of the same title by Heinrich von Kleist ultimately fomented rebellion when he failed to get justice for the appropriation of two of his horses by one of the local nobility, who had sought to impose upon Kohlhaas what the latter regarded as the imposition of an unwarranted toll charge. Equally extreme was the reaction of the German border police, Fried argues, when they shot down hostages and Palestinian guerillas alike on the airfield at Fürstenfeldbrück. This tragic sequel to the attack on the Munich Olympic village in 1972 is linked by Fried with the tale of Kohlhaas: he follows Kleist in linking Kohlhaas's name with Kohlhasenbrück near Potsdam, now in the German Democratic Republic, and – as he so often does in his poetry – permits this chance constellation of sounds and associations to relate the two episodes, calling Kohlhaas by his historical name of 'Kohlhase', suggesting that, in the words of the proverb, he is anything but 'wie ein Hase im Kohl' (in clover; literally 'a hare among the cabbages').

Fried's political horizon, then, is far from circumscribed. He consistently views history in human terms, and demands humane actions on the part of mankind. It is partly this breadth of understanding which prevents his political verses from becoming tedious sermons delivered *ex cathedra*. But there is a further, far more significant reason why his political poems – like this one on as potentially unpoetic a subject as the defoliation campaign in Vietnam – are not just a versified prose statement but a living thing:

> Wenn es
> gestattet ist
> daß man
> die Kinder
> bestattet
> dann
> ist es
> auch
> erlaubt
> daß man
> die Bäume
> entlaubt[9]

Nothing – not even passionately held convictions – is allowed to stand in the way of the poem as a work of creative art, and it is only through the perfect balance of the poem around the fulcrum of 'dann', the concentration on 'a' sounds in the first part and on 'au' in the second, the double pun (on 'gestattet' and 'bestattet', and on 'erlaubt' and 'entlaubt'), and the logicality of the second part, given the false premiss of the first (the poem bears the title 'Logik', logic), that the 'message' is allowed to emerge.

Fried is first and foremost a poet, convinced that only through addressing the whole man, emotions as well as reason, can he persuade him to think about the nature of the world we live in and of possible directions for positive change.

To this end he employs a whole range of poetic devices and forms, from pure lyricism at one extreme to experimental verse at the other. A favourite technique of his is the much-maligned pun, the play on words which to him is an extremely serious game indeed, in that the coincidences of sounds and meaning have a way of striking a spark of truth which might otherwise have remained

187

hidden or, at best, have been put across lamely and without conviction. At times, Fried takes this verbal manipulation to excess, but,
by and large, he is a master of a technique which had its greatest
flowering in Dada, especially in the poetry of Hans Arp. Here Fried
is demonstrating his skill with the word:

> Das Wort ist mein Schwert
> und das Wort beschwert mich
>
> Das Wort ist mein Schild
> und das Wort schilt mich
>
> Das Wort ist fest
> und das Wort ist lose
>
> Das Wort ist mein Fest
> und das Wort ist mein Los[10]

The word, with all its vagaries and chance associations, dominates
his work as a poet: it is 'fest' and 'lose', firm and loose, and it is his
'Fest' and 'Los', his joy and his destiny. The poem's title, 'Logos',
stresses its magical, almost transcendental, import.

This degree of experimentation – if such it should be called – is
modest by comparison with Fried's ventures into the area of the
poetic 'objet trouvé', in which entire poems are composed of word
for word quotations from newspaper articles, political speeches,
and the like. One striking illustration of the 'objet trouvé' poem is
furnished by a classified advertisement in the Berlin *Tagesspiegel*
newspaper, in which the local police president seeks to purchase
Alsation dogs for training as police animals. (*Unter Nebenfeinden*,[11]
p. 37). The division of a straight prose text into nine 'stanzas' serves
to add a commentary by accentuating certain words and phrases
and also by highlighting the basic structure of the text. This holds
true whether the context is the suggestion of police violence, the
stressing of the line of argumentation in extracts from books and
speeches on the Palestine problem, (*Höre, Israel!*, pp. 29ff) or, as
here, the descriptive material about an American book which ends
on a note of unintended irony:

> *Die lange Hoffnung*
> *(unwesentlich gekürzt)*[12]

On similar lines, Fried also employs collage, as in a poem from *Gegengift* (Antidote) (p. 50) which takes lines from the works of other poets represented in a contemporary anthology. On occasion, he also produces poems close to concrete poetry.

At the other end of the scale, there is a strong lyrical streak in his poetry which now and again, especially in his earlier work, can spill over into the realms of the fairy tale or of fantasy:

> Wenn Hunde welken
> zwischen den bellenden Blumen
> wenn Wälder arbeiten gehen
> in die Papierfabriken
> wo Menschen zerkleinert werden
>
> ist etwas aus den Fugen
> aber nicht viel
> Mit ein zwei Strichen
> kann es behoben werden
> ohne Blutvergießen
> und ohne Geld[13]

Fried can also write of love simply and honestly, in this case with great unhappiness and bitterness:

> Durch dich hat alles
> neue Namen bekommen
> . . .
> So verwandelt die Liebe
> den ganzen Menschen[14]

But, as the lines above indicate in their shift from the specific to the general, Fried rarely lingers on personal emotion as such, preferring to operate on two distinct levels, to blend thought and feeling, as in the poignant contrast in a poem about holiday-makers in Saigon, with its unanswered question as to whether lovers have a right to their happiness when outside thousands are dying:

> Morgen zählen wir sie
> jetzt ist noch Nacht

Komm
Geliebte[15]

Fried, then, explores a wide range of poetic techniques in the practice of his craft. The professional critic may or may not regard some of his more experimental work as 'art', but this would not worry Fried, who is far more concerned with selecting the most apposite method of putting across what he wishes to say.

It should not, however, be thought that the extremes of his poetry represent any kind of artistic dilletantism: on the contrary, the different facets of his poetry all reflect a preoccupation with the same basic themes and approach. In particular, the two levels on which his poetry characteristically operates are to be found throughout his work: in the contrast in the Saigon poem between private emotion and the outside world; in the way in which sound and meaning conspire to bestow a surprising profundity on his sparkling puns; and, not least, in the 'objet trouvé' poems, where the reorganization of prose text into a 'poetic' form creates a disconcerting new insight in just the same way that a play on words generates a flash of understanding, or the contrast between individual and society poses unanswerable problems. And this is a fundamental objective of his poetry: to surprise the reader into seeing personal, social and political issues with new eyes.

Fried brings all his intellectual and poetic gifts to bear on his work as a translator. He has rendered Hebrew works, as well as Sylvia Plath, Dylan Thomas, TS Eliot and others into German, but his greatest challenge and most significant achievement in this field is his translation of the works of Shakespeare (1969ff).

This is a task of extreme difficulty, not least because the Schlegel-Tieck translation has come to be regarded in Germany over the years with a veneration which can only be compared with the regard in which the English-speaking world holds the Authorised Version of the Bible. Fried has said that 'translation is an impossible task', and in this instance it is a task rendered doubly impossible because of the manner in which the Schlegel-Tieck translation has become assimilated into German culture, and considered almost to be superior to the English original. Fried has met the challenge with an acting and reading text of the plays – to date he has translated some twenty or so – which can truly be held to be the finest version without exception in German.

Fried brings to his work as a translator three qualities in particular which have served him so well as a poet and writer.

The first of these is a flexibility of approach, a refusal to be bound by artistic or ideological preconceptions, and a willingness to explore each and every means of committing what he has to say most effectively to paper. In the context of translating Shakespeare, this has meant that he has neither slavishly followed the precedent set by the Schlegel-Tieck, nor has he gone to the other extreme of rejecting it altogether and seeking to create an entirely 'new' Shakespeare. Schlegel and his collaborators owe many of the shortcomings of their version to the fact that they did not have the benefits of modern scholarship and richly annotated editions like the Arden Shakespeare series. By and large, their understanding of the English was extremely good, quite often outstripping their ability to render the text into the most apposite German. Fried has leaned on the Schlegel-Tieck where they have achieved felicitous renderings, but he has equally studied other German versions in an attempt to make a genuine advance on the achievements of past translators.

The second quality is an extremely acute sense of detail coupled with a thorough knowledge of Shakespearean English. Detailed slips, as he has pointed out, have led to serious blunders, such as the German tradition of a corpulent Hamlet, which derives from a misconstruing in the Schlegel-Tieck of Gertrud's line 'He is fat and scant of breath', which they translated as 'fett' (podgy), whereas in reality the line does no more than to assert that Hamlet is sweating – it was thought at the time that sweat was fat. Equally, he recognizes – where Schlegel-Tieck do not – the need to retain 'wound' as a rhyme-word in the couplet immediately preceding the balcony scene in *Romeo and Juliet* as an essential linking factor in the episode; he seeks to retain the continuity of meaning of the term 'ambition' in *Julius Caesar*, which Schlegel-Tieck dilute by first using 'Herrschsucht' and then, after his death, 'Ehrsucht'; in *A Midsummer Night's Dream*, he confronts the problem of retaining as much as possible of the pun in 'This is the wittiest partition' in the play within the play; and, in countless other places throughout his translations, Fried never allows himself the easy way out, by diluting the text, but attempts to keep literal meaning, imagery, poetic and dramatic effect, and above all the unity of the dramas in his mind throughout his translations.

The third, and perhaps most important, quality which Fried

191

brings to bear on Shakespeare is the fine balance within him between intellectual and poet. He puts his great poetic sensitivity to work, disciplining it through his clear understanding of the text to produce a translation which will clearly become the standard version of Shakespeare for many generations.

One section of the collection *Gegengift* bears the title 'Meine Muse hat Kanten' (My Muse has sharp edges), and that phrase aptly characterises Fried's abrasiveness, his constant challenge to received ideas, to intolerance and persecution wherever and whenever they occur. But for all that, he is essentially a poet, writing out of an inner compulsion. As the poem 'Sprachlos' (Speechless) indicates, he cannot put into words the reason why he feels impelled to function as a poet, writing for minorities about issues that should have the widest possible public airing:

> Warum schreibst du
> noch immer
> Gedichte
> obwohl du
> mit dieser Methode
> immer nur
> Minderheiten erreichst
> fragen mich Freunde
> . . .
> und ich weiß
> keine Antwort
> für sie[16]

But he keeps on writing, with great fluency, questioning and challenging, his persistency underlined by the fact that he prefers to write in cycles of poems, worrying away at a problem, not letting it go even though he knows in the last analysis that the problem is insoluble. His task is like that of Sisyphus, continually rolling the stone uphill until it is worn away to a pebble, and then what remains?

> Nichts als die Qual
> seine Qual
> überlebt zu haben[17]

The questions may be unanswered or even unanswerable, his voice lost in the wilderness, but he keeps on posing them none the less, warning his audience of the potential inhumanity of man, frequently returning to the motif of the stone:

> Zu den Steinen
> hat einer gesagt:
> seid menschlich
>
> Die Steine haben gesagt:
> wir sind noch nicht
> hart genug[18]

The ultimate reason why the questions remain without response is that man is acting out his existence against the ineluctable facts of life and death, which he can do nothing to alter, blind forces which are beyond our control or understanding. Man may seek hope, but all that comes is death:

> Wir suchen Hoffnung
> . . .
> Hoffnung vor dem Tod
> der nicht auf uns hofft
> der nicht hofft
> und der uns nicht sucht
> nur findet[19]

In the last analysis, however, Fried remains positive, almost optimistic, in the face of all the evidence, asserting rather than fleeing life:

> Schön ist der Mensch und das Leben
> Schön ist der Mensch und der Tod
> Schön ist Leben und Tod
> Schön ist der Weg[20]

And he responds to the challenge of the times with great vigour and impassioned defence of human qualities; but he is above all else a poet of considerable stature whose work will long outlive the specific problems he has explored, since he sees them in the wider context of the enduring challenges that have faced man throughout time; but still, one suspects, Fried relishes the confrontation with the severe crises of contemporary life. Perhaps the play on his own name is unintentional, but it none the less rings true that

Je ärger die Zeiten
desto friedlicher wird es in mir[21]

(I am grateful to Erich Fried for his assistance on matters of fact and interpretation in the preparation of this essay.)

NOTES

1. *Ein Soldat und ein Mädchen*, Hamburg, 1960
2. *und Vietnam und:* 41 Gedichte, Berlin, 1966.
3. *Höre, Israel!:* Gedichte und Fußnoten, Hamburg, 1974.
4. 'White hands
   red hair
   blue eyes

   White stones
   red blood
   blue lips

   White bones
   red sand
   blue sky'   *und Vietnam und*, p. 36
5. 'After nineteen centuries
   it was proclaimed in Rome
   that Israel did not bear
   collective guilt for Christ's death

   Now the dead Jews
   will in turn declare:
   We were never slain
   by Christian hands'
   			Anfechtungen: fünfzig Gedichte, Berlin, 1967, p. 40.
6. 'You used to long
   to be like the other peoples
   who were murdering you
   Now you have become as they'   *Anfechtungen*, p. 44.
7. 'I was never a Zionist, I was only religious for a while when a child . . . but the fate of the Jews is by no means indifferent to me. I even go so far as to hope that, although I do not feel Jewish race-consciousness or Israeli patriotism, I am a better Jew than those Chauvinists and Zionists who, whatever their intentions may be, are in reality driving 'their people' deeper and deeper into a situation which in the end could bring about a disaster for the Jews in present-day Israel.'
   					Höre, Israel!, p. 10.

194

8. 'And nearly all the people
to whom almost everything was done
said then almost in resignation:
"The day will come

The day on which we will do
to almost everyone almost all
that they have done to us".'

Gegengift, 49 Gedichte und ein Zyklus, Berlin, 1974, p. 9.

9. 'If it
can be done
that children
are buried
then
we also
have leave
to take
the leaves
off the trees'   *und Vietnam und*, p. 25

10. 'The word is my sword
and the word burdens me

The word is my shield
and the word scolds me

The word is firm
and the word is loose

The word is my feast
and the word is my fate.'

Befreiung von der Flucht: Gedichte und Gegengedichte, Hamburg, 1968, p. 4.

11. *Unter Nebenfeinden*: fünfzig Gedichte, Berlin, 1970.

12. *The Long Hope*
(*very slightly abridged*)
Die Freiheit den Mund aufzumachen, achtundvierzig Gedichte, Berlin, 1972, p. 22.

13. 'When dogs wilt
among the barking blooms
when woods go off to work
in the paper factories
where men are chopped up

something is out of joint
but not much
With one or two strokes
it can be put to rights
without blood-letting
and without money'   *Warngedichte*, Munich, 1964, p. 8.

14. 'Through you all things
have gained new names

195

. . .
So love transforms the whole man'
Zeitfragen, Gedichte, Munich, 1970 p. 63.

15. 'We'll count them tomorrow
now it is still night

    Come
    my love'
Zeitfragen, p. 88.

16. 'Why do you
keep on writing
poems
although you
in this way
only
reach minorities

    friends ask me
    . . .

    and I have
    no answer
    for them'
Die Freiheit den Mund aufzumachen, p. 29.

17. 'Only the torment
of having
survived his torment'
Anfechtungen, p. 13.

18. 'To the stones
someone said:
become human

    The stones replied:
    we are not yet
    hard enough'
Warngedichte, p. 121.

19. 'We seek hope
. . .
hope against death
which does not hope for us
does not hope
and seeks us not
only finds'
Zeitfragen, p. 12.

20. 'Beautiful is man and life
Beautiful is man and death
Beautiful is life and death
Beautiful is the way'
Reich der Steine: zyklische Gedichte, Hamburg, 1963, p. 18.

21. 'The worse the times
the more peaceful it becomes in me'
Anfechtungen, p. 54.

IV Crisis and Revolt

Hans Wolfschütz

In the latter half of the 1960s, the literary scene in Germany was the setting for a phenomenon whose precise cause and importance was, and still is, the subject of considerable critical dispute. Quite unexpectedly a new literary trend swept through German publishing-houses, a trend originating, somewhat surprisingly, in the quiet cultural backwaters of the Austrian provinces, in the environs of Salzburg and the sleepy, almost geriatric atmosphere of Graz. A veritable flood of controversy was unleashed by such writers as Thomas Bernhard (b. 1931) and Peter Handke (b. 1942), the two best-known and most-discussed writers of this 'wave', and Handke in particular was to play a decisive role in the development of contemporary German literature under the aegis of the so-called 'new sensibility'. 'Forum Stadtpark', the Graz group of writers with Handke and Wolfgang Bauer (b. 1941) as its most prominent members was instrumental in creating this Austrian 'literary miracle' and Graz found itself with the dubious distinction of being the 'secret capital' of contemporary German literature. Wolfgang Bauer's plays were soon firmly ensconced in the repertoire of every major German theatre, despite or rather because of their very Austrian timbre, and many other writers – Gert Jonke, Gerhard Roth, Peter Turrini, Michael Scharang, Franz Innerhofer and Gernot Wolfgruber – added to the wealth and divergent vitality of this Austrian literary renaissance.

It was not, however, just the younger generation of writers who came to the fore; Bernhard himself is, after all, almost a generation older than Handke and Bauer, as are the authors of the 'Wiener Gruppe' whose work had survived an underground existence in the 1950s with no prospect of publication and was now retrospectively dusted down and acclaimed – notwithstanding the fact that the group itself had broken up in 1964. Public enthusiasm for Austrian literature even extended to the exhumantion and belated appreciation of the works of Ödön von Horváth, and Horváth had by then been dead some thirty years! The extent of this Austrian 'incursion' onto the German literary scene is perhaps best shown by the fact that in the early 1970s Germany's most coveted literary award, the Georg Büchner Prize, was awarded to no less than four Austrian writers, writers of very different backgrounds and with widely-differing literary preoccupations, Bernhard, Handke, Elias Canetti and Manès Sperber.

There can be little doubt that it was the political developments in the Federal Republic of Germany which allowed contemporary Austrian writers to occupy such a dominant position. The unrest among the younger generation of Germans, which culminated in the student revolts of the late 1960s had led to a considerable politicization of German life and institutions and had inevitably left its mark on literature as well. Social relevance had been a prime criterion in literary criticism before this, but while in the 1950s critics thought in terms of a general moral stance, in the 1960s the demand was for a more intimate relationship between literature and political action:

> Revolutionäre Praxis verhörte die Literatur, und Literatur sah sich plötzlich mit dem, was sie immer anzugreifen schien: mit der Gesellschaft identifiziert. Gerade weil man gewohnt war, sich als moralische Instanz der Gesellschaft zu verstehen, war das für viele Autoren ein Schock, und um seine Integrität zu wahren, distanzierte man sich von der Literatur als von einem peinlichen Verdacht.[1]

Even if not everyone agreed with Hans Magnus Enzenberger that 'literature was dead' there was a general readiness to become politically involved, with such established authors as Heinrich Böll, Günter Grass, Martin Walser and Peter Weiss all making public statements on current social and political issues. At the same time the emphasis on agitprop lyric, on social documentation and didactic theatre offered enhanced opportunities for more direct political persuasion. At the other end of the spectrum a literature of radical linguistic experimentation emerged, with such figures as Helmut Heißenbüttel in its ranks. These two disparate poles, activist realism on the one hand and anti-subjectivist formalism on the other, allowed a vacuum to develop which the new Austrian literature, combining as it did linguistic awareness and a highly persona-

198

lized approach, readily filled with its own new realism.

Contemporary Austrian literature is based on different social conditions and a different literary tradition to its German counterpart. The political implications of the younger generation's revolt which swept through Germany left scarcely a ripple in Austria, and yet there can be no doubting that the aggressive, denunciatory and deliberately provocative nature of Thomas Bernhard's writing or the early works of Wolfgang Bauer and Peter Handke are just as much a part of this general reaction against the established order. In this respect these authors were wholly in sympathy with the rebellious mood of the later 1960s in Germany; the difference is that what they understood by 'change' has little to do with concrete social problems but more with the cultural superstructure of society. Thus they seem to follow a peculiarly Austrian pattern, retreating to a cultural (i.e. literary) realm, and, as Handke himself put it in 1967, becoming 'inhabitants of an ivory tower'.[2] Even so they are not seeking some aesthetic order which will provide release from a social reality devoid of meaning as had their counterparts at the turn of the century; on the contrary, the contemporary authors, by challenging established cultural norms, seek to forge a new way from their literary ghetto to the reality of the everyday world.

The origins and development of this literature are best understood as a reaction against the dominant cultural legacy of the first two decades of the Second Republic. The cultural climate of that period had sought to foster and nurture the new-found 'Austrianism' that had emerged during the war years. In the 1950s and 1960s Austrian literature had played a prominent part in this attempt to banish once and for all the spectre of the 'German nation' of the First Republic, and to create a specifically Austrian cultural identity. Thus many writers and critics took it upon themselves to isolate and identify the essential features of the Austrian literary tradition and to define the more timeless and enduring qualities of Austrian writing. Only rarely were such efforts of a purely descriptive nature; they often tended to degenerate into a rather simplistic duality of plus and minus, of 'Austrian' versus 'non-Austrian', and the result was a tendency to create stereotyped images rather than a genuine identification and presentation of the nation's cultural characteristics.

The restrictions imposed by this literary 'Austrianism' are reflected in the numerous broadsides levelled against the moral *engage-*

ment and critical stance of so many post-war writers in the Federal Republic. From the 'Austrian redoubt' such preoccupations with National Socialism and the social restoration of the Adenauer era seemed ideologically limited. Indeed, to use Doderer's phrase, they seemed the embodiment of 'Apperzeptionsverweigerung', the refusal to take the 'whole' reality into account. There was no 'Committee for Un-Austrian Affairs' as such, but the Brecht boycott in Vienna is a prime example of the narrow confines which the Austrian literary world of the 1950s drew for itself. This mental isolationism must also account for the fact that until the middle of the 1960s scarcely one play was written in Austria which enjoyed success outside the Second Republic. The creative impetus of such a gargantuan figure as Brecht, who had a decisive effect on Frisch and Dürrenmatt in Switzerland simply did not communicate itself to the young Austrian playwrights; they had to resurrect their own father-figure, Ödön von Horváth, for themselves.

In the immediate post-war years, it seemed that authors of different generations and divergent political persuasion had been able to work together peacefully and fruitfully, but the emergence of the spiritual tradition of the old Hapsburg Empire as a focal point in the 1950s, placed this harmony under considerable strain; indeed it marks the first stage of the polarization of Austrian literature into the traditionalists and the avant-garde progressives which culminated in the celebrated defection from the official Austrian PEN Club in 1972 of the 'Grazer Autorenversammlung', the Graz 'collective of writers'. The 1950s were, however, more particularly characterized by a different division in Austrian literature, and one that can not be so conveniently seen in terms of 'tradition' and 'avant-garde'. There was a marked contrast between those Austrian writers who had settled abroad, particularly in West Germany, whose works were issued by West German publishing houses, and who were acclaimed by a West German readership and critical cadre, and those authors who had chosen to remain within the boundaries of their homeland.

Paul Celan, Ingeborg Bachmann and Ilse Aichinger, whose works are very much part of the mainstream of Austrian modernism, very soon turned their backs on the literary world of their native country, while others, for example Erich Fried, simply chose not to return from exile. As a consequence, these authors were able to deal with 'Austria' and 'the Austrian way' ('Das Österreichische') with increased objectivity and were able to respond to and

200

develop the trends which emerged. Their ingrained suspicions of language and the resulting search for new aesthetic forms was instrumental in providing new impetus for literary development in the Federal Republic, and Walter Jens goes so far as to select the appearance of Bachmann and Aichinger among the writers of the 'Gruppe 47' as the signal for a move away from the realistic mode of writing that had hitherto dominated German literature towards a more formalistic mode.[3]

Austrian writers of this 'middle generation' who had remained in the Second Republic found the task of breaking down the bastions of tradition from within and using this confrontation to their own literary advantage a much more difficult undertaking. They were particularly inhibited by the presence of the older generation of writers who enjoyed considerable influence and prestige and they themselves reacted much more directly and emotionally to the power of the Austrian tradition whether they supported the current mood or whether they rejected everything 'Austrian' as had the 'Wiener Gruppe'.

Amongst those authors who found their spiritual homeland in the shadow of this tradition two names stand out, Herbert Eisenreich (b. 1925) and Gerhard Fritsch (1924–1969) although both writers on occasion adopted a more ambivalent attitude. Fritsch and Eisenreich shared the fate of the disillusioned soldier returning home after the war who found himself at odds with a general social attitude that emerged as the country began to enjoy a measure of affluence and the onset of the tourist boom. The alienation and sense of homelessness felt by both writers had little to do with political disillusionment, but stemmed from a general scepticism of progress as such and civilization as a whole. Eisenreich, for example, regarded the immediate post-war era as one of self-deception on a massive scale where cultural standards were lowered and tradition debased in the interests of the tourist trade. Gerhard Fritsch's novel *Moos auf den Steinen* (Moss-covered Stones, 1956) is no less scathing in its depiction of the contemporary situation as a 'Zeitalter des Benzins und der Verhetzung' – an age of petrol and propaganda, and the hero of the novel, a writer with autobiographical similarities to Fritsch himself, is ultimately destroyed by this new 'dark age'. Both Eisenreich and Fritsch were particularly influenced by their own personal dreams, memories and hopes for a sense of security, and their work is coloured by their readiness to contrast the chaos they experienced in reality with a consolatory vision of a more meaningful order which would resolve the dissonances of their own sense of isolation in a world they found sterile and confusing. Each in his own way sought to recreate in his work the elements he missed in society, elements which would combine to form a culture which, by rising above the conflicts and squabbles of every-day life, would shine like a beacon and provide spiritual guidance towards a higher and more meaningful form of existence.

This cultural idealism necessarily obliged both Fritsch and Eisenreich to turn away from the world about them and seek refuge where they felt such values and order were preserved; it was inevitable that they would turn to the Austrian tradition. Ironically, it was their own deep scepticism of contemporary ideologies which made them the most representative messengers of the central ideology of the Second Republic in the 1950s, the 'Austrian vision'. When conversion from such belief in traditional values comes, as it inevitably must, the consequences can be traumatic, and in Fritsch's case 'Austrian idealism' became a negative factor, as his radical volte-face in the early 1960s illustrates.

Eisenreich, for his part, survived the crisis- and turmoil-ridden 1960s without shedding his artistic creed. He held it to be the artist's responsibility to create order in himself, and in the world about him – 'Ordnung in sich und Ordnung in seiner Umwelt zu schaffen',[4] and this can be seen not only in his more traditional narrative work, but in his numerous essays which appeared in 1964 in a collection *Reaktionen. Essays zur Literatur* (Reactions. Essays on Literature). In this volume Eisenreich counters his disillusioned analysis of the cultural anonymity of the Second Republic by putting forward the consoling thesis of a continuous tradition in Austrian writing reaching from Grillparzer to the present day. The common thread for so many generations is, he argues, a 'creative scepticism'.[5] Quite clearly Eisenreich is alluding to Ilse Aichinger's *Aufruf zum Mißtrauen* but he offers a restrictive interpretation of this crucial manifesto of 1946. Where Aichinger questioned the very possibility that literature and truth had anything in common, Eisenreich restricts his interpretation of scepticism to the 'Unbehagen in der bekannten (und) das Ungenügen an der erkannten Wirklichkeit'.[6] He sees no problem in the literary quest for the 'innermost truth' which is hidden beneath the surface of the world we know and recognize and, consequently, does not accept that there is such a thing as a 'crisis in the novel'.[7] His confidence in his own ability to understand the world with the help of language remains unimpaired and he supports this view by frequent references to Doderer's concept of the 'total novel' which, for Eisenreich provides a picture of the world 'so wie sie ist: voll von disparaten Eizelheiten und doch ein organisches Ganze'.[8] He stresses this concept of universality with its capacity to resolve all contrasts and contradictions and regards the aesthetic order and structure as a reflection of an order of existence and values inherent in creation itself.

Gerhard Fritsch enjoys no such confidence. He too sees writing in the 1950s as the prime means of resolving and overcoming the dissonances in life, but his consolatory affirmative is much more vulnerable and always open to attack as a result of his own deep despair and sense of disorientation. Fritsch frequently changes direction and even when he seems to have found a negotiable route often remains unsure of himself. The first change in direction came in the early 1950s when, after a brief period of involvement with the Communist Party, he withdrew from politics and all direct involvement in the social questions of the age. In his lyric poetry he found refuge in nature and in the novel *Moos auf den Steinen* in Hapsburg Austria. Eisenreich hailed this novel as the most representative work of his generation[9] precisely because it disregards contemporary relevance and embarks on a quest for timeless values by following the well-trodden paths of Austrian writing.

The novel's title derives from the ruins which constitute the central location, a castle which has fallen into disrepair and which is gradually being overgrown and reclaimed by nature. There is little trace in the novel of Fritsch's own experiences, no mention of cities devastated by air-raids, for the novel dreams nostalgically of a bygone age which is far beyond the author's own memories and personal experience. The historical reality of the Hapsburg monarchy, symbolized by the castle, is elevated to a museum and respository of all the humanitarian values from the 'good old days' which Fritsch so sorely misses in contemporary society, but, in contrast to Eisenreich, Fritsch lacks the certainty that those values – the 'Modo Austriaco' of the central chapter of the novel – can continue into the present.

Moos auf den Steinen is in many respects typical of the Austrian reaction to history during the 1950s. The tendency to look back to the 'old Austria' with nostalgia and a touch of pathos could not help but prevent a critical assessment of the 'other', more immediate past – the civil war of the First Republic and the National-Socialist 'interlude'. There was little or no sense of the realities of the present or the future or, at best as in Fritsch's somewhat lyrical epilogue to the novel, there was a vague hope that the 'Modo Austriaco' might be revived.

Reviewing the cultural climate of this period as a whole, Paul Kruntorad aptly noted that a new, 'Austrian' optimism seemed to have gained ground, but added that it was backward-looking rather than truly positive:

> Nicht die Utopie ist das Ziel, sondern die Wiedererweckung (. . .) Man benützt die Tradition nicht als Sprungbrett nach vorn, sondern erblickt in ihr die Pforte zum Reich des Mythos, das die Größe schon per definitionem birgt.[10]

By the beginning of the 1960s more and more writers and intellectuals had come to realize that Austria was threatened by the shadow of its own past, and they began to formulate a new approach to the Second Republic as they found it, often as a direct reaction to the domestic political situation. The Second Republic enjoyed a political stability unknown to the First Republic, but it seemed all too ready to accept the status quo rather than make the effort to move forward. The Grand Coalition whose original aims had been achieved in 1955 with the signing of the State Treaty was still in office some eleven years later and stultifying both the political and cultural atmosphere. As was suggested above, in Chapter One, the net result was creeping parochialism in all aspects of Austrian life, a situation which eventually spurred pressure groups within both major political parties to work for a change in the way their country was governed.

Literature, too, was submitted to this new-found spirit of investigation and revaluation which began to emerge – and was found wanting. Claudio Magris' seminal study of the Austrian literary tradition and the 'Hapsburg myth' (1963),[11] despite a certain lack of balance, set the standard and tone for what was to follow. Herbert Eisenreich had based his vision of a literary and cultural renaissance in the Second Republic on a sense of continuity through the Austrian tradition, but Magris's sociological analysis rejected such a continuity as positively harmful. Eisenreich's acclaim of those Austrian writers from Grillparzer to Doderer who had dedicated themselves to what he termed the 'Totalität der Wirklichkeit', the complete and total reality, was rejected by Magris, who regarded them rather as working in the interests of a fixed and essentially pre-determined social and moral order. Magris believed that their view of life and their way of thinking had been excessively restricted by what he termed 'the burden of tradition'. His criticisms of earlier Austrian writers broke new ground but Humbert Fink had already castigated the prose works of the 1950s on very similar grounds. Fink's essay 'Warm und zufrieden im Provinziellen?' (Is your small-town existence cosy enough?, 1961)[12] charged the writers of this period with disregarding contemporary problems, with supporting principles and laws for no better reason than that they were there and with failing to come to grips with social ideologies at all.

It was at about the same time that Fritsch also began to reassess his own early work, distancing himself in particular from *Moos auf den Steinen* as a product of the general malaise of the 1950s, and turning his back on what he now saw as his 'escapist tendencies'. His second novel *Fasching* (1967) is a direct criticism of the Austrian tradition in which he rejects what he had earlier seen as a treasure-house of lasting values, revealing it as a mendacious fantasy, a chimera which allows the narrow-minded inhabitants of a small provincial Austrian town to hide behind a façade of bourgeois respectability. It is not that Fritsch has altered his sense of values in this aggressively sharp novel, but rather that there has been a shift in his concept of the true nature of past and present: the idealized image of 'old Austria' has been replaced by a satirical interpretation of the continuous tradition which traces a negative thread from the Hapsburg monarchy via Austro-fascism and National Socialism to the provincialism of the Second Republic.

Fritsch's 'conversion' was considerably aided by Hans Lebert's novel *Die Wolfshaut* (Wolf's Clothing, 1960) the first work to deal explicitly and at length with the sensitive problem of involvement with National Socialism. As did *Fasching, Die Wolfshaut* portrays the dilemma of a hero returning from the war and branded an outsider, who discovers the guilt lurking behind a mask of collective silence. (Lebert sets his novel in a village with the telling name 'Schweigen' – silence). In *Fasching* Fritsch dealt with the unmasking of real social aspects and ideologies, but Lebert's novel is particularly ironic in that it transcends the actual historical background and introduces a mythological and demonic element. In this it conforms to that apparently inescapable Austrian urge to move away from historical contexts to the world of myth. Fritsch's hero is enrolled in society as a helpless victim at the end of the novel, whereas Lebert allows a means of escape to remain open: his hero, having fulfilled his task and revealed 'Evil' is able to shrug off its pervasive influence.

A contrast to Fritsch's satirical interpretation of Austria's recent past and Lebert's mythological approach was provided by Helmut Qualtinger and Carl Merz in their cabaret monologue *Herr Karl* (1961). Here too the authors' concern is with 'continuity', but they give the theme a savage and ironic twist for Herr Karl is the conformist par excellence who greeted Hitler's appearance at the Heldenplatz in Vienna in 1938 with the same enthusiasm with which he later hailed the State Treaty in 1955. As Walter Weiss put it, he represents the negative aspect of this tradition:

> die Kontinuität des Egoismus, der Indifferenz, der scheinbar gemütlichen Herzlosigkeit, die sich's immer und überall richtet.[13]

Despite early objections the sketch was a huge success, not least because the Austrian audiences who saw it regarded Herr Karl as a caricature and were thus able to dispel their uncomfortable sense of identification with his outrageous interpretations of recent Austrian history by laughing at them as if there were no connection between stage and auditorium.

All three works were united in their rejection of what they saw as a parochialism and provincialism

> (der) sich mit der Einstimmung in übernommene Bilder von Sinn und Zweck des Lebens, in vorfabrizierte Weltmodelle, Weltanschauungen, Überzeugungen und Gefühlszustände zufriedengibt.[14]

Their assault on traditional images and illusory truths was taken a stage further in the provocations unleashed on the Austrian public by Thomas Bernhard. In Bernhard's work the historical background and setting of a 'real' Austria is translated into a universal model for a world bound-up with death. The crucial difference, however, is that Bernhard's assault was also mounted on a formal level and disregarded the limits of traditional writing to which both Fritsch and Lebert had adhered. Bernhard writes as one who, bowed down under the weight of tradition, seeks to throw off this burden by self-destructive aggression and by distancing himself more and more from reality through heightened artificiality. Bernhard's radical destruction of the ethos of the 'Hapsburg myth' and his deep-rooted scepticism as to the possibility of communicating effectively through language, leave him with but one solution: 'große Verweigerung', a grand negation of all he sees about him. And yet, behind the overwhelming pessimism of his work and his ritual condemnations of modern Austria there is always the impression that the author cannot help smiling at the absurdity of his own antics. This is particularly evident in an interview given for the BBC in 1976:

I would say there was a sickness and madness in this country. Things have become increasingly involved, tanged up within themselves, introspective. Here you find it expressed every day in the newspapers and in the faces of the people who read them or don't read them. The country is ruled by madmen and fools – but madmen and fools who are, on the whole, loveable and sympathetic. It's the result of history, naturally, as everything is – but the fact remains, everyone behaves as though they were sick and mad. Don't think I've escaped all this. Not at all. I too am sick and mad. It is an Austrian characteristic.[15]

Bernhard was still drawn to the traditions of the old Austria if only to deny them, but for the 'Wiener Gruppe' that ethos was completely unacceptable. The 'tradition' to which they turned was the iconoclasm of dadaism and surrealism, the termini of European modernism. The writers of the 'Wiener Gruppe' were not concerned with the 'whole man' nor with 'total reality'; their concern was with language, which they saw as the most comprehensive system for the conservation of reality. Under the influence of Wittgenstein and modern linguistic thinking they were convinced that thought, perception and social activity were the direct product of linguistic conventions and they consequently rejected symbolic language and regarded literary activity as working with language as their raw material. For them words were 'windows', (Fenster, 1968 is the title of a collection of Gerhard Rühm's work), through which reader and author saw nothing but words. This reduction from metaphor to word was sensed as liberation from the traditional and out-worn function of the writer as a 'namer of things' and, consequently as the origins of a new role for the writer in which he would manipulate linguistic structures, 'neue anschauungsformen zu provozieren, zu "verändern".'[16]

The 'Wiener Gruppe' was a most disparate entity, combining the extreme subjectivism and pure imagination of H.C. Artmann on the one hand and Friedrich Achleitner's constructivist works on the other. Their common bond was their apolitical, anti-bourgeois mantle and they came together as a result of their cultural isolation and the antipathy with which they were regarded by the cultural establishment – although it must be said that it was an antipathy they returned with interest. The 'Wiener Gruppe' constituted a private sub-culture in which reality and art, politics and aesthetics were no longer considered opposites; for the writers of the group poetry was tantamount to political activism and they planned revolution as a poetic act. They lived their art to such an extent that their appeal was inevitably restricted to a hard-core of enthusiastic initiates and it seems unlikely that this would have been any different even if there had existed any prospect of their work being published, which at that time there was not. When works by members of the 'Wiener Gruppe' did begin to appear in print the 'Group' itself had disbanded. Konrad Bayer had committed suicide, and Gerhard Rühm and H.C. Artmann had left Austria to live abroad. There was a second 'wave' of emigration from Austria at this time, with some of the writers setting up a little 'Austria in exile' in Berlin, but where the 'emigrés' of the 1950s had made their mark outside Austria, the writers of the 'Wiener Gruppe' provoked a creative response within the confines of the Second Republic.

The literary heirs to the 'Wiener Gruppe' are found not in Vienna but in Graz, and with them the Austrian literary world was effectively transported into the provinces. The process began in 1960 when the Graz City Council responded to the promptings of a group of young architects, artists, writers and intellectuals and allowed them to use an old café house in the city park. With a secure base the young avant-garde also found a forum in which to present their ideas and produced the journal *manuskripte*. Fortuitous external circumstances may have helped these young writers to come together but the group's inner strength was immeasurably helped by the howls of outraged civic pride which their earliest literary experiments provoked. In Vienna the avant-garde had felt hard-pushed to find anyone who could be provoked, in Graz provocation brought denunciation which fanned the flames of revolt and, at the same time, attracted a considerable amount of very welcome publicity for the writers. It was a pattern echoed in Salzburg when Thomas Bernhard published his first novel *Frost* in 1963.

The Graz writers adopted the theoretical and experimental impulses of the 'Wiener Gruppe' but were more inclined to use language in its familiar role as the means to an end. (This meant, of course, that they could reach a far larger public than the authors of the 'Wiener Gruppe'). Peter Handke's *Selbstbezichtigung* (Self-accusation, 1966), is one of the earliest works to reveal a systematic and socially-relevant application of the group's understanding of the 'political' nature of language as propounded by the 'Wiener Gruppe'. In this play Handke makes use of set linguistic clichés to construct the image of a man in order to reveal reality as a system of pre-determined interaction and pre-set responses 'ein geschlossenes Kombinationssystem'.[17] Like *Selbstbezichtigung*, Handke's most successful play, *Kaspar* (1968), is based on the author's realization that the way a man thinks and behaves is determined by social and moral norms that are inherent in language itself; his pantomime *Das Mündel will Vormund sein* (My Foot, My Tutor, 1969) goes one stage further, dispensing with language altogether and achieving the same effect by a system of gestures which is seen as no less conditioning.

Handke's success as a playwright runs counter to the theoretical aims he himself expressed. He had demanded that literature should achieve 'ein Zerbrechen aller endgültig scheinenden Weltbilder'[18] and in 1968 had specifically required that the theatre should be 'ein Spiel mit Widersprüchen'[19]; neither aim is achieved in these plays. For all his disparagement of Bertolt Brecht, whom Handke dismissed as a writer of trivia ('Trivialautor'),[20] all too ready to package social contradictions in a simplistic Marxist wrapping, Handke himself ends up writing parables with a very clear-cut interpretation of the world. *Kaspar*, for example, in following the progress of an individual learning to speak, provides a clear-cut presentation of the relationship between those with power (i.e. those who have the power of speech) and their victims (i.e. those who lack this power). Handke's plays are abstracts, they show man a prisoner within set norms and concepts but make no attempt to move beyond the systems delineated in the works themselves and so at the end of *Kaspar*, the unfortunate subject can do no more than make a futile gesture of anarchy.

Wolfgang Bauer is also concerned with demonstrating 'Spielregeln', the rules of the game by which his figures live out their lives. He has been repeatedly charged with using a wholly unrepresentative context, namely the world of the drop-out, to portray a sense of alienation, but it should be remembered that Bauer uses milieu and action for his own idiosyncratic purpose. Most of his plays are imitation melodamas which deliberately trivialize the traditional features they have borrowed. Bauer is thus able to create an artificial atmosphere, what might well be called theatre at second hand. His figures are not so much characters as psychological constructs, illustrators of such psychological concepts as fear, frustration or aggression, but his presentation of psychological syndroms is always linked to the social mechanisms on which society depends – the time-honoured games of oppression and dependence, of aggressor and victim, of master and slave. Even though Bauer's plays never show 'normal' bourgeois society on stage, it is the power of that society's rules and conventions which is implied by the behaviour of his figures.

Bauer's and Handke's plays, then, can be seen to illustrate the social norms and conventions governing human consciousness and behaviour but make no claim to be social documentation. The alienation they so graphically depict is not linked to specific social causes but seen rather in terms of its effect on the individual. Clearcut social references to the world outside the theatre are used only to the extent necessary to establish a particular setting and like so many young Austrian writers they seem to show no interest in reality as such. For most of this generation indeed such a 'reality' is unattainable, and the writers feel themselves imprisoned, like Handke's Kaspar, in a web of language which obstructs their vision of the world outside and prevents their gaining access to the world of objects. Handke expresses their dilemma neatly by suggesting that whereas Brecht was able to listen to political news and events and be moved by what he heard because the medium through which he heard this news, the radio, was no more than a medium, he himself feels he lives in a world full of news in which the medium has itself become 'ein Fetisch für "Wirklichkeit"' – where the medium has displaced the reality.[21]

It is in his prose-work that Handke attempts to break out of this 'prison-house of language'.[22] His narratives are more directly based on his personal experience than his plays and show him concerned from the start to reveal the true nature of traditional forms of perception and, more importantly, to shatter them. To aid him in this respect he uses well-known literary forms: the detective novel (as in *Der Hausierer* and *Die Angst des Tormanns beim Elfmeter*), the 'Bildungsroman' (as in *Der kurze Brief zum langen Abschied* and

210

Falsche Bewegung) or women's biography (as in *Wunschloses Unglück*). As Pütz comments on *Falsche Bewegung*, a film-script based on Goethe's *Wilhelm Meisters Lehrjahre*:

> Handke übernimmt das vorgeformte Geflecht eines Bildungsromans und verändert es derart, daß die Vorlage und damit die Tatsache der Übernahme ständig sichtbar bleiben, daß aber immer mehr Fäden dieses Geflechts in andere Richtungen gelenkt, zu neuen Sinnbeziehungen verknüpft werden.[23]

In contrast to his plays Handke is not merely content to unmask the implications of culturally preformed systems in which he feels our perception has become enmeshed. In most of his narratives he offers a new perception of the world that transcends ideological distortion; it is a perception conveyed by a calculated juxtaposition of traditional and borrowed features on the one hand, and descriptions of reality in precise detail on the other.

Handke's world, however, remains firmly within the confines of his own individual consciousness and defies all social definition. Even though there are still traces of social reality in contemporary Austrian literature, for writers such as Franz Innerhofer (b. 1944), Michael Scharang (b. 1941), Peter Turrini (b. 1944), Gernot Wolfgruber (b. 1944) and Helmut Zenker (b. 1949), in the 1970s developed a form of counter movement whose aims are to expose the concrete social mechanisms rather than their abstract equivalents. Admittedly, these writers still place the individual, his emotions and subjective reactions in the foreground of their work, but they are concerned not to examine these feelings in isolation, but to see them in the context of the everyday reality in and by which they are formed. Inevitably, such an approach entails a return to traditional realistic modes of writing, but far from being seen as a formal regression this development should be welcomed as a revival of the rich and varied fabric which constitutes modern Austrian writing.

NOTES

1. 'Revolutionary practice demanded that literature be investigated, and to its surprise literature found itself identified with society – the target for its own investigations! This came as a nasty shock to those writers

who had come to see themselves as arbiters of society's moral standards, and many of them sought to preserve their own integrity by distancing themselves from literature and thus avoiding any embarassing suspicions.'

Renate Matthaei, 'Vorwort' in: R.M. (ed.), *Grenzenverschiebung, Neue Tendenzen in der deutschen Literatur der 60er Jahre*, 2nd. ed., Cologne, 1972, p. 17.

2. Peter Handke, 'Ich bin ein Bewohner des Elfenbeinturms', published in a collection of essays bearing the same title, Frankfurt, 1972, pp. 19–28.

3. cf Walter Jens, *Deutsche Literatur der Gegenwart*, 2nd ed., Munich, 1966, (=dtv 172), pp. 129f.

4. Hermann Friedl, 'Herbert Eisenreich oder Schreiben, um Leben zu lernen', in *Wort in der Zeit*, 7 (1961), 6–20. This quotation p. 8.

5. Herbert Eisenreich, 'Das schöpferische Mißtrauen, oder Ist Österreichs Literatur eine österreichische Literatur?' in: H.E., *Reaktionen. Essays zur Literatur*, Gütersloh, 1964, pp. 72–104. This particular essay was written in 1959.

6. 'unease in the world we know and dissatisfaction with the world we see'. ibid. p. 86.

7. Herbert Eisenreich, 'Der Roman. Keine Rede von der Krise', in: *Reaktionen*, pp. 43–56. The essay was written in 1961.

8. 'just as it is, full of disparate entities and even so an organic whole'. Herbert Eisenreich, 'Roman und Zeitgeist' in: *Reaktionen*, pp. 115–20. This quotation p. 119.

9. Herbert Eisenreich, 'Das schöpferische Mißtrauen', in: *Reaktionen* pp. 89ff.

10. Their goal is not Utopia but resurrection . . . Tradition is not a means of moving forward but a gateway into the realm of myth and the prospect of greatness that myth by definition suggests'. Paul Kruntorad, 'Provinz der eigenen Vergangenheit', in: *Akzente*, 14 (1967), 414–19. This quotation pp. 414f.

11. Claudio Magris, *Der habsburgische Mythos in der österreichischen Literatur*, Salzburg, 1966. (This work was originally published in Italian in 1963).

12. Humbert Fink, 'Warm und zufrieden im Provinziellen?', in: *Wort in der Zeit*, 7 (1961) No. 11, 33–40.

13. 'the continuity of egotism, indifference and the jovial mask of heartlessness, which always knows how to come out on top.' Walter Weiss, 'Literatur', in: Erika Weinzierl and Kurt Skalnik (eds.), *Österreich. Die Zweite Republik*, vol. 2, Graz, Vienna, Cologne, 1972. pp. 439–76. This quotation p. 467.

14. 'quite content with the sense of harmony it derived from received images of the meaning and purpose of life, from pre-fabricated views of the world, pre-fabricated opinions, convictions and emotional attitudes.' Heinrich Vormweg, 'Überwindung eines Idols', in: *Akzente*, 14 (1967), 420–26. This quotation p. 422.

15. *The Austrian Miracle* (Presenter Charles Marowitz), BBC Radio 3, 25 April 1976, Tape No. BLN 17/041 D101.

16. 'to provoke new possibilities of expression, to effect change'. Gerhard Rühm, 'Vorwort' in: G.R. (ed.), *Die Wiener Gruppe. Achleitner, Artmann, Bayer, Rühm, Wiener. Texte, Gemeinschaftsarbeiten, Aktionen*, Reinbek bei Hamburg, 1967, pp. 7–36. This quotation p. 28.

17. Friedbert Aspetsberger, 'Sprachkritik als Gesellschaftskritik. Von der Wiener Gruppe zu O. Wieners "die Verbesserung von Mitteleuropa, Roman"', in: *Zeit-und Gesellschaftskritik in der österreichischen Literatur des 19. und 20. Jahrhunderts*, edited by the Institut für Österreichkunde, Vienna, 1973, p. 151.

18. 'the complete destruction of all those images of the world that seem to be complete'. Peter Handke, 'Ich bin ein Bewohner des Elfenbeinturms', in: *Elfenbeinturm*, p. 20.

19. 'a game with contradictions'. Peter Handke, 'Straßentheater und Theater', in: *Elfenbeinturm*, pp. 51–55. This quotation p. 53.

20. Peter Handke, 'Horváth und Brecht', in: *Elfenbeinturm*, pp. 63–64. This quotation p. 63.

21. Peter Handke, *Das Gewicht der Welt. Ein Journal*, Salzburg 1977, p. 291.

22. cf. Frederic R. Jameson. *The Prison-House of Language*, Princeton 1972.

23. 'Handke takes the fabric of a 'Bildungsroman'' and unpicks and reworks the design so that both the original model and the new version can be seen. He draws more and more threads in new and different directions, and weaves new associations of meaning.' Peter Pütz, 'Peter Handke', in: Heinz Ludwig Arnold (ed.), *Kritisches Lexikon zur deutschsprachigen Gegenwartsliteratur (KLG)*, Munich, 1978f, (= edition text und kritik).

Thomas Bernhard:
The Mask of Death

Hans Wolfschütz

Thomas Bernhard's early prose collection *Ereignisse* (*Events*, written in 1957) takes the form of a sequence of anecdotally-fashioned episodes each presenting a variation on that most central of concepts in modernist writing, the intrusion of 'Schrecken' of terror and horror, into everyday reality. In such a moment of shock the victim inevitably looks at his own existence and his relationship with the world about him in a new light, as, for example does the painter in one of Bernhard's episodes; at work on his scaffolding high above the people in the street, he is suddenly struck by the ridiculous nature of his elevated position:

> Ein entsetzlich lächerlicher Mensch! Jetzt ist ihm, als stürze er in diese Überlegung hinein, tief hinein und hinunter, in Sekundenschnelle, und man hört Aufschreie, und als der junge Mann unten aufgeplatzt ist, stürzen die Leute auseinander. Sie sehen den umgestülpten Kübel auf ihn fallen und gleich ist der Anstreicher mit gelber Fassadenfarbe übergossen. Jetzt heben die Passanten die Köpfe. Aber der Anstreicher ist natürlich nicht mehr oben.[1]

All Bernhard's characters are marked by such an 'event', whether this takes the form of some personal misfortune or shock, or has been experienced as part of a general or historical 'catastrophe'. But whereas in his early prose Bernhard is still primarily concerned with the actual moment when a sense of normality gives way to a sense of alienation, in most of his more typical work of the 1960s and 1970s the emphasis is switched to the effects of this new awareness, to the presentation of a mind and consciousness that have been wholly deranged by the experience. The connection with external reality has disappeared. Bernhard's typical character is, to use the image of the 'Anstreicher', suspended between the scaffold-

214

ing and his death in the abyss of his own inner world. He is a 'survivor' whose monomanic visions of decay and dissolution are the last hold to which he clings before his final fall.

The episode of the 'Anstreicher' also illustrates the second basic pre-condition for Bernhard's writing – the experience of the inward collapse of illusionistic art and art-forms. Bernhard's dislike for such painters of façades, who from their bird's-eye-view paint a harmonizing gloss over the world, that is his hatred of 'high art', is evident in most of his work. The grotesque image of the yellow wash running over the dead painter's body expresses an awareness of the death of such art and its artistic means, an awareness which forms the basis of the author's own iconoclastic approach to literary conventions.

Bernhard's uncompromising vision of man caught in the web of a solipsistic universe together with the far-reaching formal consequences of his defection from a belief in art as an organizing structure account for the fascination (and frustration) of his readers and critics. Critics may describe his work as akin to torture but this has not prevented them from writing extensively about it. Bernhard must rank as Austria's most widely-discussed and controversial writer, arousing such dissenting views as angry denunciations of his obsessive obscurantism or the high praise of George Steiner, who regards him as 'the most original and concentrated novelist writing in German'.[2] His status in the Austrian literary scene may be described as 'that of being at the same time a kind of "modern classic" and required reading, and, at least in the eyes of some, an *enfant terrible*, a poseur or even a charlatan'.[3]

It was not until the early 1960s that critics started to take an interest in Bernhard's writing. By then he had already published three volumes of poetry written under the haunting shadow of a serious illness which had very nearly proved fatal. These poems, for the most part an expression of his religious and mystical search for meaning, speak of a world full of suffering, brutality and coldness, but they are too close to personal experience to escape the charge of sentimental melancholia and self-indulgence. Even in the volume *In hora mortis* (1958) written several years after his brush with death, Bernhard shows but a fleeting glimpse of the rebellious self-assertion that was to become such a characteristic feature of his later writing. In these poems the lyrical 'I' is attempting to overcome his fear of death through religious faith, but without success,

for he receives no answer from his God. The cycle ends in a cry of
mental anguish that is clearly expressionististic in both idiom and
pathos:

> tot ist längst
> mein Rot
> mein Grün
> mein Stachel
> zerschnitten
> ach zerschnitten
> ach zerschnitten
> ach
> ach
> ach
> mein Ach.[4]

In his early prose work, on the other hand, Bernhard shows a
much greater control over his personal pain. *Ereignisse* illustrates
his new-found capacity to invest an individual dilemma with universal significance and to create a new norm, that of a life lived in the
aftermath of the experience of 'Schrecken'. This is particularly evident in the progression from the opening to the closing episode.
Ereignisse begins with the hasty flight of two lovers into a tower
where, in each others arms, they attempt to blot out the memory of
an unspecified horrific experience. Their flight is echoed in the final
episode, but this time it is a mass flight, the flight of a crowd seeking
sanctuary from air-raids in tunnels bored into the mountains. Bernhard's conclusion is grotesquely macabre:

> Als nun aber der Krieg zu Ende ist, geschieht etwas, das niemand
> begreifen kann: sie schütten die Stollen nicht zu, sondern gehen,
> wie es ihnen zur Gewohnheit geworden ist, hinein. Sie werden,
> solange sie leben, die Stollen aufsuchen.[5]

The escape gained by the two lovers promised a momentary release, now, at the close of the collection, there is nothing but permanent incarceration in a mind frozen by fear. Those who return to the
tunnels have become automatons controlled by a force whose
power-source has long been extinguished.[6] Having survived their
experience of war and death, life for them is but an empty ritual.

Even the narrator in *Ereignisse*, whose traditional function would involve drawing the various strands together in a meaningful pattern, is seen at the end of the sequence to be as much a 'survivor' as those whose fate he has described, and must be accounted part of the world he depicts. Thus there are no standards which might help the reader to assess the distortions portrayed. The narrator cannot interpret the world or put it into perspective but he is able to present it in a detached manner with occasional moments of grotesque and ironic lightening. This dual aspect to the narrator prefigures one of the most striking features of Bernhard's later narratives – the objective and dispassionate presentation of extremely subjective experience.[7]

Both of Bernhard's early novels *Frost* (1963) and *Verstörung* (Disturbance, 1967) follow this pattern and begin realistically enough before probing deep into the minds of their protagonists. The narrator in *Frost*, a young medical student, is given the task of observing and reporting on a painter, Strauch, who is allegedly mad and who has retreated to a mountain village. He begins his study with a fascinated and yet critical attitude but gradually loses the scientific detachment of the mere observer. By the end of the novel he can only express himself in the language and idiom of his 'case history':

> Er schiebt ganz einfach seine Hinfälligkeit in Form von Sätzen in mich hinein, wie photographische Bilder in einen Lichtbilderapparat, der dann diese Schrecken an den immer vorhandenen gegenüberliegenden Wänden meiner (und seiner) selbst zeigt.[8]

In *Verstörung* the narrator accompanies his father, a doctor, as he makes his house-calls. Their journey proceeds via stages of physical and psychological mutilation until it ends at Hochgobernitz, the seat of the mad Prince Saurau. In much the same manner as the young medical student in *Frost*, the doctor's son also suffers a process of depersonalization: he falls prey to the fascinating charm of the darker world represented by Saurau and finds himself reduced to a silent transmitter of his gigantic monologue (which covers about two thirds of the novel).

Both novels reflect Bernhard's penchant for adapting traditional elements of narrative fiction for his own idiosyncratic presentation of a monomanic world. The journey which the doctor's son undertakes for 'educational purposes' and which, as so often with Bernhard, takes him upwards, clearly echoes the structure of the *Bildungsroman*. The outcome of this educative journey is, however, not self-awareness and self-recognition but self-loss. The narrators of both novels are taken over by the characters they encounter, characters whose deranged talking it becomes their function to record and transmit.

Such a reduction of the narrator to a mere transmitter shatters the basis of traditional realism – the dialectical relationship of inner and outer reality. In most of Bernhard's subsequent narratives the narrators cease to exist as identifiable characters with recognizable features, but even so the reader remains aware of their narrative presence. It is a shadow existence, often suggested by nothing more substantial than extensive and sustained passages in the subjunctive mood, or by means of the reported speech in which they record the monologues of the central characters.

Within the hermetic world of these monologues there is nothing that exists in its own right. Topography, events and all the minor characters are merely the outward manifestation of a single psyche; thus the nightmarish village in *Frost* with its cripples, drunkards, lunatics and criminals is merely the outer shell of the disturbed workings of the painter Strauch's mind, and the house-calls in the first part of *Verstörung* are merely the first, basic, often animal-like steps towards the rarified philosophical derangements of Prince Saurau.

In much the same manner Bernhard's work as a whole presents a sequence of variations on a set of identical situations, characters and settings. There is no individuality to these settings and they are well-nigh interchangable, whether they are isolated hamlets, menacing valleys, impenetrable forests, or castles and estates which in earlier times were centres of economic power but are now no more than dilapidated anachronisms. Bernhard's central characters are shadowy figures too, for the most part psychological cripples on the threshold of madness with no hope of escape into the sanctuary of former times nor any prospect of a meaningful future; having withdrawn to the extreme solitude of some bleak mountain retreat they lead a life of total introspection and philosophical contemplation devoting themselves to such topics as the irrelevance of the state, the senselessness of historical development, the hostility of nature, disease, madness and above all, death.

Thematic and formal consistency is the hallmark of all Bernhard's work. He deliberately turns his back on such contemporary preoccupations as the relevance of literature in the political and social context, or the search for new artistic forms and methods, and concentrates on the one recurrent image of the world – an organism inescapably caught in its own vacuity. His writing thus acquires an uncanny immediacy as each new work provokes a moment of recognition when the reader detects the familiar set pieces, quotations and ideas rearranged in a new and unfamiliar context. Any 'development' there has been in Bernhard's work after the appearance of *Frost* must be seen in terms of increasing emphasis on a limited spectrum of stock-situations. In Bernhard's plays this has led to a measure of self-parody which can be seen in the shift from *Die Macht der Gewohnheit* (The Force of Habit, 1974), still largely a parable, to the sheer self-caricature and self-denunciation of *Die Berühmten* (Notabilities, 1976) or *Immanuel Kant* (1978). The shrinking world of Bernhard's narrative fiction reaches its ultimate stage in his novels *Kalkwerk* (The Limestone Works, 1970) and *Korrektur* (Correction, 1975).

Not surprisingly such an insistent pattern of repetition and variation has led many critics to charge Bernhard with increasing sterility and a consequent failure to provoke and irritate his public. His most recent narrative *Der Stimmenimitator* (The Mimic, 1978), a collection of some hundred short episodes, does, however, suggest a welcome change of direction. As Ulrich Greiner notes:

> Im *Stimmenimitator* hat Bernhard kein neues Thema, wohl aber eine neue Methode gefunden. Während er früher aus dem absolut Ungewöhnlichen die Lust des Schreckens saugte, holt er sie hier aus dem scheinbar Gewöhnlichen.[9]

In its preoccupation with the absurdities of everyday life but also in its anecdotal form and its combination of the deadly serious with elements of comedy *Der Stimmenimitator* is very reminiscent of Bernhard's first narrative work, the collection *Ereignisse*. This may well indicate that the author, by going back to his own beginnings, is searching for a way out of the solipsistic world which his literary explorations of the last twenty years have increasingly sealed off from any recognizable reality. But as Uwe Schweikert writes, 'Bernhards Werk ist ein "work in progress". Über ein solches läßt Endgültiges sich nicht ausmachen'.[10]

Bernhard's emergence from the relatively minor role of 'literary

219

talent' in the 1950s to his pre-eminence in the Austrian literary revival of the late 1960s and 1970s coincided with the spread of a new political and cultural radicalism amongst the young in the western world. It must be said that his writing has little in common with the politically inspired student revolts of the late sixties and yet both his work and his life-style are in harmony with the spirit of revolt in their anarchic rejection of preconceived ideas, their aggressive defiance of authority in any form and the delight they take in shocking 'respectable' society. Conventions and established patterns of meaning are seen as fetters from which the individual consciousness is to be liberated.

Bernhard's own rebellious streak is primarily rooted in the agony of his own existence. For him 'Vergangenheitsbewältigung', the attempt to come to terms with the past, is not a political problem but a personal one. In an essay on his childhood he describes his writing as a search for the origins of his personal disaster,[11] as an attempt to ward off the mists of despair which threaten to engulf him. Thus the act of writing becomes an expression of self-assertion; its function is therapeutic but not in a psychotherapeutic sense. While a psychoanalyst believes that the establishment of a chain of cause and effect, of action and reaction will assist understanding and enlightenment and thus help overcome the trauma of personal experience, Bernhard takes the opposite road and seeks freedom in a form of self-exorcism. It is in this sense that in a television interview, *Drei Tage* (Three Days, 1971), he described himself as a surgeon desperately performing a series of operations on himself to rid his body of the cancerous growths which keep on forming.[12]

The overwhelming negativity of Bernhard's world is the product of the writer's chosen form of therapy. Rather than search for a meaningful pattern to his personal suffering, Bernhard, through writing, intensifies his agony and raises it to an absolute and universal condition in which all traces of personal experience are lost. This attempt to transcend authentic, personal experience implies entry 'in die *andere, in die zweite, in die endgültige* Finsternis', the eternal darkness that comes when hope and illusion have had their day.[13] There is only one vantage point for such an absolute panorama: the finality of death. 'Wenn man an den Tod denkt', Bernhard suggests, everything about human life seems ridiculous.[14] Viewed from the perspective of death, he argues, everything becomes relative and is reduced to little more than the stage properties for some drawing-room comedy; from this perspective – and it is the perspective that informs all Bernhard's work – life itself, society, the state, historical development and even such personally-based experience as fear and disorientation lose their specific significance and become interchangeable elements in a uniform panoply of darkness.

It is death which enables Bernhard to escape the limitations of an objective, balanced view of the world and grants him the freedom to experiment within the framework of a world that is artificial and wholly aesthetic in its origins.

Bernhard's autobiographical novels illustrate this paradoxical attempt to assuage existential suffering by a process of intensification; it is an attempt inextricably linked to a central concept of Bernhard's writing: resistance. In the purely existentialist sense this implies a revolt against the norms of a world in which, as for example *Der Keller* (The Cellar, 1976) shows, the writer has experienced nothing but pain. *Der Keller* constantly harks back to Bernhard's decision to abandon the grammar school education envisaged for him and to take up an apprenticeship in a poky grocer's shop in the worst part of Salzburg. Only by summoning up the strength to reject an existence which Bernhard felt was being imposed on him from outside, was he able to find the conditions in which he could survive. His chosen path away from the 'normality' of a conventional career to life at the periphery of society amongst its flotsam and jetsam is an outward manifestation of the road from illusion to an all-embracing preoccupation with the 'ultimate darkness' referred to in *Drei Tage*:

> hier war alles zu finden, was die Stadt zu verschweigen oder zu vertuschen versuchte, alles, was der normale Mensch flieht, wenn er in der Lage ist, es zu fliehen, hier war der Schmutzfleck Salzburgs . . . ein einziger Schmutzfleck aus Armut und also ein Schmutzfleck zusammengesetzt aus Hunger, Verbrechen und Dreck.[15]

The road to this world beyond hope, to the extremities of society is, at the same time, a road to the inner mind, a descent into the abyss of Bernhard's own personal existence. As such it is given symbolic expression in the total isolation of his private world which he secures in *Die Ursache* (The Cause, 1975) in a narrow, stinking shoe-cupboard of the boarding-school where the young pupil sought refuge from the humiliations he suffered at the hands of his teachers and fellow pupils:

In die Schuhkammer ist nichts hineingedrungen, als ob sie hermetisch für mich und meine Phantasien und Träume und Selbstmordgedanken abgeschlossen wäre.[16]

In this 'fürchterlichsten Raum im ganzen Internat'[17], a further example of Bernhard's methodical pursuit of obscurity in all its forms, the young boy is able to allow his despair and thoughts of suicide full rein, while at the same time resolving and dispelling them through the 'creativity' of his violin which he is practising in this room. His playing is both unconventional and contrary to all instruction, but, in intensifying his morbid tendencies it also serves to counter them by consciously directing his mind from thoughts of suicide to the creative possibilities afforded by the violin. Thus the shoe-cupboard is not merely a place of extreme isolation and morbidity but one of resistance through creative activity; in this Bernhard depicts the second aspect of the motif of resistance – the resolution of existential difficulties by their transformation into an aesthetic world.

Bernhard's shoe-cupboard is a compelling image of that creative activity which depends on an almost autistic detachment from the outside world, and whose goal is the eradication of the original stimulus to such activity, namely suffering. Pure, self-sufficient aesthetic experience offers a significant prospect of release from the pain and suffering of life. In a literary context this would imply the ideal of *poésie pure*, the *absolute Prosa* which Bernhard finds in the work of Ezra Pound and above all in Valéry's *Monsieur Teste*.[18] It would be a literature in which language ceased to be a 'window on reality' and would stand or fall by its immanent possibilities. In the idiom of *Die Ursache* this would be the creative range and possibilities of the violin.

Bernhard's work testifies to this continual struggle to achieve an ideal literature constructed according to musical and mathematical principles. It is an enterprise whose roots lie in the misery of existence and which, while never fully losing contact with the existential realm, is decided on an aesthetic plane. Since language, as opposed to musical sound, is not merely an autonomous sign, but always carries a signifying element in its transmission, Bernhard must seek to destroy all those linguistic elements which threaten to communi-

222

cate by reflection and image, or, in other words, he must seek to 'musicalize' his language. To this end he uses a consciously contrived and very distinctive style of writing whose most prominent features are density and exaggeration, repetition and variation. His prose is characterized by geometrically-constructed sentence-complexes, some of which may run on for more than a page in a manner reminiscent of the formal and laborious style of official or legal documents. It is his exaggerated precision in these mammoth constructions – the abundance of conjunctions such as 'because' or 'although' – which enables Bernhard to undermine the development of logical arguments. As he himself writes:

> In meiner Arbeit, wenn sich irgendwo Anzeichen einer Geschichte bilden, oder wenn ich nur in der Ferne irgendwo hinter einem Prosahügel die Andeutung einer Geschichte auftauchen sehe, schieße ich sie ab. Es ist auch mit den Sätzen so, ich hätte fast die Lust, ganze Sätze, die sich *möglicherweise* bilden könnten, schon im vornhinein abzutöten.[19]

In his plays he achieves the same purpose of preventing the development of a logical sequence by using rhythmically accentuated blocks of paratactical sentences. A number of his public speeches have a similar effect, in that the meaning is not so much conveyed by the sentences as a whole, but by the use of selected words with clear negative overtones.

Bernhard's writing thus suggests a state of constant tension. On the one hand, by making use of language at all, he inevitably conveys meaning while with the other he retracts it, and such reflections of the world as he does create are promptly shattered. The emphasis is firmly on structure and the rhythmical patterns of language rather than on content; there is little place for the referential element in language in the systematic abstraction to which Bernhard's absolutism leads. His predilection for superlatives, his recurrent use of such adverbs as 'all', 'nothing', 'every', 'always' etc. are similar means to the ultimate goal of aesthetic redemption through pure formal experimentation. It is an ideal which, given the dual nature of language as sign and signifier, can never be wholly attained.

The consequent ambivalence in Bernhard's presentation of material from the world at large and his concealment of that reference behind a veil of methodical abstraction is particularly evident in his use of material with specifically Austrian overtones. Nearly all the settings of his works, although in themselves devoid of any clearly identifiable features, are given names of actual villages and communities in Austria. In addition, Bernhard is constantly deriding Austria, not only in his public speeches and autobiographical accounts, but in his creative writing as well. A third point of reference to Austria can be traced in Bernhard's inclusion in his work of examples of the gradual decline and dispersal of the massive estates which had been held by individual families down the ages. While granting economic freedom to their owners in former times, these estates are regarded by Bernhard's central characters as an unbearable burden of which they desperately attempt to rid themselves.

These heirs of the feudal aristocracy are depicted as inhabiting residences situated high above the realm their families used to control. Thus Festung Hochgobernitz, the world of Prince Saurau, is a typical example of these centres of former economic and cultural import. Land and property bestowed power, and the landowners themselves embodied a tradition of universal values. Like the Zoiss family in the narrative *Ungenach* (the name of an actual Austrian village; 1968), they 'made' history. Their decline is seen as the direct result of a loss of purpose, of a growing impotence and of the aggressive advances made by representatives of the 'masses' from their lowland dwellings into the feudal heights. Such an incursion is documented in the novel *Korrektur* in which the thoughts of the central figure, Roithamer, continually return to the destructive influence of his mother, who, having fought her way up from the cultural wasteland of life as a butcher's daughter to become the mistress of the Altensam estate, presides over its destruction with devastating effect.[20]

Bernhard is not, however, writing specifically Austrian versions of such family chronicles as *Buddenbrooks* or *The Forsyte Saga*. His novels have, as it were, already 'taken place' and what is presented to the reader is the product of the memory and imagination of his central characters, a pageant acted out on a stage which they themselves will never tread. Their thinking is conditioned by concepts which are inextricably linked to their own heritage, but, as they are all-too aware, their whole existence has become an anachronism and can no longer be defined in terms of belonging to a particular social environment. Prince Saurau in *Verstörung* provides a characteristic illustration of this dilemma:

Ich fühlte unter meinen eigenen Leuten, daß ich für sie längst unsichtbar geworden bin, und fühlte das immer mehr. Auf einmal war ich für sie überhaupt nicht mehr vorhanden, nicht mehr *da*.[21]

The parallel to the 'Anstreicher' in *Ereignisse* who was suddenly 'no longer up there' any more is evident, but the anecdotal reference to a purely existential problem is now presented within a historical framework. Saurau measures his own existence, as might be expected of the head of a feudal hierarchy, in terms of his property, that is of 'his own people'. 'The Prince' was indeed to have been the original title of the novel, but Saurau is a mere shadow of the pre-eminence outlined by Machiavelli in his treatise. His sense of disorientation within any meaningful external reality, his feeling that in social terms he is as good as dead, leaves him with one recourse, and that is to defy social yardsticks completely and establish his own inner standards and codes. It is a solution shared by most of Bernhard's characters, not least the doctor in *Watten* (1969; 'Watten' is an Austrian card-game), whose social alienation leads him to seek a different reality within himself:

Ich muß in der Isolierung *sein* . . . Ich gehöre nicht in die Masse, höre ich die Masse, ich gehöre in mich selbst, höre ich mich. Da die Masse mich ausscheidet, habe ich keine andere Wahl, als mich nach einem Tod in mir selbst umzuschauen . . .[22]

Like Saurau, the doctor also has an aristocratic background; however, rather than shut himself off within the walls of his inherited castle, he seeks refuge in the isolation of a forest-hut. For both characters death represents a surrogate for a social pattern that has been lost – a clear echo of Bernhard's own paradoxical step from personal alienation to what he called 'the ultimate darkness'.

The elevation of death to such absolute pitch is no mere exercise in excessive morbidity but an attempt to establish a new, abstract universality totally devoid of all reference to historical reality. It is an attempt that demands the shedding of physical and psychological limits to the experiencing mind. Thus Bernhard's central characters seek the deliberate destruction of their heritage in both the literal sense (by running-down such property as they have inherited) and the figurative (by thinking through and re-thinking their own past to the point at which it no longer has any meaning). The heir-cum-philosopher Roithamer in *Korrektur* not only allows Altensam to go to rack and ruin, but writes a treatise on the estate and everything related to it as part of his attempt to extinguish within himself all traces of the past:

> Er hatte sich den Kopf frei gemacht von Altensam und von Österreich . . . er hatte praktisch alles, was er gewesen war, aufgegeben, um alles zu erreichen, was er nicht gewesen war und schließlich geworden ist durch die übermenschliche Überanstrengung.[23]

Roithamer's almost Nietzschean 'self-correction', his attempt to achieve 'what he had not been', is at the same time matched by his equally Nietzschean attempt at absolute creativity: he plans and directs the construction of the 'Kegel', an extraordinary cone-shaped building in the middle of an impenetrable forest. This building, intended as a home for his beloved sister, represents a kind of 'counter-Altensam' and as such is the external manifestation of the new zenith of pure thought for which Roithamer is striving. As Sorg notes, the 'Kegel' is:

> konzentriertester Ausdruck einer radikalen Untergangssehnsucht, die noch einmal, vor dem Erlöschen, das Vollkommene will und plant und gegen alle und alles durchsetzt.[24]

Inevitably, Roithamer's attempt to invoke extremes of analytical thought as an instrument to achieve the destruction and annihilation of those concepts that condition his mind can only lead to self-annihilation. His final suicide leaves the 'Kegel' as a defiant symbol of unfulfilled utopia abandoned in the forest where it will be reclaimed by nature.

Most of Bernhard's characters dream of such a wholly different reality to what they perceive as a dying world. There every thought and deed is guided by the ideal of an a-directional, a-practical existence, by mystical visions permeated with concepts from a fairy-tale utopia, as described by the painter Strauch in *Frost*:

> Es gibt hier auch ganz eigensinnige Täler und in diesen Tälern Herrenhäuser und Schlösser. Man geht in diese Herrenhäuser und in diese Schlösser hinein und man sieht gleich: die Welt, aus der man ist, hat hier nichts mehr zu suchen. Das müssen Sie sich

alles ganz unwirklich vorstellen, *so wie die tiefste Wirklichkeit*, wissen Sie. Türen gehen auf, hinter denen Menschen in kostbaren Kleidern sitzen, Thronsesselmenschen . . . Einfachheit wölbt sich wie ein klarer Himmel über das, was man denkt. Nichts Phantastisches, obwohl alles der Phantasie entsprungen. Wohlhabenheit, die einfach, Menschenwärme, die ohne die Spur eines Verbrechens ist . . . Geist und Charakter sind schön in der Menschennatur vereint. Logik ist in Musik gesetzt. Das Alter plötzlich wieder zur Schönheit fähig, die Jugend wohl wie ein Vorgebirge. Die Wahrheit liegt auf dem Grund wie das Unerforschliche'.[25]

Such an utopian vision, cast as it is against the background of an aristocratic social structure, with its emphasis on the synthesis of mind and body, thought and deed, imagination and reality and man and nature in the simplicity and geometric clarity of a new order, is clearly indebted to the specifically Austrian tradition which sought to escape from historical reality into an abstract order.[26]

Even so, Bernhard cannot be seen as a latter-day exponent of that literary trend which Claudio Magris so tellingly designated 'the Hapsburg myth'. There is no one explanation of Bernhard's idiosyncratic approach. The socio-historical perspective, his realization that a social class and indeed a whole historical era has come to an end, would, in a political sense, undoubtedly label him as a conservative defector into the ranks of anarchy. Yet this is but one of so many different perspectives ranging from the purely existential to the metaphysical and philosophical. Bernhard's literary explorations defy all categorization; he hints at solutions while at the same time throwing a veil of mystery around their implications – 'Die Antwort muß ausbleiben'.[27] His style, his linguistic abstractions and the circular structure of his works leads to a broad spectrum of interpretations which are at the same time congruent yet disparate.

This is well shown in the play *Die Macht der Gewohnheit*. This comedy turns on the vain, artistic ambitions of an ageing ringmaster in a small family circus. For the past twenty-two years he has been unsuccessfully attempting to bring his small troupe of artistes to the point at which they can achieve a perfect performance of Schubert's quintet 'The Trout' – an activity clearly echoing Roithamer's projected perfect home, the 'Kegel'. Despite the ringmaster's awareness that he can never achieve such an ideal of universal beauty he refuses to give up. On this level the play appears to be little more than a straight-forward parable in the absurd manner employing the familiar absurdist circus metaphor and an equally familiar bleak message conveyed to the audience by the ringmaster himself:

> Wir wollen das Leben nicht / aber es muß gelebt werden . . .
> Wir hassen das Forellenquintett/ aber es muß gespielt werden[28]

Die Macht der Gewohnheit is so overloaded with such 'universal truths' that the validity of individual statements is immediately cast into doubt. While clearly an absurdist parable at base, the play could equally well be seen as a political parable or as a parody of the very Salzburg Festival for which it was written. It is to music, however, that the reader should look for the most telling parallel, to the musical structure of Schubert's quintet with its central theme woven around with a sequence of variations. From this point of view *Die Macht der Gewohnheit* ceases to be piece of literature 'about' something; with its rhythmically reiterated set of phrases and actions it comes closest to Bernhard's ideal of musicalized writing and its theme, if indeed it can be said to have one, is the death of meaning.

Bernhard's obsession with death suggests a close affinity to that Austrian modernism which turns aside from reality in favour of introspection and the cultivated pursuit of melancholy, ascribing to death a mythical quality as the ultimate source of truth. It is, however, open to question whether Bernhard's apocalyptic visions suggest that the 'purgatory' at present experienced will in fact necessarily lead to 'paradise'. In the speech he gave when receiving the Austrian State Prize, Bernhard insisted that all thinking was 'second-hand', and in this he must have included thinking and speaking about death. Thus he sees speaking as a form of speaking in inverted commas, a form of role-playing within a carefully-set theatre, and he includes both his own work and his own public image in this definition. By choosing to live in the solitude of an out-of-the-way farm he not merely reflects the isolation of his characters, but his infrequent public appearances to receive prizes or to give interviews show him obsessed with death and apparently unable to talk about anything else. It is as if he were constantly quoting from his own work.

Bernhard's fine sense of the theatrical is well-shown in the speech he prepared for his receipt of the Wildgans Prize in 1968. He was

228

not allowed to deliver this speech lest this too might provoke yet another of the many scandals surrounding his public appearances. What he had written was a fairly lengthy speech, yet another variation on the theme of death, the end of which seems to parody 'memento mori':

. . . und mit dem Hinweis darauf, daß nämlich alles mit dem Tode zu tun hat, daß alles der Tod ist, das ganze Leben ist ja nichts anderes als der Tod, werde ich Ihnen einen guten, möglicherweise einen merkwürdigen Abend wünschen und aus diesem Saal hinausgehen, fortgehen aus Wien, aus Österreich eine Zeit fortgehen an das Vergnügen und an die Arbeit und ich . . . erinnere Sie noch einmal nachdrücklich an den Tod, daran, daß alles mit dem Tode zu tun hat, vergessen Sie den Tod nicht . . . vergessen Sie ihn nicht, vergessen Sie ihn nicht . . .[29]

The evening which Bernhard, cast in his role of voice crying in the wilderness, would have given his culturally-polished audience, would have been memorable indeed. Those listening would have found themselves presented with what was tantamount to a play, but one whose conclusion was still unclear, so that they would not have known whether they were being given answers to the problems of life (or the realization that there are no answers) or made to witness a brilliant piece of clowning.

There is a similar deliberate 'staginess' in much of Bernhard's work, a staginess with strong morbid overtones. The dark overtones of his story *Ja* (Yes, 1978) conceal the mystery of the affirmative title, so untypical of Bernhard's style, until the very last sentence. At the end of the story the narrator is recalling a series of conversations he had had with a woman, who, he has just learned, has committed suicide. This news reminds him that he had asked her during a discussion about suicide whether she had ever considered the possibility that she might take her own life:

Darauf hatte sie nur gelacht und *Ja* gesagt.[30]

In this, the last sentence of the story, Bernhard uses the grotesque element in this paean of self-destruction as a counter to the gloomy seriousness and philosophical profundity of what has gone before. As in the grotesque climax to the episode of the 'Anstreicher' in *Ereignisse*, the author fuses comic and tragic elements into a new

229

and original union.

Ultimately, the reader realizes that Bernhard's preoccupation with death is a pose in which he plays the part of the poet of death, transcending mundane social and political considerations to draw hidden treasures of truths from the shadows for all to experience. His relationship to the literary tradition, his life and work, are first and last a game played at the edge of the abyss, a game which not only reflects the loss of any objective value-system, but also the demise of that modernist view which sees the artist as the interpreter and sooth-sayer of a disjointed and fragmented world. There is no better phrase to describe his attitude than the romantic 'höheren Witz' to which he refers in *Der Keller*.[31]

Bernhard's sceptical attitude to the possibilities of artistic integrity and meaningful interpretation is the paradoxical conclusion to that Austrian tradition whose roots lie in the linguistic and philosophical dilemmas of the turn of the century. Hugo von Hofmannsthal, despite the despair of the Chandos Letter, still believed in a new form of poetic language and in the possibility of salvation through art; for Bernhard this avenue is no longer open. Language does not bring contact with the world but, on the contrary, re-emphasizes the isolation of the individual:

Ich spreche die Sprache, die nur ich allein verstehe, sonst niemand, wie jeder nur seine eigene Sprache versteht.[32]

Here too, as in so many other Austrian writers, we find an echo of Wittgenstein's solipsistical 'The limits of my language signify the limits of my world'.

Even so Bernhard is not the value-free observer of the world that Wittgenstein would have his new philosopher be, nor is he the mere recorder of phenomena as Robbe-Grillet sees the new writer in the technological era. Bernhard maintains the humanistic tradition of searching for meaning, he remains an interpreter of the world, but always keenly aware that the artist can create nothing but lies and deceit. The ringmaster in *Die Macht der Gewohnheit* grandly proclaims his belief that anyone who trusts art is a fool, and yet he pursues his obsessive quest for perfection through art in much the same way as Bernhard continues to write. It is another character in the comedy – the juggler – who may well provide the clue to Bernhard's artistic goal:

Das Leben besteht darin/Fragen zu vernichten[33]

It is not just that Bernhard refuses to provide answers, leaving the search for meaning in some absurd vaccum, but rather that he makes the validity of the very act of questioning the focal point of his work. However, whereas some other younger writers have abandoned altogether the search for a justification of life and reality, Bernhard, while doubting the existence of any justification, is nonetheless peculiarly susceptible to this basic human aspiration to attach meanings to all phenomena and experiences. Like Beckett, his work

> retains a link with traditional western rational humanism by virtue of its felt sense of the pathos of this tradition's demise. Such literature may be said to affirm an objective order of values, not by permitting the assumption that such an objective order actually exists, but by assuming that the loss of such an order is deprivation.[34]

In its manic obsession with death, Bernhard's 'anti-literature' may be said not to deal with death itself, but rather with the death of meaning and truths, including the absurdist meaning of the meaninglessness of the world. There is here more than an echo of Nietzsche's dictum that all truths are illusions, only mankind has forgotten this fact. Bernhard's writing is closely involved with his own country and its own traditions; it is a fluctuating love-hate relationship that is perhaps inevitable in one steeped as he is in the Austrian tradition which, on the one hand lays claim to culture as the ultimate repository of human values and truths, and on the other, breeds scepticism and radical self-doubt in its creative offspring.

An author such as Bernhard, who questions the validity of his own role as writer, can find himself in a paradoxical cul de sac. In attempting in his own very peculiar way to take the mystique out of art he cannot but see himself caught in the cultural process he derides. This vicious circle is neatly illustrated in the three plays written for the Salzburg Festival, perhaps *the* shrine of the Austrian cultural myth. It is surprising enough, perhaps, that Bernhard should write these plays, but, despite parting company with the festival on the bitterest of terms, he then had them published in a single volume under the collective title of *Salzburger Stücke*!

NOTES

1. 'A horribly ridiculous person! Now it seems to him as if he were plunging into this awareness, deep into it and down, at tremendous speed, and cries are heard and when the young man lies crumpled on the ground all the people run apart. They see the turned-up paint pot fall on him and all at once the painter is covered in yellow. Now the passers-by look up, but, naturally, the painter is no longer up there'.
   Thomas Bernhard, 'Ereignisse', in: Thomas Bernhard, *An der Baumgrenze*, Munich, 1969 (= sonderreihe dtv 99), pp. 41–91. This quotation pp. 57f.

2. George Steiner, 'Conic sections', in: *The Times Literary Supplement*, 13.2.1976.

3. A.P. Dierick, 'Thomas Bernhard's Austria: Neurosis, Symbol or Expedient?', in: *Modern Austrian Literature*, 12 (1979), No.1, 73–93. This quotation p. 73.

4. 'Long since dead/ my red/ my green/ my sting/ broken/ oh broken/ oh broken/ oh/ oh/ oh/ my oh'.
   Thomas Bernhard, *In hora mortis*, Salzburg, 1958, p. 30.

5. 'Now that the war is over, something inexplicable happens and no-one knows why. Instead of closing up the tunnels, they keep going back into them. It has become a habit. Every day, at the same time they go back into them. As long as they live they will keep on returning to the tunnels'.
   Bernhard, 'Ereignisse', in: *An der Baumgrenze*, p. 91.

6. In *Die Ursache* (The Cause, 1975) Bernhard reveals the documentary basis for these tunnels. He describes them as air-raid shelters used by the citizens of Salzburg during the Second World War, and shows that these places of refuge are themselves filled with the presence of fear and death and devoid of all hope of safety.

7. cf. Uwe Schweikert, '"Im Grunde ist alles, was gesagt wird, zitiert"', in: Heinz Ludwig Arnold (ed), *Thomas Bernhard*, Munich, 1974 (= Text und Kritik 43), pp. 1–8.

8. 'He slips his vulnerability into me in sentences like slides into a projector, which casts these terrors onto the ever present walls of my (and his) self'.
   Thomas Bernhard, *Frost*, Munich/Zurich, 1965, (= Knaurs Taschenbuch 80), p. 257.

9. 'The *Stimmenimitator* does not represent a new theme for Bernhard but rather a new method. In his earlier work he was drawn by the horrific elements in existence which were wholly out of the ordinary, but now he depicts them in a context which has all the appearance of everyday reality'. Ulrich Greiner, 'Thomas Bernhards gewöhnlicher Schrecken', in: *Frankfurter Allgemeine Zeitung*, 21.11.1978.

10. 'Bernhard's work is "work in progress". There is nothing definite that could be said about it'.

Uwe Schweikert, op. cit., p. 8.

11. cf. Thomas Bernhard, 'Unsterblichkeit ist unmöglich. Landschaft der Kindheit', in: *Neues Forum*, 15(1968), 95–97.

12. cf. Thomas Bernhard, 'Drei Tage', in: Thomas Bernhard, *Der Italiener*, Munich, 1973, (= sonderreihe dtv 122), pp. 78–92. This reference p. 80.

13. Bernhard, 'Drei Tage', in: *Der Italiener*, p. 89.

14. 'If we think of death . . .' Thomas Bernhard, 'Rede', (On receipt of the Austrian State Prize for Literature, 1968) in: Anneliese Botond (ed), *Über Thomas Bernhard*, Frankfurt/M., 1970 (= edition suhrkamp 401), p. 7.

15. 'Here was everything which the city would rather forget or gloss over, everything from which the normal individual would flee if he had the opportunity, here was the garbage-can of Salzburg . . . one huge garbage-can of poverty, of hunger, crime and filth'.
Thomas Bernhard, *Der Keller, Eine Entziehung*, Salzburg, 1976, p. 34.

16. 'Nothing could penetrate the shoe-cupboard, it was seemingly hermetically sealed so that I could indulge in my fantasies and dreams and think of suicide'.
Thomas Bernhard, *Die Ursache, Eine Andeutung*, Salzburg, 1975, p. 78.

17. 'the most terrible room in the whole boarding-school', Bernhard, *Die Ursache*, p. 15.

18. cf. Bernhard, 'Drei Tage', in: *Der Italiener*, p. 87.

19. 'Whenever I see a story about to take shape, or catch a glimpse of a story lurking somewhere in the distance behind a mountain of words, I reach for my revolver. It's the same with sentences – I get this strong desire to take sentences which might just take shape and wring their necks before they have a chance to breathe'.
Bernhard, 'Drei Tage', in: *Der Italiener*, pp. 83f.

20. Here and elsewhere (as, for example, in *Ungenach*) Bernhard links the decline of a former ruling-class to the intrusion of women into the sphere of male domination and patriarchal rule.

21. 'Even amongst my own people I felt I had long since become invisible as far as they were concerned. I simply did not exist any more. I just wasn't *there*'.
Thomas Bernhard, *Verstörung*, Frankfurt/M., 1967, p. 134.

22. 'I must exist in my isolation. I don't belong to the masses when I hear the masses, I belong to myself when I hear myself. Since the masses have closed their ranks against me, I have no option but to seek out a death within myself'.
Thomas Bernhard, *Watten, Ein Nachlaß*, Frankfurt/M, 1969 (= edition suhrkamp 353), p. 23.

23. 'He had rid his mind of Altensam and Austria (. . .), he had as good as given up everything which he had been, in order to achieve what he had not been, and this he finally achieved through his superhuman effort'.
Thomas Bernhard, *Korrektur*, Frankfurt/M., 1975, p. 39.

233

24. 'a highly concentrated symbol for a radical death-wish which, before the final collapse, seeks to achieve perfection and lays its plans and carries them through against all opposition'.
Bernhard Sorg, *Thomas Bernhard*, Munich, 1977 (= Autorenbücher 7), p. 181.

25. 'There are quite wilful valleys here too, and these valleys have castles and manors. If you go into these manor-houses and into these castles you can see at once that the world you have come from is another world completely. But you have to imagine things in a quite unreal way, *as if it were absolute reality*. Doors open and reveal people sitting there in precious clothes, fit for a throne . . . Everything you think is beautifully simple, like a cloudless sky. Nothing strikes you as being fantastic but it is all fantasy. There is a simple well-being and a genuine human kindness without a touch of wrong-doing . . . Mind and character have been harmoniously united in human nature and logic has become music. Old age can regain its youthful beauty and youth seems no more than a foothill. And truth lies around like some unfathomable puzzle'.
Bernhard, *Frost*, p. 193f.

26. cf. Herbert Gamper, *Thomas Bernhard*, Munich, 1977 (= dtv 6870), pp. 43ff.
Hans Höller, *Kritik einer literarischen Form. Versuch über Thomas Bernhard*, Stuttgart, 1979, (= Stuttgarter Arbeiten zur Germanistik 50).

27. 'There cannot be any answer'.
Bernhard, *Der Keller*, p. 157.

28. 'We do not want life /but we have to live it. We hate 'The Trout'/but we have got to play it.
Thomas Bernhard, *Die Macht der Gewohnheit*, Frankfurt/M., 1974 (= Bibliothek Suhrkamp 415), p. 43.

29. '. . . and with the reminder that everything has to do with death, everything is death, the whole of life after all is nothing but death, let me wish you a good, perhaps even remarkable and strange evening. I leave this hall, leave Vienna, leave Austria, to pursue my pleasure, pursue my work for a time, and let me say again . . . let me again remind you quite expressly of death, of the fact that everything has to do with death; don't forget death, don't forget death . . . don't forget death . . .'
Thomas Bernhard, 'Der Wahrheit und dem Tod auf der Spur. Zwei Reden', in: *Neues Forum*, 15(1968), No. 173, p. 349.

30. 'Thereupon she had laughed and answered 'Yes''
Thomas Bernhard, *Ja*, Frankfurt/M., 1978 (= Bibliothek Suhrkamp 600), p. 148.

31. 'I speak a language which I alone understand, and everyone else speaks their own private language as well'.
Bernhard, *Der Keller*, p. 156.

32. Bernhard, *Der Keller*, p. 156.

33. 'Life is a question of destroying questions'.
Bernhard, *Die Macht der Gewohnheit*, pp. 144f.

34. Gerald Graff, 'The Myth of the Postmodernist Breakthrough', in:

Malcolm Bradbury (ed.), *The Novel Today*, Glasgow, 1977, pp. 215–249. This quotation p. 226.

From the 'Wiener Gruppe' to Ernst Jandl

Michael Butler

The emergence of the 'Wiener Gruppe' can only be adequately understood in relation to the political and socio-cultural background of post-1945 Austria and its capital city, in particular. In a situation where powerful conservative forces seemed intent on establishing the concept of an historic Austrian 'continuity' – as if the authoritarian Dollfuss régime, the Civil War of 1934 and the Hitler dictatorship had been temporary, if embarrassing interruptions in a natural evolution from Imperial grandeur to Second Republic – the young artists of what came to be known as the 'Wiener Gruppe' could only see themselves as rebels and outsiders. They found themselves in a country which was fragilely poised between the victorious Great Powers and concentrating its energies on the development of a system of concensus politics, designed to achieve stability and national independence. Together with an increasing emphasis on materialism, this naturally involved the gradual stifling of opposition and the discreet obfuscation of such 'unpatriotic' questions as the nature of Austrian fascism and the problem of opportunist Nazi collaboration. The cultural atmosphere generated in such circumstances was marked by an entrenched provincialism and a hostility to experimentation of any kind. It is not surprising, therefore, that the members of the 'Wiener Gruppe' (H.C. Artmann, Gerhard Rühm, Konrad Bayer, Oswald Wiener and Friedrich Achleitner) looked for an alternative cultural tradition outside the officially sanctioned limits. They located it, in fact, amongst those European artists who had been denounced as 'degenerate' by Hitler and viciously proscribed throughout the Nazi Empire: the Expressionists, the Dadaists and the poets of Surrealism. In Konrad Bayer's words: 'We had to master these movements of the past in order to ward off the pre-past that was threatening to engulf us.'[1] Thus, almost inevitably, these young writers adopted a stance of anarchic individualism as they tried to catch up with those significant areas of

236

European art from which the *Anschluß* and its aftermath had excluded them.

Held together by ties of friendship rather than by any firm programme or rigid theory, the 'Wiener Gruppe' surfaced as a recognizable entity in the early 1950s, but its roots stretch back to the progressive 'Artclub', founded in 1946 in Vienna, which rapidly became a magnet for every avant-gardist in the capital. It was not, however, until 1952 that H.C. Artmann and Gerhard Rühm came into contact, to be shortly joined by Bayer and Oswald Wiener, and finally by Friedrich Achleitner. A period of intense collaboration ensued which culminated in 1957 in the Group's first public reading at Vienna's 'Intimes Theater'. There followed a series of regular readings which led to the formation of the 'Literarisches Cabaret'. In retrospect, the two performances of the latter in 1958–9 can be seen as the climax of the 'Wiener Gruppe's' activities. In fact, Artmann had already left the Group by 1958, and with Wiener's departure a year later the early 1960s mark its slow dissolution. By 1967, when Rühm published his important anthology *Die Wiener Gruppe* (significantly in West Germany), the Group had clearly become an historical fact, albeit one barely acknowledged within official Austrian cultural circles. The latter, indeed, could still manage an outraged protest when presented with a modest selection of the work of Rühm and Bayer in the February 1964 number of the State – supported *Wort in der Zeit* – an editorial indiscretion which eventually cost Gerhard Fritsch his job.[2]

The spirit of revolt against bourgeois conventions and restorative tendencies in society and literature, which characterized the 'Wiener Gruppe's' work, was most clearly enunciated in Artmann's *Acht-Punkte-Proklamation des poetischen Actes* (1953) with its provocative opening assertion: 'Es gibt einen Satz, der unangreifbar ist, nämlich der, daß man Dichter sein kann, ohne auch irgendjemals ein Wort geschrieben oder gesprochen zu haben.'[3] Together with this aggressive demotion of the traditional concept of the 'Dichter' as Poet-Seer – nowhere stronger than in Austria – in favour of artistic endeavour and achievement as a state of mind or attitude, Artmann stressed the freedom of the 'poetic act' from all bourgeois criteria of individual quality, permanence and marketable value. Art was to be spontaneous and independent of public acclaim or criticism. The emphasis on the value-free, extempore and irrational nature of artistic production shows very clearly Artmann's debt to the Surrealists whose exploration of the subcon-

237

scious and whose aleatory techniques were later to fascinate all the members of the Group. That Artmann and his friends were well aware of the political dimension of such attitudes can be seen not only in the various 'happenings' and 'poetic demonstrations' they promptly organized in various little cellar theatres and, on one occasion, on the streets of Vienna, but also in the sharp attack on Austrian rearmament launched by Artmann in his *Manifest* of 17 May, 1955, which was signed by twenty-five colleagues.

The specific assault on the hierarchy principle in regard to the artist and his products was continued a year later with the publication of Oswald Wiener's *Coole Manifest* which was signed by all the members of the Group except Achleitner (who had not yet joined). The original document has unfortunately been lost, but judging from recollections by Rühm and Wiener himself, the Manifesto – or anti-Manifesto, as it declared amongst other things the uselessness of such proclamations – went further than the somewhat loose programme drawn up by Artmann. For Wiener appears to have believed at this time that no serious statement could be made through art; 'events' were to be created merely as opportunities to handle emotions coolly and objectively like tools to fashion aesthetic effects. Rühm, whilst not entirely accepting, or perhaps perceiving, the full implications of Wiener's ideas, records that the *Coole Manifest* was an attempt to redefine the whole concept of 'literature': puns, deliberately pointless jokes, the language of business signs and bureaucracy, the vocabulary of crossword puzzles and advertisements, fragments of used blotting-paper, random illustrations from books and medical treatises, combined with suitably shocking texts etc., were all potential literary material in the struggle to unmask the pretentious falsity and crippling restrictions of bourgeois aesthetics. This anarchic eclecticism, with its strong echoes of Kurt Schwitters' similar reversal of the normal categories of banality and significance, was aimed at freeing the imagination and thus precisely those creative energies which were trapped by the multifarious control mechanisms of the social system. In this respect, the 'Wiener Gruppe' anticipated by almost a decade the radical questioning of literature and its values which took place in West Germany in the 1960s.

The common denominator which links all the manifestations of the 'Wiener Gruppe' both to each other and to the twentieth-century European tradition of experimental literature, is to be found in the Group's critical attitude to *language*. The ancient claim of language to be the means by which man orientates himself in, and makes sense of, the world had already received its first major literary challenge from Austria in the shape of Hofmannsthal's 'Chandos-Brief', published in 1902. Hofmannsthal's crucial insights into the crisis of language and thus of personal identity were developed by the Expressionists – and nowhere more consistently than by the circle gathered round Herwarth Walden in Berlin. It was the poets and artists associated with the latter's influential magazine *Der Sturm* who primarily interested the 'Wiener Gruppe'. It was there in 1912 that the German version of Marinetti's *Manifesto technico della letteratura futuristica* was published – the first fully worked-out programme for a radical assault on language. Far more than relatively isolated precursors such as Scheerbart, Mallarmé or Morgenstern, Marinetti's concept of 'Parole in libertà', that is, the release of words from the straight-jacket of linearity and traditional syntax, has exerted a continuous influence on experimental literature, from his immediate contemporary August Stramm, through the Dadaists to the 'Wiener Gruppe' and other post-war avant-gardists. For Marinetti's theories point vividly to the connection between man's socio-cultural environment and the language he speaks.[4] If man's conceptual ability is related to and shaped by his linguistic capacity – an idea which was also fascinating Wittgenstein at that time – any fundamental attempt to get to grips with linguistic phenomena must imply a fundamental analysis of man. Furthermore, if the grammatical and syntactical arrangements of language are historically and socially determined, a rigorous attack on those arrangements should both help to reveal the true structures of the world and correct man's perception of them. For the latter, so the argument goes, has been progressively obscured by the ossification of linguistic conventions and the social system that reflects them. In this way man's alienation from his innate creative sources can be explained and the possibility of his emancipation revealed. Such, at least, were the ideas that attracted the 'Wiener Gruppe' towards radical linguistic experimentation in the 1950s.

Their individual attitudes to language also help to differentiate the members of the Group from each other. Whereas, for example, Rühm and Achleitner – the former trained as a musician, the latter as an architect – were more interested in the Constructivist aspects of experimentation and, together with Wiener, saw themselves soberly as 'Sprachingenieure' and 'Sprachpragmatiker', Bayer, like

Artmann, was clearly more related to the fantastical tradition of French Surrealism. It was Artmann, in fact, who was the first to detach himself from the Group, and the reason for his departure can be detected in his reluctance to follow his friends into a position of extreme language scepticism to which Wiener, in particular, was leading them. For despite his love of the grotesque, the macabre quality of his imagination and his anti-bourgeois stance, Artmann never lost his confidence in language or his role in the creative process, however distant the latter might be from conventional typology: 'Worte haben eine bestimmte magnetische Masse, die gegenseitig nach Regeln anziehend wirkt; sie sind gleichsam 'sexuell', sie zeugen miteinander, sie treiben Unzucht miteinander, sie üben Magie, die über mich hinweggeht, sie besitzen Augen, Facettenaugen wie Käfer und schauen sich unaufhörlich und aus allen Winkeln an. Ich bin Kuppler und Zuhälter von Worten und biete das Bett . . . ich rede nicht von meinen Gefühlen; ich setze vielmehr Worte in Szenen und sie treiben ihre eigene Choreographie.'[5] Thus Artmann, whilst remaining fully open to the irrational as a creative principle, nevertheless retained a sense of irony and humour which, though sometimes close to whimsy, was strong enough to protect him from the cultural pessimism which in the end claimed both Wiener and Bayer.

Bayer, in particular, fell victim to an all-corrosive despair when faced with what he ultimately saw as the impossibility of language to communicate anything beyond trivial phenomena: 'wir haben mit dem vokabular künstliche kategorien gezüchtet, haben die erregung des unbestimmten als gefährlich einbalsamiert, können leichtfertig sagen, haha eine maus, und haben keine ahnung, jedes wort ein schlechter vergleich . . .'[6] Like Artmann, Bayer saw no distinction between art and life, but he lacked his mentor's secure faith in the imagination as an effective counter to the pressures of bourgeois society. He therefore plunged headlong, like a latter-day Rimbaud, into experiments with drugs, yoga, zen buddhism, spiritualism – anything which might help him to break through into a world of absolutes. In his paradoxical desire to escape solipsism via the intensification of subjective experience Bayer looks back to a particular Dionysian trend in German Expressionism – and indeed beyond to the 'poète maudit' tradition of Baudelaire and Gérard de Nerval.[7]

Oswald Wiener's approach to language was more systematic than Bayer's. Possibly the most rigorous mind in the 'Wiener Gruppe',

Wiener was the one who tried to get to grips with the shifting complexity of Wittgenstein's philosophy. His extraordinary novel *Die Verbesserung von Mitteleuropa*, not published until 1969, sums up much of the work completed before his break with the Group in 1959 and is deeply influenced by the development of Wittgenstein's thought. Its central theme is the basic discrepancy between the *need* to express and the inadequacy of the means at the writer's disposal. Equipped with an impressive knowledge of experimental art, information theory and linguistic philosophy, Wiener's book is really an anti-novel – a self-ironizing treatise complete with a monstrous academic apparatus. His apparent aim is to bring language and reality into as sharp a confrontation as possible. The result is a text of chaotic richness, shot through with flashes of stringent socio-cultural criticism. In effect, a massive erudition is marshalled in a sustained attack on its own cultural foundations.

In contrast to the later work of Bayer and Wiener (the latter destroyed most of his previous texts on leaving the Group), the earlier experiments of the 'Wiener Gruppe' appear less frenetic and decidedly more positive. They cover four major areas of experimentation: dialect poetry, concrete poetry, 'Montagen', and attempts to create a form of 'total theatre' – the 'Literarisches Cabaret'.

Without doubt the most original contribution of the 'Wiener Gruppe' to contemporary avant-garde literature lies in its experiments with dialect poetry. Far from continuing the folklore tradition of dialect literature, Artmann, Rühm and Achleitner were attracted to dialect initially by the plasticity and directness of local (especially Viennese) speech and the visual 'alienation effect' of such language when transcribed phonetically. At the same time, of course, the conjunction of literary experiment with speech forms hitherto relegated to light entertainment or provincial humour was bound to appeal to the non-conformist spirit of the Group. Thus dialect poetry became part of the 'Wiener Gruppe's' increasingly methodical reflection on the nature of language itself. It did not aim at a mimetic reproduction of everyday reality but at a critique of the linguistic structures that mediate that reality. Not surprisingly, it was Artmann, above all, who seized on the characteristically rich sounds and nuances of Viennese dialect in order to explore its surrealistic and humorous possibilities. His first collection of dialect poems *med ana schwoazzn dintn* (Written in Black, 1958) immediately reached a wide public and brought him a totally unexpected success. The commercialization of his work, however, effectively marks the point at which Artmann began to withdraw from the 'Wiener Gruppe' – he took no part, for example, in the Group's Cabaret performances. On the other hand, this breakthrough enabled the three friends a year later to publish elsewhere a representative group of their dialect poems *hosn rosn baa*, which contained a number by Artmann deemed too aggressive by the conservative publisher of the earlier volume.

Its primary concern with language as 'raw material' naturally led the 'Wiener Gruppe' into further experiments with its basic elements – sentence, word, syllable, letter – which anticipated or rather coincided with similar investigations being undertaken on an international scale by diverse groups of writers who, on the initiative of Eugen Gomringer in Switzerland and the Noigandres Group in Brazil, were to assume the name of 'concrete poets'.[8] Just as Kandinsky had reduced painting to its essentials of point, line and plane, and by freeing it from its representational function had discovered new expressive potentialities of abstraction, so concrete poets, by concentrating on the medium of their art, hoped to relocate the latent energy beneath the rigidity of historically and socially determined forms. The work of Rühm and Achleitner, in particular, relates to this aspect of concrete poetry. Thus Rühm's 'Konstellationen' ('constellations'), like Gomringer's, explore the poetic possibilities of isolated words or word-groups, using the space around them as a structural agent. They follow the fundamental principle of all concrete poetry: maximum clarity and variation with the minimum of means. In a similar fashion, his 'Textbild', 'Jetzt', consists of this single word repeated twelve times in a variety of type faces and sizes. The precise positioning on the page produces a three-dimensional, imploding/exploding effect which in a highly graphic manner conveys a freshened sense of the complex and relative nature of simultaneity. Other poems seek to release the semantic echoes of individual words or fragments of words by surprising juxtapositions, sometimes in random groups, sometimes in tightly organized grids or matrices.

Such experiments – especially in the closely related area of sound poetry – plainly reveal Rühm's musical and Achleitner's architectural interests, and it is against the backcloth of the theories of serial music and the functional requirements of architectural design that the 'Wiener Gruppe' turned to permutational methods of creating texts. In this connection it developed the idea of 'methodischer Interventionismus'. Sharing Artmann's iconoclastic attitude towards the 'Dichter' syndrome in Germanic culture, they were interested in methods of fashioning poetic texts, based on objective mathematical principles, which could be applied to linguistic material by anyone. In Rühm's words: 'das sprachliche material sollte, aus einem kausalen zusammenhang gelöst, in einen semantischen schwebezustand geraten, auf "mechanischem" wege überraschende wortfolgen und bilder erzeugen.'[9]

A further dimension to the attack on conventional syntax can be seen in the Group's use of the 'Montage'. This technique, in particular, lent itself to collaborative effort, and the 'Wiener Gruppe's' first experiment on these lines sprang from Artmann's typically chance discovery of an 1853 Primer on the Bohemian language. By translating fragments of this book and reassembling them in a-logical sequences, Artmann, Bayer and Rühm produced a number of texts which recall Ionesco's *La Cantatrice Chauve*: disconnected conversational phrases, idioms, lists of vocabulary and clichés are welded together and thus 'alienated' in a manner calculated to challenge the reader's (or audience's) culturally conditioned expectations. Other 'Montagen' were constructed from telephone directories (incorporating the puzzled responses to random calls!), military training manuals, old encyclopaedias and so on – 'ready-made' material to be manipulated sometimes by aleatory, sometimes by strictly serial methods of composition.

The close collaboration among the members of the 'Wiener Gruppe' had already led to the application of concrete and 'Montage' principles to longer 'Hörtexte' and short plays; it was therefore a logical extension of the Group's activities to assemble representative selections of their work in the framework of an attempt to create 'total theatre'. With a conscious nod in the direction of the Dadaist 'Cabaret Voltaire' in Zürich, the 'Wiener Gruppe' set up their own 'Literarisches Cabaret' which, however, gave only two performances – on 6 December 1958 and 15 April 1959, both in Vienna. The overall aim of these events was to challenge the essentially passive nature of the audience/performer relationship. An anarchic farrago of sound poems, polemical chansons, mini-happenings, inspired (and at times infantile) clowning, together with some abuse of the audience itself, aimed at provoking the latter into new modes of participation and perception. Owing to the Group's decision to allow chance occurrences to develop, the planned programme was not completed on either occasion. Nevertheless, and despite the presence backstage of the police on the second evening, the two performances were apparently well received by packed houses – thus demonstrating the potent theatrical attraction that can be generated by a mixture of absurdist humour, bad taste and constant unpredictability. Whether this was quite what Rühm, Achleitner, Bayer and Wiener and their associates intended, may be considered doubtful. The fact remained that beyond these audiences – who in any case may be presumed to have been broadly sympathetic to avant-garde experiments – the 'Wiener Gruppe' found little response in the established cultural and social circles of Vienna. It was as much this depressing 'Echolosigkeit' as much as waning inventiveness on the part of its individual members that led to the break-up of the Group. Its last appearance in April 1964 in a newly opened Viennese night club merely emphasised the fact that the four friends had already decided to go their own ways: Rühm left Vienna altogether to continue his work in the more stimulating atmosphere of West Berlin; Bayer retired to Lower Austria to work on his novel *Der sechste Sinn*, (The Sixth Sense) but committed suicide later in the year; Achleitner went back to architecture and Wiener to a successful career with Olivetti, where he was able to pursue his increasing interest in cybernetics and computers.

If the impact of the 'Wiener Gruppe' on official culture in Austria can be said to have been minimal in the 1950s and 1960s, that is not true of its influence on a large number of writers who emerged during those years in Vienna and the provinces. The poets, artists and musicians, for example, who gathered round the 'Forum Stadtpark' Arts Centre, established in 1960 in Graz, openly acknowledge their debt to the pioneering efforts of the 'Wiener Gruppe'. Peter Handke's early work, in particular, shows how quickly the techniques and principles first evolved by the Group were assimilated. In Vienna itself the 'Wiener Gruppe's' activities naturally attracted many artists who shared its refusal to conform to accepted literary and social conventions. Andreas Okopenko, Friederike Mayrökker and Ernst Jandl are just three of the younger poets who, whilst never formally members of the 'Wiener Gruppe', maintained loose and regular contact with it. In effect, together they formed a mutually beneficial and supportive 'underground' culture.

In the last fifteen years, however, it is Ernst Jandl who seems to have developed the ideas of the 'Wiener Gruppe' most consistently and successfully. Jandl's texts – including some of the most inventive sound poems to have appeared so far – possess one distinct

244

advantage: accessibility. For despite the 'Wiener Gruppe's' desire to democratise the arts and dissipate the aura and mystique of the 'Dichter', it remains true that much of its work is relatively obscure without some foreknowledge of its aesthetic principles and intentions. This applies, of course, also to Jandl to a degree, but his best work has an impact and immediacy of appeal surpassed only by Artmann – significantly, the least theoretical of the Group. Although Jandl does not go so far as Friederike Mayröcker (with whom he frequently collaborates) in rejecting theory altogether, his strength lies in deriving theoretical positions from practice in a non-systematic way. Thus his 'work-shop' statements are refreshingly free from jargon and pomposity and owe more to his sound knowledge of Anglo-Saxon empiricism than to the European avant-garde.

Nevertheless, Jandl sees his work as firmly situated in the experimental tradition followed by the 'Wiener Gruppe', in particular by Artmann and Rühm whom he first met in 1956 and with whom he has remained in friendly contact ever since. Indeed, Jandl combines in a unique mixture Artmann's love of the surreal with Rühm's versatility in exploring the structural possibilities of concrete poetry. In common with them and concrete poets in general he stresses the primacy of language as 'raw material' rather than as a tool for description: concrete poems are *objects* in the first instance, not statements *about* objects. At the same time, the creation of such poem-objects is seen as an assertion of individual freedom in a hostile environment: 'Die Manipulatoren einer weitgehend gleichgeschalteten Gesellschaft sehen ihr System gefährdet durch den Anspruch der modernen Kunst auf einen Bereich, wo ohne Lenkung von außen immer wieder neue Modelle der Freiheit entstehen. Bedrohlich erscheint ihnen, daß Kunst zu einem Muster für Gesellschaft werden könnte, einer Gesellschaft, in der zahlreiche gleichzeitig daran sind, sich jeder sein eigenes Modell von Freiheit zu zimmern.'[10]

Jandl's experimental poetry – which dates from the middle 1950s – has little to do with self-absorbed aestheticism (a charge sometimes levelled at concrete poets). It is consciously situated on the one hand between the linguistic patterns of everyday speech and those of art, on the other between the normative grammar of the textbooks and the fluid structures preferred in practice. Distinctions are blurred in order to jolt language (and thus perception) out of stereo-typed modes of expression. For the enemy of creativity –

245

whether that of the poet or of his audience – is *habit*, and it is to challenge habitual ways of reading or listening that Jandl conducts his three-dimensional – semantic, phonetic, visual – explorations of language.

'Moritat' (from *Der künstliche Baum*, The Artificial Tree), for example, concentrates on the inherent ambiguities of German grammatical forms:

> die der das taten waren
> der die das taten war
> der die das tun sah war
> das die der taten war . . .

Eleven more stanzas, conventionally arranged, pursue the possible permutations and force eye and ear to examine afresh the relationships of verb, noun and pronoun. In a different way, a tired proverb 'Eile mit Weile' ('Make haste slowly') is turned into a strange but evocative play on words by the methodical change of a single letter:

> eile mit feile
> eile mit feile
> auf den fellen
> feiter meere . . .
> ('étude in f' from *Laut und Luise*, Sound and Luise)

Or in contrast to this poem with its resonant echoes of a nostalgic lyricism, a 'kleine Sprechmaschine' (little speech machine) i.e. Jandl, comments wittily on the expression 'how time flies' (from *Sprechblasen*, Speech bubbles)

> die zeit vergeht

> lustig
> luslustigtig
> lusluslustigtigtig
> luslusluslustigtigtigtig
> lusluslusluslustigtigtigtigtig
> luslusluslusluslustigtigtigtigtigtig
> lusluslusluslusluslustigtigtigtigtigtigtig
> luslusluslusluslusluslustigtigtigtigtigtigtigtig

Here the human voice, geared like a metronome, checks the notion of time passing enjoyably by stressing the ambiguity of the syllables 'lust-ig' ('Lust/Verlust', 'pleasure/loss') which point to it ticking remorselessly past. The poem also looks back to seventeenth-century Baroque experiments with its graphic suggestion of sand piling up in an hour-glass. Thus a playful method with the elements of language produces an unexpected fusion of form and content.

Wit and skill with words, used physically like the parts of a jigsaw, are also fundamental to a number of sound poems ('Sprech-gedichte') which can be classified as 'political'. Perhaps Jandl's best known poem is 'schtzngrmm' (from *Laut und Luise*) in which he conveys both the excitement and the futility of war by the elision of every vowel – as Jandl puts it himself: 'War does not sing!' Built on the single word 'Schützengraben' ('trench'), the poem produces the sounds and rhythms of warfare in a vocal crescendo, culminating in a single stark syllable: 't-tt' (= 'tot', 'dead'). Similarly, his 'ode auf N', from the same collection, starts unintelligbly:

> lepn
> nepl
> lepn
> nepl
> lepn
> nepl
> o lepn
> o nepl
> nnnnnnnn
> lopn
> paa
> lopn
> paa . . .

but gradually builds up to a fierce expression of mockery, centred on the extended syllable 'naaaaaaaaaaaa' (= 'Narr', 'fool'), before unleashing the name 'Napoleon' in a donkey-like bray. As a score for solo voice, the poem possesses an extraordinary power, and Jandl's comment on man's perennial weakness for heroes and the necessity for their debunking is as unmistakeable as Brecht's.

Although Jandl is best known for such sound poems, where the human voice becomes a subtle instrument to bring out the semantic richness of the text, his work also includes visual poems which exert their appeal primarily in 'painterly' terms, for example, 'oeö' (from *Sprechblasen*):

```
                    e
                   ee
                  eee
         oooooooooooöööööoooooooo
         ooooooooooööööööoooooooo
         ooooooooööööööööoooooooo
         oooooooööööööööööoooooooo
         oooooöööööööööööööoooooooo
         ooooöööööööööööööööoooooooo
         oooöööööööööööööööööoooooooo
         ooöööööööööööööööööööoooooooo
         oöööööööööööööööööööööoooooooo
         öööööööööööööööööööööööoooooooo
         eöööööööööööööööööööööööoooooooo
         eeööööööööööööööööööööööööoooooooo
         eeeeeeeeeeeeeeeeeee
```

A poem-object of this sort, of course, depends more than most on type-face, quality of paper and ink, but it demonstrates how the smallest particle of language can be used to illustrate amusingly the nature of vowel-shift as a phalanx of bold 'e's moves through a field of passive 'o's. A more complex concrete poem in this category, however, is the delightful 'erschaffung der eva', from a group of love poems in *Laut und Luise*.

As in the 'Konstellationen' of Rühm and Achleitner, space is used structurally. The poem's spine descends from the Godhead on the Alpha-Omega analogy to lend a core of stability to the centrifugal activity at its foot. The creation of Eve from Adam's rib (not, it may be remarked, the tranquil, painless affair of Biblical tradition!) leads to a lightness and restoration of balance and harmony – and thus towards a knowledge of God. The poem is an excellent example of Jandl's belief in 'gründliche Simplizität' as an artistic principle: 'Alles so einfach wie möglich zu machen, um gerade dadurch die Vielschichtigkeit von allem wirklich deutlich zu machen, könnte man gründliche Simplizität nennen, im Gegensatz zu einer oberflächlichen, die ein Verkleinern und Verniedlichen ist, während in der gründlichen alles seine Erwachsenheit behält:'[11]

<pre>
g   o   tt
                     p
                     q
                     r

          adam s
     ripp   e
          dam   a
     ipp   et
          am   a   d
     pp   e
          m u
     p   e   a   d   a
          eva   d   a   m
</pre>

Whether one accepts a religious interpretation of 'erschaffung von eva' or prefers to take a more ironic, detached view, the fact remains that the poem offers the reader/viewer an aesthetically pleasing structure in which he can freely move, an opportunity to explore his own creativity in a way radically different from, but nevertheless relating to, traditional poetic patterns. For it is especially true of Jandl that his work – despite the initial impression – does not turn its back on the past. As Helmut Heißenbüttel points out in his 'Nachwort' to the new Reclam edition of *Laut und Luise* (1976), Jandl's experiments with language and form can be seen as a critical evaluation and thus one possible continuation of tradition: examples of the 'Lied', love and nature poetry, the epigram, didactic and political verse can all be found in this first comprehensive collection of his experimental work. In Heißenbüttel's view, Jandl's poetry reflects the crisis in language which has become increasingly evident since the beginning of the twentieth century; and it is certainly true that the sources of his inspiration are similar to those of the 'Wiener Gruppe': Expressionism, Marinetti, Stramm, the Dadaists, as well as Gertrude Stein, Joyce and Pound – that is, poets who were all acutely conscious of a cultural crisis rooted in language. But it is also true that Ernst Jandl's ability to

249

locate areas of the past which are still capable of stimulating growth and experiment is a creative achievement in itself. His work is an open invitation to pause and consider coolly the verbal barrage to which contemporary man is daily exposed; and in the face of much linguistic imprecision and dangerous abstraction, it puts forward concrete but non-prescriptive models as confident and optimistic alternatives.

NOTES

1. 'The Vienna Group', *The Times Literary Supplement*, 3.10.1964.
2. The opposition to the 'Wiener Gruppe' and the avant-garde generally was widespread and persistent. In 1958 no less a respected figure than Heimito von Doderer resigned his post on the conservative *Wiener Kurier* when refused permission to print examples of the Group's work in the paper's 'Feuilleton'. The Graz magazine *manuskripte*, which published the 'Wiener Gruppe' from its first issue in 1960, was actually accused of 'disseminating degenerate' literature and 'poisoning the healthy sensibilities of our young people'! See: Peter Laemmle/Jörg Drews (eds.), *Wie die Grazer auszogen, die Literatur zu erobern*, Munich, 1975, p. 19.
3. 'There is only one inalienable principle, namely that anyone can be a poet without ever having written or uttered a single word.'
4. The socio-cultural situation of the Italian Futurists presents striking similarities with that of the 'Wiener Gruppe'. Both groups felt stifled by the sheer weight of their countries' immense cultural heritage. Although the Austrians did not share the extreme *tabula rasa* attitude of the Italians, it is sobering to reflect that radical aesthetic revolt does not necessarily imply left-wing social radicalism – as Marinetti's espousal of Fascism indicates.
5. 'Words have a precise magnetic mass which exerts mutual attraction according to set laws; they are, as it were, "sexual", they procreate with one another, they fornicate with one another, they exercise magic powers which ignore me, they possess eyes, multi-facetted eyes like a beetle's, they never cease watching each other from every corner. I am a procurer and pimp of words and provide the bed . . . I do not speak of my feelings, rather do I put words on the stage where they devise their own choreography.' 'Ein Gedicht und sein Autor' in: *The Best of H.C. Artmann*, Frankfurt/Main, 1970, p. 375f.
6. 'We have used our vocabulary to breed artificial categories, we have embalmed the excitement of the indefinite as something dangerous, we can say thoughtlessly, haha, a mouse, and we have no idea, every word a wretched comparison.' Quoted in: Renate Matthaei (ed.), *Grenzverschiebung. Neue Tendenzen in der deutschen Literatur der 60er Jahre*, Cologne, 1970, p. 51.

7. Oswald Wiener has recalled his friendship and experiences with Konrad Bayer in an article: 'Einiges über Konrad Bayer. Schwarze Romantik und Surrealismus im Nachkriegs-Wien', in: *Die Zeit*, 17.2.1978, p. 39.

8. For an introduction to the international phenomenon of concrete poetry, see my article: 'Concrete Poetry and the Crisis of Language', *New German Studies* 1 (1973), 99–115.

9. 'Released from its causal context, linguistic material was to be suspended in a semantic balance and via a "mechanical" method produce surprising word-sequences and images.' *Die Wiener Gruppe*, Reinbek bei Hamburg, 1967, p. 14.

10. 'The manipulators of an extensively coordinated society see their system threatened by the claim of modern art to a domain where new models of freedom continually arise without outside control. It seems ominous to them that art might become a pattern for social organization, a society in which a large number of individuals are simultaneously busy fashioning their own models of freedom.' In: 'Voraussetzungen, Beispiele und Ziele einer poetischen Arbeitsweise. Ein Vortrag', *Protokolle. Wiener Jahresschrift für Literatur, bildende Kunst und Musik*, Heft 2 (1970), p. 25. (Reprinted in: *Für alle*, Darmstadt/Neuwied, 1974, pp 234–48.)

11. 'To make everything as simple as possible in order thereby to reveal the multiplicity of everything might be called radical simplicity, in contrast to the superficial kind which represents a diminution and a trivialisation, whereas in radical simplicity everything retains its mature qualities.' *Die schöne Kunst des Schreibens*, Darmstadt/Neuwied, 1976, p. 50, and see also p. 25.

The 'Grazer Gruppe',
Peter Handke and Wolfgang Bauer

Hugh Rorrison

Graz galt immer als verträumte Stadt . . . eine Stadt der Stadt-
poeten, für sentimentale Bewunderer, für feines Schrifttum
oder für natonale Blut- und Bodenparolen, mit denen man das
Lokale ins Völkische hochstilisierte und so überlokal zu werden
gedachte.[1]

This Graz was slumbering in contented provincialism in 1958 when
an action group mooted converting the derelict Cafe Stadtpark into
a literary club and arts laboratory. By 1962 the writers of the firmly
established 'Forum Stadtpark' felt sure enough of their literary
identity to designate themselves the 'Grazer Gruppe'. In 1968 Peter
Handke publicly chastised the powerful 'Gruppe 47' and took
Experimenta, the Frankfurt drama festival, by storm with *Kaspar*,
and Wolfgang Bauer began his conquest of the German stage with
Magic Afternoon at Hanover. Graz seemed, having outdistanced
Vienna, bent on gingering up the entire German-speaking literary
scene.

Avantgarde literature could not have flourished in this conservative corner of Austria without the 'Forum Stadtpark' as a talking-
shop and working space for the arts. Literature came to dominate
the Forum's activities, largely due to the success of the house magazine, *manuskripte*, which appeared as a cyclostyled hand-out when
the Forum opened in 1960, and under the editorship of Alfred Kolleritsch and Günter Waldorf, developed into the leading little
magazine for new writing in German. The second issue featured the
Wiener Gruppe whose pioneering work on language, dialect poetry
and drama and concrete poetry, as well as their black, anti-
bourgeois humour strongly influenced the young Grazer. This 'degenerate art' provoked local opposition but the Forum weathered
the storm with liberal support and *manuskripte* has prospered with
the pluralistic, progressive editorial policy.

252

The Group is heterogeneous. Apart from Michael Scharang, the socialist author of an 'Arbeiterroman', the worker's novel *Charly Traktor* (1973), their work is oppositional rather than ideological. They reject Alt-Österreich, be it nostalgia for the monarchy, be it the celebration of traditional folk life in regional literature à la K.H. Waggerl. G.F. Jonke's *Geometrischer Heimatroman* (1969) parodies the regional novel, making a structural pattern of the spatial and social relationships round the village square. Alfred Kolleritsch's *Die Pfirsichtöter* (The Peach Killers, 1972) has a half-concealed picture of genteel, pre-war country life shimmering behind the structured philosophizing of its plotless disconnected chapters, Handke's *Die Hornissen* (The Hornets, 1966) and *Wunschloses Unglück* (Sorrow Beyond Dreams, 1972) are negations of the country idyll, which survives only as the rubble foundation on which daring avantgarde structures are built from salvaged components of traditional literary forms as the group explores the nature of language. Gerhard Roth strings together selected persons and sentences from Joseph Roth's *Der Stumme Prophet* (The Mute Prophet) as a short novel *Der Ausbruch des Ersten Weltkriegs* (The Outbreak of the Great War, 1972), and penetrates the world of madness in the fractured objectivity of *die autobiographie des albert einstein* (The autobiography of Albert Einstein, 1972). Barbara Frischmuth's *Das Verschwinden des Schattens in der Sonne* (How the Shadow was Lost in the Sun, 1974), shows how immersion in a Turkish milieu sharpens the heroine's command of her native language as an instrument for self-orientation.

The group, notably Wolfgang Bauer, has exploited dialect for the stage, as in Harald Sommer's *A unhamlich Schtorka Obgaung* (A Helluva Powerful Exit, 1970), a housemaid's tale of persecution, told with a fine fantasy. Franz Buchrieser's *Das Produkt* (1976) uses dialect in a realistic setting to plead for an ex-convict, the deformed 'product' of the penal system.

The 'Grazer Gruppe' is not defined by its style or themes, but by its concern to give experimental literature a hearing. A literary pressure group rather than a school.

Peter Handke studied law in Graz from 1961 to 1965, and *manuskripte* published his earliest pieces. In 1966 he was recruited by the Suhrkamp Verlag and moved to Düsseldorf. With his flair for self-advertisement and his nose for new trends Handke attracted wide publicity over the next five years. (He is now trying to live it down.) He created his first sensation at the Princeton meeting of the

253

'Gruppe 47' which, by 1966, was a kind of unofficial academy of post-war German letters. On the final day, the long-haired Handke delivered a scathing attack from the floor on the assembled company's 'Beschreibungsimpotenz', its inability to see beyond its own 'piffling and idiotic' brand of descriptive prose. To his delight his outburst was featured in *Der Spiegel*. 'The delicate beatle from Graz' had arrived.

In *Zur Tagung der Gruppe 47 in USA* (Gruppe 47 meets in the USA) Handke, a compulsive and lucid self-commentator, explained that his main objection was to the Group's neo-realist view that language was an inert medium in which the facts might be suspended for examination. Language for him was not a glass (Sartre's term) for viewing social and political events, and the critics merely compounded the misconception if they were content to assess the accuracy of an author's selection and presentation of facts. Language was on the contrary an active medium, words manipulate matters for individual and social ends, and literature should be concerned with language and its use rather than facts and their presentation. Handke's return to the avant-garde's perennial preoccupation with the artist's medium is coloured by an awareness that the media today quickly absorb and debase innovation, hence his exaggerated demand for literary revolution in permanence in his assertion, 'Eine Möglichkeit besteht für mich jeweils nur einmal.' (Each possibility only exists once for me) As Handke saw it the novels of the 'Gruppe 47' had come to work in terms of conditioned responses to hackneyed stimuli – Hitler, Auschwitz, Berlin, napalm – which left him cold. Handke's assertiveness at this stage was symptomatic of a generation that was immune to the sense of collective guilt that had pre-occupied postwar German, and to a lesser extent Austrian literature, and was about to articulate its frustrations and aspirations in the Student Movement, though Handke himself, in his ironically professed ivory tower, is bolshy rather than committed or partisan when it comes to politics.

Before Princeton Handke published his experimental novel, *Die Hornissen*, a prose puzzle in sixty-seven non-sequential chapters with a kind of key at the end. One might compare it to a jigsaw puzzle without a picture to work from, were it not that Handke's aim is not to assemble a story/picture but to look at his subject, a day of family life, from various angles, using different techniques to describe the facet of his own, or his narrator's experience of that day on which attention is momentarily focussed, while reminding the reader constantly of the essentially mediated nature of prose communication. The narrative perspective shifts freely between the writer and the blind narrator, who cites other witnesses and sometimes appears to be quoting a literary account of his experience. Two things happened that day, the narrator went blind and his brother drowned, and neither event is depicted, though the latter is the subject of a chapter entitled 'Die Ertrinkungsgeschichte' (The story of the drowning), which tries out conventional autobiography, 'Ich war der älteste von drei Brüdern . . .' (I was the eldest of three brothers . . .) then anecdote, 'Wir pflegten einen Bach entlang zur Schule zu gehen. Eines Tages aber . . .' (We used to go to school along a stream. Then one day . . .) and abandons both as samples of mere storytelling. The narrative is handed over to a third party, 'Ich beende nun aus zweiter Hand die Erzählung . . .' (I now hand the story over to somebody else to finish . . .) who tells us how the narrator and his brother on their way to school taunt one another to swing Tarzan-style across a ravine on a liana, clearly fictional parody, given the scarcity of tropical vegetation in Carinthia. Without being particularly gripping, this shows the evasive technique Handke uses to remind us that what we are reading is a form of words, not to be confused with reality. He teases with deliberate omissions, (*Der vergessene Gegénstand*) (The forgotten object), exasperates with elaborate irrelevancies like the full fire procedure in the local cinema (*Die Alarmanlage*) (The fire-alarm), defying the reader to make sense of the linguistic game he is playing.

Though Handke had at this point pronounced plot unnecessary, he had not managed to eliminate it from *Die Hornissen*, whose penultimate chapter, 'Zur Entstehung der Geschichte' (How the story came to be written), explains the point of departure for the preceding narrative:

Das Buch erzählt von zwei Brüdern, von denen später der eine, als er allein nach dem abgängigen zweiten sucht, erblindet; es wird aus der Erzählung nicht ganz klar, durch welchen Ereignis der Knabe erblindet; es wird nur mehrmals gesagt, daß ein Kriegszustand herrsche; die näheren Angaben über das Unglück jedoch fehlen, oder er hat sie vergessen. Es wird davon ausgegangen, daß der Blinde, als er schon erwachsen ist, eines Sonntages erwacht und durch etwas, dem er mit den Gedanken nicht mehr beikommen kann, an seinen abwesenden Bruder gemahnt wird. Fortan wechseln in seinem Gehirn die Stellen, an die er sich zu erinnern glaubt, ohne Ordnung durcheinander.[2]

The blind adult narrator is moved one Sunday to reconstruct a November day in his childhood in deepest Austria, in a setting similar to Handke's native village as described in *Wunschloses Unglück*. Since the events the narrator summarizes are those of *Die Hornissen*, it is reasonable to assume that the book in question is not a separate source-novel, but the novel which Handke and his narrator have at this point almost completed, and which seems to be an effort to exorcise a lingering sense of guilt by piecing together the half-forgotten events from which that guilt may derive. A further passage explains the process of random recall which is at the same time the process of composition:

> Sogar der Ort und die Jahreszeit, zu welcher die Handlung spielt, sind ihm entgangen. Weil er zwar das alles nicht mehr weiß, oder doch nur zerbrochene Stücke davon innezuhaben glaubt, weil er aber gewiß ist, daß er das Buch einmal gelesen hat, deshalb und von daher setzt es ihm zu und macht es ihm begierig zu wissen. Das hat seine Gedanken auf den langen Gang gebracht. Jedoch hat seine Erinnerung keine Beweiskraft; was er ausgedacht hat, braucht nicht wahr zu sein, in dem Sinn, daß es mit den Vorgängen im Buch glaubwürdig übereinstimmt; es braucht nur möglich und vorstellbar zu sein, dadurch, daß es an sich glaubwürdig ist; eine falsche unnatürliche Aussage würde von der Erfahrung ab- und zurückgewiesen.[3]

The novelist/narrator, reflecting on the story, now becomes his own putative reader, just as perplexed in the face of the fragmented, incoherent account as is the narrator in the face of his memories of the events. He equates the effort of setting down the truth of his memories with the effort of making sense of the narrative. The intractable material is a challenge to the reader's tenacity, and he may read any sense into it which is imaginable, credible and consonant with his experience. A doggedly experimental novel for determined readers.

Going a stage further, *Der Hausierer* (The Hawker, 1967), Handke's next novel, was an arabesque on the detective story in which chapters of formal analysis alternate with illustrative blocks of random sentences of a sort found in crime fiction. The author considers this experiment a failure.

By the mid-sixties the pop generation had developed a vital sub-culture and turned its back on institutionalised art. Handke voiced their rejection of 'Grandpa's theatre' in *Publikumsbeschimpfung* (Offending the Audience, 1966), a 'Sprechstück' or speech-play without a plot, characters or setting.

The audience, expecting a play, was confronted by four men in jeans who delivered an hour-long tirade debunking the theatre and theatre-going:

> Sie sitzen in Reihen . . . Sie schauen uns an, wenn wir mit Ihnen reden . . . Sie hören uns nicht zu, Sie hören uns an . . . Hier wird dem Theater nicht gegeben, was des Theaters ist . . . Ihnen wird nichts vorgespiegelt . . . Das Licht, das uns beleuchtet, hat nichts zu bedeuten . . . Wir sind keine Spaßmacher . . . Sie sind das Thema . . . Sie werden von uns gemustert . . . Dieser Raum täuscht keinen Raum vor . . . Von beiden Polen hier, sind Sie der ruhende Pol . . . Sie sehen bezaubernd aus . . . Aber Sie sind nicht abendfüllend . . . Das ist kein Drama . . . Hier oben gibt es keine Ordnung . . . Hier hat nicht jedes Ding seine Zeit.[4]

These are the first lines of some of the play's sixty-six paragraphs which explore in a reiterative, spiral progression the themes set out in the first few paragraphs, namely that the piece is not a play but a prologue to the audience's future theatregoing, the stage is just a stage and does not stand for anywhere else, the time is the time it takes to perform the script, the actors and the audience are two groups of people thinking independent thoughts, nothing has a symbolic or metaphorical meaning, and the audience is the central concern of the evening.

The lines are not attributed and the director is left to orchestrate their delivery using his four 'speakers' – Handke does not call them actors – at will, bearing certain suggested models in mind: football crowds, a cement mixer starting up, Ringo Starr on the drums (Handke was an ardent pop fan), monkeys mimicking people at the zoo, Lee J. Cobb and Gary Cooper (he was addicted to Hollywood second features too), the Radio Luxembourg Hit Parade. Handke is a compulsive recorder of casually significant gesture in art and life, and has recently published a collection of such *gestes trouvés, Das Gewicht der Welt* (The Weight of the World, 1977). These banal details strike him as significant, somehow right but *not* symbolic, and his instructions to his speakers, as well as clarifying their attitude to the audience, are probably intended to sharpen their awareness of the aural and visual texture of life about them, which will then somehow feed back into their technique. The phrasing of the piece is based on the aggressive, repetitive rhythms of rock music. *Publikumsbeschimpfung* turns the clichés of theatre-appreciation against the theatre itself. It is a joke which works once, and then only with serious theatregoers who know what is being travestied.

The function of language is the theme of Handke's most successful play, *Kaspar* (1967), whose bleak message is that the process of language acquisition is a process of indoctrination. Like Kaspar Hauser who emerged from solitary confinement in 1828 with only one sentence at his disposal, Kaspar can only say: 'Ich möcht ein solcher werden wie einmal ein andrer gewesen ist' (I want to be somebody like somebody else once was), a modification of the Nuremberg original which seems to express his will to be an integrated person rather than to be like somebody in particular. The play is full of echoes of Wittgenstein's *Tractatus logico-philosophicus*, and the dictum, 'The limits of my language signify the limits of my world,' (5.6) neatly defines Kaspar's predicament. With his one sentence he has almost no world, hence his lack of physical co-ordination as he stumbles over the stage props at the start like a marionette with its strings slack. The play not only has a named protagonist, a concession to tradition in the context of the *Sprechstücke*, it also has a multiple antagonist in the 'Einsager', the invisible persuaders who address Kaspar through loudspeakers in the impersonal, artificial tones of telephonists, TV-announcers, football commentators, or crowd-marshalls with megaphones. As in *Publikumsbeschimpfung* careful modulation of rhythm and volume is essential to the success of the piece, for the play is not a dialogue but a pattern of stimulus and response. First, with a sophisticated commentary on the nature of words and sentences, the 'Einsager' break down Kaspar's sentence into words, syllables, isolated sounds until he is finally silenced, whereupon he is trained with word-drills to speak properly, until, by the interval, he is co-ordinated and articulate and has taken possession of and tidied up the chaotic stage. But, ominously, other identical Kaspars have appeared.

The play might equally well be called speech-torture, Handke tells us, and in the second half the 'Einsager' enumerate violent methods of keeping order until Kaspar, taking stock of his situation, realizes to the cacophonous accompaniment of the secondary Kaspars, that he has been standardized. Far from enabling him to express himself, the speech-material he has absorbed has trapped him within the restrictive code of the 'Einsager's' world.

The stage directions prescribe a cat-mask, a parti-coloured jacket, baggy trousers and clumsy shoes for Kaspar, a circus costume with a touch of commedia dell' arte, but to counteract any playfulness, they also tell us that he resembles Frankenstein or King Kong, part man-made monster, part creature of the wild translated into a technological society. Kaspar's plight is that of modern man, and is not the result of one particular political system, though the pronouncements of the 'Einsager' are steeped in bourgeois values. Handke's aim is not to portray the historical Kaspar Hauser, but to use his predicament as a metaphor to show how an individual can be manipulated by a process of linguistic engineering.

Society imposes on individuals, individuals impose on one another. Competition means subjugation, which can be achieved without words as Handke demonstrates in *Der Mündel will Vormund sein* (My Foot, My Tutor, 1969), which is one long stage-direction describing a series of silent aptitude tests, from tying laces to topping turnips with a ferocious agricultural guillotine, in which the eager ward/pupil always comes off worse than the smug guardian/teacher. *Der Ritt über den Bodensee* (The Ride across Lake Constance, 1971), explores the tyranny of language, using comic possibilities of theatrical posturing, while his last play, *Die Unvernünftigen sterben aus* (They're Dying Out, *1973*), an examination of the soul-searching of a capitalist *malgré lui*, is almost a conventional drama.

Handke's prose has also become less formally experimental, though he continues to feel threatened in his authorial authenticity by literary convention, making a mannerism of avoiding mannerism. With *Wunschloses Unglück* (1971) it became clear that even an obscure piece like *Die Hornissen* had an autobiographical core, and self-scrutiny has become more explicit in his recent work, so that it is worth recalling the function he attributed to literature in 1967:

Literatur ist für mich lange Zeit das Mittel gewesen, über mich selber, wenn nicht klar, so doch klarer zu werden. Sie hat mir geholfen zu erkennen, daß ich da war, daß ich auf der Welt war

. . . Die Wirklichkeit der Literatur hat mich aufgeklärt über mich selber, und über das, was um mich vorging.[5]

Der kurze Brief zum langen Abschied (Short Letter, Long Farewell, 1972) with its titular echo of Chandler's *Long Goodbye* is a fictitious account of a trip across the USA in which an Austrian writer is pursued by his estranged wife who is bent on murdering him. It ends with a visit to John Ford, the film director, after which they part in peace. A response, one might say to the break-up of Handke's marriage, but also a voyage of self-discovery. The hero/narrator sees America as the most foreign of foreign parts, he observes, a propos of performances of Schiller's *Die Räuber* and Ford's film *Young Mr Lincoln*, that Americans expect grand gestures and actions of their heroes; they do not expect them to play roles, because in America anybody can play a role. Not so the Austrian narrator who has been trapped within complexes caused by the deprivations of his childhood. The American experience, part of which is a kind of Proustian intimation of ANOTHER TIME, triggered off by dice instead of a madeleine, prises him away from his tortured past by means of a kind of creative recall which bypasses the shame, anxiety, fear and disgust which have hitherto haunted his memories. In discovering America he has discovered himself.

The impoverished, oppressive world of his childhood, as described in *Wunschloses Unglück*, written under the impact of his mother's suicide, is the antithesis of the vigorous, idyllic rusticity of the 'Heimatroman'. His mother's vitality was ground down by an inescapable routine of drudgery – childhood, motherhood, decrepitude – which Handke sums up in the children's rhyme 'Müde / Matt / Krank / Schwerkrank / Tot.' (Tired / worn out / ill / seriously ill / dead.). It is a life-story with plot and pathos enough for conservative readers who once shied away from the wayward experimenter. Yet with these emotive facts, Handke is consciously picking his way between straight record and the conventions of biography:

> Diese zwei Gefahren – einmal das bloße Nacherzählen, dann das schmerzlose Verschwinden einer Person in poetischen Sätzen – verlangsamen das Schreiben, weil ich fürchte, mit jedem Satz aus dem Gleichgewicht zu kommen.[6]

When he senses that the pathos of the story is taking over, that it is

260

beginning to tell itself, he lets it taper off in short, disconnected musings and recollections.

The autobiographical angle in *Die linkshändige Frau* (The Left-handed Woman, 1976) is more oblique. The story was conceived as a film scenario, but was published as a slim, typographically inflated volume and became an instant best-seller – Handke now had a large popular following, and this was an objective, even bald and unproblematic tale. A woman dismisses her husband in an impulsive moment to take up translating again and live independently with her son, a study of going it alone. We could see it as a fanciful projection of what his mother might have been, or as a role-reversed image of Handke himself, coping with his writing and his daughter when his wife, Libgart Schwarz, left him and returned to the stage. In an interview with *Le Monde* (18.5.78) Handke has invoked Rousseau's *Promeneur Solitaire* and suggested analogies to Chandler's Philip Marlowe, or the Western hero. As the latter rides or strides impassively to his destiny, so Handke's heroine moves, self-contained, through her environment. When she has a bath with her son, Handke suggests, there are echoes of our cowboy abluting in the saloon tub at the end of a rugged trail. Whether Handke's story, or his slow intense filming of it, achieve the mythical dimension is debatable; what is clear is that his need to filter, objectivize and intellectualize his experience remains constant. A myth is more than just a story.

The second member of the Graz Group with an international reputation, Wolfgang Bauer, presents a contrast to Handke, the tortured, fastidious intellectual who settled in Paris as a cosmopolitan exponent of the New Inwardness (Neue Innerlichkeit). Bauer, a spontaneous, hard-drinking bohemian has remained faithful to Graz and its 'Zentrum für zeitgenößische Zersetzungskultur' (Centre for Contemporary Cultural Blight)[7], and is at his best when describing the antics of its adepts.

Bauer's first short *Mikrodramen* (Microdramas, 1963), partly in the absurd vein, were performed at the 'Forum Stadtpark', where in 1965 he founded his own underground movement, the 'Happy Art and Attitude'. With *Party for Six* (1969), first seen at Innsbruck in 1967 he found the subject he was to make his own, intellectuals at play. Fery, the host, chats with Friedrich over the latest pop record as they wait for the other guests, Franzi, Frieda, Fanny and Fifi:

Friedrich: Du. Stimmt des, dos da Franzi die Fanny scho übanommen hot?

Fery: Gsogt hot er. Oba iiii glaub holt . . .

Friedrich: I hob imma glaubt bei der geht nix.

Fery: Nana. Im Gegenteil. Wannst in richtigen Schme auf-
ziagst, host scho so an Riß bei dea. Oba daß da
Franzi . . .

Friedrich: Des man i jo!

Fery: I glaub holt net. Wieso, Stehst auf sie?[8]

Already there is a touch of permissiveness, but more important is the deftly transcribed dialect, more precisely the argot, of the young Graz generation, which Bauer was to develop to give not only local but also contemporary colour to his plays.

In *Party for Six* almost nothing happens, but to great comic effect. The audience sees a hallway leading to the toilet and front door. Characters drift out from the intermittently audible jollifications backstage, flush loudly, sometimes to be accosted by other characters on the way back. Bauer's joke is to humour the audience with a minimum of music and dialogue while depriving it of the play it came to see, but he is content to amuse them with their own tolerance, without explicitly querying, like Handke in *Publikumsbeschimpfung* , the validity of their expectations as theatregoers.

In the ironically titled *Magic Afternoon* (1969) an unproductive writer tells his girl-friend 'Ich kann höchstens ein Stück schreiben, wo zwei auf der Bühne sitzen und Platten hören . . . a Platten nach der andern.'[9] This aptly describes Bauer's play – an afternoon session with a pair of intellectual sensualists in their late twenties, hooked on hash, liquor and sex. Their boredom and frustration are punctuated by occasional violence. It is a hot day ('a Luft wie bei Tennessee Williams') (This heat could be in Tennessee Williams), and the two pad around half dressed in a room which defines their world – shelves of books, crap to throw at one another, 'Scheiß-Dürrenmatt, Scheiß-Pinter, Scheiß-Albee' down to the 'Scheiß-Klassiker'; a bed surrounded by bottles and records. Birgit and Charly cast around for something to do. A film? A play? A swim? A screw? Nothing turns them on so they put on another record, dance, spar playfully before fighting outright as a storm breaks outside. Blood flows and the director is invited to make the most of it. 'Jetzt kommt die Schlacht – bitte, Herr Regisseur.' (Now the set-to, do your stuff, director.) Exit Charly and Birgit, enter their even more brutal friends, Joe and Monika, who strip (partially) and get into bed, casting aside a stray copy of Wittgenstein. Monika taunts Joe, '. . . Na kleiner . . . süßer Teddybärli? Willst mich net vergewaltigen?' (. . . Well . . . my sweet little teddy-bear. How about a spot of rape?) It is a game they play, but Joe, in obliging, inadvertently breaks her nose and packs her off to the hospital. The conversation takes a philosophical turn on the return of Birgit with Charly who observes, 'Die Wölt is unhamlich schiach' (The world is a total cock-up), whereupon the two men attempt to flush a globe down the toilet, concluding when they fail, 'Die Wölt is ewig' (The world will go on for ever). Shifting from ludicrous symbolism to macabre melodrama Joe and Charly, high on hash, finally play matadors to Birgit's bull, until, in desperation, she stabs Joe. Charly concurs limply when she insists it was self defence. He rolls the corpse in a rug and huddles in the wardrobe as she leaves.

Magic Afternoon examines neurotic behaviour in a static situation, *Change* (1969) has a plot. Fery, a feckless painter and Reicher, a journalist, meet Blasi, an amateur artist up in Vienna from the country, and decide to market him as the new 'naive realist.' The manipulation (*Manipuläschn*) will culminate in Blasi's suicide when the women and drugs he is to be plied with are withdrawn. For Fery who conceives the scheme this is an art form, playing with life, rather than just words or paint – besides which his photodocumentation of Blasi's career will make a million. The plot misfires when Blasi turns out to be a latter day version of Brecht's Baal who can take care of himself. The final scene is a hash party with a game of 'total change'. The characters swap roles and re-enact the manipulation, until Fery (as Blasi) completes his own plot by hanging himself in the toilet.

Embedded in this black farce which is reminiscent of Joe Orton in its studied outrageousness – Guggi, highly pregnant by Blasi, finds the latter on her mother on the kitchen floor and fetches her demented father who expires at the sight – is a satire on the commercialized Viennese art scene.

Playing with reality takes another form in *Silvester, oder Das Massaker im Hotel Sacher* (1974). Wolfram Bersenegger, poet and dramatist, bugs a suite at the Sacher, invites an arty crowd to a New Year party, and at midnight hands a tape of the lurid proceedings to Burgtheater director Stögersbach for transcription as his new play. More sceptical reviewers wondered whether this was how Bauer got his dialogue; in fact this electronic version of Dada's automatic writing shows Bauer's fixation on the notion of infinite regression as

263

he writes plays about characters writing plays about etc, etc. Fred, the poet in *Gespenster* (Ghosts, 1974), comments:

> ' . . . dann hab ich das Gefühl, ich hab was ganz selbständiges erzeugt, irgendetwas was lebt und was mit mir selber nix mehr zu tun hat . . . sowie a Perpetuum mobile . . . mir ham scho als Kind immer die – nachn Krieg hats es gebm – die Schuhpasta-schachteln von der Firma Solo imponiert, wo auf der Schachtel wieder die Schachtel und auf der Schachtel wieder und wieder und wieder . . .'[10]

The idea of transferring the creative process to one of the characters and launching the play as a self-perpetuating mechanism is not unlike the idea behind Handke's *Die Hornissen*, except that there the narrator shields the author, whereas here the internal author draws attention to the dramatist.

Bersenegger's party ends with a My Lai massacre 'happening', after which the half-insane Robespierre castigates the guests' jocular response to the Vietnam atrocity and shoots himself. This is one of the few explicit social comments in Bauer's plays, and, significantly, it is provoked by something outside the routine of boredom and amusement. Vietnam is another world, but it puts Bauer's characters in perspective. Can we then conclude that his presentation, ambivalent though it is, of these characters' self-indulgence tends to criticise rather than celebrate their life-style? To suggest that these children of affluence conceal an implicit criticism of capitalism is going too far.

In *Gespenster* the literary bohemians are four years older, and have reverted from drugs to alcohol for stimulus. Sober, they fall to pieces 'like crumbling mosaics'. For three acts the play is a drunken, blowsy conversation piece. The characters muse about their lives, their writing, their roles. Fred and Robert have rejected classic middle-class backgrounds, but Fred is uneasy as an artist. He has abandoned his adaptation of Ibsen's *Ghosts* in which the characters were to 'dry' and deviate from their rôles after twenty minutes. His projected novel is called *Rôle-Juggler*. Life has become a sexual game, Schnitzler's *Reigen* reduced to permutated pairs within a small circle of friends. Insiders know the rules, and Lore, surprising Fred and Robert deep in conversation hesitates to intrude, sensing the 'vibes' between them ('ihr habts so a Feld aufbaut zwischen euch') (You've really got something going here), but outsiders don't. Magda, a vulnerable Swiss girl who has moved in with Fred blithely tries to join the game and is destroyed playing 'total bourgeois dinners', a parodistic ritual in which she is cast as maid, humiliated, made to drink a tumbler of schnaps and eventually taken off raving in a straitjacket. Robert comments, 'Puh . . . des war das härteste Spul, was i jemals gspült hab . . .' (That was my toughest game yet . . .).

These plays are comedies of manners which document the lifestyle of the Graz avantgarde, posing in elegant, nihilistic boredom, experimenting with consciousness and framing their lives as an affront to bourgeois decency. Like Handke's, Bauer's director has to be a disc-jockey, generating audience excitement with the sounds of the Beatles, Wilson Pickett, the Rolling Stones et. al. Dialect, Bauer demonstrates, need not be quaint and folksy. The plays are built round a solid framework of vernacular realism, which Bauer abandons at his peril as demonstrated by *Magnetküsse* a weak surrealist pastiche of the stage thriller.

NOTES

1. 'Graz has always been a dreamy place . . . a town for local poets and sentimental admirers, for genteel literature or nationalist 'blood and soil' slogans which were used to turn local trivia into folk art in the hope of giving it wider significance.'
   Quoted in *Wie die Grazer auszogen, die Literatur zu erobern*, ed. Peter Laemmle and Jörg Drews, Munich, 1975, p. 13.
2. 'The book tells of two brothers, one of whom later, searching alone for the other lost brother, goes blind; it does not emerge clearly from the story what event causes his blindness; it is stated several times that it is wartime; but all details of the misfortune itself are omitted, or he has forgotten them. The story begins with the blind brother, now a man, waking up one Sunday and being reminded by something which eludes him when he tries to think of it, of his missing brother. From that point the bits he thinks he can remember go through his brain, but without any semblance of order.'
   Peter Handke, *Die Hornissen*, Hamburg, 1968, p. 149.
3. 'Even the place and time of year in which the plot is set elude him. Because he does not know all this any more, or rather is only in possession of bits of it here and there, because he is certain that he read the book at some time he is spurred on and wants to know the whole story. This is what set him off on his long quest. But things remembered are not things proved; what he has conjured up need not be true in the sense that it corresponds plausibly with events in the book, but it does have to be possible and imaginable by being credible in its own

265

right, any false or unnatural utterance would be spurned and rejected by experience.' ibid. p. 150.

4. 'You are sitting in rows . . . You are looking at us when we talk to you . . . You hear us but you are not lstening . . . The theatre is not getting its due here tonight . . . We're not putting on anything for you tonight . . . These lights shining on us don't mean a thing . . . We're not comedians . . . You are the subject of the evening . . . You're to get the once-over from us . . . This space doesn't stand for any particular space . . . If there are two poles here, you are the one that is stationary . . . You look entrancing . . . But you don't add up to an evening's theatre . . . This is not a drama . . . There is no order up here . . . There isn't a time and place for everything up here.'
Peter Handke, *Publikumsbeschimpfung*, Frankfurt, 1966.

5. 'Literature for me has long been the means of getting myself a little clearer, even if that still is not very clear. It has helped me to recognise that I exist, that I am part of the world . . . The reality of literature cleared up my ideas about myself, and about what was happening around me.'
Peter Handke, *Ich bin ein Bewohner des Elfenbeinturms*, Frankfurt, 1972, p. 19.

6. 'These two dangers, on the one hand simply telling it as it happened, on the other the painless dissolution of the person into poetic sentences – make writing a slow process because I am afraid of losing my balance at each sentence.'
Peter Handke, *Wunschloses Unglück*, Frankfurt, 1975, p. 44.

7. See the satire by P. A. Schmidt, *Fünf Finger im Wind* in *manuskripte*, Graz 1977, no. 57, pp. 57–62.

8. 'Friedrich: Say, is it true that Franzi has pulled Fanny already?
Fery: That's what the man says. Not that I believe a word.
Friedrich: Never thought she would lay.
Fery: Huh! On the contrary. Touched up right she's hot stuff. But whether Franzi's got the . . .
Friedrich: That's the point!
Friedrich: I'd say he hasn't. Why? Do you fancy her?
Wolfgang Bauer, *Party for Six*, Cologne, 1969, p. 124.

9. 'The best I could do would be write a play about two people sitting on the stage listening to records . . . one record after another,'
Wolfgang Bauer, *Magic Afternoon*, Cologne, 1969, p. 14.

10. 'Then I have the feeling I've created something independent, with a life of its own, which no longer has anything to do with me . . . like a perpetuum mobile . . . Even when I was a boy those shoe-polish tins you got just after the war, Solo the stuff was called, made a big impression on me. The tin had a picture of another tin with the picture of another tin, and so on . . .'
Wolfgang Bauer: *Gespenster*, Cologne, 1974, p. 37.

General Bibliography

a) The most comprehensive account of the political, historical, sociological and cultural developments of the Second Republic is:
Erika Weinzierl/Kurt Skalnik (eds), *Österreich Die Zweite Republik*, vol. I and II, Graz/Vienna/Cologne, 1972.
An excellent critical analysis of the political system of Austria is:
Heinz Fischer (ed), *Das politische System Österreichs*, 2nd rev. ed., Vienna, 1977.
Other useful works include:
William B. Bader, *Austria between East and West 1945–1955*, Palo Alto, 1966.

Elizabeth Barker, *Austria*, London/Basingstoke, 1973.

William T. Bluhm, *Building an Austrian Nation. The Political Integration of a Western State*, New Haven/London, 1973.

Erich Bodzenta (ed), *Die österreichische Gesellschaft. Entwicklung, Struktur, Probleme*, Vienna, 1972.

Walter Goldinger, *Geschichte der Republik Österreich*, Vienna, 1962.

Karl Gruber, *Ein politisches Leben. Österreichs Weg zwischen den Diktaturen*, Vienna, 1976.

Karl Gukas/Alios Brusatti/Erika Weinzierl, *Österreich 1945–1970*, Vienna, 1970.

Bruno Kreisky, *Neutralität und Koexistenz*, Munich, 1975, (=neue edition List).

Bruno Kreisky, *Österreich und Europa*, Vienna, 1963.

Norbert Leser/Richard Berczeller, *Als Zaungäste der Politik. Österreichische Zeitgeschichte in Konfrontationen*, Vienna/Munich, 1977.

Klaus W. Mayer, *Die Sozialstruktur Österreichs*, Vienna, 1970.

Adolf Schärf, *Österreichs Erneuerung 1944–1955*, Vienna, 1955.

Heinrich Siegler, *Austria – Problems and Achievements since 1945*, Bonn/Vienna/Zurich, 1969.

Karl R. Stadler, *Austria*, London, 1971.

Alfred Verdross, *The Permanent Neutrality of Austria*, Vienna, 1978.

Alexander Vodopivec, *Die dritte Republik. Machtstrukturen in Österreich*, Vienna/Munich/Zurich, 1976.

Kurt Waldheim, *Der österreichische Weg*, Vienna, 1971.

b) A very full, highly readable and often controversial account of modern Austrian writing, complete with illustrations, is:

Hilde Spiel (ed), *Die zeitgenössische Literatur Österreichs*, Zurich/Munich, 1976, (=Kindlers Literaturgeschichte der Gegenwart).

See also:

Heinz Ludwig Arnold (ed), *Kritisches Lexikon zur deutschsprachigen Gegenwartsliteratur (KLG)*, Munich 1978f, (=edition text und kritik).

H. Kunisch, *Handbuch der deutschen Gegenwartsliteratur*, Munich, 2nd ed., 1970. Frederick Ungar (ed), *Handbook of Austrian Literature*, New York, 1973; many of the entries of this edition have been translated from the German version edited by Kunisch.

Hans F. Prokop, *Österreichisches Literaturhandbuch*, Vienna/ Munich, 1974.

Victor Suchy, *Literatur in Österreich von 1945–1970*, Vienna, 1971.

Walter Weiss, 'Literatur', in: Erika Weinzierl/Kurt Skalnik (eds), *Österreich, Die Zweite Republik*, vol. II, Graz/Vienna/Cologne, 1972, pp. 439–479.

The following anthologies provide a useful introduction to Austrian writing since the war:

Dimension, Contemporary German Arts and Letters, vol. VIII, Nos 1 and 2, 1975 (a valuable collection of parallel texts – English/German – of contemporary Austrian writers, edited by the University of Texas at Austin).

Milo Dor (ed), *Die Verbannten. Eine Anthologie*, Graz, 1962.

Otto Breicha/Gerhard Fritsch (eds), *Aufforderung zum Mißtrauen. Literatur, Bildende Kunst, Musik in Österreich seit 1945*, Salzburg, 1967.

Walter Weiss/Sigrid Schmid (eds), *Zwischenbilanz. Eine Anthologie österreichischer Gegenwartsliteratur*, Salzburg, 1976.

268

Invaluable introductions and background for the cultural atmosphere of the post-war period will be found in:

W. M. Johnston, *The Austrian Mind. An Intellectual and Social History 1848–1938*, Berkeley/Los Angeles/London, 1972.

C. Magris, *Der habsburgische Mythos in der österreichischen Literatur*, Salzburg, 1966.

Walter Strolz (ed), *Dauer im Wandel. Aspekte österreichischer Kulturentwicklung*, Vienna/Freiburg/Basle, 1975.

C. E. Williams, *The Broken Eagle. The Politics of Austrian Literature from Empire to Anschluß*, London, 1974.

BIOGRAPHICAL NOTES

ILSE AICHINGER

Aichinger was born in Vienna on 21 November 1921. She spent her early childhood near Linz before she returned to Vienna to receive her secondary education. The 'Anschluß' of March 1938 hit her in a very personal way: her mother, whom she stayed with after the divorce of her parents, was Jewish. Whilst Aichinger's twin sister managed to escape to Britain, she herself stayed with her mother and saw almost all of her relatives and friends taken away to concentration camps. In 1945 she started studying Medicine but after two years she gave up her studies and became a reader for S. Fischer Verlag, the publishing house which had published her first work *Die größere Hoffnung*. In the early 1950s Aichinger collaborated in the founding of the Academy for Design in Ulm/Württemberg. In 1953 she married the German poet Günter Eich. The couple lived in various Bavarian villages before they moved to Austria and settled in Groß-Gmain near Salzburg, where Ilse Aichinger continued to live after Eich's death in 1972.

Aichinger was a member of the Group 47 which awarded her its prize in 1952. In the same year she received the 'Förderungspreis des österreichischen Staatspreises'. Other major literary awards include the Bremen Prize for Literature (1955) and the Austrian State Prize for Literature (1975).

Select Bibliography

A detailed bibliography (including translations of Aichinger's work) has been compiled by Irmelat Holtmeier and can be found in *Ansprachen und Dokumente zur Verleihung des Kulturpreises der Stadt Dortmund 'Nelly-Sachs-Preis' am 12. Dezember 1971*, (=Mitteilungen aus dem Landesarchiv Dortmund, 3).

Most of Aichinger's narratives are collected in three volumes: *Nachricht vom Tag*, Frankfurt/M., 1970 (=Fischer Bücherei 1140). *Dialoge, Erzählungen, Gedichte*, Stuttgart, 1971 (=Reclam 7939). *schlechte wörter*, Frankfurt/M., 1976.

(The two latter volumes are accompanied by short introductory essays, both written by Heinz F. Schafroth).

The most comprehensive collection of Aichinger's poetry is: *Verschenkter Rat*, Frankfurt/M., 1978.

See also:

James Charles Alldridge, *Ilse Aichinger*, London, 1969 (=Modern German Authors: Texts and Contexts 2).

Carol B. Bedwell, 'Who is the bound man? Towards an interpretation of Ilse Aichinger's *Der Gefesselte*', in: *German Quarterly*, 38 (1965), 30–37.

Carol B. Bedwell, 'The ambivalent image in Aichinger's *Spiegelgeschichte*', in: *Revue des langues vivantes*, 33 (1967), 362–368.

Werner Eggers, 'Ilse Aichinger', in: Dietrich Weber (ed), *Deutsche Literatur seit 1945. In Einzeldarstellungen*, 2nd rev. ed., Stuttgart, 1970, (=Kröners Taschenausgabe 382), pp. 252–70.

Helga M Gerresheim, 'Ilse Aichinger', in: Benno von Wiese (ed), *Deutsche Dichter der Gegenwart*, Berlin, 1973, pp. 481–96.

Wolfgang Hildesheimer, 'Ilse Aichinger. *Der Querbalken*. Mit einer Einführung und Illustration', in: *Merkur*, 17 (1963), 1179–85.

Hellmuth Himmel (ed). 'Ilse Aichingers Prosastück *Der Querbalken*. Vier Interpretationsversuche', in: *Sprachkunst*, 5 (1974), 280–300.

Rainer Lübbren, 'Die Sprache der Bilder. Zu Ilse Aichingers Erzählung *Eliza Eliza*', in: *Neue Rundschau*, 76 (1965), 626–36.

Peter Horst Neumann, 'Über Wissen und Nicht-Wissen im Werk Ilse Aichingers', in: *Neue Zürcher Zeitung*, 5.12.1971.

Ernst Oldemeyer, 'Zeitlichkeit und Glück. Gedanken zu Texten von Ilse Aichinger', in: Götz Großklaus (ed), *Geistesgeschichtliche Perspektiven. Festgabe für Rudolf Fahrner*, Bonn, 1969, pp. 281–307.

Heinz F. Schaffroth, 'Teil eines stärkeren Widerstandes. Ein Gespräch mit Ilse Aichinger', in: *Basler Nachrichten*, 27.5.1972 (including also an interpretation by Lilly Spring of Ilse Aichinger's narrative *Queens*).

Jürgen P. Wallann, 'Ilse Aichinger und ihre Dichtung', in: *Universitas*, 28 (1973), 41–45.

Roderick H. Watt, 'Ilse Aichingers Roman *Die größere Hoffnung*. Versuch einer literaturkritischen Würdigung', in: *Studia Neophilologica*, 50 (1978), 233–51.

Werner Weber, 'Ilse Aichinger', in: Klaus Nonnemann (ed), *Schriftsteller der Gegenwart. Deutsche Literatur. 53 Porträts*, Olten and Freiburg, 1963, pp 11–18.

INGEBORG BACHMANN

Bachmann was born at Klagenfurt on 25 June 1926 and proved a gifted child. Her studies at Austrian universities culminated in a doctorate on Heidegger in 1950. She spent some time working for radio in Vienna and then began to attract critical attention with collections of poetry, radio plays and opera libretti. She has also worked in the academic field and was a visiting lecturer at the University of Frankfurt (1959–1960). She died in Rome on 17 November 1973.

Select Bibliography

Ingeborg Bachmann, *Werke*, (edited by Koschel, Weidenbaum and Münster), 4 vols, Munich, 1978.

Gedichte, Erzählungen, Hörspiel, Essays, Munich, 5th. edition, 1974.

A comprehensive bibliography of Bachmann's works is:

Otto Bareiss, Frauke Ohloff, *Ingeborg Bachmann, eine Bibliographie*, Munich, Zurich, 1978.

See also:

Text und Kritik, No. 6, 3rd edition, May 1976.

Interpretationen zu Ingeborg Bachmann, Munich, 1976.

M. B. Benn, 'Poetry and the Endangered World: Notes on a Poem by Ingeborg Bachmann: "Freies Geleit"', in: *German Life and Letters*, New Series, 19 (1965/66), 61–67.

J. K. Lyon, 'The Poetry of Ingeborg Bachmann: A Primeval Impulse in the Modern Wasteland', in: *GLL* (NS) 17 (1963/64),

206–15.

E. Marsch, 'Ingeborg Bachmann', in: Benno von Wiese (ed.), *Deutsche Dichter der Gegenwart. Ihr Leben und Werk*, Berlin, 1973, pp. 515–30.

H. Pausch, *Ingeborg Bachmann*, Berlin, 1975.

G. C. Schoolfield, 'Ingeborg Bachmann', in: B. Keith-Smith (ed.), *Essays on Contemporary German Literature*, London, 1966, pp. 185–212.

E. Summerfield, *Ingeborg Bachmann. Die Auflösung der Figur in ihrem Roman 'Malina'*, Bonn, 1976.

M. Triesch, 'Truth, Love and the Death of Language in Ingeborg Bachmann's Stories', in: *Books Abroad* 39 (1965), 389–93.

THOMAS BERNHARD

Bernhard was born in Heerlen (Holland) on 9 February 1931 of Austrian parents. He spent his early childhood with his grandparents in Vienna, near Salzburg and in Traunstein (Bavaria). In 1943 he was sent to a boarding-school in Salzburg where he experienced the air-raids and bombing of the city, the end of the war and the chaos of the immediate post-war years (cf. his first autobiographical novel *Die Ursache*, 1975). In 1947 he left the grammar-school to become an apprentice in a grocer's shop in a Salzburg suburb (cf. the second autobiographical novel, *Der Keller*, 1976). In 1948 a serious illness brought him close to death (cf. his latest autobiographical novel, *Der Atem*, 1978) and he had to spend some considerable time in a sanatorium; it was here that he began to try his hand at creative writing. His grandfather, the Austrian writer Johannes Freumbichler died in 1949; this was a considerable blow, for Freumbichler had had a profound influence on Bernhard's intellectual development and had been the model on which Bernhard fashioned the typical male character in his work. A second blow came in 1950 with the death of his mother. Between 1952–57 Bernhard studied music and drama at the Academy Mozarteum in Salzburg and during the same period he also reported court-hearings for a Salzburg newspaper. After spending some time abroad, particularly in Poland and England, Bernhard settled on a farm in Upper Austria and became an independent writer. He has received a number of major awards, including the Bremen Prize for Literature (1965), The Austrian State Prize for Literature (1968) and the Georg Büchner Prize (1970).

Select Bibliography

In hora Mortis, Salzburg, 1958.

Frost, Frankfurt am Main, 1963.

Verstörung, Frankfurt am Main, 1967.

Ungenach, Frankfurt am Main, 1968, (es 279).

Ereignisse (written 1957), Berlin, 1969.

Watten. Ein Nachlaß, Frankfurt am Main, 1969,(es 353).

Das Kalkwerk, Frankfurt am Main, 1970.

Die Macht der Gewohnheit, Frankfurt am Main, 1974.

Die Ursache, Eine Andeutung, Salzburg, 1975.

Korrektur, Frankfurt am Main, 1975.

Der Keller, Eine Entziehung, Salzburg, 1976.

Der Atem, Salzburg, 1978.

Der Stimmenimitator, Frankfurt am Main, 1978.

Ja, Frankfurt am Main, 1978.

Immanuel Kant, Frankfurt am Main, 1978.

Die Erzählungen, Frankfurt am Main, 1979.

Comprehensive bibliographies for Thomas Bernhard can be found:–

Gerhard P. Knapp, 'Bibliographie', in: Anneliese Botond (ed), *Über Thomas Bernhard*, Frankfurt/M., 1970, (= edition suhrkamp 401), pp. 144–149.

Thomas B. Schumann, 'Bibliographie zu Thomas Bernhard', in: Heinz Ludwig Arnold (ed), *Thomas Bernhard*, Munich, 1974 (= Text und Kritik 43), pp. 50–55.

Bernhard Sorg, 'Thomas Bernhard', in: Heinz Ludwig Arnold (ed), *Kritisches Lexikon zur deutschsprachigen Gegenwartsliteratur (KLG)*, Munich, 1978f, (= edition text und kritik).

See also:–

Heinz Ludwig Arnold (ed), *Thomas Bernhard*, Munich, 1974, (= Text und Kritik 43).

Anneliese Botond (ed), *Über Thomas Bernhard*, Frankfurt/M., 1970 (= edition suhrkamp 401).

(Both of these volumes are collections of a number of worthwhile essays on Thomas Bernhard)

Alfred Barthofer 'The Plays of Thomas Bernhard – A Report', in: *Modern Austrian Literature*, 11 (1978), No 1, 21–48.

D.A. Craig, 'The Novels of Thomas Bernhard. A Report', in: *German Life and Letters*, NS 25 (1971/72), 343–53.

A.P. Dierick, 'Thomas Bernhard's Austria: Neurosis, Symbol or

Expedient?', in: *Modern Austrian Literature*, 12 (1979), No. 1, 73–93.

Josef Donnenberg, 'Zeitkritik bei Thomas Bernhard', in: *Zeit und Gesellschaftskritik in der österreichischen Literatur des 19. und 20. Jahrhunderts*, ed. by the Institut für Österreichkunde, Vienna 1973, pp. 115–143.

Josef Donnenberg, 'Thomas Bernhard und Österreich. Dokumentation und Kommentar', in: *Österreich in Geschichte und Literatur*, 14 (1970), 237–251.

Herbert Gamper, *Thomas Bernhard*, Munich, 1977, (= dtv 6870).

Hans Höller, *Kritik einer literarischen Form, Versuch über Thomas Bernhard*, Stuttgart, 1979, (= Stuttgarter Arbeiten zur Germanistik 50).

Erich Jooß, *Aspekte der Beziehungslosigkeit. Zum Werk von Thomas Bernhard*, Selb, 1976.

Manfred Mixner, *Thomas Bernhard*, Königstein, 1979.

Wendelin Schmidt-Dengler, 'Thomas Bernhard', in: Dietrich Weber (ed), *Deutsche Literatur der Gegenwart. In Einzeldarstellungen*, vol. II, Stuttgart, 1977, (= Kröners Taschenausgabe 383), pp. 56–76.

Bernhard Sorg, *Thomas Bernhard*, Munich, 1977, (= Autorenbücher 7).

Jens Tismar, *Gestörte Idyllen. Über Jean Paul, Adalbert Stifter, Robert Walser und Thomas Bernhard*, Munich, 1973.

Benno von Wiese, 'Thomas Bernhard', in: Benno von Wiese (ed), *Deutsche Dichter der Gegenwart*, Berlin, 1973, pp. 632–646.

CHRISTINE BUSTA

Busta is a pseudonym of Dimt. Busta was born in Vienna on 23 April 1915 in poor family circumstances. She worked as a teacher and subsequently as librarian of Vienna's public libraries (from 1950).

Select Bibliography

Jahr um Jahr, Vienna, 1950
Der Regenbaum, Vienna, 1951 (2nd. edition 1977)
Die bethlehemitische Legende, Salzburg, 1954
Lampe und Delphin, Salzburg, 1955

Die Scheune der Vögel, Salzburg, 1958
Die Sternenmühle, Salzburg, 1959
'*Unterwegs zu älteren Feuern*', Salzburg, 1965
Unveröffentlichte Gedichte, Salzburg, 1965
Salzgärten, Salzburg, 1975
Die Zauberin Frau Zappelzeh, Salzburg, 1979
Viktor Suchy, *Conversation with Christine Busta*, Tape 199 A1, Dokumentationsstelle für neuere österreichische Literatur, 24 June 1968
Horst Fassel, 'Zerreißprobe des Natürlichen', in: *Literatur und Kritik*, 122 (1978), 103–109.

ELIAS CANETTI

Canetti's biography is unusually cosmopolitan. He was born on 25 July 1905 in the town of Ruse (Rutschuk) on the lower reaches of the Danube in what is now Bulgaria. It was a place where many cultures came together and where many languages were spoken. His parents were Jews of Spanish extraction, so that the language he first spoke was an archaic form of Spanish. In 1911 his parents moved to Manchester, where his father joined the business of his brother-in-law and where the young boy received his first school education in English. On the sudden death of his father in 1913 his mother took her three sons to Vienna, which had long been a city of cultural longing for her. For Canetti himself this involved the painful learning of German for the first time. In 1916 his mother's illness provided the opportunity to leave wartime Vienna for neutral Switzerland, where Canetti's schooling continued until 1920, when his mother decided he was leading too easy a life and so took him off to Frankfurt to experience 'reality' during the inflationary years in post-war Germany. In 1924 he returned to Vienna as a student, gaining a doctorate in the natural sciences. At the same time his literary interests were renewed and his career as a writer began. Not only did he embark here on the studies that were eventually to lead to the monumental work *Masse und Macht*, but he wrote his novel *Die Blendung*, in 1930 and 1931, and two of his plays. In November 1938 he left Austria, moving first to Paris and then, in 1939, to London, which was to be his home for well over thirty years. Here he devoted most of his energies to the completion of *Masse und Macht*, consciously restricting his purely literary activities. More recently he has moved to Zurich, the scene of his boyhood paradise.

Select Bibliography

Die Blendung. Munich, 1963.

Dramen. Munich, 1964.

Die Provinz des Menschen: Aufzeichnungen 1942–1972. Munich, 1973.

Der Ohrenzeuge: Fünfzig Charaktere. Munich, 1974.

Masse und Macht. Munich, 1976, second edition = Reihe Hanser 124–125.

Das Gewissen der Worte: Essays. Munich, n.d. (1976?).

Die gerettete Zunge: Geschichte einer Jugend. Munich, 1977.

Annemarie Auer, 'Ein Genie und sein Sonderling – Elias Canetti und *Die Blendung*', in: *Sinn und Form*, 21 (1969), 963–83.

Dagmar Barnouw, *Elias Canetti*, Stuttgart, 1978.

Mechthild Curtius, 'Das Groteske als Kritik', in: *Literatur und Kritik*, 65 (1972), 294–311.

Dieter Dissinger, 'Der Roman *Die Blendung*', in: *Text und Kritik*, Nr. 28 (1970), 30–38.

Manfred Durzak, 'Versuch über Elias Canetti', in: *Akzente*, 17 (1970), 169–91.

Ernst Fischer, 'Bemerkungen zu Elias Canettis *Masse und Macht*', in: *Literatur und Kritik*, 7 (1966), 12–20.

Erich Fried, introduction to Elias Canetti, *Welt im Kopf*. Graz and Vienna, 1962 (= Stiasny Bücherei 102), 5–22.

Herbert G. Göpfert (ed.), *Canetti lesen: Erfahrungen mit seinen Büchern*. Munich, 1975 (= Reihe Hanser 188). (This volume contains numerous essays on Canetti as well as a comprehensive bibliography up to 1975.)

Manfred Moser, 'Zu Canettis *Blendung*', in: *Literatur und Kritik*, 50 (1970), 591–609.

Idris Parry, 'Elias Canetti's novel *Die Blendung*', in: *Essays in German Literature*, I, ed. F. Norman. London, 1965, 145–66.

Peter Russell, 'The vision of man in Elias Canetti's *Die Blendung*', in: *German Life and Letters*, NS. 28 (1974–5), 24–35.

Marion E. Wiley, 'Elias Canetti's Reflective Prose', in: *Modern Austrian Literature*, 12 (1979), No. 2, 129–40.

PAUL CELAN

Celan is a pseudonym; the poet's real name was Paul Antschel. He was born on 23 March 1920 in Roumania, the only son of Jewish parents, where he lived and was educated up to university level. Then he travelled to Tours in France to take up his studies in medicine. That was in the year 1938; when war broke out, he interrupted his studies, returning home to resume them but this time he took up Romance languages and literatures. Celan himself was not interned, but his parents both met their death in a concentration camp. When the war was over, Celan found himself in Bucharest working for a publisher, and it was there that his first poetical works appeared. At the end of 1947, Celan moved to Paris, once again as a student, this time of German literature and language. He graduated in 1950. A succession of slim volumes of poetry appeared, reflecting in language often difficult, terse and obscure, his sufferings, wanderings and strange blend of backgrounds. He remained in Paris until his death by drowning in the river Seine in late April 1970. It is presumed that he took his own life.

Select Bibliography

Paul Celan, *Gedichte*, edited by Beda Allemann, 2 vols, Frankfurt am Main, 1976 (= Bibliothek Suhrkamp 412, 413).

Paul Celan, *Ausgewählte Gedichte. Zwei Reden*, (ed. Beda Allemann), Frankfurt am Main, 1962 (= es 262).

The standard critical work on Celan is:-

Gerhard Buhr, *Celans Poetik*, Göttingen, 1976.

Two special issues are devoted to Celan:-

Etudes Germaniques, 25 (1970).

Text und Kritik, 53/54 (1977).

See also:

Hermann Burger, *Paul Celan. Auf der Suche nach der verlorenen Sprache*, Zurich, 1974.

J. Glenn, *Paul Celan*, New York, 1973 (contains a good bibliography).

J.K. Lyon, 'The Poetry of Paul Celan: An Approach', in: *Germanic Review*, 39 (1964), 50–67.

J.K. Lyon, 'Paul Celan and Martin Buber: Poetry as Dialogue', in: *PMLA*, 86 (1971), 110–20.

D. Meinecke, *Wort und Name bei Paul Celan. Zur Widerruflichkeit des Gedichts*, Berlin, Zurich, 1970.

D. Meinecke (ed.), *Über Paul Celan*, Frankfurt am Main, 1970.

P.H. Neumann, *Zur Lyrik Paul Celans*, Göttingen, 1960.

S. Prawer, 'Paul Celan', in: B. Keith-Smith (ed.), *Essays on Contemporary German Literature*, London, 1966, pp. 161–84. (with bibliography).

G-M Schulz, *Negativität in der Dichtung Paul Celans*, Tübingen, 1977.

J. Schulze, *Celan und die Mystiker*, Bonn, 1976.

A. Staples, 'The Concept of "Nebenwelt" in Paul Celan's Poetry', in: *Seminar*, 9 (1973), 229–52.

K. Voswinckel, *Paul Celan, Verweigerte Poetisierung der Welt*, Heidelberg, 1974.

M. Winkler, 'On Paul Celan's Rose Images', in: *Neophilologus*, 56 (1972), 72–78.

HEIMITO VON DODERER

Doderer was born at Weidlingau near Vienna on 5 September 1896 into a family with roots in Austria, Germany, France and Hungary. He was taken prisoner in Russia in World War I, escaped and crossed the Kirghiz steppe on foot, returning home in 1920 where he unsuccessfully tried to establish himself as a painter. He then read history at the University of Vienna, taking his doctorate after four years study in 1925. He met Gütersloh for the first time in 1924 and thereafter was preoccupied with his 'master' as seen in *Der Fall Gütersloh*, 1930. Doderer also worked as a journalist for a time, but his own literary efforts went unremarked. He joined the illegal Austrian Nazi party in 1933 and though he burned his membership card in 1938 he was still proscribed after the war and forbidden to write until 1948. Doderer's dissociation from National Socialism is reflected in his conversion to Catholicism in 1940 – an attempt to regain and enhance his sense of humanity. After the war success still eluded him as a writer until the publication of *Die Strudlhofstiege in 1951*. Once his own reputation was assured Doderer used his position of eminence assiduously on others' behalf. He was long regarded as the authority on Gütersloh and was particularly concerned to encourage the younger generation of writers, showing a broad-mindedness and sympathy for their new ideas and experiments. He was awarded the Great Austrian State Prize for Literature in 1958. His first marriage ended in early divorce, he remarried

278

in 1952 and thereafter lived in Landshut and Vienna. He died in
Vienna on 23 December 1966.

Select Bibliography

The standard edition of Doderer's work is published by Biederstein
Verlag Munich, 1950ff. A comprehensive bibliography for Heimito
von Doderer can be found:-

W. Schmidt-Dengler, 'Bibliographie. Sekundärliteratur zu Heimito von Doderer' in *Literatur und Kritik*, 80 (December 1973),
615–20.

See also:-

A. Barker, 'Closely observed trains' – some thoughts on Heimito
von Doderer's use of the railway theme', in: *FMLS*, 10 (1974),
357–64.

'Heimito von Doderer and the Meaning of Memory', in: GLL NS
32(1978/79), 30–39.

'Heimito von Doderer and the "Science of Physiogonomy"', in:
NGS 5(1977) 91–109.

H. Hatfield, 'Vitality and Tradition in two Novels by Heimito von
Doderer', in: HH, *Crisis and Continuity in Modern German
Fiction*, Ithaca, London, 1969, pp. 90–108.

International Symposium in Memory of Heimito von Doderer
(1896–1966), in: *Books Abroad*, 42 (1968).

I. Ivask, 'Poet of the Vibrant Equilibrium: The Austrian Novelist
Heimito von Doderer at 70', in: *Books Abroad*, 40 (1966), 415–
18.

'Heimito von Doderer, An Introduction', in: *Wisconsin Studies
in Comparative Literature* 8 (1967), 528–47.

D.L. Jones, 'Proust and Doderer as Historical Novelists', in: *Comparative Lit. Studies*, 10 (1973), 9–24.

C. Magris, *Der habsburgische Mythos in der österreichischen
Literatur*, Salzburg, 1966.

'Doderers erste Wirklichkeit' in: *Literatur und Kritik*,
114 (May 1977), 209–26.

W. Paulsen, 'Deutsch–Österreichischer Zeitroman; zu Doderers
Roman *Die Strudlhofstiege*', in: *Symposium* 10 (1956), 217–30.

H. Politzer, 'Heimito von Doderer's "Demons" and the Modern
Kakanien Novel', in: R. Heilner (ed.), *The Contemporary Novel
in German*, Austin, 1967, pp. 37–62.

A. Reininger, *Die Erlösung des Bürgers. Eine ideologie-kritische*

Studie zum Werk Heimito von Doderers, Bonn, 1975.

W. Schmidt-Dengler, 'Die Thematisierung der Sprache in Heimito von Doderers *Dämonen*', in: *Sprachthematik in der österreichischen Literatur des 20. Jahrhunderts*, ed. Institut für Österreichkunde, Vienna, 1974, pp. 119–34.

'"Analogia entis" oder das "Schweigen unendlicher Räume"? Theologische Themen bei Heimito von Doderer und Thomas Bernhard', in: *Gott in der Literatur*, (Linzer Philosophisch-Theologische Reihe 6) Linz, 1976, pp. 93–107.

F. Slawik, 'Literatur von Innen. Heimito von Doderer und das Selbstverständnis der modernen Literatur', in: *Literatur und Kritik*, 114 (May 1977), 227–41.

M.W. Swales, 'The Narrator in the works of Heimito von Doderer', in: *MLR* 61 (1966), 85–95.

F. Trommler, 'Doderer und Gütersloh', in: F.T., *Roman und Wirklichkeit: Eine Ortsbestimmung am Beispiel von Musil, Broch, Roth, Doderer und Gütersloh*, Stuttgart, 1966.

H.M. Waidson, 'Heimito von Doderer's Demons', in: *GLL*, NS 11 (1957/58), 214–24.

D. Weber, *Heimito von Doderer. Studien zu seinem Romanwerk*, Munich, 1963.

C.E. Williams, 'Down a Steep Place. A Study of Heimito von Doderer's *Die Dämonen*', in: *FMLS*, 7 (1971), 76–82.
The Broken Eagle. The Politics of Austrian Literature from Empire to Anschluß, London, 1974, pp. 132–147.

ERICH FRIED

Like so many of his contemporaries, Fried has suffered much through the war years and experienced exile, in his case an exile which has become voluntary and extends to the present day. For many years now he has lived in London, as a full-time writer and translator. Born on 6 May 1921 in Vienna, he was brought up there. His parents were arrested and interned in 1938; when his father was released a month later, he died as a result of injuries received during interrogation. A year later, his mother was released, and the two of them made their way to England. After working at a variety of different kinds of employment, Fried turned his attentions to creative writing, and from 1946 onwards concentrated his attentions on poetry, prose, translating and freelance journalistic work.

He is best known for his political verse and his extremist political affiliations, as well as for his caustic views of West German democracy; but it should also be remembered that he is a distinguished translator, particularly of the works of Shakespeare.

Select Bibliography

Ein Soldat und ein Mädchen, Hamburg, 1960.

Reich der Steine, Hamburg, 1963.

Warngedichte, Munich, 1964.

Überlegungen, Munich, 1964–65.

Kinder und Narren, Munich, 1965.

und Vietnam und, Berlin, 1966.

Anfechtungen, Berlin, 1967.

Befreiung von der Flucht, Berlin, 1968.

Zeitfragen, Berlin, 1968.

Unter Nebenfeinden, Berlin, 1970.

Höre, o Israel!, Berlin, 1974.

A representative collection of Fried's poems, translated by Stuart Hood, appears in *100 Poems without a Country*, London, 1978.

See also:

Harald Hartung, 'Lyrik als Warnung und Erkenntnis. Zur Zeitlyrik Erich Frieds', in: Heinz Ludwig Arnold (ed.), *Geschichte der deutschen Literatur aus Methoden – Westdeutsche Literatur von 1945–1971*, Vol. 3, Frankfurt am Main, 1972, pp. 71–77.

Walter Hinderer, 'Sprache und Methode: Bemerkungen zur politischen Lyrik der 60iger Jahre. Enzensberger, Grass, Fried', in: *Revolte und Experiment. Die Literatur der 60iger Jahre,* Heidelberg, 1972, pp. 98–143.

Hans Rochelt, 'Erich Fried, Dichtung und Klassenkampf', in: *Literatur und Kritik*, 3 (1968), No. 30, 618–21.

THE 'GRAZER GRUPPE'

A. Holzinger and G. Scheuer, *Literatur in der Steiermark von 1945– 1976*, (a catalogue of the 'Landesausstellung', Graz, 1976).

P. Laemmle and J. Drews (eds.), *Wie die Grazer auszogen, die Literatur zu erobern*, Munich, 1975.

WOLFGANG BAUER

Wolfgang Bauer was born in Graz on 18 March 1941, and left the city for the first time when he went to study Drama, Romance Languages, Law and Philosophy at Vienna. It was here that he made contact with the 'Wiener Gruppe'. He was a founder member of the 'Forum Stadtpark' in Graz and published his first work there in *manuskripte*. The success of the première of *Magic Afternoon* at Hanover in 1968 made his name known to a wider public. Apart from a brief stay in Berlin he has remained faithful to Graz, where he makes his living as a gutsy, hard-drinking writer. In 1970 he was awarded the Franz Theodor Csokor Prize by the Austrian PEN Club, and in 1973 he was instrumental in founding the 'Grazer Autorenversammlung' in opposition to the predominantly conservative Vienna PEN Club.

Select Bibliography

Die Sumpftänzer, Cologne, 1978 (Prose, poetry and drama from two decades; this volume contains most of Bauer's work with the exception of the collection *Gespenster . . .*)

Gespenster, Silvester oder Das Massaker im Hotel Sacher, Film und Frau, Cologne, 1974.

H.L. Arnold (ed.), *Wolfgang Bauer*, (*Text und Kritik*, 59), Munich 1978.

G. Melzer, *Wolfgang Bauer*, Kronberg, 1978; contains a full bibliography.

P. Haberland, 'Duality, the Artist, and Wolfgang Bauer', in: *Modern Austrian Literature*, 11 (1978), No. 1, 73–86.

BARBARA FRISCHMUTH

Barbara Frischmuth was born in Altaussee on 5 July 1941. She trained as an interpreter in Turkish and Hungarian at the Dolmetsch Institut in Graz, and at Erzurum and Debrecen, and later studied Oriental Languages at Vienna University. She is a member of the 'Grazer Autorenversammlung' and lives as a writer and translator at Oberweiden.

Select Bibliography

Die Klosterschule, Salzburg, 1968.

Das Verschwinden des Schattens in der Sonne, Salzburg, 1973.

Haschen nach Wind, Salzburg, 1974.

Amy oder Die Metamorphose, Salzburg, 1978.

PETER HANDKE

Peter Handke was born in Griffen, a small village in Carinthia, on 6
December 1942. His early years were spent in the ruins of post-war
Berlin, but from the family's return to Griffen in 1948 until 1961 his
experience was restricted to the remote country life of his birth-
place, where he went to primary school before moving to a Catholic
boarding school near Klagenfurt and then to grammar school in
Klagenfurt itself, the capital of Carinthia. He turned to literature to
escape from the repressive atmosphere of his boarding school and
claims to have wanted to be a writer from the age of twelve. From
1961 he studied law at Graz University, but his energies mainly
went into writing and he abandoned his degree in 1965. He
published in *manuskripte*, the house magazine of the 'Forum Stadtpark', and by 1966 with the publication of his first novel, *Die Hornissen* and his diatribe against the 'Gruppe 47' at Princeton he had
become the *enfant terrible* of German literature, an image which the
performance of *Publikumsbeschimpfung* that June confirmed.
Handke left Graz for the cities – Berlin, Paris, a commuter suburb
of Frankfurt and finally Paris again where he lived for six years. In
1979 he settled in Salzburg. Personal experience is the source of his
writing and the birth of his daughter Anima in 1969, his separation
from his wife Libgart Schwarz, his mother's suicide in 1971, and his
trips to the USA are all obliquely or directly documented. He was
awarded the Gerhart Hauptmann Prize in 1967 and the Büchner
Prize in 1973.

Select Bibliography

Prosa, Gedichte, Theaterstücke, Horspiel, Aufsätze, Frankfurt am
Main, 1969.
Stücke, Frankfurt am Main, 1972, (*Publikumsbeschimpfung,
Weissagung, Selbstbezichtigung, Hilferufe, Kaspar*).
Stücke II, Frankfurt am Main, 1973, (*Das Mündel will Vormund
sein, Quodlibet, Der Ritt über den Bodensee*).
Die Hornissen, Frankfurt am Main, 1966.
Der Hausierer, Frankfurt am Main, 1967.
Die Angst des Tormanns beim Elfmeter, Frankfurt am Main, 1970.
Chronik der laufenden Ereignisse, Frankfurt am Main, 1971.
Der kurze Brief zum langen Abschied, Frankfurt am Main, 1972.
Wunschloses Unglück, Salzburg, 1972.

283

Ich bin ein Bewohner des Elfenbeinturms, Frankfurt am Main, 1972.
Als das Wünschen noch geholfen hat, Frankfurt am Main, 1974.
Die Unvernünftigen sterben aus, Frankfurt am Main, 1973.
Die Stunde der wahren Empfindung, Frankfurt am Main, 1975.
Falsche Bewegung, Frankfurt am Main, 1975.
Die linkshändige Frau, Frankfurt am Main, 1976.
Das Gewicht der Welt, Salzburg, 1977.
Langsame Heinkehr, Frankfurt am Main, 1979.
H.L. Arnold (ed.), *Peter Handke*, (*Text und Kritik*, 24/24a), Munich, 1976.
G. Heintz, *Peter Handke*, Stuttgart, 1971.
       Peter Handke: Analysen, Munich, 1976.
Nicholas Hern, *Peter Handke*, London, 1971.
M. Mixner, *Peter Handke*, Kronberg, 1977.
    This volume contains a full bibliography.
R. Nägele and V. Renate, *Peter Handke*, Munich, 1978.
M. Scharang (ed.) *Über Peter Handke*, Frankfurt am Main, 1972.
U. Schultz, *Handke*, Velber, 1974.

GERT JONKE

Gert Friedrich Jonke was born at Klagenfurt on 8 February 1946. He studied briefly at Vienna University before becoming a writer and spending long periods of residence in Berlin and London before finally settling in Klagenfurt. It was Peter Handke's review of his first novel, *Geometrischer Heimatroman*, in the magazine *Der Spiegel* which first brought Jonke to the attention of the reading public. He is a member of the 'Forum Stadtpark' and of the 'Grazer Autorenversammlung'.

Select Bibliography
Geometrischer Heimatroman, Frankfurt am Main, 1969.
Beginn einer Verzweiflung, Salzburg, 1970.
Schule der Geläufigkeit, Frankfurt am Main, 1977.

ALFRED KOLLERITSCH

Alfred Kolleritsch was born at Brunnsee on 16 February 1931. He is a school teacher and university lecturer and has been editor of the journal *manuskripte* from its inception, as well as being the third

President of the 'Forum Stadtpark' in Graz. In 1978 he was awarded the Petrerca-Prize.

Select Bibliography
Die Pfirsichtöter, Salzburg, 1972.
Die grüne Seite, Salzburg, 1974.
Einübung in das Vermeidbare, Gedichte, Salzburg, 1978.

GERHARD ROTH

Gerhard Roth was born in Graz on 24 June 1942. He studied medicine but later worked as an organizational manager at the Graz 'Rechenzentrum'. He lives as a writer at Graz.

Select Bibliography
Die autobiographie des albert einstein, Frankfurt am Main, 1972.
Der Ausbruch des Ersten Weltkriegs und andere Romane, Frankfurt am Main, 1972.
Der Wille zur Krankheit, Frankfurt am Main, 1973.
Der große Horizont, Frankfurt am Main, 1974.
Ein neuer Morgen, Frankfurt am Main, 1976.
Winterreise, Frankfurt am Main, 1978.
Menschen, Bilder, Marionetten – Prosa, Kurzromane, Stücke, Frankfurt am Main, 1979.

MICHAEL SCHARANG

Michael Scharang was born at Kapfenberg on 3 February 1941. His background is working-class. He studied Theatre Science, Philosophy and Art History at Vienna University. He is a member of the 'Forum Stadtpark' in Graz, and joined the Austrian Communist Party in 1973. He lives as a writer in Vienna.

Select Bibliography
Charly Traktor, Darmstadt/Neuwied, 1973.
Einer muß immer parieren, Darmstadt/Neuwied, 1973.
Der Sohn eines Landarbeiters, Darmstadt/Neuwied, 1976.

*   *   *

ALBERT PARIS GÜTERSLOH

Gütersloh's real name was the equally dactylic A. Conrad Kiehtreiber. He was born in Vienna on 5 February 1887 and educated by Benedictines and Franciscans at Melk and Bolzano. He remained a lifelong catholic though his religious orientation is noticeable more in his general outlook on life than in his free-spirited, avant-garde style of art. He lived mostly in Vienna and its immediate vicinity, working as a painter and author, but also as a stage setter, director and even as an actor until his work was deemed 'entartet' by the Nazis and he was forbidden to paint or write. During World War I Gütersloh saw active service before joining the war press headquarters in Vienna as a journalist. Here he met Franz Blei with whom he published the journal *Die Rettung* in the years 1918–19. After the war he wrote prolifically, being awarded the Theodor Fontane Prize in 1923. He was appointed to the Viennese Kunstgewerbeschule in 1929, and lectured enthusiastically on the works of Gobelin, receiving the Grand Prix from Paris on two occasions for tapestry design. He also gained the Austrian State Prize for painting. After 1945 Gütersloh's support for modern art intensified and he tried to bridge the gap between pre-war modern artists and the post-war generation. He was an instigator of new trends in Austrian art after 1945, particularly the Viennese art school of phantastic realism. He was appointed to the teaching staff of the Akademie der bildenden Künste in Vienna in 1945 and was its dean from 1953 to 1955. He was for many years president of the International Vienna Artclub, a forum for the leading artists in Europe and the birth-place of the literary 'Wiener Gruppe.' He was married twice; his first wife died in childbirth in 1916, the second marriage ended in divorce after ten years in 1931. Gütersloh received many national and international awards after the war, including the State Prize for Painting in 1952, and for Literature in 1961. He died in Baden near Vienna on 16 May 1973.

Select Bibliography

Albert Paris Gütersloh, *Sonne und Mond, ein historischer Roman aus der Gegenwart*, Munich 1962.

Albert Paris Gütersloh, Autor und Werk, Munich (Piper), 1962, has an extensive list of Gütersloh's publications; see also Herbert Eisenreich's brief account in the *Handbook of Austrian Literature*, pp. 105–7.

H.F. Prokop, 'Albert Paris von Gütersloh: Bibliographie' in: *Literatur und Kritik*, 68 (October 1972), 483–92.

E. Bonfatti, 'Albert Paris Gütersloh: *Sonne und Mond*', in: *Literatur und Kritik*, 79 (October 1973), 540–48.

H. von Doderer, *Der Fall Gütersloh: Ein Schicksal und seine Deutung*, Vienna, 1930, reprinted: Munich, 1961.

A. Focke, 'Versuch über Albert Paris Güterslohs Materiologie', in: *Literatur und Kritik*, 68 (October 1972), 466–72.

A. Focke, 'Grabrede für Gütersloh', in: *Literatur und Kritik*, 78 (September 1973), 449–53.

E. Fuchs, 'Über Gütersloh', in *Literatur und Kritik*, 68 (October 1972), 480–82.

I. Ivask, '*Sonne und Mond*', in: *Books Abroad* 37 (Summer 1963), 304–5.

E. Jooß, 'Zu Güterslohs *Sonne und Mond*', in: *Literatur und Kritik*, 94 (May 1975), 193–200.

A. Obermayr, 'Bemerkungen zu Albert Paris Güterslohs Romanfragment *Tandaradei*', in: *Literatur und Kritik*, 112 (1977), 140–42.

H. Rieder, 'Jenseits des Romans: A. P. Güterslohs *Sonne und Mond*', in: H. R., *Österreichische Moderne*, Bonn, 1968, pp. 109–17.

W. Schmidt-Dengler, 'Die Anfänge des "Falles Gütersloh"', in: *Literatur und Kritik* 68 (October 1972), 472–79.

F. Theiner, *Albert Paris Gütersloh. Studien zu seinem Romanwerk*, Bern, 1970.

F. Trommler, 'Doderer und Gütersloh', in: F. T., *Roman und Wirklichkeit: Eine Ortsbestimmung am Beispiel von Musil, Broch, Roth, Doderer und Gütersloh,* Stuttgart, 1966, pp. 109–17.

FRITZ HOCHWÄLDER

Fritz Hochwälder was born in Vienna on 28 May 1911, where he lived and worked until 1938. He earned his living as a craftsman, an interior decorator, not as a writer and after the *Anschluß* his antipathy to Nazi ideology and his Jewish background made it essential that he leave Austria. Like so many other would-be refugees, however, he found it impossible to gain an entry visa to a 'safe' country and so entered Switzerland illegally in August 1938 by the simple, if dangerous method of swimming across the frontier. He was interned and forbidden to take up gainful employment (i.e. as an interior decorator) and was thus able to indulge in his hobby of writing. After a satire on the story of Esther (1940) he wrote *Das Heilige Experiment* whose success enabled him to survive as a writer financially. After the war Hochwälder chose to remain in Switzerland while retaining Austrian citizenship. His popularity was at its zenith in the decade after World War II when he seemed to mirror the sentiments of audiences all over Europe. He has received a number of significant awards, including the Austrian State Prize for Literature in 1966, being awarded the title of 'Professor' by the Austrian President in 1964 and the 'Ehrenring' of the City of Vienna in 1972. He lives as an independent writer in Zurich.

Select Bibliography

A detailed bibliography has been complied by James Schmitt and can be found in *Modern Austrian Literature*, 11 (No. 1) 1978, 63–74. The most recent collection of Hochwälder's plays is Fritz Hochwälder, *Dramen*, 3 vols, Graz (Styria Verlag) 1975ff which contains all the major plays. *Lazaretti oder der Säbeltiger* was also published separately by the same publishers in 1975. An earlier two volume collection is: *Dramen*, Munich/Vienna, 1959/64; both these volumes are accompanied by worthwhile forewords, by Hans Weigel and Paul Hübner respectively.

Cf. also Fritz Hochwälder, *Der Befehl*, (Stiasny Bücherei 170) 1967, for essays by Hochwälder 'Über mein Theater', Csokor 'Zu Hochwälders *Der Befehl*', and Adorno, 'Reflexionen über das Volksstück'. 'Über mein Theater' was originally published in *German Life and Letters*, NS 12 1958/9, 102–114; the Stiasny version is a modification and up-dating of the original. Cf. also Fritz Hochwälder 'Vom Versagen des Dramas in unserer Zeit', *Maske und Kothurn*, 8 (1962), 19–30, and FH 'Kann die Freiheit überleben?', Styria, Zurich, 1976, the text of a lecture given to the Friends of the Burgtheater in October 1974.

See also:-

E. Alker, Der Dramatiker F. H., in: *Österreich in Geschichte und Literatur*, 15(1971), 466–69.

P. Demetz, *Post-war German Literature*, New York, 1970. pp. 109–12.

O. M. Fontana, 'F. H. zum 50. Geburtstag', in *Wort in der Zeit*, 7 (1961), Heft 5 pp. 10–14.

J. Foster (ed.), Introduction to *Das Heilige Experiment*, London (Harrap), 1957.

Introduction to *Der Öffentliche Ankläger*, London (Methuen), 1962.

A. J. Harper, 'Tradition and Experiment in the Work of Fritz Hochwälder', in: *New German Studies* (Hull), 5 (1977), 49–57.

M. P. Holdmann, *The Concept of Order in the Drama of Fritz Hochwälder*, (Diss) City University, New York, 1976.

I. Loram, F. H., in: *Monatshefte* 57 (1965), 8–16.

J. Schmitt, 'The Theater of F. H.: Its Background and Development,' in: *Modern Austrian Literature*, 11 No. 1, (1978), 49–62.

R. Thieberger, 'Macht und Recht in den Dramen F. H.'s' in: *Deutsche Rundschau*, 83 (1957), 1147–52.

Introduction to *Donadieu*, London (Harrap), 1967.

H. Vogelsang, 'Das klassizistische Ideendrama F.H.'s', in: *Österreich in Geschichte und Literatur*, 2 (1958), 224–32.

G. Wellwarth, 'F. H.: The Drama within the Self', in: *Quarterly Journal of Speech*, 49 (1963), 274–81.

The Theater of Protest and Paradox, New York, 1971, pp. 207–21.

E. R. Wood, Introduction to *The Strong are Lonely* (adapted by Eva Le Gallienne from the French version by J. Mercure and R. Thieberger), Hereford Plays Series, London (Heinemann), 1968. (= *Das Heilige Experiment*)

ÖDÖN VON HORVÁTH

Ödön von Horváth was born at Fiume on the Adriatic on 9 December 1901. His father was an Austrian diplomat whose frequent postings meant that the young Horváth spent his first few school years changing languages as well as schools. By the time Horváth came to Munich in 1913 he had suffered four such changes and could not speak a word of German. Shortly before the end of the war the family returned to Budapest where Horváth began to dabble in national-revolutionary politics. Between 1919 and 1922 Horváth was back in Munich at the University and beginning to write seriously. He moved to Berlin in 1924 and while sifting material in the offices of the German League for Human Rights came across details of the secret trials carried out by the extreme right-wing 'Schwarze Reichswehr'. Part of this material was later incorporated into his play *Sladek oder Die schwarze Armee* (1928). His activities soon brought him into conflict with the Nazis, he gave

289

evidence against them in a case dealing with a political brawl in 1931, and from then on was a clear target for Nazi denunciation. The award of the Kleist Prize in the same year did nothing to lessen Nazi animosity towards him. Horváth left Germany in 1933 for Budapest where he acquired Hungarian citizenship, enabling him to return to Germany with some safety. Gradually as Nazi influence grew and spread, Horváth found himself on the move until by 1938 he left Budapest for Paris, probably en route for the United States. Always a highly superstititious man he is reputed to have been told by a fortune-teller that a significant experience awaited him in the French capital. On 1 June while sheltering from a storm under a tree opposite the Théâtre Marigny, he was killed when the tree collapsed.

Select Bibliography

Ödön von Horváth, *Gesammelte Werke*, 4. vols., edited by Traugott Krischke and Dieter Hildebrandt, Suhrkamp, Frankfurt am Main, 1970–71. (An eight volume paperback edition was published as 'Werkausgabe der edition suhrkamp' by the same editors in 1972).

Individual plays, each with draft material, variants and commentary are available in the *Bibliothek Suhrkamp* series. Interested students should also consult the *edition suhrkamp* list for 'Materialien' to a number of the plays (esp. *Geschichten aus dem Wiener Wald, Kasimir und Karoline*). A detailed bibliography of primary texts will be found in: Traugott Krischke. *Ödön von Horváth. Ein Lesebuch*, Frankfurt, 1978. See also T.K. and Hans F. Prokop, *Ödön von Horváth. Leben und Werk in Daten und Bildern*, Frankfurt am Main, 1978.

The following volumes in the edition suhrkamp are highly recommended for the valuable primary and secondary material and bibliographical information they contain:

Traugott Krischke (ed), *Materialien zu Ödön von Horváth*, ed. suhrkamp 436, Frankfurt am Main, 1970.

Dieter Hildebrandt and Traugott Krischke (eds), *Über Ödön von Horváth*, ed. suhrkamp 584, Frankfurt am Main, 1972. (with detailed bibl. of secondary lit.)

Secondary Literature

There is now almost a plethora of criticism on Horváth both in English and German; the following titles will prove a useful addition to the bibliography in *Über Ödön von Horváth* (1972).

A. Bance, 'Ödön von Horváth's *Kasimir und Karoline*', in: *FMLS* 13 (1977), 177–89.

K. Bartsch, U. Baur, D. Goltschnigg (eds.), *Horváth Diskussion* (Monographien Literaturwissenschaft 28), Kronberg, 1976.

A. Doppler, 'Dramatisches Geschehen als sprachliches Arrangement, *Geschichten aus dem Wiener Wald*', in: A.D., *Wirklichkeit im Spiegel der Sprache*, Vienna, 1978, pp. 150–71.

A. Fritz, *Ödön von Horváth als Kritiker seiner Zeit: Studien zum Werk in seinem Verhältnis zum politischen, sozialen und kulturellen Zeitgeschehen*, Munich, 1973.

D. Goltschnigg, 'Das Individuum als geknechtete Kreatur in der Gesellschaft. Die Spuren von Büchners Woyzeck in Ödön von Horváths dramatischem Werk', in: *Modern Austrian Literature*, 8 3/4 (1975), 113–25.

H. Jarka, 'Zur Horváth-Rezeption 1929–38', in: *Literatur und Kritik* 109 (1976), 542–62.

S. Kienzle (ed.), *Ödön von Horváth Colloquium*, Berlin, 1977.

V. R. Kling, 'The Conflict of Eros and Politics in some dramas of Ödön von Horváth', in: *Modern Austrian Literature*, 6 (1973), 182–90.

H. U. Lindken, 'Illusion und Wirklichkeit in Ödön von Horváths Volksstück *Geschichten aus dem Wiener Wald*', in: *Modern Austrian Literature*, 9 1/2 (1976), 26–43.

G. Melzer, *Das Phänomen des Tragikomischen. Untersuchungen zum Werk von Karl Kraus und Ödön von Horváth*, Kronberg, 1976.

S. Parkes, 'The dramatic art of Ödön von Horváth', in: *New German Studies*, 5 (1977), 111–23.

P.M. Potter, 'Death and Guilt in the Works of Ödön von Horváth', in *German Life and Letters*, New Series 32 (1978/79), 148–52.

H. Scheible, 'Verschollene Bürgerlichkeit. Ödön von Horváth: Jargon und gesellschaftliche Immanenz', in: *Neue Rundschau*, 88 (1977) 365–85.

P. Stenberg, 'The last of the magicians . . . Horváth's 'Zauberkönig' and his ancestors', in *GLL* NS 28 (1974/75), 395–405.

M. Swales (ed.), *Symposium on Ödön von Horváth*, (Austrian Institute), London, 1977.

M. Walder, *Die Uneigentlichkeit des Bewußtseins: zur Dramaturgie Ödön von Horváths*, Bonn, 1974.

K. Winston, 'The Old Lady's day of judgement. Notes on a mysterious relationship between Friedrich Dürrenmatt and Ödön von Horváth', in: *GR* 51 (1976), 312–22.

K. Winston, 'The Unbuttoned Nightgown of Anna Schramm: Dress and Undress in the plays of Ödön von Horváth', in: *Modern Austrian Literature*, 11 2 (1978), 53–72.

CHRISTINE LAVANT

Lavant was born on 4 July 1915 as Christine Habernig, in the Lavant valley from which she took her pseudonym. She started writing at an early age, gained several prizes (including the Trakl Prize in 1964), but despite her fame chose never to leave her home region. She died on 8 June 1973.

Select Bibliography

Christine Lavant, Kunst wie meine ist nur verstümmeltes Leben, Armin Wigotschnigg and Johanna Strutz (eds.), Salzburg, 1978. (A collection of poems, prose and letters 'aus dem Nachlaß' and a selection of poems from various earlier editions with the exception of the following collections: *Die Bettlerschale, Spindel im Mond* and *Der Pfauenschrei*.

Die unvollendete Liebe, Bläschke, 1949.

Das Krüglein, Erzählung, Bläschke, 1949.

Baruscha, Drei Erzählungen, Bläschke, 1952.

Die Bettlerschale, Gedichte, Salzburg, 1956.

Spindel im Mond, Gedichte, Salzburg, 1959.

Der Pfauenschrei, Salzburg, 1962.

Hälfte des Herzens, Bläschke, 1967.

Nell, Vier Erzählungen, Salzburg, 1969.

W.V. Blomster, 'Christine Lavant', *Symposium*, 19 (1965), 19–37.

K. Fleischmann, 'Mystisches und Magisches bei Christine Lavant; Versuch einer Deutung der Sammlung *Die Bettlerschale*', in: *Literatur und Kritik*, 109 (1976), 524–41.

G. Lübbe-Grothues, 'Zur Gedichtsprache der Christine Lavant', in: *Zeitschrift für deutsche Philologie*, 87 (1968), 613–30.

GEORGE SAIKO

Saiko was born on 5 February 1892 in Seestadtl, Bohemia, An art historian by profession, he published academic articles and various translations from Russian. He was a close friend of Hermann Broch from the late twenties. During the Second World War he played a key part in preserving the treasures of the Vienna Albertina from destruction and pillage and after the war became its director until conflict with the authorities led to his premature retirement in 1950. He was a withdrawn figure, deeply interested in philosophical, theological and psychological issues and was particularly drawn to Mediterranean climes and cultures. His literary career proper did not begin until after 1945. He was a member of the Austrian PEN Club and the Deutsche Akademie für Sprache und Dichtung but his failure to win recognition embittered him and he tended to shun the 'culture industry' which might have made him familiar to a wider audience. He was awarded the prize of the Theodor Körner Foundation in 1957, the Prize of the City of Vienna in 1959 and lived just long enough to be awarded the Austrian State Prize for Literature in 1962 on the recommendation of Heimito von Doderer. Saiko died in Rekawinkel (Lower Austria) on 23 December 1962 and retains the stigma of being an esoteric, 'difficult' writer.

Select Bibliography

The standard edition of his work is published by the Benziger Verlag, Zürich in three volumes – *Auf dem Floß* (1970), *Der Mann im Schilf* (1971) and *Erzählungen* (1972). For a representative selection of his theoretical and publicistic essays, see the Bibliography attached to the article on Saiko by Robert Mühlher in *Handbuch der deutschen Gegenwartsliteratur*, edited by Hermann Kunisch, revised by Herbert Wiesner, 2nd edition, Munich 1970.

Kurt Benesch, 'G.S. – Ein unbekannter Autor?', in: *Wort in der Zeit*, 8 (1962), no. 8, 39–41.

Kurt Benesch, 'In Memoriam G.S.', *Wort in der Zeit*, 9 (1963), No.2, 1–5.

Alfred Doppler, 'Historische Ereignisse im österreichischen Roman' in: *Geschichte in der österreichischen Literatur des 19. und 20. Jahrhunderts*, edited by the Institut für Österreichkunde, Vienna 1970, pp. 73–91.

Jeannie Ebner, 'Hermann Broch und G.S.', in: *Literatur und Kritik*, 54/55 (1971), 262–70.

Claudio Magris, 'Die Rundung und der Kreis', in: *Literatur und Kritik*, 70 (1972), 586–89.

Janko Musulin, 'G.S.', in: *Schriftsteller der Gegenwart*, ed. K. Nonnenmann, 1963, pp. 267–74.

Heinz Rieder, 'Ein magischer Realist', in: *Wort in der Zeit*, 8 (1962), No. 1, 15–19.

Heinz Rieder, *Der magische Realismus. Eine Analyse von 'Auf dem Floß'* von G.S., Marburger Beiträge Bd. 22, 1970. (Rieder has published extensively on the theme of Saiko in the periodicals *Literatur und Kritik* and *Österreich in Geschichte und Literatur*, as well as in his book *Österreichische Moderne*, Bonn, 1968).

Zsuza Széll, 'George Saikos Wirklichkeit', in: *Literatur und Kritik*, 99 (1975), 553–61.

F. Wernigg, Introduction to G.S., *Die dunkelste Nacht* (an anthology), Stiasny-Bücherei, Bd. 92, Graz/Vienna, 1961.

THE 'WIENER GRUPPE'

H. Hartung, *Experimentelle Literatur und Konkrete Poesie*, Göttingen, 1975.

G. Rühm (ed.), *Die Wiener Gruppe. Achleitner, Artmann, Bayer, Rühm, Wiener. Texte, Gemeinschaftsarbeiten, Aktionen*, Reinbek bei Hamburg, 1967.

Two editions of the literary periodical *Text und Kritik* (edited by H.L. Arnold) have been devoted to experimental and concrete poetry:

No. 25 (January, 1970) 'Konkrete Poesie I – experimentelle und konkrete Poesie'

No. 30 (April, 1971) 'Konkrete Poesie II – kritische Ansätze zur Konkreten Poesie'.

(This latter contains a useful 'kommentierte Auswahlbibliographie' by Jörg Drews of primary and secondary literature, including work by the 'Wiener Gruppe'.)

Roger Bauer, 'Die Dichter der Wiener Gruppe und das surrealistische Erbe', in: *Grillparzer Jahrbuch* 12 (1976), pp 11–25.

M. Wulff, *Konkrete Poesie und sprachimmanente Lüge. Von Ernst Jandl zu Ansätzen einer Sprachästhetik*, Stuttgart 1979 (= Stuttgarter Arbeiten zur Germanistik 44).

FRIEDRICH ACHLEITNER

Friedrich Achleitner was born on 23 May 1930 in Scholchen/

Oberösterreich. After school in Salzburg he studied architecture at the 'Akademie der Bildenden Künste' in Vienna. He worked as an independent architect in Vienna from 1953–1958 and belonged to the 'Wiener Gruppe' from 1955 to its dissolution in 1964. Since 1963 Achleitner has taught at the Academy of Fine Art in Vienna.

Select Bibliography
prosa, konstellationen, montagen, dialektgedichte, studien, Reinbek bei Hamburg, 1970.
Quadratroman, Reinbek bei Hamburg, 1974

HANS CARL LAERTES ARTMANN

H.C. Artmann was born on 12 June 1921 in Vienna, where he spent his youth. He was wounded during the Second World War and then served as an interpreter for the American Army from 1945–49. After this period he studied comparative linguistics. Artmann was a member of the 'Wiener Artclub', joined the 'Wiener Gruppe', and in the 1970s he was a founder-member of the 'Grazer Autorenversammlung'; he was elected President of this group in 1975. He spent a number of years abroad, in Sweden and in Berlin and currently lives as an independent writer in Salzburg. He was awarded the Austrian State Prize for Literature in 1974.

Select Bibliography
The Best of H.C. Artmann. Lyrik, Theater, Prosa, Theoretisches, Frankfurt/Main, 1970.

KONRAD BAYER

Konrad Bayer was born on 17 December 1932 in Vienna; he committed suicide on 11 October 1964. He had a number of careers, working in a bank, playing music in a bar, acting and as a guide in art galleries. He joined the 'Wiener Artclub' in the years immediately after the war and was a founder-member of the 'Wiener Gruppe' in 1952.

Select Bibliography
Das Gesamtwerk, ed. Gerhard Rühm, Reinbek bei Hamburg, 1977.

ERNST JANDL

Ernst Jandl was born on 1 August 1925 in Vienna; he was taken prisoner by the Americans during the war and after 1945 studied German and English in Vienna. He completed his studies by taking his teaching exam. and gained his doctorate with a dissertation on the 'Novellen' of Arthur Schnitzler. Since 1949 (with some interruptions) he has taught at a grammar school in his native Vienna. His first literary attempts were published in 1952. He was part of the circle around the 'Wiener Gruppe' and was later a member of the 'Forum Stadtpark' in Graz and a founder-member in 1973 of the 'Grazer Autorenversammlung'. In 1968 he was joint winner (with Friederike Mayröcker) of the 'Hörspielpreis der Kriegsblinden'; in 1974 he was awarded the Georg Trakl Prize for Poetry and in 1976 the City of Vienna Prize for Literature.

Select Bibliography

Laut und Luise, Stuttgart, 1976. (This is a reprint of the edition published in 1966 by Walter Verlag, Olten/Freiburg).
Sprechblasen, Neuwied and Berlin, 1968. (2nd. edition 1970).
Der künstliche Baum, Neuwied and Berlin, 1970. (5th ed. 1975).
Für Alle, Darmstadt and Neuwied, 1974.
Die schöne Kunst des Schreibens, Darmstadt and Neuwied, 1976.
die bearbeitung der mütze. gedichte, Darmstadt and Neuwied, 1978.

GERHARD RÜHM

Gerhard Rühm was born on 12 February 1930 in Vienna. He studied piano and composition at the Academy of Music in Vienna, lived for a short period in Beirut where he studied oriental music. Rühm was a founder-member of the 'Wiener Gruppe'; from 1954 he has lived as an independent writer in Vienna. After the dissolution of the Group he moved to West Berlin.

Select Bibliography

gesammelte gedichte und visuelle texte, Reinbek bei Hamburg, 1970.
Ophelia und die Wörter. Gesammelte Theaterstücke. 1954–1971, Neuwied and Darmstadt 1972.

OSWALD WIENER

Oswald Wiener was born in Vienna on 5 October 1935. He studied Law, Music, African Languages and Mathematics. After having left the 'Wiener Gruppe' in 1959 he started a career as a data processor and later became director of a data processing company. Since 1969 he has been an independent writer and innkeeper in West Berlin.

Select Bibliography
Die Verbesserung von Mitteleuropa, Reinbek bei Hamburg, 1969.

INDEX

Hitler, Adolf, 2, 4, 7, 92, 94, 96, 99, 104, 206, 236, 254
Hochhuth, Rolf, *Der Stellvertreter*, 48
Hochwälder, Fritz, 23, 24, 30f, 37, 38, 40f, *44–62*, *287ff*; *Der Befehl*, 30,
  46, *56ff*; *Donadieu*, 46, 51, 53f; *Donnerstag*, 53; *Esther*, 53; *Das Heilige
  Experiment*, 30, 44, 45, 46, 47, *48ff*, 53, 54; *Die Herberge*, 45, *53ff*; *Der
  Himbeerpflücker*, 30, 45, 46, 47, 48, 55, *56f*, 58; *Lazaretti oder Der
  Säbeltiger*, 44, *46f*; *Meier Helmbrecht*, 30, 53; *Der öffentliche Anklä-
  ger*, 30, 46, *51f*, 53, 54; *Der Unschuldige*, 53, 54; *1003*, 53
Hochzeit, Die (Canetti), *88*
Hofmannsthal, Hugo von, 'Ein Brief', 33, 83, 128, 230, 239; *Das Märchen
  der 672. Nacht*, 79, 81; *Der Turm*, 98
'Holzfahrscheine' (Aichinger), *169*
Höre, Israel! (Fried), *185f*, 188
Hornissen, Die (Handke), 253, *254ff*, 259, 264
Horváth, Ödön von, 23, 26f, 33, 40f, 44, 87, *108–127*, 198, 200, *289ff*;
  Geschichten aus dem Wiener Wald, 26f, 40, 108, 109, *117ff*; *Glaube Liebe
  Hoffnung*, *112f*, 118; *Italienische Nacht*, *113ff*; *Kasimir und Karoline*,
  122ff; *Sladek der schwarze Reichswehrmann*, 113

Ibsen, Henrik, *Ghosts*, 264
In hora mortis (Bernhard), *215f*
Innerhofer, Franz, 197, 211
Ionesco, Eugène, *La Cantatrice Chauvre*, 243
Italienische Nacht (Horváth), *113ff*

Jandl, Ernst, 236, *244–250*, 296; 'erschaffung der eva', *248f*; 'étude in f',
  246; 'a kleine Sprechmaschine', *246f*; *Der künstliche Baum*, 246; *Laut
  und Luise*, 246, 247, 248, 249; 'Moritat', 246; 'ode auf N', *247*; 'oeö',
  248; *Sprechblasen*, 246f, 248; 'schtzngrmm', *247*
Jeanne d'Arc (Mell), *37f*
Jonas, Franz, 22
Jonke, Gert Friedrich, 197, 253, *284*; *Geometrischer Heimatroman*, 253
Joyce, James, 24, 107, 249

Kafka, Franz, 24, 35, 38, 60, 83, 90, 94, 98, 135, 136, 163; *In der Strafko-
  lonie*, 90; *Der Prozeß*, 35; *Das Schloß*, 35, 90, 98; *Die Verwandlung*, 163
'Kakanien', 25, 26
Kandinsky, Wassilyi, 242
Kasimir und Karoline (Horváth), *122ff*
Kaspar (Handke), 171, *209*, 210, 252, *258f*
Keller, Der (Bernhard), *221*, 230
Klaus, Dr. Josef, 16
Kleist, Heinrich von, 164, 186; *Michael Kohlhaas*, 186
Kolleritsch, Alfred, 252, 253, *284f*; *Die Pfirsichtöter* , 253
Komödie der Eitelkeit (Canetti), *88f*, 90
Korrektur (Bernhard), 219, 224, *226f*,
Kraus, Karl, 23, 33, 87, 94
Kreisky, Dr. Bruno, 11, 16, 18, 19
Kroetz, Franz Xaver, 40, 124

Turrini, Peter, 197, 211

und Vietnam und (Fried), 137f, *184ff*, 187
Ursache, Die (Bernhard), *221f*, 232

Valéry, Paul, *Monsieur Teste*, 222
Verbesserung von Mitteleuropa, Die (Wiener), *241*
'Vergangenheitsbewältigung', 9, 30f, 34, 55, 160, 200, 203f, 220
Verstörung (Bernhard), *217f*, 224f
'Vögel' (Busta), *143*
'Volksstück', 40, 44f, 50, 54, 56, 57, 60, 108, 109, *110ff*, 113, 117, 118, 124
Von Schwelle zu Schwelle (Celan), *149*

Waggerl, Karl Heinrich, 253
Walden, Herwarth, 239
Waldheim, Dr. Kurt, 13
Waldorf, Günter, 252
Walser, Martin, 198
Weigel, Hans, 23, 24f, 39, 128
Weinheber, Josef, 140
Weiss, Peter, 198
Werfel, Franz, 23, 25, 101; *Der Abituriententag*, 25; *Das Trauerhaus*, 25
Wie eine Träne im Ozean (Sperber), *31ff*
'Wiener Gruppe', 197, 201, *207f*, *236–242*, 245, 252, *294ff*; *hosn rosn baa*,
    242; 'Konstellationen', 242, 249
Wiener, Oswald, 236, 237, *238*, 239, *240f*, 244, *296*; *Die Verbesserung von*
    Mitteleuropa, *241*
Wilder, Thornton, 24
Wittgenstein, Ludwig, 133, 146, 207, 230, 239, 241, 258, 263
Wo ich wohne (Aichinger), *166ff*
Wolfgruber, Gernot, 197, 211
Wolfshaut, Die (Lebert), *205f*
Wunschloses Unglück (Handke), 211, 253, 256, *259*, *260*,

Zeitfragen (Fried), 189f, 193
Zenker, Helmut, 211
Zuckmayer, Carl, 24
Zweig, Stefan, 23, 85, 95